Rudyard Kipling
A Life

By the Same Author

Fiction
People Like Us

Non-Fiction

Talking About Ourselves:
Interviews with New Zealand Poets

Poetry

Coming Here
Coming Under Scrutiny
How Things Are
(with Adrienne Jansen, J.C. Sturm, Meg Campbell)
A Brief History of New Zealand Literature
13 Ways
Nothing to Declare

Anthologies

How You Doing?
A Selection of New Zealand Comic and Satiric Verse

RUDYARD KIPLING

A Life

HARRY RICKETTS

CARROLL & GRAF PUBLISHERS, INC.
NEW YORK

First Carroll & Graf edition 2000

Carroll & Graf Publishers, Inc.
19 West 21st Street
New York, NY 10010-6805

Library of Congress Cataloging-in-Publication data is available.
ISBN: 0-7867-0711-9

Manufactured in the United States of America

To my parents and David

Contents

Illustrations

The author and publishers are grateful for kind permission to reproduce the following illustrations: The National Trust (Bateman's, Sussex) 1, 3, 7, 9, 14, 20, 25, 26; Lord Baldwin 2, 4, 5, 10; Haileybury College Governing Body 8; The Library of Congress, Washington D.C., 11, 17; The Houghton Library, Harvard University 13 (pf MS Am 1094), 23 (pf MS Eng 696(2)), 24 (pf MS Eng 696 (18)), 30 (pf MS Eng 696 (19)); The Howard C. Rice Jr Collection, Marlboro College, Vermont 15, 16, 18; The National Portrait Gallery, London 19; the Library of the Groote Schuur Estate, Cape Town 21; Radio Times Hulton Picture Library 22, 31; the Kipling Archive, Sussex University, Brighton, 25, 26; Julia McSwiney 27.

Preface

On 18 March 1891 Kipling, twenty-five and newly famous, sent a hand-written note to an autograph-hunter in Florence. The name 'Rudyard Kipling', he told her, could be written in three entirely different ways – as he demonstrated before signing the note with a different signature again. To give five separate, self-cancelling versions of his autograph was a characteristic game, witty, high-spirited and evasive. It suggests too something of Kipling's chameleon nature, the ability he celebrated in characters like Mowgli and Kim to cross boundaries and switch identities. At every stage of his life, a number of 'Rudyard Kiplings' co-existed in varying degrees of compatibility with each other: devoted son/damaged 'orphan', precocious aesthete/apprentice sahib, scholar gipsy/rule-bound conformist, would-be American/Empire Tory, innovative craftsman/fervent jingoist, doting father/bellicose tub-thumper – to mention only a few of the most obvious. In this new life, I have tried to bring out the full range of these diverse Kiplings, so fascinating and at times so frustrating.

Kipling himself would have disowned the attempt. He always claimed to hate 'this here biography and "reminiscence" business', which he pungently dubbed the 'Higher Cannibalism' – with the emphasis on the 'higher'. Yet he gave his aunt Georgie every assistance with her memoir of her painter husband and he read his Lytton Strachey with rapt if disapproving attention. Besides, as the creator of the Elephant's Child, he understood that we are all naturally full of 'satiable curiosity' and want to know what the Crocodile had for dinner.

My own curiosity about Kipling began when as a child my mother read me the *Just So Stories* and the *Jungle Books*. It quickened when, as a teenager, a master at school pointed out that Kipling was not all pith helmets and pukka sahibs, and it dimly occurred to me that my father, a deeply conscientious British Army officer, was the sort of person Kipling sometimes wrote about. Reading Kipling became one of those half-guilty pleasures, a holiday from the more 'mature' worlds of Forster or Sartre or Grass. Later, casting about for a subject for a postgraduate thesis, I thought 'Why not Kipling?' It was then that I began to realise that he was not only a wonderfully varied and subtle writer, but something rarer – a writer who, when things get tough, can be guaranteed to see you through long days and longer nights. This extra-literary quality, this sense of relationship which turns certain authors into friends, is what sends us back to regular re-readings of their work, confident of finding old pleasures and from time to time discovering new ones. Like any friend, Kipling can be irritating and dismaying, but he has never disappointed me during the writing of this biography.

Harry Ricketts, Wellington, 1998

1

Ruddy is Coming

Kipling adored his parents.

His mother, Alice Macdonald, was lively, witty and talented; in a Jane Austen novel she would have been called accomplished. She wrote and published poems, arranged songs, sang and sewed and knew how to run a household. Her racy, gossipy letters captured acquaintances and social situations in phrases that flickered between mischief and malice. Frederic, her younger brother, thought her 'keen, quick and versatile' beyond anyone he had ever known. She 'saw things at a glance,' he recalled, 'and dispatched them in a word'.[1] Her poems showed another side, revealing a deep strain of melancholy, which she shared with her mother and three of her four sisters.

Alice also had a flair for family melodramatics. Packing up on one of the Macdonalds' triennial moves – her father was a Methodist minister – she came across an envelope containing a lock of John Wesley's hair. 'See!' she exclaimed, throwing the holy relic on the fire. 'A hair of the dog that bit us!'[2] She liked to startle the family with her talent for table-turning, an enthusiasm which led later in life to a more serious involvement with spiritualism.

As a young woman she was considered a flirt and had already been engaged a number of times before she met her future husband: once, even perhaps twice, to William Fulford, a friend of her other brother Harry, and once to the Irish poet William Allingham of 'Up the airy mountain,/

1

Down the rushy glen'. 'Alice,' observed her youngest sister Edie, 'never seemed to go on a visit without becoming engaged to some wild cad of the desert.'[3] From the few surviving photographs – she hated having her picture taken – Alice appears full of face and solidly built. It was apparently her bright eyes, variously described as blue or grey, which were her chief fascination: 'they could both flash and sparkle,' said her friend Edith Plowden.[4]

Alice met her husband, John Lockwood Kipling, either late in 1862 or early in 1863. She was on a visit to her brother Frederic, then just beginning his first circuit as a Methodist minister at the Swan Bank Wesleyan Chapel at Burslem in Staffordshire. Frederic had recently made friends with Lockwood, who was in Burslem liaising between his employers at the Department of Science and Art, South Kensington, and manufacturers in the Potteries. Lockwood, like Alice, was twenty-six and in his much quieter way had an equally purposeful personality. Five foot three, he was already bald – and that and a long golden beard gave him a distinctly Socratic appearance. Intellectual curiosity, patience and an air of safety were the hallmarks of his character. 'All things interested him,' recalled Frederic. 'He seemed to know something about everything, as well as everything about some things.'[5] As a couple, Frederic considered Alice and Lockwood ideally suited.

The story of how they became engaged deserves a place in any anthology of courtship. The occasion was a picnic with friends at Rudyard Lake in Staffordshire in the summer of 1863. There was a meal, followed by a walk. An old, gaunt-looking horse was spotted in a nearby field. '"Thrust out past service from the devil's stud,"' suggested Lockwood. '"He must have been wicked to deserve such pain,"' returned Alice, immediately recognising the quotation from Robert Browning's 'Childe Roland to the Dark Tower Came', and capping it with a line from the next stanza. 'It was done in that moment,' she later observed.[6]

If the story sounds too literary to be true, it gains support from the entries the couple made a few years later in an *In Confession* book: although differing on every other point, both agreed that Robert Browning was their favourite poet. As an off-the-cuff glimpse into their tastes and preferences, other entries in the book make equally interesting reading. Alice's pet aversion was tripe, Lockwood's cold weather. Her favourite virtue was constancy, his patience. Becky Sharp was appropriately her favourite fictional heroine, while he preferred Balzac's Eugénie Grandet and Beatrice from *Much Ado About Nothing*. Her favourite real-life hero was Rajah Brooke of Sarawak; he plumped for St Vincent de Paul and Christopher Columbus. Her idea of happiness was freedom from care, his a ripe mango in his bath, with a cheroot.[7]

One further courtship story handed down by the family tells how Lockwood, still at that time known by his first name, John, arrived on a visit to the Macdonalds during the course of evening prayers. The lesson, from the first chapter of St John's Gospel, contained the sentence, 'There came a man sent from God, whose name was John.' And the Macdonalds apparently took this as Biblical approval of Alice's choice.

But although Lockwood was enthusiastically received as a prospective son-in-law, his immediate prospects were not considered good enough for the marriage to go ahead at once. In fact, it was not until the end of 1864, when Lockwood was appointed to one of the three new posts for artist-craftsmen at the Sir Jamsetjee Jeejeebhoy School of Art and Industry in Bombay, that the wedding was finally arranged. Events then moved swiftly, and the couple were married on 18 March 1865 at St Mary Abbots Church in Kensington. The ceremony was by choice a modest affair. None of Lockwood's family was present and only a smattering of Alice's many relations: her sisters Aggie and Georgie, Georgie's husband the painter Edward Burne-Jones, her brother Frederic and an aunt or two.

'Alice looked very nice,' wrote Aggie to Louie, another sister, who did not attend, 'her bonnet became her very well, and she had a plain tulle veil.' The service was followed by one of those improbable-sounding Victorian wedding breakfasts: cakes, potted meats, ham, tongue, reindeer tongue, oyster patties, crystallised fruit, macaroons and apricots. One present that the newly married couple wisely decided against taking with them (and passed on to Lockwood's mother) was 'an electro-plated palm tree out of which [rose] a tall glass of flowers'.[8]

The honeymoon was spent with Lockwood's mother and sisters in Skipton, Yorkshire, where Rud was presumably conceived. Then there were a few last hectic days in London before the departure for India. Aggie, with evident relish, reported to Louie on the full horror of a 'desert hat' which Alice had bought. It was, she wrote, 'of the foulest appearance ... The mind of man recoils from the sight of that hat: it is nearly as large as a beehive, you can see none of her face when it is on, and her voice sounds a mile off. There is also a green veil about a yard square which completes the costume.'[9] On 12 April, Alice and Lockwood set sail on the SS *Ripon* for Bombay and the start of their new life.

That Alice and Lockwood had both been brought up in devout Methodist families, and had then lapsed, formed a significant additional bond between them. Not only Alice's brother but also her father and grand-father had served as ministers; indeed, from 1784 to 1928, the three of them covered 144 years of unbroken ministry. Her grandfather, James Macdonald, converted by John Wesley, was a man of formidable learning. A good Latin scholar, he read the Bible in the original Greek and Hebrew, knew Italian and Spanish and spoke French fluently. He edited the *Methodist Magazine* and, among other books, wrote a life of the Reverend Joseph Benson. He died in 1833 at the age of seventy-two, his health broken by twenty-seven circuits as a minister.

Alice's father, George, married twice and by his second wife, Hannah, had eleven children. Seven of these survived into adulthood: two sons, Harry and Frederic, and five daughters, Alice, Georgie, Aggie, Louie and Edie. George Macdonald was an eloquent preacher, a good storyteller and a cheerful, broad-minded workaholic. 'Offspring, spring off,' he would say when his children disturbed his work by climbing on his knee. And as long as they grew up to be good Christians, he claimed not to mind whether they were Methodist or not. This tolerant attitude was perhaps just as well, since all his children except Frederic were to turn their backs on his faith. The peripatetic life of the ministry eventually wore George out too, though he did live long enough to see his grandson Rud.

Alice's mother, Hannah, possessed a more troubled temperament than her husband. Even Frederic, always generous in his estimation of others, felt compelled to mention 'the touch of sadness that was never far away from even her brightest moments'.[10] Edie, Hannah's youngest daughter, was more specific, claiming that her mother's early Methodist training had encouraged an unhealthy introspection and a 'melancholy tinge in the religious teaching which she gave to her children'.[11] This melancholy tinge found its way into Hannah's diaries, as in this entry from August 1874, the year before her death:

Once a cherished wife, Mother of a numerous family, Mistress and

Centre of a large household. Now a lonely widow, my children, all but one precious daughter, married and scattered over the earth: but I thank God, that with much sadness, there is no bitterness. My dear children are all good to me; and now that my own proper life seems to have terminated, I live in their joys and sorrows, as I once did in my own.[12]

Of Alice's two brothers, the elder, Harry, was a failure, the younger, Frederic, a success. Harry (1835–91) seemed destined for great things when he left St Edward's School, Birmingham, with a scholarship to Corpus Christi, Oxford. But at Oxford he fell in love, lost direction and went down after two years without taking a degree. He moved to New York in the hope of making his fortune, but his early promise quickly faded. At school and at Oxford one of his most intimate friends was Edward Burne-Jones, and it was this friendship that led to the close ties between his sisters and the Pre-Raphaelite circle. Frederic (1842–1928), less obviously brilliant, certainly less highly strung, rose high in the Wesleyan Church, becoming President of the Conference and earning the affectionate sobriquet 'The Admirable Crichton of the Methodist ministry'.

Alice had two older sisters who died young. Of the four who survived, Georgie (1840–1920), three years younger than Alice, would prove the family mainstay in times of emotional crisis. After Burne-Jones proposed to her in front of the Arthur Hughes painting *April Love*, the couple were married in 1860. The marriage had its troubles, particularly in the late 1860s when Edward had an affair with the Greek heiress Maria Zambaco. But they stayed together, and their home, The Grange, North End Road, Fulham, became one of the chief meeting-places for Morris, Rossetti and the other Pre-Raphaelites, besides featuring prominently in the lives of Georgie's sisters. After Georgie came Aggie (1843–1906), the family beauty. She married another painter, the Academician Edward Poynter. Their wedding in August 1866 took place on the same day that Louie (1845–1925), the family hypochondriac, married the Worcestershire ironmaster Alfred Baldwin. Edie (1848–1937), the youngest of the five surviving sisters, was the only one to remain single. In marrying Alice, Lockwood had joined a clannish, socially ambitious and increasingly distinguished family.

5

Lockwood himself came from more modest stock. The Kiplings had been small-holding farmers around Lythe in North Yorkshire for generations before his father Joseph (1805–62) decided to break away and join the Wesleyan ministry in the early 1830s. Joseph, like his son and grandson, was a short man but, unlike them, shy and retiring. An unusually sweet singer and fond of gardening, he was said to be singularly devout, though not an impressive preacher. Impressive or not, the title of one of his sermons, 'The Eternal Nature of Hell's Torments', sounds promising. In 1836 Joseph married Frances Lockwood, fathered six surviving children, and died three years before the birth of his famous grandson.

His wife, Frances, was equally devout but much livelier, with a sense of humour which she kept to the very end. During her last illness, the doctor, who was taking her pulse, asked her whose hand he was holding. 'The hand of youth and beauty' came the whimsical reply.[13] It was, incidentally, from Frances's side of the family that Kipling inherited the famous eyebrows that featured so prominently in photographs of him in later life.

Lockwood, Joseph and Frances's eldest child, was born in Pickering on 6 July 1837, a couple of months after his future wife Alice. Following the family tradition of calling Kipling sons alternately John and Joseph, he was christened John and only started calling himself Lockwood at the time of his marriage. At the age of seven he was sent to Woodhouse Grove School, an establishment set up for the education of the sons of Wesleyan ministers. Clothes, shoes and six years' schooling were provided virtually free, but conditions were fairly spartan. Lockwood later remembered the school as 'dreary' and claimed to have been beaten by the headmaster for his 'stoical apathy'.[14] His attitude to other aspects of his Wesleyan upbringing can be gauged from his unpublished romance *Inezilla*, in which the narrator caustically describes how he has bowed his head 'in baize-lined pews of dissent' and marvelled 'at the ravings of Methodist ranters round weeping and snuffling victims at the penitent bench'.[15]

It was a visit to the Great Exhibition in 1851 that determined Lockwood's future career as artist and craftsman. He was taken on as an apprentice by Pinder, Bourne & Co., earthenware manufacturers of Burslem in Staffordshire, while concurrently studying (and winning prizes) at Stoke and Fenton School of Art. After two years working in London and elsewhere for an architectural sculptor, he joined the

Department of Science and Art at South Kensington. It was during his four years with the Department that, going to and fro between London and the Potteries, he met Frederic Macdonald and became engaged to Alice. By the time he applied for the job at the Sir Jamsetjee Jejeebhoy School of Art and Industry in Bombay, Lockwood could claim an extensive 'practical knowledge of Gothic as well as Italian ornament' and a wide 'acquaintance with the various processes of Pottery'; and it was these areas of expertise that secured his appointment.[16] The contract that Lockwood was offered, and accepted, was initially for three years at a salary of 400 rupees a month (about £36), plus whatever fees he could pick up from pupils and apprentices.

The Bombay in which Alice and Lockwood arrived in May 1865 was a flourishing city, soon to be known as 'The Gateway of India' with the opening of the Suez Canal. Their new home on the Esplanade was a whitewashed bungalow just across the compound from the School of Art. In the early summer the bungalow was surrounded by a colourful jungle of plants and scrub, which shrivelled into a dust bowl as the heat increased, then turned into a swamp when the rains came.

Life at first cannot have been easy. While Lockwood had his new job to engross him, Alice had to set up a household in conditions very different from any she had previously experienced. Packing cases sent ahead had gone astray, and a dinner service had, expensively, to be bought. An array of servants, far more than in England, had to be employed and their castes and duties understood. Sanitary arrangements were primitive, fever frequent and the spicy food unfamiliar. The intricacies of the Anglo-Indian social hierarchy, in which the Kiplings occupied a low position, were not always easy to grasp. She suffered from homesickness and morning sickness.

Their son was born at ten o'clock on the evening of 30 December 1865, after six days of labour – 'as long as it took for the creation of the world,' as Alice later quipped.[17] The servants sacrificed a goat to assist a safe delivery and quick recovery. The child was christened Joseph Rudyard Kipling – Joseph following the Kipling family tradition, and Rudyard, on Aunt Louie's suggestion, to commemorate the couple's engagement at Rudyard Lake. Had Rud been a girl, his name, less memorably, would have been Margaret Macdonald Kipling (which would have given him the same initials as another English writer about India, M M Kaye).

A carte-de-visite of Rud as a baby showed him, white as a snowflake, asleep on his *ayah*'s lap. Uncle Frederic, when he saw the photograph, pretended to mistake the *ayah* for Alice and joked, 'Dear me, how dark Alice has become!'[18] In another early photograph Rud, now a year old, sat on Alice's knee, smiling up at her raised finger. The deeply cleft chin was already clearly in evidence, though not of course the eyebrows or the slight cast in one eye. Rud made his presence felt from the beginning. Lockwood, writing to his sister-in-law Edie just before Rud's first birthday, described him as 'a great lark' and how it was 'the quaintest thing in the world to see him eating his supper, intently watched by three dogs to whom he administers occasional blundering blows with a little whip & much shouting'. From the same letter it appears that, socially speaking, the Kiplings were now starting to find their feet. At a recent party they had met Lady Frere, the Governor's wife, and 'various swells', and Alice had 'sung in the choruses and duets like a bird'. They were becoming assimilated into Anglo-India in other ways too. 'A Hindoo,' Lockwood went on, 'makes a shot at the right thing & he hits or misses by chance . . . a strange and curious imperfection & falling short attends everything . . . I don't suppose if I were to talk for a week I could make you quite realise how far the brains of the native take him and where the inevitable clog of his indolence & that'll-do-ishness stop him short.'[19]

When Alice again became pregnant in the autumn of 1867, they decided that she should return to England to have the baby, taking Rud with her. Given the difficulties of his birth, the decision was entirely understandable, although it must have severely stretched their finances.

Alice and Rud reached London on 10 March 1868, and after a fortnight with Georgie and Edward Burne-Jones at The Grange went on to stay with Alice's parents, who were by now living in Bewdley in Worcestershire. As soon as they arrived, the two-year-old Rud made a rapid survey of the house's sleeping arrangements and announced indignantly that his grandparents had 'tooken the best room for themselves'.[20] With Alice's father, George, bedridden and dying, it was not an auspicious beginning.

On 10 May Alice returned to Georgie's to have the baby, leaving Rud with her parents and her sister Louie, who lived nearby at Wilden. The baby was delivered a month later on 11 June. She was christened Alice after her mother, but was soon known by Lockwood's nickname for her, Trix. Weighing eleven pounds, she was born with a black eye and a broken arm and looked, according to Georgie, 'like a Blake baby so big and white'.[21] In fact, everyone assumed that she had been born dead until, after much slapping from the doctor, she started to breathe. Rolled up in a blanket, she was then placed on a chair in Burne-Jones's studio, where a large prospective buyer was only just prevented from sitting on her.

Alice stayed on at Georgie's for another month after the birth. While his mother was away, Rud would apparently walk down the street in Bewdley, shouting 'Ruddy is coming!' or, if anyone got in his way, 'An *angry* Ruddy is coming!'[22] It was not a story that Louie thought to pass on to Alice when the latter wrote, asking for news of her son. Indeed, as Louie informed Aggie, she would have been perfectly happy to send Alice 'some Ruddy anecdotes . . . but since he has not had his retentive memory crammed with rhymes & so on, he really says nothing funny, and is a very usual little boy'.[23]

Soon after Alice's return to Bewdley with Trix, Rud did in fact say something funny. On his mother remarking that Trix looked 'like a Rubens lady', he agreed in his newly acquired Worcestershire accent that 'ur be very like Reuben' – Reuben being Louie's coachman and Rud's current hero.[24] Louie, writing again to Aggie, did not mention this particular exchange but did say that the baby was proving 'terribly cross and troublesome', while Rud was being 'good and nice', and that for the first time she felt 'very fond of the child'.[25]

During August and September Alice took the children on a visit to Lockwood's mother at Skipton. In early October they returned to the Macdonalds at Bewdley for a final few weeks before leaving on the first leg of the journey back to Bombay. The departure from Bewdley on 2 November did not go well. Hannah noted in her diary that 'Ruddy, after being sweet & pleasant for a little while, screamed horribly just before leaving, which had the effect of drying our tears. I cannot think how his poor Mother will bear the voyage to Bombay with an infant, and that self-willed rebel. I hope his Father will train him better.'[26] A week later, in another letter to Aggie, Louie was more waspishly sententious: 'Sorry as we were to lose [Alice] personally, her children turned the house into such a bear-garden, & Ruddy's screaming tempers made Papa so ill we were thankful to see them on their way. The wretched disturbance one ill-ordered child can make is a lesson for all time to me.'[27] (A sobering reflection when one recalls that Louie had recently given birth to a future Prime Minister, Stanley Baldwin.) On 13 November, a few days after Alice and the children had set sail, George Macdonald died.

From the surviving evidence of this nine-month trip it has been suggested that Rud may have been the toddler from Hell. This is patently absurd – although at times he was no doubt quite as noisy, unruly and tyrannical as his grandmother and aunt claimed. Reading Hannah's almost daily accounts in her diary of her husband's failing health, and remembering that for much of the time she also had to contend with a turbulent two-year-old, it is impossible not to feel very sorry for her. For instance, the entry for 9 October reads simply: 'Poorly and depressed beyond my power of expression, and I would not express it if I could.'[28] In the circumstances it was natural enough for her to find Rud's tantrums intolerable. And yet one should feel sympathy for Rud too. He was after all a very young child, staying in completely unfamiliar surroundings among strangers, one of whom was slowly and painfully dying. In addition, his mother was absent a good deal and was preoccupied with the new baby. That he should sometimes have been 'ill-ordered' and given to 'screaming tempers' is hardly surprising. It would have been far more surprising had he always been 'good and nice'.

Rud's earliest memories probably dated from his return to Bombay. He remembered lying awake in his cot, listening to the sound of the rain in the monsoons, and, when it was too hot to sleep, getting up and untucking the mosquito-net and getting bitten to death.[29] He remembered 'vast green spaces and wonderful walks through coconut woods on the edge of the sea where the Parsees waded in and prayed to the rising sun'; going to the fruit market in the early morning with his Roman Catholic Goanese *ayah* and Trix in her pram; with Meeta, his bearer, 'assisting with offerings at some Hindu wayside temple' where, being below the age of caste, he 'could trot in and out without offence'.[30]

His *ayah* and Meeta and the other servants formed the centre of his inner kingdom. With them he was Rud-*baba* and spoke in Hindi, and was lulled to sleep by their stories and songs. In one story a Ranee turned into a tiger; in another a potter's son married a princess. Listening to the servants' talk, he learnt 'the elementary facts of life so discreetly veiled from the young in the west' and was surrounded by warmth, safety and unconditional affection.[31]

On the borders of this world existed his parents. With them he spoke English, 'haltingly translated out of the vernacular idiom that one thought and dreamed in'.[32] He would wander across the compound on his own to the School of Art to see his father. On one such occasion, he later recounted:

> I passed the edge of a huge ravine a foot deep, where a winged monster as big as myself attacked me, and I fled and wept. My Father drew for me a picture of the tragedy with a rhyme underneath –:
>
> There was a small boy in Bombay
> Who once from a hen ran away.
>   When they said: 'You're a baby,'
>   He replied: 'Well, I may be:
> But I don't like these hens of Bombay.'
>
> This consoled me.[33]

Without wanting to make too much of the incident, this was probably Rud's first experience of the consolations of literature. Less portentously, a pupil of Lockwood's, Pestonjee Bomanjee, recalled years afterwards how Rud would come into the room where they were modelling and would pelt the students with clay, before being forcibly removed by his father.[34] Rud also remembered Pestonjee Bomanjee and preserved his name in the *Just So* story 'How the Rhinoceros got his Skin'.

Near the Kiplings' bungalow rose the ominous Towers of Silence, on top of which dead bodies were exposed to the vultures. One day Alice found a child's hand in the garden. Rud, naturally curious, wanted to see the hand; Alice, naturally upset, told him not to ask questions. Already an adept at knowing whom to pump for necessary information, he found out from his *ayah*. When Rud developed whooping cough, however, Alice's imagination and good sense rose to the occasion. He had been prescribed an emetic to be taken before going to bed, and Alice devised a ritual whereby after the nightly dose she would choose an interesting storybook and begin to read. Rud would then raise his hand at the crucial moment as a sign for her to stop. Less dramatically, she wrote to a friend of how, after desperately coveting a donkey, Rud had come to her saying, 'Never mind of that donkey. I've seen a little white horse' and had gone on to tell her exactly how few rupees it would cost. Alice was particularly struck by her four-year-old son's unusual description of the horse as looking 'rather like a bicycle'.[35]

It is not known exactly when Lockwood and Alice decided that Rud and Trix should be sent to live in England. Why they chose to do so would not have surprised any of their fellow Anglo-Indians; in fact, the reason would have seemed too obvious to mention. If an explanation had to be given, it was usually that, at a certain age, white children became particularly susceptible to the rigours of the Indian climate. This, however, was a convenient euphemism, a broad-spectrum rationale, masking other concerns – since, medically, there was no reason why children of five and three, like Rud and Trix, should have been more at risk from the climate than children even younger.

What were those other concerns? Two at least seem straightforward enough. Anglo-Indians did not want their children to grow up thinking of India as home: home, or 'Home' as they usually referred to it, was England. Nor did they want their children to acquire sing-song, chi-chi accents, the almost inevitable consequence of prolonged exposure to the servants' English. In addition, there were less obvious anxieties, again involving the influence of the servants. Maud Driver in her 1909 book The Englishwoman in India was one of the first publicly to express these less mentionable fears. According to her, it was necessary to send Anglo-Indian children 'Home' in order to remove them from 'the promiscuous intimacy of the Indian servants, whose propensity to worship at the shrine of the Baba-log [the children] is unhappily apt to demoralise the small gods and goddesses they serve'.[36]

In other words, while Anglo-Indian parents were happy enough for their children, when very young, to be cosseted and worshipped by the servants, they did not want them to grow up unmanageable and, in the case of their sons, unmanly. And, strictly in its own terms, such an attitude makes sense. There is plenty of evidence, not least among Kipling's

12

stories, to support the idea that the little sahibs were often extremely indulged and tyrannical. In his own case, his sister Trix remembered how the servants used to treat him as one of themselves, calling him (as he was later to call his character Kim) 'Little Friend of all the world'. She added that he was also 'rather noisy and spoilt'.[37] More obliquely, Maud Driver also hinted at something more problematic than simple over-indulgence. Her phrase 'promiscuous intimacy' suggests that the real demoralisation she had in mind was of a sexual nature: that, through such close and extended contact with the servants, white children ran the risk, at an early age, of finding out about the facts of life and of knowing more than was good for them. Kipling's own testimony bears this out, and he certainly came to feel that in India 'it was inexpedient and dangerous for a white child to be reared through youth'.[38]

After five years in India, Lockwood and Alice probably fully shared and endorsed these concerns. But in their case two other factors contributed to their decision to send Rud and Trix to England. On 18 April 1870 Alice had given birth prematurely to another son who did not survive. Whether as catalyst or corroboration, that loss must have played its part. The other reason was more pragmatic: without the children, Alice would be better able to concentrate her very formidable social skills towards the advancement of Lockwood's career. So, in the circumstances, the decision to send Rud and Trix to England was nothing out of the ordinary. What seems puzzling, and requires some explanation, is why the couple should have decided to send the children to live with strangers and not with any of their numerous relations.

Alice, who obviously had a monopoly on the domestic decision-making, must take responsibility for this. Edith Plowden recalled her later saying that 'She had never thought of leaving her children with her own family – it led to complications.'[39] Alice could hardly have been unaware of the bad impression that Rud's behaviour had made on her mother and sister Louie during the 1868 visit. Understandably, she would have wanted to avoid any possible repetition. Other worries probably also affected her thinking. While she and her sisters were undeniably close, their letters and Louie's diary show that they could be intensely competitive and at times extremely jealous of each other. Did Alice fear that if she sent her children to live with members of her own family, they might in time transfer their primary allegiance away from herself? The prospect of parting with Rud and Trix would have been painful enough in itself; to part with them to strangers might well have appeared a less threatening prospect than the risk of 'losing' them to one or other of her tough, charming sisters. Towards the end of her life, Trix suggested that the obvious solution would have been for Rud and her to have gone to Lockwood's family at Skipton. But once Alice had discounted her own side of the family, clearly Lockwood's had to be discounted too; that would only have led to other complications.

As it turned out, Alice and Lockwood chose Pryse Agar and Sarah Holloway of Southsea as the future 'foster parents' for their children. Whether the original contact was made through an advertisement in an English or Indian newspaper or through some other channel has never been discovered. Presumably letters and references were exchanged and considered satisfactory. At any event, all the necessary arrangements must have been made long before Alice, Lockwood and the children set off for England in April 1871.

One final anecdote of Rud as a very young child survives. Told by his parents of the creation of the world in six days, he commented thoughtfully, 'If God had half-made the world and then made a man how *terrified* he would have been.'[40]

2

The House of Desolation

The Kiplings landed at Southampton on 13 May 1871, put up for a night or two at the Railway Hotel and then travelled to London to the Burne-Jones family at The Grange. Louie, who saw them there, commented in her diary that Rud was 'much grown and improved' and that Alice had to undergo a painful operation to remove a big toenail.[1]

The next five months were full of activity. There were visits to Hannah and Edie at Bewdley; to Louie, her husband Alfred and son Stan at nearby Wilden; to Lockwood's mother and sisters at Skipton; further visits to the Burne-Joneses. Lockwood and Alice spent a day at the International Exhibition in South Kensington; toured Alfred Baldwin's iron-works to watch tin-plate making; had dinner with Aggie and her husband. For Lockwood, who had been away for six years, it was an especially exhilarating and stimulating trip, apart of course from the prospect of leaving the children.

On 13 October Alice took Rud and Trix down to Southsea and settled them in for a few days with the Holloways at Lorne Lodge before rejoining her husband in London. A month later, on 18 November, they sailed on the *Moolton* back to Bombay. Neither of them saw the children again for over five years. How much, one wonders, did Alice and Lockwood really know about the couple with whom they were leaving their children?

Pryse Agar Holloway was the fourth son and seventh of fifteen children of

15

Benjamin Holloway Esquire and his wife Georgina. He was born on 28 June 1810 (or perhaps 1811) at the family home, Lee Place, Charlbury in Oxfordshire. Rebuilt at the beginning of the eighteenth century on an earlier site, Lee Place was a large, handsome establishment surrounded by its own grounds. Pryse Agar's grandfather had bought the house in 1772 from Robert Lee, when the latter succeeded to the Earldom of Lichfield and moved to Ditchley Park. In 1832, on the death of Benjamin Holloway, Lee Place was sold to Benjamin Whippy, High Sheriff of Oxfordshire and the husband of Jane Holloway, one of Pryse Agar's sisters. It is now a summer residence of the Duke of Marlborough.

So, whatever Pryse Agar's circumstances by 1871 – and he must by then have been relatively hard-up to be taking in other people's children – he was born and raised in the affluent world of the English upper-middle classes. His five brothers all had careers that ranged from the distin-guished to the solidly successful. Benjamin, the eldest, was a solicitor in Woodstock. Edward rose to Lieutenant-Colonel in the Madras Army. Thomas served in the Royal Marines and finished up a Knight Commander of the Order of the Bath. Henry was a clergyman and Octavius a Fellow of New College, Oxford. By contrast, Pryse Agar's own career, in so far as it can be reconstructed, was much more modest.

He joined the Royal Navy on 13 June 1824 as a Volunteer, First Class, entering HMS *Brisk*, a sloop with a complement of seventy-five men and two supernumerary boys.[2] He served on the *Brisk* under Captain Charles Hope from 1824 to 1829, except for two brief spells on loan to HMS *Gloucester* and HMS *Warspite*. Promoted to midshipman on 18 November 1825, much of his five years' naval service was spent on patrols in the Mediterranean. He took part in the Battle of Navarino in October 1827 and was paid off, still a midshipman, on 3 June 1829. Although he was subsequently known as 'Captain Holloway', this was probably one of those honorary titles that ex-sailors often acquire.

The decade after Pryse Agar left the *Brisk* is largely a blank. Perhaps, as has been suggested, he joined the Merchant Navy, though there is no evi-dence to support this. It seems likely that for a time he was a whaler. Kipling recalled how as a child he used to stare with 'horrified interest' at a 'dry, black scar' on the 'Captain's' ankle, which he was told was the result of being pulled overboard by 'a harpoon-line while whale-fishing'.[3] It is hard to imagine him inventing so specific a detail.

However Holloway earned his livelihood during the 1830s, he was back in the Oxford area by 1844. On 6 January of that year, he was elected Inspector of Weights and Measures for Oxfordshire at the Quarter Sessions and on 2 March duly inspected Charlbury's Weights and Measures at the Crown Inn, from ten o'clock in the morning till five o'clock in the afternoon.[4] He then disappeared again from view for another eleven years. At some point in the intervening period he must have moved to London, because the Navy Records for 1855 list him as joining the Coastguards from Cox and Co., the Army agents and bankers, who had their offices in Craig's Court off Whitehall. His position at Cox's cannot have been a very elevated one, since the firm's records fail to mention him; perhaps he worked there as a clerk.

On 15 December 1855 he was appointed to the Coastguard Station at Sizewell Gap, Aldeburgh, Suffolk, probably as Chief Officer – if not, he was soon promoted to that rank. He married Sarah Slatter on 10 August 1859 at nearby Dunwich and their son Thomas Henry Pryse Holloway was born the following year on 16 June.[5] On 9 February 1866, Holloway was granted the tenancy of the Rose and Crown Inn, Charlbury, presumably as an absentee-tenant, since he continued to serve as Chief Officer of Coastguards at Sizewell Gap until his superannuation on 23 August 1869. Then or soon afterwards he and his family moved to Southsea, rented Lorne Lodge and advertised to take in children.

By the time he met Rud and Trix in October 1871, Pryse Agar was in his sixties, tall, grey and lame, and probably already showing the effects of the liver cancer that was to kill him three years later. Born apparently with every social advantage, he had spent a large part of his life shifting from job to job before finally finding his niche as a coastguard. Whether his lack of material success was due to a restless temperament or limited ability, it is impossible to know. Perhaps he was just less ambitious than his high-achieving brothers.

Of his wife Sarah, who was to become such a key figure in the lives of Rud and Trix, only two statements can be made with certainty: she was over ten years younger than her husband and she came from much lower down the social ladder. The eldest daughter and second of five children of Thomas and Nance Slatter, she was born in Oxford towards the end of 1822. According to her baptismal record, her father was a tailor and the family lived in the High Street.[6] One imagines that she and Pryse Agar

17

must have originally met in or around Oxford, or at least that Oxford somehow provided the initial link. At the time of their marriage he was pushing fifty and she forty. Perhaps it was a middle-aged romance, based on an earlier attraction; perhaps he simply wanted someone to look after him, and she wanted a husband. Either way, the discrepancy in class seems a more fruitful area for speculation, since it lends support to Kipling's later hints that social tensions, and Sarah's disappointed hopes of a legacy from Pryse Agar's brother Thomas, were important factors in the household dynamics at Lorne Lodge.

Kipling wrote a number of accounts of his Southsea years – the earliest being the fictional 'Baa Baa Black Sheep' in 1888, the latest the opening to his autobiography *Something of Myself* in 1935, only months before his death. In addition, he drew widely on the experience in his work, often in a transmuted form and in unexpected contexts. Trix, who stayed at Southsea even longer than her brother, also produced her own versions of their time at Lorne Lodge. Both told a story of extreme emotional abuse. While there is no reason to doubt the general truth of their accounts, or many of the specific details they mentioned, it is likely that things only went seriously wrong after Holloway's death in the autumn of 1874. That the acute misery and suffering that Rud, in particular, endured after the 'Captain's' death should have come in time to dominate their memories of the entire period is hardly surprising.

Lorne Lodge, Rud and Trix's new home, was a thin, three-storeyed house, covered in stucco and standing at the very end of a street then called Havelock Park, later changed to Campbell Road. At the front was a scrap of garden with a bank of St John's wort, at the back a tiny lawn, some Portugal laurels and a few flowers. Inside, off a short, narrow hall-way, was a drawing-room, described by Rud as having 'a buried-alive smell', and to the right a dining-room with a highly polished table.[7] Leading out from the dining-room was a small greenhouse with pink oleanders, the only things of colour and beauty in the whole of that drab house. The kitchen was downstairs in the basement, as was the 'play-room', where no fire was ever lit and anything left in the wall-cupboards quickly went blue with mildew. In later life, Trix would always be reminded of that 'mushroom-smelling den' whenever she was unwell, and it haunted her dreams.[8]

Back upstairs on the first floor were two bedrooms: Pryse Agar's at the back and the one shared by Sarah and Trix at the front above the drawing-room. Trix recalled 'a brass bed with a stiff white honeycomb quilt and a nightdress case with GOOD NIGHT braided on it in red, to match the SOILED LINEN bag that hung behind the door, and the BRUSH AND COMB bag on the toilet table. The wallpaper was a dull grey, patterned with small purple roses . . .'[9] Up a further flight of stairs were three attic bedrooms: Rud and the Holloways' eleven-year-old son Harry shared one, the current servant-girl had another, and the third was presumably a workroom or spare-room.

Mrs Holloway quickly annexed the three-and-a-half-year-old Trix as the daughter she had always wanted, and even if between Sarah and Rud it was dislike at first sight, the effects of this were kept in check while her husband was alive. Pryse Agar clearly warmed to the boy and went to considerable trouble to amuse and interest him. He told Rud of his days as a midshipman at Navarino and allowed him to play with a model of the *Brisk*. He took him for long walks in and around Portsmouth, discussing the ships and the docks, and sowing the seeds of Rud's later enthusiasm for the Navy. Kipling always remembered with relish his use of the expression 'Shiver my timbers!' and, as an ex-coastguard, Pryse Agar no doubt had smuggling stories to tell. The impression emerges of a kind, patient man whom Rud, a naturally affectionate child, accepted readily enough as a father-substitute.

When Alice's mother Hannah and her sisters Georgie, Aggie and Louie paid a visit at the end of August 1872, almost a year after the separation, they found no cause for alarm. On the contrary, Hannah, who saw the children frequently over the following three weeks, taking them for drives and to the beach, recorded in her diary that both were 'well and happy'.[10] Louie was even more enthusiastic. She thought 'the little Kiplings . . . very well & happy, improved in every way & Mrs Holloway a very nice woman indeed'.[11] Even allowing for best behaviour on all sides, two such critical eye-witnesses are hard to gainsay. And one can be sure that Louie, mindful of the 'bear-garden' of four years earlier, would not have asked Rud to come on to Wilden for a month's stay had she had any misgivings.

This visit too was a success. Hannah spent a peaceful Sunday with her grandson, 'reading the Scriptures & repeating hymns' while the others were at church.[12] Louie referred to him more than once in her diary as 'dear little Ruddy' and commented on how 'beautifully' he and her son Stan behaved.[13] On 16 October Rud was taken to Oxford to rendezvous with Mrs Holloway. This arrangement was probably so that Sarah could conduct some family business, but as far as Rud was concerned, the highlight of the trip was being shown 'an Ancient of Days, who, I was told, was the Provost of Oriel; wherefore I never understood, but conceived him to be some sort of idol'.[14] The idol was the celebrated don Edward Hawkins, then in his eighties, who had been Provost since 1828. He seems to have made a deep impression on Rud, since both his Carrollian title 'Provostoforiel' and his habit of unashamedly nodding off in company were to find a place in the 1895 story 'The Brushwood Boy'.

It may have been the Christmas of that year or more likely the next, 1873, that saw the first of Rud's annual visits to the Burne-Joneses at The Grange. Arriving at the house, he would, he recalled, 'reach up to the open-work iron bell-pull on the wonderful gate that let me into all felicity'.[15] On the Christmas Eve of his first visit, Aunt Georgie and Uncle Ned assembled a group of friends and relations 'who could if needed still romp with a will'.[16] The Morrises, William and Jane, were there with their daughters, Jenny and May; so too was Rud's uncle, Edward Poynter, with his son Ambo; and the family friends Charles Faulkner, William De Morgan, William Allingham and Sir Frederick Burton. With their pranks, games and stories, the grown-ups ensured that the children had an evening they never forgot.

In his autobiography Kipling offered a vivid collage of the excitement, affection and sheer fun of this and subsequent Christmases at The Grange. He would climb the mulberry tree in the garden to hatch plots with his cousins, Phil and Margaret, or they would improvise a toboggan-slide in the nursery out of a table and two chairs. The house seemed always full of visitors only too happy to share in the children's games. William Morris, known to Rud as 'Uncle Topsy', would turn up at all hours to try out new ideas for designs and poems on Ned and Georgie. Once, failing to find them and desperate for an audience, he unearthed Rud and Margaret in the nursery, climbed on to the rocking-horse and, pulsing backwards and forwards, poured out 'The Story of the Ere-Dwellers', a Norse saga he was currently translating, while the children listened spellbound. The only visitor to ignore the children entirely was, ironically, Robert Browning, whose poetry – besides being the catalyst that had brought Rud's parents together – was to prove a major influence on Kipling's own development as a writer. Uncle Ned's paintings were of course all over the house, propped up wherever there was space, and 'whiffling down from the big studio on the first floor' came the 'most wonderful smells of paint and turpentine'.[17]

Evenings were best of all. The children sprawled on sofas, sucking toffee and calling each other 'Ho Son' and 'Daughter of my Uncle' and 'O True Believer', while Aunt Georgie read them Walter Scott's *The Pirate* or stories from *The Arabian Nights*. Sometimes Uncle Ned would stop work and join in. On one occasion he shrouded himself in rugs and pretended to be 'Norna of the Fitful Head' (from *The Pirate*), answering the children's questions and thrilling them 'with delightful shivers, in a voice deeper than all the boots in the world'. Another time he appeared, brandishing a tube of 'Mummy Brown' paint, and announced that as it was 'made of dead Pharaohs', it must be buried forthwith. So they all processed into the garden to dig a ceremonial grave. At bedtime the children would lean over the banisters, listening to what Kipling later claimed was 'the loveliest sound in the world – deep-voiced men laughing together over dinner'.[18]

It was probably during that initial Christmas at The Grange that Rud wrote his first surviving letter, a note to Aunt Louie, thanking his cousin Stan for a card and Uncle Alfred for a copy of *Robinson Crusoe*. The note marked the beginning of a lifelong habit of decorating letters with drawings: here a picture of Cordelia and a map of Lilliput and 'Bromdignag'. It may also have been on this visit that he wrote the fragment 'Will Briarts Ghost'. 'It was a dark stormy night of the goodwins,' began the first chapter, showing a firmer grasp of atmospherics than spelling, before going on to describe the dastardly murder of Captain Briart by one of his crew. Chapter 2, of which only a few lines survive, would presumably have gone on to recount the return of the Captain's ghost: 'The scene is the beach of Deal it is midnight and one of the coastguard men is on the lookout he paces to and fro quickly to warm himself when suddenly he becomes aware of . . .'[19] The presence of the coastguard suggests that as a child Rud probably knew of Pryse Agar's former occupation, and the story itself may even have been one that he had been told by the old man. The fragment was published in the *Sydney Morning Herald* after Kipling's death by his cousin, Hugh Poynter, with a note claiming that it was written at the age of eight. If so, 'Will Briarts Ghost' was Rud's earliest surviving literary effort.

Compared to Lorne Lodge, The Grange must have seemed like a paradise. Small wonder that when Kipling finally settled down at Bateman's, he should have begged Georgie for its iron bell-pull to hang by the front door, 'in the hope that other children might also feel happy when they rang it'.[20]

And then, on 29 September 1874, the 'Captain' died, and without him the whole balance of the household at Southsea changed. For Rud, his death was in effect a second 'abandonment', following that of his parents three years earlier. For Sarah, too, her husband's death brought irreversible consequences. In addition to her feelings of loss, she now had to manage the three children on her own and probably on a reduced income, since it is likely that Pryse Agar had been drawing a small pension.

Of course to suggest that before his death the situation at Lorne Lodge had been more or less under control does not preclude the strong possibility that undercurrents already existed, or that there had been problems from the start. When Rud first arrived, he was bumptious and wilful and, according to his sister, extremely spoilt.[21] Indulged by the Indian servants and his mother, he was quite unused to female authority and no doubt reacted to Mrs Holloway's attempts to discipline him with cheeky contempt. Even someone of a more equable nature than Sarah – and she apparently had 'a violent temper, and enjoyed making scenes' – would have found it hard not to resent such treatment.[22] Moreover, her husband's kindness towards the boy, though it helped to provide a stabilising influence, was probably also a source of jealousy. If Rud felt displaced, it is likely that the Holloways' son Harry did too. Social resentments almost certainly played their part. What did Sarah feel about a boy left in her charge whose background and connections implied so much more auspicious a future than any awaiting her own son? Was there disapproval of parents who chose to leave their children in another's care and could afford to do so? In any case, what sort of parents were they, when they had not even taken the trouble to teach their nearly six-year-old boy to read? And, a crucial element, Sarah was intensely religious.

Lorne Lodge, Kipling archly observed in his autobiography, was 'an establishment run with the full vigour of the Evangelical as revealed to the Woman'.[23] 'Evangelical' in the nineteenth century was a broad term, covering members of a wide range of 'enthusiastic' Low Church sects, both inside and outside the Church of England. Congregationalists were, for instance, Evangelicals and so were Plymouth Brethren. The essence of Evangelical belief lay in its particular view of salvation. Evangelicals believed that, as a result of the Fall, human nature was inherently sinful and depraved and that the Bible, not the Church, carried sole authority in matters of doctrine. Salvation was to be gained neither through good works nor through observance of the Sacraments, but exclusively through faith in the atoning death of Christ. Evangelicals were also keenly interested in the destiny of an individual's soul: at death, they believed, there was either eternal life or eternal damnation. Not surprisingly, reactions to Evangelicalism were often sharply divergent. George Eliot in *Middlemarch* (published while Rud was at Southsea, though set some forty years earlier) was not alone in thinking that 'Evangelicalism had cast a certain suspicion as of plague-infection over the few amusements which survived in the provinces'.[24] Less scathingly, Dr Arnold of Rugby defined an Evangelical as 'a good Christian, with a narrow understanding'.[25] Both descriptions seem to fit Mrs Holloway's brand of Evangelicalism. She had the Puritan's killjoy attitude to innocent pleasure, while at the same time being 'theoretically . . . a good woman' and well-respected at the local church. 'Lack of imagination', in Trix's view, was her cardinal fault.[26]

Since some Methodists were also Evangelicals, it is possible that Hannah Macdonald's impression that her grandchildren were in good hands with the Holloways may have been somewhat coloured by Sarah's evident devoutness. At any event, her narrow, fixed views clearly dominated her attitude towards Rud and determined how she treated him. Alice and Lockwood, lapsed Wesleyans and purely nominal churchgoers, had given their son little or no religious instruction. It was Mrs Holloway who first introduced him to Hell 'in all its terrors', and when he mixed up the Biblical version of Creation with his *ayah*'s stories, she was profoundly shocked.[27] Here, she must have felt, was a child, deep in sin, whose soul it was her duty to save. 'Baa Baa Black Sheep' provided an example of the sort of methods she used. Punch (Rud's alias in the story) was ordered to play and under no circumstances to read. He rigged up an elaborate arrangement of bricks and a table, which he could work one-handed to make it sound as though he was playing, while holding a book in his other hand. Caught out 'acting a lie', he was beaten by Aunty Rosa (Sarah) and confined in the playroom: 'It was a revelation to him. The room-door was shut and he was left to weep himself into repentance and work out his own gospel of life.'[28] Here, as elsewhere in the story, the heavily ironic religious phrasing – revelation, repentance, gospel of life – made it plain that the Sarah character was an Evangelical, though she was never specifically identified as such.

Since there is nothing to indicate that Pryse Agar shared his wife's beliefs, the full effect of these probably did not come into force until after his death, when Sarah was trying to maintain control over the increasingly dysfunctional household. From that point, however, whatever Rud said or did was subjected to a regular inquisition from Mrs Holloway and her son, Harry, who seems to have enjoyed acting as informer-cum-assistant-torturer. Rud and Trix both remembered Harry with a loathing even deeper than the hatred they felt for his mother. 'I was a real joy to him,' recalled Kipling bitterly:

for when his mother had finished with me for the day he (we slept in the same room) took me on and roasted the other side. If you cross-examine a child of seven or eight on his day's doings (specially when he wants to go to sleep) he will contradict himself very satisfactorily. If each contradiction be set down as a lie and retailed at breakfast, life is not easy.

That Rud was a pathological liar became an *idée fixe* with both Sarah and Harry. In another bitter memory, Kipling told how:

Coming out of church once I smiled. The Devil-Boy [Harry] demanded why. I said I didn't know why, which was child's truth. He replied that I *must* know. People didn't laugh at nothing. Heaven knows what explanation I put forward; but it was duly reported to the Woman as a 'lie'. Result, afternoon upstairs with the Collects to learn. I learned most of the Collects that way and a great deal of the Bible.[29]

Kipling claimed in his autobiography that the culmination of this obsession with 'lying' came one day when he threw away a bad school report and pretended never to have received it. (He was by then attending nearby Hope House, which he described as a 'terrible little day-school'.) 'My web of deceit,' he continued, 'was swiftly exposed . . . and I was well beaten and sent to school through the streets of Southsea with the placard "Liar" between my shoulders.'[30]

The authenticity of this particular humiliation, also mentioned in 'Baa Baa Black Sheep', has been questioned and its similarity to an episode in Dickens's *David Copperfield* pointed out. Might not Kipling, perhaps unconsciously, have 'borrowed' the incident to heighten the impact of Punch's sufferings in the story and then, nearly fifty years later, have remembered *that* version when he came to write *Something of Myself*? This is possible. Trix, who learnt to read quicker than her brother, would recall telling him the plot of *David Copperfield* at Lorne Lodge. And certainly David's persecution in the novel by the Evangelical Murdstones did bear a marked resemblance to Sarah and Harry's persecution of Rud. A case of self-identification leading to appropriation? Against this, there is Trix's detailed recollection of trying to help her brother remove the placard.[31] But then her memory could have failed her, just as his could have failed him. (Both she and Rud remembered Alice *and* Lockwood taking them down to Southsea, while Hannah's diary makes it clear that only their mother accompanied them.) Or she could simply have been backing up her brother as loyally in death as she seems to have done in life. And yet is the whole 'Liar' incident so very implausible? After all, Wilde's witticism about Life imitating Art only works because it reverses our *usual* assumptions.

Rud was sustained through his period of acutest suffering and mistreatment by Trix's affection (despite attempts by Sarah to alienate the two), by his annual visits to The Grange and by his development of intricate, imaginative games using 'natural magic'. One of these games, acted out in the mushroom-smelling playroom, was based on Uncle Alfred's gift of *Robinson Crusoe* and, with Rud in the role of trader, involved a 'coconut shell strung on a red cord, a tin trunk and a piece of packing case which kept off any other world. Thus fenced around, everything inside the fence was quite real . . . If a bit of board fell, I had to begin the magic all over again . . . The magic, you see, lies in the ring or fence that you take refuge in.'[32] It sounds as though the object of this particular game was, by

enactment of a highly precise and complicated ritual, to create an alternative, safe world from which the uncontrollable realities of Lorne Lodge
could be temporarily shut out. Another game by which he tried to avoid
his surroundings was to make 'a charm . . . out of old bones stuffed with
wool & camphor-scented'.[33] Unfortunately, he does not say how this
charm was supposed to work, nor what or whom it represented. An earlier
variation, according to Trix, was to tell her stories of their lost kingdom
in Bombay and to teach her Hindi words for use as a private language.
One of these words was *Kuch-nay* (or, more accurately, *Kuch-nahi*), meaning 'nothing', which became their accepted code name for Mrs
Holloway.[34]

His main form of escape, however, was reading. This had not come
without a struggle. He was put off initially by being forced to read by
Sarah and by the fact that his sister picked it up much more quickly than
he did. Trix recalled how, when she was already a fluent reader and Rud
was still only spelling out the letters, he tried, in typical older-brother
fashion, to play down her accomplishment. 'No, Trix,' he would say,
'you're too little to see . . . I want to know, *why* "t" with "hat" after it
should be "that".'[35] But once he had grasped the essentials, new worlds
opened up.

In 1919 Yeats's friend Lady Gregory recorded a conversation with
Kipling about childhood reading, in which he insisted that 'one could not
think too much of the influence of books read in early years'.[36] Since so
much of what he read in the Southsea period was later to bear fruit, it is
interesting to consider even a short list of what he then so eagerly
devoured. There were copies of *Aunt Judy's Magazine*, including Mrs
Ewing's *Six to Sixteen*, a story of Anglo-Indian children sent back to
England to be brought up; 'I owe more in circuitous ways to that tale than
I can tell,' Kipling later remarked.[37] There was F E Paget's *The Hope of the
Katzekopfs*, the preface quoting from Bishop Corbet's poem beginning
'Farewell rewards and fairies'; George Macdonald's *The Princess and the
Goblin*, used in the story 'Wee Willie Winkie'; James Greenwood's *King
Lion*, an acknowledged source for the *Jungle Books*; Louisa Alcott's *Little
Women* and *Little Men*; the fairytales of Andersen and Grimm; Lewis
Carroll's *Alice* books; the hunting novels of Surtees, alluded to frequently
in *Stalky & Co.* and in later stories like 'Little Foxes' and 'My Son's Wife';
and poems by Wordsworth, Scott and Tennyson. Even a magazine like

Sunday at Home, apparently Mrs Holloway's idea of suitable reading matter, later provided Rud with the title for a story, 'My Sunday at Home'. And there were the Collects and the Bible, which he was made to learn by heart.

In addition to what was available at Lorne Lodge, Rud had once a year the run of the library at The Grange. It was clearly the stimulus and example he absorbed during these Christmas visits that encouraged him to start writing himself. Alice and Lockwood's friend, Edith Plowden, recalled how in early 1877 letters arrived in Bombay containing some of the children's literary efforts. One of Rud's pieces, part of an attempted novel, described a heroine on a sofa, 'the snowy whiteness of her face hands and feet proclaim[ing] her aristocratic birth'. There was also a love poem (addressed to his cousin Margaret?), with the less than haunting refrain 'Margaret, Margaret I love but thee!' and the lines 'Up to its feathered head the barb/ Has pierced my heart'.[38] To judge by the watermark on the paper, two other poems, 'The Carolina' and 'The Legend of Cedar Swamp', also dated from this time. Both show definite promise for a child of just eleven. The following extract from 'The Carolina' suggests that 'The Rime of the Ancient Mariner' and older, traditional ballads like 'Sir Patrick Spens' were among Rud's discoveries at The Grange:

> A vessel from the harbour came
> The Carolina was her name
> With Stun'sails set and royals too
> Over the billows she lightly flew
> Three hundred souls bou[n]d for London town
> Each one doomed Alas! to drown
> For o'er the deck Death's dark shape hung
> Loud and weird were the songs he sung . . .
> Down, down, she lies full 50 fathom down
> Does the Carolina bound for London town.[39]

That Christmas of 1876 was to prove a turning-point in other ways. Rud's deep unhappiness finally became apparent to Georgie, who promptly wrote to Alice, urging her to come over as soon as possible. Back at Lorne Lodge, Rud's eyesight started to fail – he was to need strong glasses for the rest of his life – and the eleven-year-old suffered some sort of nervous breakdown. By the beginning of April 1877 Alice had reached Southsea and removed the children (though Trix was subsequently to return for intervals over the next few years). Kipling recalled his mother telling him afterwards how 'when she first came up to my room to kiss me goodnight, I flung up my arm to ward off the cuff that I had been trained to expect'.[40]

Why had it taken so long for Rud's problems to come to light? Part of the reason has already been suggested: that although he himself recalled the entire Southsea period as one of misery and persecution, it was more probably the last two and a half years that were really traumatic. Before the Christmas of 1875, say, there may have been little of note for even so concerned a relation as Aunt Georgie to detect; and of course after the 1872 visit none of the family had actually been down to Lorne Lodge to see the children. There is also the explanation that Kipling offered in his autobiography:

> Often and often afterwards, the beloved Aunt [Georgie] would ask me why I had never told any one how I was being treated. Children tell little more than animals, for what comes to them they accept as eternally established. Also, badly-treated children have a clear notion of what they are likely to get if they betray the secrets of the prison-house before they are clear of it.[41]

This makes sense in terms of a child's view of the world. It is only as adults that we achieve any perspective on our upbringing and come to realise that what has happened to us was not necessarily in the normal order of things. Kipling was right too that abused children often only 'tell' much later on. So it is perfectly understandable that at the time he said little or nothing about his sufferings to his mother or anyone else. To have escaped from Sarah and Harry, and to know that he did not have to return, would have been relief enough.

That said, the legacy of his Southsea years remained with Kipling always. He may have claimed, and genuinely believed, that the whole experience 'drained me of any capacity for real, personal hatred for the rest of my days', but the facts hardly bear this out.[42] Not only was he capable of intense hatred for individuals (and groups, races and nations), but hatred recurred again and again as a mainspring of his mature work. On a personal level, this may have been regrettable, but for him as a writer it had considerable imaginative gains. Hatred, and its conse-quences, formed the core of some of his greatest stories, and it was a sub-ject that he explored with an insight and an honesty few others have matched.

Orphanhood too was a condition he had learnt to understand inti-mately, and it is hardly coincidental that his two best-known child heroes, Kim and Mowgli, were orphans. So powerfully did the idea possess Kipling that in one poem he even went so far as to conceive of Heaven as the ultimate orphanage, where dead children pluck at 'the radiant robes of passers-by' and plead, 'Ah, please will you let us go home?'[43] For him the word 'home' always held profoundly dislocating implications. In part, of course, these can be attributed to the conflict experienced by many Anglo-Indian children between 'home' (India) and 'Home' (England), but in his case inner displacement and 'homelessness' were feelings that ran far deeper. The original source of these feelings was his time at Lorne Lodge, the 'home' that he came to think of as 'the House of Desolation'.[44]

Visiting Lorne Lodge today, it is hard to imagine that such suffering could ever have taken place there. It looks just an ordinary house in an ordinary street. And yet, downstairs in an alcove off the once mildewy basement-room where Rud and Trix used to play, deeply scored into the white-washed wall in capital letters, is the single word HELP.

3

Beetle in Love

The years of confinement at Lorne Lodge were followed by nine months of complete freedom. Alice took the children on a round of visits to relations and friends and then the three of them settled down for an extended holiday at Golding's Hill, a farm on the edge of Epping Forest. Here Rud and Trix quickly made friends with the farmer and his family, and with a local gipsy called Saville who allowed them to ride on his donkeys, taught them how to set snares for game and took them on expeditions deep into the forest. They climbed trees, played in the barn when it was wet, and Rud made up stories for Trix that 'started from an old log in the duck-pond, or a ruined cottage half seen in the Forest, and then became wildly exciting'.[1]

In the autumn they were joined by Stanley Baldwin, sent by Aunt Louie to escape an outbreak of scarlet fever. According to Trix, Stan tried but utterly failed to convert his cousins to cricket and soon became 'the wildest of the three'.[2] Together they raced hoops down a nearby hill, and the boys conducted a 'self-sacrificing war against a wasps' nest on a muddy islet in a most muddy pond', sustained by an enormous roly-poly pudding looted from the farm kitchen.[3] For Hallowe'en, Mr Dally, the farmer, gave the children wurzels out of which they carved lanterns, and on Guy Fawkes Night they 'pranced and capered like happy demons round and through the flames' of a huge bonfire in which they roasted potatoes, and 'no potatoes were ever so delicious'.[4] They were also joined for a time by

Alice's youngest sister, Edie. She strongly objected to the children coming into the kitchen reeking of the farmyard and telling her in graphic detail about pig-killing, but in lighter moments she was quite prepared to play the miming, rhyming game 'dumb crambo'.[5]

In November, Alice, worn out by months of unaccustomed child care, succumbed to shingles and her sister Georgie came down to Golding's Hill to look after her. Rud and Trix were despatched to 'an ivory-faced, lordly-whiskered ex-butler and his patient wife, who lived at 227 Brompton Road in London.[6] Here again they discovered exciting new ways to entertain themselves. They had a toy theatre, let off indoor-fireworks with exotic names like 'Pharaoh's Serpent' and fired a tin pistol with real caps. They dangled blobs of meat on bits of string to entice the army of cats that lived on the steep slate-roofs. They dropped alluringly wrapped packets, containing a lump of coal or a walnut-shell, down on to the street below and watched the surprised reactions of passers-by who stopped to pick them up.

When Alice rejoined them in December, she sensibly bought the children season tickets to the South Kensington Museum, where they became fascinated by the figure of a vast, bronze Buddha with a little door in its back into which, as Rud explained to his mother, 'the priests used to go . . . to work the miracles'.[7] The Buddha also featured in Rud's fantasy for a great jewel heist, with his sister concealed in its back while he hid further down the gallery in a pulpit. He pored over the manuscript of a Dickens novel, surprised that such a famous writer could have been so careless, 'leaving out lots which he had to squeeze in between the lines afterwards'. His own voracious reading continued: Wilkie Collins's novels, Bret Harte's stories, Ralph Waldo Emerson's poems and, a Pre-Raphaelite favourite, Johann Meinhold's *Sidonia the Sorceress*. He learnt that his mother wrote poems and his father pieces for the Indian newspapers and that 'one could take pen and set down what one thought, and that nobody accused one of "showing off" by so doing'.[8]

Among so many new and wonderful experiences, the strangest was the occasion when, as he later eerily put it, 'the night got into my head'. He got up and wandered for hours about the silent house, before slipping out into the garden to see the dawn. It was only when he crept into his mother's bedroom to give his pet toad Pluto a drink and dropped the water-jug that his night-wandering was discovered and 'very much was said'.[9] This kind of experience would recur throughout his life, and Kipling was later to associate it with the operation of his personal literary daemon.

On 16 January 1878 twelve-year-old Rud unwillingly took the train down to North Devon and his new school, United Services College. USC had been established four years earlier as a limited company by a group of Army and Navy officers. Whereas most public schools of the period still saw themselves primarily as nurseries for Oxford and Cambridge, the principal aim of USC (as its name implied) was to prepare its pupils for direct entry into the Services. The recent introduction of examinations meant that public schoolboys destined for the Army frequently had to spend time at an expensive crammer in order to have a chance of passing into Sandhurst or Woolwich. By cutting out the need for the crammer, the founders of USC hoped to fill a gap that had opened in the market, while providing their own sons with a relatively cheap education. Casting about for a suitable location for the school, they decided on Westward Ho!, a failed Devonshire seaside resort, optimistically named after the Charles Kingsley novel of 1855. A block of twelve semi-detached houses was purchased and cheaply converted into dormitories and classrooms. Alice and Lockwood's decision to send their son to a school with such a strong Service rationale might seem surprising. In fact, their reasons are not hard to guess. On their income, the fees (sixty to seventy-five guineas per year) were attractively affordable; and even more importantly, they were close friends with the headmaster, Cormell Price.

A schoolfriend of Alice's brother Harry, Price studied law at Oxford in the 1850s and became a member of the Morris/Burne-Jones group, contributing articles to the *Oxford and Cambridge Magazine* and, with Rossetti, Burne-Jones and others, painting the frescos on the walls of the Oxford Union. After Oxford and a brief spell as a medical student, Price went to St Petersburg as private tutor to the son of a Russian nobleman. Back in England in 1863, he turned to schoolmastering and ran the Modern Languages Department at Haileybury before being appointed the first headmaster of USC. Over the years, Price maintained his Pre-Raphaelite connections and was a regular visitor to The Grange. There he met Rud one Christmas and, like William Morris, became accepted as one of the boy's deputy-uncles. By sending their son to Uncle Crom's school, Alice and Lockwood could feel confident not only that Rud would receive an adequate education, but that they would be kept reliably informed about his progress.

Many years later Kipling was to describe Price as 'a lean, slow-spoken, bearded, Arab-complexioned man' much loved by his pupils, many of whom continued to seek his advice long after they had left school.[10] Like his Pre-Raphaelite friends, Price was a liberal and an aesthete, and thus something of an anomaly as headmaster of a school like USC. (In addition, he was not in Holy Orders – unlike most nineteenth-century public school headmasters.) Anomaly or not, the school flourished under Price's headship, maintaining an average enrolment of 200 pupils during his twenty-year reign, and there is little doubt that he was a shrewd judge of boys. This is attested not only by his subsequent steering of Rud towards a career in journalism, but also by a story told by Lionel Dunsterville (soon to become one of Rud's two closest friends at USC).

Dunsterville, unhappy at school, ran away. After a few days, starving but full of a sense of his own daring, he returned and was escorted into the headmaster's study. Much to his surprise, Price entirely ignored him and went on with what he had been doing. When he did notice the boy, he acted as though Dunsterville no longer belonged at the school and asked him what he wanted. This unexpected reaction broke down Dunsterville's self-assurance far more effectively than any accusations or reproaches would have done, and he burst into tears. After making sure that he was 'given plenty of good things to eat', Price then gave him 'a public licking before the whole school in solemn assembly, which somewhat restored my assurance. And there the matter ended.'[11]

It was in Price's friendly company that Rud travelled down to North Devon at the beginning of his first term. He would later associate 'that terrible first night' with the 'soft smell of escaping gas' and 'the odour of trunks and wet overcoats'.[12] Lonely and depressed, he was soon bombarding his mother with letters – sometimes as many as four a day. It was, Alice confided to Price, 'the roughness of the lads that he seems to feel most'.[13] And rough many of them were. According to Dunsterville, it was not uncommon for younger boys to be dangled by their ankles from top-storey windows or dropped down a central stairwell on a rope in an early form of bungy-jumping, known as 'hanging'.[14] While there is nothing to suggest that Rud himself was either dangled or hung, he did subsequently claim to have been bullied a good deal during his first few terms.

In his reminiscences Dunsterville did not record what he thought of Rud as a new boy. The only first impressions to survive are those of Rud's other close friend at school, an Irish boy called George Beresford. Unfortunately, Beresford, later a civil engineer, photographer and antique dealer, is not an ideal source. From his sourly facetious memoir, *School-days with Kipling* (published after Kipling's death), it is clear that Beresford was someone permanently disgruntled with life, and his book, though lively and entertaining, was little more than an attempt to cash in on his old chum's reputation. For all that, it contained a number of details not available elsewhere, including a first glimpse of Rud on his arrival at school. He appeared, said Beresford, 'a cheery, capering, podgy, little fellow, as precocious as ever he could be. Or, rather, a broad smile appeared with a small boy behind it, carrying it about and pointing it in all directions.'[15] Above the smile was a pair of glasses, which quickly earned Rud the nickname of 'Giglamps' or 'Gigger', though he was also occasionally known as 'Beetle'. Beresford did not mention Rud being bullied, but implied that his friend had been a bit of a coward, avoiding physical confrontations by caution and tact. If true, this suggests that some of the lessons so bitterly learnt at Lorne Lodge were proving useful. In addition to his glasses, diplomacy and smile, Rud arrived at USC with what was then a reasonable academic grounding: in mathematics, he had covered the first four books of Euclid and the first twelve rules of Algebra; in Latin, he had reached the second book of Caesar.[16] More unusually for a boy of twelve, he was widely read and already had a distinctly visible moustache.

Although, like many public schoolboys before and since, Rud remembered his first term as deeply unpleasant, by March he was writing more cheerfully to his mother. Then the Easter holidays brought an unexpected bonus. Alice was in Italy meeting Lockwood; so Rud remained at school. Instead of the miserable time he had anticipated, he found that under 'Uncle Crom's' benign influence the older boys also staying behind were suddenly transformed into tolerant older brothers, sharing delicacies with the younger ones at tea-time and taking an interest in their hobbies. School, he decided, was not so bad after all. Better still, during the summer term, he was given permission to accompany his father to the Paris

Exhibition. Lockwood had moved from Bombay to Lahore in 1875 to become Principal of the Mayo School of Art and Curator of the Lahore Museum. He was now a well-respected expert on Indian Arts and Crafts and had been put in charge of the Indian Section at the Exhibition. It was over six years since he had last seen his son, but he found him 'a delight-fully amiable and companionable little chap', if somewhat prone to 'vagueness and inaccuracy'.[17] He allowed Rud the run of the Exhibition, gave him Jules Verne to read in the original and, putting a few francs in his pocket, encouraged him to explore Paris.

By the end of his first year at USC, Rud was thoroughly engrossed in school life. A letter to his cousin Stan catalogues the remarkable range of pets kept by the boys. Jackdaws were popular, so too were dormice. Blackbirds and thrushes, though easy to procure, were a nuisance to look after. One boy had five young hawks, another a bull-terrier. Rud himself had kept a mole, but preferred blind-worms because they were 'very pretty' and 'very little trouble to keep'.[18]

Beresford, at least in his own estimation, was Rud's only really close friend during his first year. Initially, they were drawn together by a love of litera-ture and a strong antipathy to the school chaplain, 'Belly' Campbell. Campbell, who was Rud's first housemaster, seems to have been one of those sado-sentimental Victorian schoolmasters who thrashed boys one minute and preached at them the next. (Kipling later claimed to have received a few 'lickings' from 'Belly' and to have hated him.[19]) When Campbell left the following year, he delivered a particularly lachrymose farewell sermon. The other boys were all suitably moved; Rud was not. 'Two years' bullying is not paid for with half an hour's blubbering in a pul-pit', as he tough-mindedly pointed out.[20] He later settled his score with Campbell by giving his name to one of the bullies whom Stalky and Co. torture in 'The Moral Reformers'.

Sometime during Rud's second year, he and Beresford formed the famous alliance with Dunsterville. When Kipling later fictionalised the trio's escapades in *Stalky & Co.*, he cast Dunsterville (Stalky) as the undisputed leader, with himself (Beetle) and Beresford (M'Turk) as more or less willing sidekicks. This was partly natural modesty, partly because by then he wanted to present Stalky as the schoolboy prototype of the kind of officer that he felt the British Army desperately needed. The reality was almost certainly rather different. As Dunsterville remembered it, each of the three contributed essential qualities that the others lacked. Rud's intelligence and 'shrewd guidance', Beresford's 'extraordinarily mature judgement' and 'malicious ingenuity' were just as crucial to the alliance as his own cunning, or 'stalkiness' as they called it. 'Beresford and I,' Dunsterville claimed, 'had our fair share of brains, but Kipling had a great deal more than his fair share, and added to it the enormous asset of knowledge – intuitive and acquired.'[21] However formidable they may have become, in the earliest reference to the trio they emerged as typical schoolboys, doing nothing more sensational than breaking bounds and growing lettuces in a secret cave until caught by a master.

That August Rud sent 'The Dusky Crew', a poem describing these early exploits, to the New York children's journal, *St Nicholas Magazine*. Although the poem was pretty feeble (and was rejected), the attempt to get published – and in America – showed enterprise. At thirteen and a half, Rud was beginning to see himself as a writer.

In fact, by then he had already had something 'published' – and not a poem but a story. The previous November, William Morris's daughter, May, and Georgie's children, Phil and Margaret, had started *The Scribbler*, a hand-written home-magazine which appeared once or twice a month until March 1880. The two issues for June 1879 included 'My First Adventure' by Nickson, Rud's first surviving pseudonym and his first sustained attempt at fiction.

The story began with a school cricket match in which, in a last-wicket stand, the narrator and another boy scored the forty-nine runs required for victory. (Given Rud's poor eyesight and general lack of aptitude for games, these cricketing heroics were presumably intended as a private family joke, but their inclusion also hinted at a degree of wish-fulfilment.) Feeling faint after his exertions, the narrator was taken off to the school sick-room, became delirious and that night decided to go fishing. Down at the nearby river he saved an elderly gentleman from drowning and, in his now torn and bloody nightgown, danced around the old man, gibbering at him not to be frightened. The old man, imagining his rescuer to be a ghost, became even more terrified. At length the narrator left him and returned to the sick-room. Some years later at a farmer's 'ordinary', he overheard the same elderly gentleman recounting how he was once rescued from drowning by 'a monster reeking with gore'. The narrator took him aside and tried without success to explain what really happened. The next day he received a letter from the old man, imploring him 'not to repeat your version of what we two know the rights of, because mine has the sanction of time and has been produced with much satisfaction in many companies where I was ever considered respectable and highly creditable'.[22]

'My First Adventure' was carried off with great gusto and could justly be called 'promising'. Its real interest, however, lay in the fact that it contained, in embryonic form, so many features characteristic of Kipling's mature work: the figure of the child, for instance, trying to put the adult right; the preoccupation with abnormal mental states; the delight in farce; the use of cryptic personal references; above all, the confident and skilful parodying of different styles. Rud seems to have submitted no more stories to *The Scribbler*, but 'The Pillow Fight', a poem in knockabout Miltonics, appeared in a later issue; and when the magazine finally folded – killed off by an interminable serial-novel called *The Queen of the Adriatic* – three other poems of his were among the material under consideration.

The year 1880 was to prove a momentous one for Rud. By the end of it, he was firmly ensconced in a study with Dunsterville and Beresford. This tiny, L-shaped room with just enough space for a table and three chairs became their pride and joy. They decorated it with cheap curios from nearby Bideford, and when Alice came for a visit before returning to India that November, they initiated her into the mysteries of a study 'brew'. Poems too were beginning to flow, mostly parodies of whomever Rud happened to be reading: Swinburne, Shelley, Keats. And, sometime during that summer, he fell in love.

Trix was back with Mrs Holloway in Southsea, and when Rud paid her a visit, he found that Lorne Lodge had a new inmate, Flo Garrard. She was sixteen, a student at a local art school and kept a pet goat called Becquot, which, to Rud's delight, used to butt Mrs Holloway. Trix in later life offered this vividly ambiguous portrait of Flo: 'the heavy rope of brown hair that hung to her knees – the head that was too small for even her tall thin frame – the ivory face too small for the head – & the features too small for the face – all except the grey eyes – clotted with black lashes – & they were too big'.[23] Rud's response at the time was more straightforward: he fell for Flo at once, and was to consider himself in love with her for at least the next four years.

That much seems definite; most of the rest remains conjecture. How often did they actually manage to see each other? Probably not very often, given that Rud was still a fourteen-year-old schoolboy when they first met. Letters then must have played a major role, though none survives, and the relationship itself must have been predominantly a long-distance affair. Did Rud simply turn Flo into a *princesse lointaine*? To an extent, he must have done. And at some level the idea that he had found Love in the 'House of Desolation' must have seemed enormously appealing to so literary an adolescent. That his passion was probably more real in the letters and poems he wrote to Flo than in the flesh did not mean that his feelings were any the less genuine or intense. To an outsider it might seem so, but not to a teenager who believed himself in love.

One teasing relic of the liaison that does survive is a sketch-book of Flo's in the Berg Collection, New York Public Library, which contains some drawings of her by Rud. These give no strong sense of what she looked like, but show her in long skirts with an easel, pursued by a bull and starting a fire with a dropped cigarette. A private joke? A clue to Rud's view of the relationship? Whatever else, the presence of the cigarette does, for the early 1880s, suggest someone with a certain sophistication. Guesswork aside, what is certain is that Lockwood and Alice were quickly aware of (and concerned about) the attachment and that Rud was soon writing Flo love poems, of which 'The Lesson' is probably the earliest:

> We two learned the lesson together,
>   The oldest of all, yet so new
> To myself, and I'm wondering whether
>   It was utterly novel to you?
>
> The pages – you seemed to have known them,
>   The pictures that changed 'neath our eyes;
> Alas! by what hand were you shown them,
>   That I find you so womanly wise?
>
> Is it strange that my hand on your shoulder

In the dusk of the day should be placed?
Did you say to yourself, 'Were he older
   His arm had encircled my waist'?

If it be so, so be it, fair teacher;
   I sit at your feet and am wise,
For each page of the book is a feature,
   And the light of the reading, your eyes.

We have met, and the meeting is over;
   We must part, and the parting is now;
We have played out the game – I, boy-lover,
   In earnest, and you, dearest, how?[24]

Alice sent the poem to Lockwood. He was impressed, astutely recognising the lines as an emotional as well as a literary portent of things to come. Writing to Edith Plowden, he remarked with a touching mixture of fatherly pride and concern that:

> it would be affectation to ignore his very decided talents and powers. He sends me (or rather Mrs Kipling sends) a copy of verses – 'The Lesson' which might be to the address of Miss Flora Garrard or possibly to you. In any case they are prettily turned and show that he has started on a round of spoons [sentimental love-play] which he will follow up till his death. There is no help for this sort of thing once it is begun . . . If I could only lend Ruddy some notions or take some of the trouble he has to go through, it would be well, but it is hopeless. He must learn by the intolerably slow & painful processes of experience.[25]

That was on 5 October 1880. A month later Alice had rejoined her husband in Lahore and she too was soon writing to Edith to express her own worries. After three years away, she was finding it hard to readapt to Anglo-Indian life and was full of complaints. Their fourteen-bedroom house on Mozung Road was terribly dusty, and so big that she and Lockwood seemed to 'rattle' around in it. The other women were even more stupid and dreary than she remembered. Worst of all, Rud was not sending her his latest poems. Would Edith pass on any copies that came her way? Otherwise, 'as time and distance do their fatal work I am sure his Mother will know less of him than any other woman of his acquaintance'.[26] Alice was obviously as anxious as her husband about their son's recent infatuation.

If all this were not enough, his parents were also uneasy about Rud's new holiday arrangements. Before leaving England, Alice had moved her daughter back to London and installed Trix at 26 Warwick Gardens, South Kensington, with three old ladies, Miss Winnard and Georgiana and May Craik. There was every reason to think that Trix, who enjoyed the company of older people, would fit in without any problem. Rud, on the other hand, with his swings of mood might flare up and prove 'unparliamentary', as Lockwood laconically put it.[27] In the event, Rud found his holidays at Warwick Gardens perfectly congenial. The household was quiet and bookish; the old ladies had known Thomas Carlyle, were on friendly terms with writers like Christina Rossetti and Jean Ingelow, and Georgiana Craik was herself a prolific, if minor, novelist. Just as importantly, they were happy to act as an audience for Rud's poems.

During 1881 it is doubtful whether Rud saw much of Flo. He still considered himself in love, however, and continued to write poems for her. He was despatching copies of his work for comment to Aunt Edie and Edith Plowden. And, despite her fears, Alice too was receiving regular consignments. By December she had made a collection of twenty-three of her son's poems, which she had privately printed in Lahore under the title *Schoolboy Lyrics*. For some reason she decided not to tell Rud about the publication. Perhaps she hoped to surprise him; perhaps she suspected that he would resent such maternal interference. If so, she was right. According to Trix, when he eventually found out about the volume a year later, Rud was furious and told his mother sulkily that 'she had taken and made use of something he needed and valued'.[28]

If his reaction sounds typically adolescent, the poems themselves were not. There were a few weak ones ('The Dusky Crew' and 'The Song of the Sufferer', a jokey parody of Swinburne) and a couple of the others were merely melodramatic or sentimental: a condemned murderer in 'The Night Before' watched the darkness melt, 'In the corpse-like light on the face of day'; a couple in 'Solus Cum Sola' walked by the sea in silent 'communion divine'. But these aside, *Schoolboy Lyrics* was a distinctly accomplished collection, notable for its tight rhythmic and verbal control and particularly for a very evident reaching after objectivity. One poem at least, 'Credat Judaeus', was dauntingly good for a fifteen-year-old:

FIRST COUPLE

Three couples we were in the lane,
Keeping our walks and turning again;
    At the point where we meet
    The roar of the street
Like the sound of a beast in pain
    Comes faintly. Here all is sweet.

Who were the others? I did not see.
    Why should I look at the men at all?
Why should their partners interest me?
    I'm sure that I loved mine best of all.

    Perfect in beauty and grace,
    Perfect in figure and face,
She with her eyes divine!
    The present for just us two;
Eternity makes her mine,
    Our love is eternal and true!

SECOND COUPLE

Watch them, dearest, cheek to cheek,
    Arm in arm; when years are past
    Will their love like our love last,
Still so fond, still cheek to cheek?

There is one true love below;
    We have found it! Others kiss
    For a little, part and miss,
Grieve awhile, then lightly go.

These in earnest! I have seen

41

Many such; the years will fly,
Leave us loving, you and I,
While they talk of what has been.

THIRD COUPLE
I wanted them walks so bad
With you, and missus is mad
'Cos she says I gad out at night;
No doubt but what she's right.

Well, I can't stay long, but see,
Promise to 'old to me,
    An I'll 'old to you for hever!
Them people may court a bit –
    They don't love like we two!
    Oh, George! I've got no one but you.
'Old by me! Promise it!
    And I'll never leave you, never!

I, the writer that made them speak,
    Laughed aloud as I passed the three,
Strong in a passion to last a week,
    For Love that is real was given to me![29]

As the couples insisted in turn on the uniqueness of their love, each spoke in a carefully differentiated idiom (upper-class, middle-class, working-class). Their identical claims progressively undermined one another, while the shifts in the rhyme scheme unobtrusively underlined the changes in register. In a final ironic twist, the 'writer', no less triumphantly, asserted (and undermined) the uniqueness of his own passion: 'For Love that is real was given to me!'

Almost as impressive was 'Overheard', in which the narrator, hot and bored at some show, found himself eavesdropping on a young, rather cosmopolitan prostitute telling her story to a potential customer:

'Tried for luck in London –
                    Voilà tout!

Failed, lost money, undone;
Took to the streets for a life.
                    Entre nous,
It's a terrible uphill strife,
Like all professions – too filled.
And now I'm in lodgings hard by,
Au quatrième, up in the sky.
Visit me by and by,
They're furnished, but oh – so cold,
                    So cold!'[30]

When Swinburne was belatedly shown the collection by Aunt Georgie in early 1884, his reaction was generally lukewarm:

Dear Georgie, I have read the little book carefully through, with interest on account of your recommendation. Some of the verses show signs of ability for possible good work in future, but I never think it fair or kind to offer any positive opinion on the attempts of very young people, as it is so impossible to tell which way they will develop – up or down. There are clever and promising touches, I think, here and there – and some things not so promising.[31]

While his guardedness is understandable, it is not easy to think of anyone else around 1880 who was writing poems quite like 'Credat Judaeus' or 'Overheard'. They form a kind of missing link between the dramatic monologues and dialogues of Robert and Elizabeth Barrett Browning twenty years earlier and Thomas Hardy's 'satires of circumstance' thirty years later. The attempt to give a voice to working-class women, without any trace of condescension, was also remarkable, anticipating a crucial element in Kipling's later work.

At USC not even Beresford and Dunsterville were allowed to read Rud's serious poems; these – like Flo – were part of his secret life, hidden away between the covers of the Russian-leather, gilt-edged, cream-laid manuscript books which, according to Beresford, 'were never opened by careless or unworthy hands'.[32] What Rud's schoolfellows did see were his parodies and light verse; which, together with his knowledgeable air, had by now gained him the reputation of school aesthete, and made him the butt of one particular master. William Crofts, a gifted teacher with a violent temper and an acid tongue, taught Classics and English. Kipling later claimed that he owed him two particular debts. One was 'to loathe Horace for two years; to forget him for twenty, and then to love him for the rest of my days and through many sleepless nights'. The other, more immediately, was the revelation that 'words could be used as weapons, for he did me the honour to talk at me plentifully; and our year-in year-out form-room bickerings gave us both something to play with'. During one of their verbal jousts Crofts hurled a copy of Robert Browning's *Men and Women* at Rud's head, with the gibe that he was 'Gigadibs the literary man' – a neat put-down of his literary pretensions coupled with a pun on his nickname, 'Gigger'. To judge by the influence that Browning was already exerting on Rud's poems, he would have had no difficulty spotting the allusion to 'Bishop Blougram's Apology', nor its sarcastic application to himself. He probably returned the compliment in kind by including a caricature of Crofts in the personalised 'Inferno' he was writing – 'into which', he would recall, 'I put, under appropriate torture, all my friends and most of the masters'.[33]

When, during the winter term of 1881, a weekly Literary and Debating Society was established, Rud was elected Secretary and he and Beresford were among the most prominent speakers (Dunsterville was later President). Over the next couple of terms the society debated such topics as 'the present [Liberal] Government is unworthy of the confidence of the country' (carried); 'the advance of the Russians in Central Asia is hostile to the British Power' (also carried, though the headmaster, Price, spoke against it); and 'the civilisation of Modern Europe is not superior to that of ancient times and oriental nations' (lost). Rud invariably spoke for the motion and Beresford, inevitably, against. The trio also acted in the school's annual Christmas play, which that year was Sheridan's *The Rivals*, with Rud as Sir Anthony Absolute, Beresford as Sir Lucius O'Trigger and Dunsterville as Mrs Malaprop. Rud's was judged 'a capital performance, somewhat marred by an obvious catarrh and a voice too slender'.[34]

Details of the threesome's other 'extracurricular' exploits remain sketchy. They built various huts outside school bounds where they could read and smoke undisturbed. (Smoking was a privilege reserved for the

Sixth Form, a concession to the fact that the school was in competition with the crammers, where smoking was usual.) They conducted duels with 'Sallies' (saloon-pistols) in the bunkers of the local golf-course. They divided their homework on a 'co-operative' basis – Dunsterville doing the Maths, Beresford the Latin and Rud the English – and from time to time they pursued vendettas against other boys. One of these involved 'frosting' the outside of the windows of a lower study with chunks of greasy bacon fat suspended on bits of string; another involved deafening their neighbours with a contraption made out of a pair of bellows, a length of rubber tubing and a penny whistle.[35] Among the staff, their housemaster, M H Pugh, a large man with big feet and a habit of prying into his charges' affairs, was a regular target. Of Dunsterville's individual Stalkyisms, only a few examples survive. Apparently he would sit during an examination, ostentatiously hiding a sheet of paper on his lap which, when challenged, would turn out to be blank. Or, ducking out of the procession into Sunday Chapel, he would rejoin the queue as it filed out at the end of the service, resplendent in top hat and gloves and carrying a prayer-book. The point of these tricks was that he always had a cast-iron alibi and never left any incriminating evidence. It was these two elements that Kipling was to make the basis of the ingenious escapades in *Stalky & Co.*

Although it is extremely unlikely that the boys themselves ever got up to anything as elaborate as their fictional counterparts, they were clearly a force to be reckoned with. Beresford recorded two of their joint hoaxes which, allowing for his usual distortions, seem to contain more than a modicum of fact. In the first, the trio, at the height of their passion for curio-collecting, apparently decided that all the bric-à-brac with which they had so lovingly decorated their study was worthless junk. The problem was how to offload the rubbish and buy pieces of real value. Their cunning solution was to declare themselves bankrupt and, seemingly with the utmost reluctance, to organise an auction of their effects. Dunsterville, inspired in the role of auctioneer, whipped up the school into such a frenzy of excitement that the other boys were conned into paying exorbitant prices for the trashy items, and on the proceeds the threesome went into Bideford on a spending spree.

The details of the second hoax are not so easily unravelled; Beresford's account must be balanced against Dunsterville's earlier version, which, in turn, must be measured against Kipling's reaction to Dunsterville's. For Beresford, Rud was the central figure. He had mortally offended Crofts by claiming that Milton's 'Lycidas' would be improved by extensive rewriting. Crofts's response was to set the whole class an extremely stiff examination paper on the poem, with the aim of exposing Rud's ignorance and literary hubris. The plan backfired when Beresford accidentally came across a jellygraph (an early form of photocopy) of the exam paper. He passed on the contents to Rud who, to Crofts's intense annoyance, was able to answer all the questions correctly. Dunsterville in his memoir, published in 1928, eight years before Beresford's, had already told essentially the same story but with an entirely different emphasis (he also remembered the Milton text they were studying as *Comus* rather than 'Lycidas'). For Dunsterville, the whole point of the jape was nothing to do with Rud's rivalry with Crofts, but was 'to see whether, when one of us was able to answer every question in full, [Crofts's] pet pupil would still emerge top – and he did'.[36] Kipling, in a letter to Dunsterville, corroborated this version, naming Powell as the pet pupil, but also complicated the issue slightly by claiming that he and Dunsterville should both have come out top, since both of them cheated.[37] From the fact that all three of them so vividly recalled the jellygraph incident, it is obvious that some form of hoax took place; the discrepancies in their versions, however, are a reminder of the fallibility of fifty-year-old memories.

All this time Price had been keeping an avuncular eye on Rud, but it was not until the summer of 1881 that he took a step that would have far-reaching consequences. By now it was becoming increasingly obvious that while his eyesight debarred Rud from a career in the Services, he was equally unlikely to get into Oxford or Cambridge, even if his parents could have supported him there. There was no question that he was clever but, as his father had already noticed, he could be vague and inaccurate; and, crucially as far as Oxbridge was concerned, there were serious doubts about his Latin. A career in journalism, on the other hand, offered distinct possibilities.

With the clear-sightedness that shows why he was so highly regarded as a headmaster, Price decided to revive the defunct school magazine, the *United Services Chronicle*, with himself as nominal editor and Rud as his assistant. The decision had a number of advantages. It kept Rud constructively occupied: he produced no fewer than seven issues of the magazine between June 1881 and the following July when he left school, and wrote most of the contents himself. In addition, collaboration over the *Chronicle* allowed Price to spend more time with Rud, keeping an eye on him and extending his literary horizons. He gave the boy the run of his own study and library and would drop in for editorial chats that branched off into readings from the Elizabethan and Jacobean dramatists, the writings of Marco Polo, Sir John Mandeville and Richard Hakluyt, and Walter Savage Landor's *Imaginary Conversations*. In a more gossipy vein, Price would also tell stories of his early days with the Pre-Raphaelites.

No particularly high claims can be made for Rud's contributions to the *Chronicle*, but his presence in the seven issues that he edited was everywhere apparent: in editorials, sporting notes (usually fairly brief), poems and a number of humorous descriptions of aspects of school life. Of these humorous sketches, 'Life in the Corridor' and its companion piece, 'Life in the Studies', were the best sustained and are still mildly amusing. The former's opening sentence conveys the general tone and flavour: 'The Corridor-Caution is the most interesting of our small deer, and cannot be confounded, even by a tyro, with the common sloper, tho' alike in many points.'[38]

All in all, it was valuable experience, and Rud's parents soon began to explore the idea of getting him newspaper work in India, sounding out old friends like James Walker (proprietor of Lahore's *Civil and Military Gazette*) and George Allen (founder of the Allahabad-based *Pioneer*). There were other reasons too why they were now increasingly eager to have their son living with them. 'I must confess,' Lockwood wrote to Price on 23 October 1881, 'from what I have seen of Ruddy it is the moral side I dread an outbreak on. I don't think he is the stuff to resist temptation.'[39] Unfortunately he did not elaborate further, and it is far from clear what sort of moral outbreak he had in mind. Had Georgie or Edith Plowden or Price himself been sending disquieting reports? Was Lockwood worried that the kind of experience so knowingly portrayed in a poem like 'Overheard' might be the prelude to a walk on the wild side? Was he perhaps remembering the temptations of his own adolescence?

For all Lockwood's anxieties, there seemed to be no immediate solution, and Rud began 1882 with every prospect of another full year at United Services College. He quickly resubmerged himself in work on the

Chronicle and also began turning out articles on gas and sewerage for the local newspaper. As usual, he was inundating his mother and others with poems, and sometime that year he presented Flo with a collection of older and newer pieces, inscribed '1882 FEBRUARY SUNDRY PHANSIES WRIT BY ONE KIPLING'.[40] Interestingly, the poems he was now writing represented something of a backward step from the virtuosity of *Schoolboy Lyrics*. This regression can largely be explained by the fact that Rossetti, Morris and the Shakespeare of the *Sonnets* had temporarily supplanted the Brownings in his literary pantheon. Such a shift in poetic allegiance was natural enough – Rud was in love, after all – but the results were just as predictable. In place of the colloquial ease and tonal precision of the best of *Schoolboy Lyrics*, the new poems were stilted in feeling and full of archaisms – in fact, rather boring. There were, however, two striking exceptions, 'Donec Gratus Eram' and 'Ave Imperatrix!'. Between them, these poems staked out what would become his future poetic territory: on the one hand, the playful and the demotic; on the other, the rhetorical and the imperialistic.

'Donec Gratus Eram', a translation into Devonshire dialect of the famous Horace ode, looked forward to the great soldier ballads, which ten years later established Kipling's reputation as a poet:

HE

So long as 'twuz me alone
   An' there wasn't no other chaps,
I was praoud as a King on 'is throne –
   Happier tu, per'aps.

SHE

So long as 'twuz only I
   An' there wasn't no other she
Yeou cared for so much – sure*ly*
   I was glad as glad could be.

HE

But now I'm in lovv with Jane Pritt –
   She can play the piano, she can;
An' if dyin' 'ud 'elp 'er a bit
   I'd die laike a man.

SHE

Yeou'm like me. I'm in lovv with young Frye –
   Him as lives out tu Appledore Quay;
An' if dyin' 'ud 'elp 'im I'd die –
   Twice ovver for he.

HE

But s'posin' I threwed up Jane
   An' nivver went walkin' with she –
An' come back to yeou again –
   How 'ud that be?

SHE

Frye's sober. Yeou've allus done badly –
   An' yeou shifts like cut net-floats, yeou du:
But – I'd throw that young Frye ovver gladly
   An' lovv 'ee right thru!⁴¹

In total contrast, 'Ave Imperatrix!' (modelled on the very different Oscar Wilde poem of the same title) was a response to the recent assassination attempt on Queen Victoria. The fourth quatrain read:

Such greeting as should come from those
   Whose fathers faced the Sepoy hordes,
Or served you in the Russian snows,
   And, dying, left their sons their swords.⁴²

The tone of this was so utterly different from anything else in Rud's early work that it is hard to know how to take it. Not too seriously, perhaps. Dunsterville recalled that the poem was written 'in French class at the end of a French textbook'; and a letter from the same month as the assassination attempt and the poem was in quite a different key.⁴³ 'The school – to put it mildly – is intensely amused with the attempt of the Queen's life,' he wrote. 'I'm afraid we are scarcely loyal and patriotic enough – but anyhow three parts of us laughed and the Democratic quarter seemed to be sorry. At all events we got a holiday on the strength of it. So I am very well contented.'⁴⁴ This suggests that when he wrote it,

49

Rud probably intended 'Ave Imperatrix!' as a loyalist spoof. Even so, its note of measured patriotic rhetoric uncannily anticipated his later poems on major public events. For instance, the cadence of parts of 'Recessional' would closely echo the lines from 'Ave Imperatrix!' quoted above:

> If, drunk with sight of power, we loose
> Wild tongues that have not Thee in awe,
> Such boastings as the Gentiles use,
> Or lesser breeds without the Law . . .[45]

The letter that so light-heartedly dismissed the Queen's escape was to a new friend, Mrs Perry. Little is known of her except that she was thirty-two, her husband, John Tavenor Perry, was an architect and the couple lived in Putney. What is clear from the tenor of Rud's surviving letters to Mrs Perry, or 'Dearest Mater' as he was soon addressing her, is that for a time she became a kind of mother-substitute and also his principal confidante about Flo. At the end of May he was confessing that 'everything that ever existed between myself and the fair F.G. is *entirely at an end* . . . A youth has just swallowed his first bitter pill: and you must excuse him if he finds it a little harsh in his mouth.' Despite the attempt to sound stoically resigned, his real distress was given away by a reference to his eyes 'feeling a little weak' – already a telltale sign of nervous strain and exhaustion.[46]

In his letters to Mrs Perry, he was also enclosing poems, mostly sonnets. 'Discovery', sent on 28 May 1882, could easily have been the text for a lost painting by Uncle Ned:

> We found him in the woodlands – she and I –
> Dead, was our teacher of the silver tongue,
> Dead, whom we thought so strong he could not die,
> Dead, with no arrow loosed, with bow unstrung.
> And round the great, grey blade that all men dread,
> There crept the waxen-white convolvulus –
> And the keen edge that once fell hard on us
> Was blunt and notched and rusted yellow red.
> And he, our Master, the unconquered one,

Lay, in the nettles of the forest place,
 With dreadful open eyes and changeless face
Turned upward, gazing at the noon day sun.
Then we two, bent over our old, dead, king,
 Loosed hands, and gave back hope and troth and ring.[47]

The dating suggests that the poem must refer to the break-up with Flo, mentioned in the same letter. And yet a version of the same poem, almost identical except for the final line, seems to have been around for at least two or three months. On 18 March Trix had written to Rud from the house of the old ladies at Warwick Gardens:

I showed your new poem – 'A Discovery' – to Mrs Winnard and Miss Georgie, and thereby hangs a tale funnier than any of Oscar's. I thought it was simple to the verge of childishness – obvious is the word I mean – but the dear ladies summoned me to a conference! Miss Winnard said – 'The verses are musical but—'

'It's a sonnet', I said foolishly – 'Yes dear, we know that, but what does it mean? Do you know?' I said I thought I did – it was fairly clear – and looked at Miss Georgie – She said in in [sic] her gentle voice that they understood that a beloved cage-bird had flown away and been found dead, but the emotion expressed was disproportionate – exaggerated.

'But it is not a bird – it's a kind of allegory – it means dead love – Cupid you know.'

'Did your brother explain that to you?'

'No, he only said it was a new poem, and he wanted to know if you liked it . . .'

Then Mrs Winnard said in her 'more in sorrow than in anger' voice – 'Really Trixie I hoped we had eradicated your unfortunate tendency to think yourself wiser than your elders, but I fear we have only repressed it. Do you seriously think a little girl of your age can understand somewhat abstruse verse better than two educated and mature ladies?'

'Oh no – of course not. Only I know Ruddy so well, and the way he thinks and writes, that I feel I can understand him better than anyone.'

'Well I can hardly agree with you. But Georgie shall write to him at once.'[48]

If this exchange sounds just too ludicrous, a note of Rud's a couple of years later confirmed that something like it took place. Alongside 'Discovery' he wrote in one of his notebooks: 'Cheap; Miss Winnard said that the King was a dead canary, for which mistake (a genuine one) I find it hard to forgive her.'[49] The existence of the earlier version of the poem suggests that the relationship between Rud and Flo was probably always precarious, that he was the one who kept it going and that he could have written poems about their 'dead love' at more or less any time. Trix's letter is also interesting as evidence of the close sympathy that continued to exist between brother and sister. At not yet fourteen, Trix already had an impressive grasp of how her brother's mind worked, not to mention a nice sense of comedy.

Back in India, Lockwood and Alice were being kept considerably less well informed, and not only about their son's emotional state. In March Alice was complaining to Edith Plowden about lack of news from other members of her family. Her sister Aggie, at thirty-nine, had recently given birth to a second son, Hugh. The first Alice knew of the birth, and probably the pregnancy, was through a paragraph in the World, which rather unsubtly implied that Aggie's labour-pains had started while she and her husband Edward were out at a dinner-party. Understandably irritated, Alice derived what comfort she could from imagining her sister's social embarrassment and from Rud's amused response. 'Est ce que mes Tantes sont donc folles?' he had written. 'Suppose the other Aunts indulge in second editions! Shan't we become venerable! At first I had a confused idea that I was an Uncle or a grandpapa, but on mature reflection I find that I am only another cousin. Never mind. I ain't cut out of any expectations and I wish her joy. Can you imagine Uncle Edward's face?'[50]

The following month still nothing definite had been settled about Rud's future, but now his sister was the one causing Alice alarm. Trix had begun having her periods, and since then her letters to her parents had been 'depressed or melancholy'. Furthermore, as Alice told Edith, 'She seems to have got – who knows how or where – some morbid religious notions and is tormenting herself with the fear that we shall be disappointed in her in some way . . .'[51] This was the first hint of the instability that was later to lead to Trix suffering a number of serious breakdowns. Although at the time Alice could hardly have been expected to make the connection, the combination of menstruation-guilt and morbid religious notions looks very much like a legacy of Lorne Lodge and, in particular, of the corrosive after-effects of Sarah Holloway's Evangelicalism.

Sometime during the next couple of months Rud's future suddenly took shape. Stephen Wheeler, the editor of the *Civil and Military Gazette*, was over in London from Lahore. A meeting with Rud was arranged and proved so satisfactory that on 17 June Lockwood wrote to Price that Wheeler wanted his sixteen-and-a-half-year-old assistant editor to come out and start work as soon as possible. Within six weeks Rud's schooldays were over; and on 20 September, after visits to Grandmother Frances at Skipton and to the Burne-Joneses at their second home in Rottingdean near Brighton, he set sail on the *Brindisi* from Tilbury. Though he was to remain close friends with Dunsterville for the rest of his life, this marked the end of his friendship with Beresford, who later claimed that Rud left England with very mixed feelings. There is probably some truth in this. The *World* had just accepted a sonnet, appropriately entitled 'Two Lives', and the prospect of leading a bohemian life in London may well have seemed more alluring than becoming a cub journalist in India. Also, according to Trix, he and Flo were by now unofficially engaged.

4

Echoes

On 18 October 1882 the *Brindisi* docked at Bombay. During the month on board ship Rud had grown a set of whiskers, borrowed Arthur Clough's title 'Amours de Voyage' for a couple of new poems and, passing through the Suez Canal, caught a glimpse of the military control that the British had begun to establish in Egypt. Then, stepping off the boat, he was back once more among the scenes of his early childhood. 'It was,' he later told a friend, 'a return to a previous existence.' Memory led him through rebuilt streets to the place where he was born. The house itself had gone, but 'all that life returned to me with the sights and specially the smells: so that I found myself uttering automatically sentences and phrases of the meaning of which I was ignorant'.[1]

A few days north on the train and he was in Lahore, reunited with his parents in their large bungalow on Mozung Road, which friends jokingly referred to as Bikaner House, because its dusty, shrubless compound reminded them of the Bikaner Desert. Here he had his own room, servant, horse, cart and groom, and the pleasure of being treated as an adult and an equal. His mother he found 'more delightful than all my imaginings or memories'; his father 'not only a mine of knowledge and help, but a humorous, tolerant, and expert fellow-craftsman . . . I do not remember the smallest friction in any detail of our lives.' That at least was how he would recall his 'joyous home-coming' years later.[2] At the time the reunion is unlikely to have been quite as 'frictionless'. Within an hour of his arrival, his mother had made him remove the whiskers he had grown on the voyage and, if Trix is to be believed, it was not long before Alice was given a sharp reminder of her son's moodiness, when he found out about the publication of *Schoolboy Lyrics*.

There were other adjustments to be made. As an Anglo-Indian child in Bombay, Rud had been able to wander about more or less at will, talking to whomever he pleased; life in Lahore was much more circumscribed. The European community amounted to about seventy persons in all. They lived in their own quarter separated from the old, walled Mohammedan city by a wide mall that contained the museum where Lockwood was curator. Out beyond the walled city and the canal stood the fort of Mian Mir, permanently manned by a battalion of British infantry and a battery of artillery. Nearer in, though still outside the city itself, were shops, colleges, schools, the Punjab Club and, in two wooden sheds, the offices of the *Civil and Military Gazette*. The normal radius of travel was about six miles in any direction. For a teenager, it was a small world with few amusements.

In November, after a week or two helping his father at the museum, Rud began work as sub-editor at the CMG, the 'daily' which served the Punjab Province. He and his chief, Stephen Wheeler, comprised the entire editorial staff, managing a labour force of 160 Indians, which performed the more menial and mechanical tasks. At first all went well, and after a fortnight Rud was enthusiastically outlining his duties to the Reverend George Wilkes (Campbell's successor as chaplain at USC). His working hours were from 10.00 in the morning to 4.15 in the afternoon, and from the start he oversaw 'every scrap of the paper' except for the first two pages. His responsibilities included general proof-reading, writing reports and reviews, checking local Indian papers for usable snippets and extracts, 'subbing' all correspondence, preparing local notes, picking up information about forthcoming events like garden parties, polo games, official dinners and dances, and being on hand to receive special telegrams and visitors. For this he received a starting salary of 150 rupees a month (the equivalent of £135 a year) with half-yearly increments. The work, he told Wilkes, left him no time for his own writing but was full of variety.[3]

Rud, it is obvious, was enjoying his first job immensely. Then, just before Christmas, he was plunged into the middle of an emergency.

Wheeler fell off his horse, was badly concussed and ordered to take a week's rest. To Rud's excitement and alarm, he found himself in sole charge of the newspaper. With his parents' help, he weathered the crisis and was able to report to Uncle Crom that 'altogether, I find that this sort of life suits me down to the ground'.[4]

Although 1882 ended on a high note, the first few months of 1883 brought a change, as the monotony of life in a small station began to take hold. The brunt of Rud's frustration fell on his mother. Towards the end of February, Alice was plaintively confiding to Edith Plowden that although her son was well enough in health, he was 'if possible – less than ever inclined to Lahore itself' and was 'at times very trying in his moods – being subject to sudden fits of the blues'.[5] Lockwood, more laconically, took the view that Rud was 'better here than anywhere else where there are no music-hall ditties to pick up, no young persons to philander about with, and a great many other negatives of the most wholesome description. For all that makes Lahore so profoundly dull makes it safe for young people.'[6] All of which was no doubt true, but not much help to a bored and frustrated seventeen-year-old.

Contributing to Rud's moods was the fact that he and his editor (the 'Amber Toad', as he was known among the family) did not get on. The reasons for their mutual antipathy are easy enough to imagine: in age, temperament and outlook the two were poles apart. Wheeler was a married man in his late twenties, a stickler for detail and quick to take offence. His young assistant, fresh from England, was full of literary ambition and no doubt starting to chafe at the drearier aspects of his daily round. The suspicion that the boy's father had pulled strings to get him the job cannot have eased relations between the two nor, if Wheeler was as prickly as he sounds, can the competent way in which Rud had handled the Christmas crisis. The result was that Wheeler went out of his way to give his deputy a hard time. Even Lockwood, never averse to the improving effects of hard work, was soon suggesting that Wheeler's extreme tetchiness and irritability were putting Rud in 'training for heaven as well as for Editorship'.[7] As for Rud himself, there was little he could do except try to make the best of the situation. With his new boss he could hardly resort to the kind of retaliatory jape he had used against masters and other enemies at school. The only option was to work hard and keep his head down. However, he took what small, private revenge he could by sarcastically referring to Wheeler as 'my eternal pal' in 'The Pious Sub's Creed', a piece of light verse which he kept safely out of sight in his notebook.[8]

In the midst of this tension at work and frustration at home, an event occurred that was to have a profound effect on Rud's political views and on his poetry. During the early 1880s the policies of the Government in India, championed by the Viceroy, Lord Ripon, became increasingly Liberal and pro-Indian. In February 1883, the Legal Member of Council, Sir Courteney Ilbert, put forward a bill specifically designed to address anomalies in the existing Criminal Procedure Code. One of its more radical proposals was to remove 'the present bar upon the investment of native Magistrates, in the interior, with power over British subjects'.[9] In other words, native Indian magistrates were to be granted powers equivalent to those of their local British equivalents. What many Anglo-Indians took this to mean was that native judges would not only be given jurisdiction over white planters in outlying districts, but – far more controversially – would be empowered to try white women. With memories of the Indian Mutiny (1857–8) still lingering, the bill was seen as the thin end of the wedge, a measure certain to weaken British supremacy in India.

Initially Rud's own paper had come out strongly against the Ilbert Bill, but it was soon forced to back down due to pressure from its larger sister-paper, the *Pioneer*. One evening after work Rud walked into the Punjab Club in Lahore to find himself 'hissed' by all the other members, because that day's CMG carried a leader by Wheeler, voicing general support for Government policy – and by implication approval of the bill. Many years later Kipling offered a vivid re-enactment of the scene and of the impact it made upon him:

It is not pleasant to sit still when one is twenty [in fact, seventeen] while all your universe hisses you. Then uprose a Captain, our Adjutant of Volunteers, and said: 'Stop that! The boy's only doing what he's paid to do.' The demonstration tailed off, but I had seen a great light. The Adjutant was entirely correct. I was a hireling, paid to do what I was paid to do, and – I did not relish the idea. Someone said kindly: 'You damned young ass! Don't you know that your paper has the Government printing-contract?' I *did* know it, but I had never before put two and two together.[10]

That evening in the club was one of the turning-points of Rud's life – and not simply because of the revelation that he was a paid lackey, working for a paper with vested interests. At his age and in his situation, few would have been able to stand out against such an unequivocal display of public feeling; and Rud, who up till then had had no particular political allegiances, had no desire to stand out – on the contrary, he desperately wanted to fit in.

Again, characteristically, he channelled his response into verse. Publicly, the title, 'A New Departure', alluded to the Viceroy's recent removal from Calcutta to Simla to decide whether, or in what form, the Ilbert Bill should proceed. Privately, it registered Rud's awareness that he was taking a new poetic direction. Using the pseudonym, 'The Other Player', he sent the poem to the *Saturday Evening Englishman*, which published it. Even more gratifyingly, the poem was reprinted on 29 March in his own paper, presumably with Wheeler's approval. What probably started out as little more than an attempt to work off his mortification at being hissed at the club turned into a minor personal triumph:

> He had said, in a Viceregal homily,
>   (Alas for the sternness of rhyme!)
> 'I surmise British law's an anomily,
>   Give place to Bengal for a time.'
> These words were the pith of his homily
>   And Calcutta considered them crime.
>
> From the City of Baboos and *bustees*,
>   From that sorrowing City of Drains,
> Came the cry: – 'Oh my friend, let us trust he's
>   But mad, through long stay in the plains;
> Perplexed with the stench of our *bustees*,
>   His reason has reeled in the plains.'
>
> And the Planters who plant the Mofussil,
>   With Indigo, Coffee, and Tea,

Cried out, when they heard: – 'Blow that cuss he'll
    Come down on such folk as we be,
Our coolies will "boss" the Mofussil,
    With his pestilent A.C.P.C. [Amendment to the
    Criminal Procedure Code]'

But the Baboos that browsed in each office
    Of Subordinate Civil Employ
Cried 'Hurrah for our Viceregal novice!
    Hurrah for the Brahminee boy!
Let the "mean white" be silent, and doff his
    Pith hat to Brahminee boy!'

And the papers they print in Calcutta,
    And the journals men read in Madras,
Were known in their pages to utter
    Some hints that he might be an . . .!
And this spread, from the sinks of Calcutta,
    And the swamps of benighted Madras,
Till the thought set the land in a flutter –
    'Ye Gods! *was* His Lordship an . . .?'

For his notions of natives *were* curious,
    So India objected, and rose,
And, when India was properly furious,
    He remarked, 'This discussion I close,
The heat to my health is injurious,
    I hie to Himalayan snows.'

With the tact that belonged to his station,
    With a suavity solely his own,
He had set by the ears half a nation
    And left it – to simmer alone.
With his maudlin *ma-bap* legislation,
    He had played merry Hades and – *flown*.[11]

At the time probably only Lockwood and Alice realised that this was the work of a seventeen-year-old newcomer, equally anxious to win acceptance and to show off his literary credentials. In fact, from a strictly aesthetic point of view, these twin impulses in the poem tended to get in each other's way. In the opening stanzas Rud did not make it clear whom he was attacking. First the satire seemed aimed at the Viceroy, then at the Planters, then at the Baboos. Each was mocked in turn as Rud flaunted his technical virtuosity, mixing Byronic mannerisms with scraps of Anglo-Indian slang and an ingeniously sustained use of self-rhyme. Only in the final two stanzas did it become obvious that the Viceroy had, in fact, been the target all along. Although this uncertainty weakened the overall effect of the satire, its wavering aim perfectly reflected Rud's mixed motives. The furore over the Ilbert Bill continued until the following year, when the legislation was eventually passed in a modified form that satisfied no one; 'whites', it was decided, could be tried by Indian magistrates but would be allowed the right to claim a half-European jury.

Rud's first hot season now set in. Temperatures soared and even under the punkah it was 86° Fahrenheit. He kept up his correspondence with Wilkes and Uncle Crom, informing them that he now had his own office and that his pay had risen sharply to £240 a year. He floated plans for an Old Boys' dinner and suggested an advertisement for United Services College in the CMG to attract pupils, which Price duly sent. This desire to maintain links with his old school implied a continuing homesickness, which came out openly in his letters to Aunt Edie. 'Homesickness is bad enough,' he told her, 'when you are within two hundred miles of any "haven where you would be", but to get it in all its beauty you must be seven thousand miles away from anywhere, and then you realise what it is to be properly, completely and thoroughly "home sick".'[12] Work, he added, was the only cure.

A verse-letter of 12 June repeated the same theme, mixing comic vignettes of his daily routine with nostalgia for a lost life in England. The cumulative effect of the lolloping couplets was both funny and rather moving. The letter ended:

Oh, what is 'two hundred a month', and half-year 'rises' to come,
To a fellow with hairs in his pen, and lizard-tails in his gum;
His ink putrescent and loathsome, a paste of corrupting flies,

His spectacles dimmed and steamy, and goggles over his eyes.
'Oh give me a London *trottoir*, some byewalk damp and muddy.
In place of this wholesome heat' is the cry of your washed out

Ruddy[13]

Wheeler was ill with fever that month, leaving Rud once more in charge. By July he badly needed a break himself and was granted a month's leave in Simla, where he stayed with one of the paper's proprietors, James Walker. It was a first glimpse of another side of his new world.

Situated 7,000 feet up on the lower slopes of the Himalayas, Simla effectively became the seat of Government for half the year. The Viceroy, the Governor of the Punjab and the Commander-in-Chief of the Army all used it as their summer headquarters, and during these months Simla turned into the social centre of Anglo-India: the place to seek advancement, amusement, romance, or simply to escape from the heat of the Plains. Rud was later to make it the setting for many of his stories and poems, but on this first, brief visit what he wanted was rest and recreation. He found both, thanks to the Walkers' generosity. After a whirl of picnics, dances and theatricals, he was back in Lahore by mid-August, cheerfully describing to Edie how he had 'flirted with the bottled up energy of a year on my lips'. 'Don't be horrified,' he reassured her, 'for there were about half a dozen of 'em and I took back the lacerated fragments of my heart as I distributed my P[our].P[rendre].C[ongé]. cards and returned the whole intact, to Flo Garrard's keeping as per usual.'[14]

From then until just before Christmas, Rud was mostly on his own in Bikaner House, fighting off boredom and loneliness. Alice had gone to England to fetch Trix, while Lockwood was away arranging the Punjab exhibits for an international exhibition in Calcutta. Left to his own resources, Rud tried to remain purposeful. Outside office hours he rode, played tennis and whist, learnt elementary Urdu and dined regularly at the club with the handful of members not away on leave. He also joined the 1st Punjab Volunteers. Ironically, given his later enthusiasm for the Army, this experiment with military life was a complete disaster – after repeated failure to attend parade, he was asked to resign.[15]

In November he nerved himself to send a letter to Crofts, enclosing 'some specimens of the stuff I write daily' and asking him 'to pass sentence upon them, in due form'. Apart from mentioning another pay rise (to

£300 a year) and that Wheeler was again absent sick, the letter to Crofts supplies further evidence of Rud's emerging gospel of work. 'Your theory about "giving a boy more work than he can do and he'll do it" works beautifully out here,' he told his old Classics master, 'though I didn't believe it in the Latin set. I have nearly always a little more than I can do on my hands and consequently it gets done.'[16] At the same time, the fact that he was still writing poems with titles like 'A Ballad of Bitterness' and 'The Song of An Outsider' suggests that as yet work provided only a makeshift bulwark against loneliness and homesickness.

On 18 December, Alice arrived back in Lahore with Trix, thus re-forming what they affectionately called the Family Square. Trix at fifteen and a half was tall and good-looking. The few surviving photographs show a sensitive face with a wistful, introspective expression. By contrast, her parents commented on her gaiety and would drop her witticisms into letters to friends. One *bon mot* that Lockwood especially prized was Trix's description of a Mrs Mason as 'a white cow in a tiger skin', which, he informed Edith Plowden, was very apt.[17] Rud too was delighted to be reunited with his sister and immensely proud of her. 'We two "frivol" like babies,' he was soon telling Aunt Edie and added that he was teaching Trix to ride: 'This morning she and I went out into the open and trotted back as hard as we could come . . . If you had seen her with the colour in her cheeks, her hair down and blowing about in the wind, and her hat jammed at the back of her head you would have seen her at her loveliest – and that's a big order.' He and his parents were, he admitted, 'spoiling the maiden sadly – but she won't spoil easily and brightens up the domestic shanty like a "Swan's incandescent".'[18]

Since his sister was initially considered too young to dine out, Rud would keep himself free on evenings when their parents were engaged. Trix later recalled some of the games they played and the fun they had. One game, Yadasi, required players to say 'By my knowledge' each time they received something from someone else. 'It is quite simple,' she later observed, 'but it goes on all the time, until one of the players dies – or goes mad.' Eventually the game got so out of hand that their father put a stop to it, because 'we could hardly help ourselves to dishes at the table without murmuring, "By my knowledge".'[19]

Other games were more literary. Sometimes they would have a

Shakespeare evening, with only quotations from the Bard allowed and no checking of references until the following morning. Part of the fun was to see how much fake Shakespeare they could get away with undetected. Rud, already an accomplished pasticheur, was especially good at coming up with plausible lines such as:

> My liege of Westmoreland, the pinnace stays
> To give you waftage to the further shore

which, if challenged, he would airily assign to '"the Richards" or "the Henrys"'.[20] Or they might spend the evening making up spoofs of their favourite English and American poets. Their model was the American parodist Bayard Taylor's *The Echo Club, and other Literary Diversions*, pages of which Rud knew by heart, and which he later claimed spurred him 'to the joyful labour of writing parodies on every poet between Wordsworth and Whitman'.[21] Soon he and Trix had enough material for a slim volume, which, with a nod to Taylor, they entitled *Echoes, By Two Writers*. In August the volume duly appeared.

Granted the importance of games in his childhood, it was no coincidence that Rud's first real book should have developed out of collaborative play. During the miserable Southsea years, he had invented elaborate rituals that involved secret knowledge and private codes. These games, played either on his own or with his sister, had been both a survival tactic and a way of creating a sense of self. That same spirit, rekindled in happier circumstances, now found new expression. It is easy to see why Rud found literary parody so appealing. An outsider longing to be an insider, he could show that he at least knew his way around 'the realms of gold', however difficult he might sometimes find the worlds of India and Anglo-India. Besides, away from the daily drudgery of the CMG, here was an area where he could safely show off his wit and ingenuity. One can also see in these parodic games with Trix an early anticipation of his later success as a writer of fiction, for adults as well as for children. His stories derive much of their power from his ability to charm the reader into feeling like a co-conspirator, even a co-author, sharing fascinating secrets, swapping privileged information.

In *Echoes* Rud may well have co-operated with Trix in another sense. Which of them, for instance, was responsible for 'Jane Smith', a neat parody of Wordsworth's 'Alice Fell'? In presentation copies to Aunt Edie and Aunt Louie, Trix claimed 'Jane Smith' as hers – which seems clear enough, except that Rud later included the poem in both the Outward Bound and De Luxe editions of his work. A case of fraternal appropriation? Memory lapse? Or was 'Jane Smith' a combined effort? If so, were there other collaborations? Very likely. In July, writing to Aunt Edie about the still unpublished *Echoes*, Rud described the joint collection as 'all parody work for which T. shows a great facility being her mother's daughter where verse is concerned'.[22] Trix would recall how, choosing pieces for republication, her brother subsequently 'found it difficult to disentangle my work from his'.[23]

Although not immediately obvious, nearly half of Rud's contributions to *Echoes* were not new. Of the thirty-one poems in the volume that were almost certainly his, fourteen or so had been written the previous year or had been culled from his old notebooks. A few of these had always been intended as parodies, but many had not. 'Commonplaces' and 'His Consolation', both written at school, started out as serious poems – the first in the manner of Heine, the second of Browning. Comments in his notebooks show that Rud was already aware how derivative several of these early pieces were; now he realised that he could pass them off as playful imitations.

A number of the new poems merely burlesqued a particular writer's mannerisms. 'The Flight of the Bucket' Rud described to Aunt Edie as 'a psychological poem on Jack and Jill, in Browning's vein'.[24] In fact, it was simply a take-off of Browning's habit of complicating a simple story with endless parentheses:

> Well, Jack and Jill – God knows the life they led
> (The poet never told us, more's the pity)
> Pent up in some damp kennel of their own,
> Beneath the hillside; but it once befell
> That Jack or Jill, niece, cousin, uncle, aunt
> (Some one of all the brood) would wash or scour –
> Rinse out a cess-pit, swab the kennel floor,
> And water (*liquor vitae*, Lawson calls,
> But I – I hold by whisky. Never mind;
> I didn't mean to hurt your feelings, sir,

And missed the scrap o' blue at buttonhole –)
Spring water was the needful at the time,
So they must climb the hill for't . . .[25]

Other poems contained a heavily disguised biographical underlayer.
Echoes not only allowed Rud to recycle older work as intentionally parodic, but provided him with a ready-made mask for his private emotions.
'The City of the Heart' was probably the clearest example. Ostensibly a
parody of Longfellow, the last two quatrains in fact portrayed the current
state of Rud's feelings for Flo and his rather desperate attempts to keep
them battened down. Here the 'echoes' were quite as much personal as
literary. The final two quatrains read:

> I passed through the streets of my haunted heart,
>   In the hush of a hopeless night;
> And from every gully a dog would start
>   And bay my soul with affright.

> But I smote with the dog-whip of Work and Fact
>   These evil beasts on the head,
> Till I made of my heart a wholesome tract,
>   Empty and garnishèd.[26]

In a few cases the new poems were not parodies at all but used an existing
poem or form as a starting-point. 'Nursery Rhymes for Little Anglo-
Indians' adapted well-known nursery rhymes to portray aspects of Anglo-
Indian life, as in the waspish reworking of 'I had a little nutmeg':

> I had a little husband
>   Who gave me all his pay.
> I left him for Mussoorie,
>   A hundred miles away.

> I dragged my little husband's name
>   Through heaps of social mire,
> And joined him in October,
>   As good as you'd desire.[27]

Less flippantly, Tennyson's 'The Vision of Sin' became the springboard for 'A Vision of India'. Rud's version borrowed the verse-form of Part IV of Tennyson's poem and adapted its opening lines, but otherwise lifted free of his original to paint a grim picture of the lot of the average Anglo-Indian civilian:

> Mother India, wan and thin,
>   Here is forage come your way;
> Take the young Civilian in,
>   Kill him swiftly as you may . . .
>
> Brown and Jones and Smith shall die;
>   We succeed to all their places,
> Bear the badge of slavery,
>   Sunken eyes and pallid faces.
>
> Laughter that is worse than tears
>   Is our portion in the land,
> And the tombstones of our peers
>   Make the steps whereon we stand.[28]

In general, however, this stark tone and outlook were not typical of Rud's new work in *Echoes*. For the most part, bravado was the keynote, the sense of a young writer gleefully picking out figures in the poetic landscape and showing how neatly they could be travestied.

Of the other poems that Rud published during 1884, 'Lord Ripon's Reverie' and 'The Story of Tommy' warrant a brief mention. Both appeared in the CMG while he was again left in charge. 'Lord Ripon's Reverie' he described to Aunt Edie as 'a parody of Locksley Hall, which . . . has disturbed the Pioneer who wanted to say something nasty about Lord Ripon's retirement but only came out with a ponderous leader no one read'.[29] After the uproar over the Ilbert Bill and the Government's subsequent climb-down, Ripon had decided to resign and return to England. It was a sign of Rud's increasing confidence that, using the pseudonym E.M., he farewelled the Viceroy with a breezy satire. He presented Ripon petulantly reflecting on the frustrations of his viceroyship

and anticipating, with some relish, the problems that awaited his successor, Lord Dufferin:

> So *you*'ve got it now, dear Duffy. Don't imagine East is West.
> Come and rule it ('tis your duty); try to kick it from its rest.[30]

The verses appeared on 15 September. Two weeks later E.M. was in print
again, describing how a young soldier, dosed with rum to ward off fever,
was hanged for accidentally shooting the barrack-room *punkah-wallah*.
Technically not as accomplished as 'Lord Ripon's Reverie', 'The Story of
Tommy' is of note because it marked the start of Rud's sympathetic
interest in the life of the Other Ranks in India.

His other writing too was beginning to gain focus and momentum. In
February 1884 he mentioned work on 'a novel of sorts' to Cormell Price
(although nothing more was heard of this).[31] In March his paper sent him
to do a 'special' on Lord Ripon's state visit to the Maharajah of Patiala on
the opening of the Mohindar College, and he produced four substantial
articles covering the event. In May he began a series of pieces for the
CMG called 'A Week in Lahore', which ran intermittently for the next
two years. Again he signed himself Esau Mull or E.M. Esau, the character
in the Old Testament who sold his birthright for 'a mess of pottage' was,
like Rud, 'an hairy man'. 'Mull', short for mulligatawny, the famous Indian
soup or pottage, was also a term for failing exams and, according to the
OED, 'a distinctive sobriquet [applied] to members of the service belonging to the Madras Presidency'. The pseudonym was one of Rud's private
games, code for 'reluctant wage-slave', with a hint that hack work like the
'Week in Lahore' series was a bit beneath him, a betrayal of his art.

Another pseudonym was the mock-pedantic 'Jacob Cavendish, M.A.'.
As the latter, he had fun in June composing a letter to the CMG on the
subject of 'Music for the Middle-Aged'. This spill-over from *Echoes*
announced a 'scheme, imperfect as yet, for the regeneration of after-
dinner music', which purported to show how the words of popular drawing-room songs might be brought into 'perfect harmony with our
every-day life' – citing, as an example, 'Come under the Punkah, Maud'.[32]
Three months later, 'Jacob Cavendish' was again in action, this time less
successfully as an Anglo-Indian Robinson Crusoe relating a dreary week
in station life.

September also saw the appearance in the CMG of Rud's first real Indian story, 'The Gate of the Hundred Sorrows'. Here in the opening sentence was the instantly recognisable Kipling voice: 'This is no work of mine. My friend, Gabral Misquitta, the half-caste, spoke it all, between moonset and morning, six weeks before he died; and I took it down from his mouth as he answered my questions. So: –' Without further interruption, Gabral then told the story of his life as an opium addict in the Gate of the Hundred Sorrows. His narrative slowly unwound, slowly circled back on itself, as obsessive details and phrases repeated themselves: the timber-construction job he had 'hundreds and hundreds of years ago' in Calcutta; the sixty rupees, a legacy, that came 'fresh and fresh each month' to support his habit; the black and red dragons on his 'wadded woollen headpiece' that shifted and fought after he had had a few pipes; the contrast between the old days, when Fung-Tching ran the Gate, and its present decline under his nephew; and always the recurring assertion that 'Nothing matters much to me', except 'the Black Smoke'.[33]

As a story, 'The Gate of the Hundred Sorrows' already displayed many of the traits that were to become quintessentially Kiplingesque: the presence of the reliable reporter, apparently just passing on a story he had been told; the penchant for peculiar names; the interest in misfits; the exploration of abnormal states of mind; the nonchalant handling of arcane detail; not least, the fascination with a ritualised life conducted in a world reduced to a small space. Since the story was almost entirely a dramatic monologue, the debt to Browning was obvious; and yet, so completely had his influence been absorbed that the effect was of something quite new. In Browning, some implicit moral judgement was usually passed on the speaker. Not here, however. Here the reader followed the languorous coiling and uncoiling of Gabral's voice, and when it stopped, so did the story. From a literary point of view, 'The Gate of the Hundred Sorrows' looked forward rather than back. The story's intimate mirroring of a consciousness preoccupied exclusively with itself had more in common with T S Eliot's 'The Love Song of J Alfred Prufrock' than it did with Browning's 'My Last Duchess' or 'Andrea del Sarto'.

How far, if at all, Rud based his portrayal of Gabral Misquitta on an actual person it is impossible to guess. His later practice was often to take someone he had met, or something he had heard, as a starting-point; so the dying addict may have had a real-life counterpart. What the details of the story do strongly suggest is that, with his parents at Simla and Trix at Dalhousie, Rud had begun his night-ramblings in the old, walled Mohammedan city – the City of Dreadful Night as he later called it, borrowing the title from one of his favourite poems. These rambles between sunset and dawn, together with aspects of his newspaper work, introduced him to the intricate complexities of a world of which many of his fellow Anglo-Indians remained ignorant and largely oblivious. That these excursions became a regular feature of his life in Lahore is clear from his autobiography:

> Often the night got into my head as it had done in the boarding-house in the Brompton Road, and I would wander till dawn in all manner of odd places – liquor-shops, gambling and opium-dens, which are not a bit mysterious, wayside entertainments such as puppet-shows, native dances; or in and about the narrow gullies under the Mosque of Wazir Khan for the sheer sake of looking . . . One would come home, just as the light broke, in some night-hawk of a hired carriage which stank of hookah-fumes, jasmine-flowers, and sandalwood; and if the driver were moved to talk, he told one a good deal. Much of real Indian life goes on in the hot weather nights.[34]

In short, Rud knew at first-hand the world he was starting to write about.

That he took opium at around this time probably provided an additional impetus to 'The Gate of the Hundred Sorrows'. Writing to Aunt Edie on 17 September, he briefly alluded to the story. He also told her that the previous night his servant (afraid that Rud might be coming down with cholera) had insisted that he smoke as much opium as he could: 'Presently I felt the cramps in my legs dying out and my tummy more settled and a minute or two later it seemed to me that I fell through the floor.' This letter was written nine days before the appearance of 'The Gate of the Hundred Sorrows' in the CMG. Oddly, he wrote to his aunt as if the story had already appeared. He talked of it having 'stirred up the easy going clericals here to a state of virtuous horror'. Was he imagining the shocked reaction he hoped the story would provoke, or deliberately obscuring the connection between his opium experience and the story? That he told his aunt that he had not 'written a word to the mother about last night's experiences' suggests that he was probably covering something up.[35]

Rud undertook several other activities during 1884. In February he was offered, and refused, his first bribe. An old Afghan who had fought against the British during the Second Afghan War of 1879–80 and was now under a form of house-arrest in Lahore tried to get him to use his influence as a journalist to secure his return to Kabul. The inducements included money, jewels, horses and a 'very handsome and beautifully dressed' Kashmiri girl. But, as Rud remarked to Aunt Edie, 'I didn't quite see how she was to be introduced into an English household like ours.'[36] In April he was to have acted the part of Chrysal in W S Gilbert's *The Palace of Truth*, but at the last minute had to pull out through ill health. (The previous December he had played Desmarets in *Plot and Passion*, to some acclaim, and throughout his Indian years was in regular demand for local theatricals.) During the spring he saw a good deal of a Miss Coxen, who had acted the part of Palmis in *The Palace of Truth*. Probably there was a mild flirtation: in June, just before she left Lahore, he sent her a verse-letter as if from his horse Joe, and in September wrote to tell her of Joe's death at Dalhousie. Dalhousie, or 'Dullhouses' as it was known, was the hill station where Trix and Alice spent much of the hot season that year, and Rud joined them there for his annual month's holiday in August.

Sometime during the first half of 1884, Flo formally broke off their understanding. Exactly when she did so is hard to establish. However, in June 1886 Rud confided in a letter to his cousin Margaret Burne-Jones that it was two years since Flo had given him his 'jawâb' or dismissal. He had been 'very unhappy' and felt that 'the bottom had tumbled out of the Great Universe'. None of his surviving correspondence from 1884 explicitly alluded to the break-up. There were, however, a few submerged hints in a July letter to Aunt Edie, in which he described how 'for one weary week my fear in the daytime was that I was going to die, and at night my only fear was that I might live to the morning'. That despair about Flo lay behind his traumatic week is suggested by another reference to eye-trouble; at school problems with his eyes had been closely linked to crises with Flo. Now they were up to 'their old tricks again', and he had been feeling 'so utterly unstrung . . . that they bothered me a good deal'. He went on to tell Aunt Edie that he had avoided 'the shadows' and cured 'the blue devils' by working sixteen hours a day on 'original matter and much précis writing'.[37] He had, in other words, been employing 'the dog-whip of Work and Fact'.

The relationship with Flo may never have amounted to much in itself, and may have been largely a product of Rud's imagination, but that does not mean that its ending was any the less devastating. For four years she had provided a kind of emotional anchor or safety-net; now he was once again adrift and even more reliant on work and the Family Square. Well might he envy his cousin Stanley Baldwin 'in the Sixth at Harrow . . . with a University Education to follow'.[38]

Following the break-up with Flo, Rud spent 1885 in a state of emotional turmoil. During that year he intermittently kept a diary, the only one of his to survive. Although it is often extremely cryptic, and at times completely impenetrable, it does offer tantalising clues to his private thoughts about sex and marriage, and hints of what he tried to do about them.

From mid-April to mid-August he was based at Simla, partly on leave but mostly in a new role as the CMG's '*chroniqueur* of a Gay Season in the hills', as he dismissively described it to Aunt Edie.[39] In early May he took a short walking holiday in the Himalayas, recording in his diary that the women at Kotgurgh were 'very pretty' and that the local padre had had 'a charge of fornication preferred against him by non-converts'. 'Should like to be Padre in these parts,' he mused on 6 May.[40] For the next two and a half months there are relatively few entries and none remotely confessional. Then, on 1 August, his father arrived in Simla to join the rest of the family, and the resultant congestion led to Rud that same day accepting another invitation to stay at the Walkers'. This time, given a room next to a couple called Hayes, his stay quickly revealed unforeseen complications.

For once, his diary entry was explicit. 'Wish they wouldn't put married couple next door to me with one ½ plank between,' he noted, adding plaintively, 'Saps ones morality.' The first two sentences of his entry for the next day, 2 August, were positively desperate: 'Same complaint. This is really ghastly.' At this point the entries for a three-week period became increasingly cryptic:

TUESDAY 4 AUGUST:	My own affair entirely. A wet day but deuced satisfactory.
WEDNESDAY 5 AUGUST:	Begin to think I've been a fool but aint certain . . .
SATURDAY 15 AUGUST:	Got to go down. W[heeler]. dekks ??? too much to make it comfortable for me. Confound the man. But I must go. Cheerful exchange of telegrams all day.
SUNDAY 16 AUGUST:	On this day I left Simla for Lahore. It was a pleasant three and a half months and taught me much.
MONDAY 17 AUGUST:	In train from morn to dewy eve with one Gempertz on his way to kill things in Kashmere. A nice person but more lecherous than is safe for those parts. May he return safe *and sound* . . .
THURSDAY 20 AUGUST:	Too savage to swear. Not a soul worth looking at in the Station . . . *Mem*. Must really make my diary a working one. Went home and thought a good deal.
FRIDAY 21 AUGUST:	. . . Usual philander in Gardens. Home to count the risks of my resolution.
SATURDAY 22 AUGUST:	A heavy day: concluding with dinner at the Wrenchs' – or at least beginning. Then a fall into the mire . . .
MONDAY 24 AUGUST:	Club. work. anticipation.
TUESDAY 25 AUGUST:	I wonder! Club. Work of sorts. ? and gardens
WEDNESDAY 26 AUGUST:	Gardens and talk with T. Young. He is sanguine and hopeful. I also. More anticipation.
THURSDAY 27 AUGUST:	First period probation over. Mind easier. Now to look about me.
FRIDAY 28 AUGUST:	Band after dinner when I did look about. Went round with Mrs L. which did not fill me with delight.[41]

A reconstruction, albeit incomplete, is possible. Aroused to a state of intense sexual frustration from listening to the Hayes making love, Rud (still a virgin?) went to a local brothel and the next day worried that he might have picked up a venereal infection. Nevertheless, he left Simla generally buoyed up by the experience. On the train to Lahore, he fell into conversation with one Gempertz, who, boasting about his past and future sexual exploits, brought back Rud's anxiety that he himself might not be 'safe *and sound*'. On his own once more in the narrow, all-too-familiar world of Lahore, he started to contemplate marriage, both as a solution to loneliness and as a means of assuaging his heightened sexual feelings. He may even have imagined that getting married would in some way 'save' him. On the look-out for a possible wife, he went a number of times to the 'Gardens' (probably the Shalimar rose gardens, four miles outside Lahore) and did a spot of exploratory flirting. On 26 August he was still concerned that he might have a venereal infection and sought a professional opinion from Tarleton Young, a surgeon and professor at the Lahore Medical College. Young was 'sanguine and hopeful'. He told Rud that by now he would certainly know if he had gonorrhoea, since the symptoms were painfully obvious. He also informed him that the initial genital sore denoting syphilis could appear up to ninety days following intercourse, but that the first three weeks or so usually constituted the most critical period, and the signs were therefore encouraging. Reassured at getting through this 'first period probation', Rud again began to 'look about' for someone to marry.

Such a reconstruction is compatible with what little can be deduced of the nature of Rud's relationship with Flo. For the previous four years, he had been using his 'engagement' to her as an emotional inoculation, to keep himself clear of other entanglements. At times he had come close to acknowledging this, as when he told Aunt Edie in 1883, 'I took back the lacerated fragments of my heart . . . and returned the whole intact, to Flo Garrard as per usual.' Now, in the aftermath of his dismissal, he found himself tormented by feelings and urges that he could no longer suppress or displace. Moreover, any fantasy he had constructed about a future with Flo could no longer be sustained. Hence, at the age of nineteen, his 'resolution' to 'look about' for a new safety-net, a wife.

In addition to the hints in his diary, Rud made an oblique reference to some recent entanglement in a letter to Margaret Burne-Jones in late September. 'Your paragraph about my keeping my "old eyes open" made me blush all to myself in the empty house,' he confided to his cousin:

> For it is a lamentable fact that I, R. Kipling, have been done, dished, had, taken in, made an ass of, bamboozled – anything contemptible you please by a 'Daughter of Heth in Silk Attire'. And it served me jolly well right for I was attempting to work the D. of H. to my own and the Old Rag's ends. She knowed it all along and I got a note – a delicately spiteful one such as only a woman could write – from her hand the other day pointing out exactly where I had failed. It's a long story and of no interest to anyone but the Principals but oh Lord! Lord! how I have abased myself in sackcloth and ashes and sworn never to pit my poor wits against a woman again . . . I told the Mummy of course . . . and she wrote that she would have done just the same if she had been the woman.[42]

Like his account of taking opium, this curious tale of being ditched does not quite ring true. The arresting phrase 'Daughter of Heth in Silk Attire' was another of Rud's bits of code, made by running together the titles of two novels by the Scottish writer William Black: A Daughter of Heth and In Silk Attire. (The expression 'a daughter of Heth' referred to 'a loose woman from outside the tribe', and 'in silk attire' meant an actress.) In recent letters to Margaret, Rud had taken to addressing her as 'the Wop of Europe' and signing himself 'the Wop of Asia' in homage to the high-spirited minister's son in A Daughter of Heth, nicknamed The Whaup. Now he used Black to devise a different kind of shorthand to hint at his involvement with (presumably) an Indian prostitute – though whether his cousin had any idea that was what he meant seems unlikely. Which was probably the main point. As with his opium-taking, Rud desperately wanted to tell someone conveniently far away that something momentous had happened to him, but he wanted to do it in such a way that there would be no awkward repercussions.

Less ambiguously, his letter to Wop showed just how much the idea of marriage was on his mind. He had begun, he told her, 'to understand faintly why so many good men perpetrate matrimony' and had warned his mother that a return of fever would certainly drive him 'into instant matrimony or some officiating arrangement' until her return. He then dropped the mask and the facetious tone, and added simply, 'All the same living alone is in every way abominable.'[43]

5

Anglo-Indian Attitudes

The year of 1885 was not only one of great emotional ferment for Rud; it was also the year in which he did what every young writer is supposed to do – he started a novel. By late July he had written 237 pages and told Aunt Edie:

> It's not one bit nice or proper but it carries a grim sort of moral with it and tries to deal with the unutterable horrors of lower class Eurasian and native life as they exist outside reports and reports and reports. . . . Trixie says it's awfully horrid: Mother says it's nasty but powerful and I *know* it to be in large measure true. It is an unfailing delight to me and I'm just in that pleasant stage where the characters are living with me always.

Mother Maturin was never published and probably never finished, though Kipling may have quarried parts of it for *Kim* before destroying the manuscript. A friend who read the manuscript of the novel described it as 'the story of an old Irish woman who kept an opium den in Lahore but sent her daughter to be educated in England. She marries a Civilian and comes to live in Lahore – hence a story, – how Govt. secrets came to be known in the bazar and vice versa'.[1] Although *Mother Maturin* doubtless had its moments, there is little reason to mourn its disappearance, or to imagine that it was the great lost Anglo-Indian novel.

*

Hard on the heels of his venereal panic in September, and accompanying the challenge of writing his novel, Rud's life in the autumn of 1885 was dominated by the apparently innocuous process of compiling, with Trix and his parents, a Christmas collection of stories and poems. In late September, he told Wop that the family had 'a magazine in hand for Xmas – a collection of Indian stories published as some sort of supplement to the Old Rag [the CMG]. Makes people take an interest in the paper you know.' This Christmas supplement, by 'Four Anglo-Indian Writers', was *Quartette* and included two powerful new stories of Rud's, 'The Strange Ride of Morrowbie Jukes' and 'The Phantom 'Rickshaw'. However, before it could be published, the supplement ran into problems – problems that Rud described in a lengthy letter to Margaret written between 28 November and 11 January. Consciously or otherwise, he offered a portrait of a stern-minded, duty-following, intensely practical Anglo-Indian in the making. The implied contrast was with Margaret herself, set up by her cousin to represent the English, liberal values that he was now renouncing. In anticipating her surprise at – and forestalling her objections to – his new attitudes, Rud was trying to persuade himself of their validity. In outlining to her the 'manifold contradictions' of life in India, he was outlining them to himself.[2] And in attempting to justify to her his new Anglo-Indian stance in the face of these contradictions, he was performing an act of self-justification.

The problems began in early December as Rud tried desperately to meet his production deadline of the 15th. Unfortunately, he was told by Ram Dass (the Hindu head printer), it could not be done. This led Rud on 6 December to spend a cold Sunday in the office, cajoling the work-force and, with a mixture of proverbs and flowery insults, keeping Ram Dass at it. He quoted to Margaret examples of his exhortatory methods:

'Oh Ram Dass! I have been now three years eating the salt of this newspaper and I thought (lit: it was in my mind) that the Hindus worked as well as the Mahommedans. But I now find that I have made a mistake and that the Hindus are weak and childish without spirit (ûkhàl is difficult to translate exactly – it means all that goes to make up a Man) and (this hurt his feelings most of all) nearly as worthless as a Bengali babu.'

Rud's command of native idiom did the trick – 'I hadn't no more bother that Sunday about "Quartette"'.[3]

His mastery of Indian proverbs displayed in miniature the central contradiction of his attitude to India. On the one hand, his admirable desire to understand an alien way of life, which he recognised as rich and compelling; on the other, his growing conviction that he could only justify this interest for its practical usefulness, as a secret code that the smart young Sahib needed to crack. The extent to which Rud's Anglo-Indian attitudes were still very much a front he was trying out became apparent when the mask momentarily slipped. While 'delivering these little homilies on the sanctity of toil', he confided to Margaret, he was unable to restrain 'an illtimed grin of self derision' at the thought that only three years before he himself had been devoting 'enormous energy' to 'shirking' his own 'work' at school.[4] At such moments one remembers with a jolt just how young he was.

By 16 December, *Quartette* still not having appeared, Rud was seriously annoyed. He had done everything he could, 'working in office till seven or eight at nights and taking a large share of the business arrangements' on himself – yet it was 'two days late already'. The natives had let him down, and once more he spelt out to Margaret (and himself) the familiar Anglo-Indian moral: 'Remember Wop in spite of what good lies in the native he is utterly unable to do anything finished or clean, or neat unless he has the Englishman at his elbow to guide and direct and put straight.' All so-called progress in India, Rud insisted, was 'boosted', 'propped-up' and 'held up' by Englishmen; but it was the English 'who take the blame if anything goes wrong'. Now thoroughly worked up, Rud's tone to his cousin became archly hysterical:

> without that aid – you would get – well anything mismanaged, ill directed, scamped, helpless and careless that you please. And a mismanaged nation is not a sweet thing I believe – 'never had one myself tho'; Ram D. and his kin taxing my patience and long suffering to the verge of lunacy.

It was as if, in his own mind, his day-to-day battles with *Quartette* had become synonymous with the Anglo-Indian story of India, and his own work-force had become the Indian 'nation' which, as an Anglo-Indian, it was his duty to 'manage'. The intense pressure and anxiety of the situation (his own and, by association, that of Anglo-India in general) lay just below the surface. What if his work-force had become 'a mismanaged nation'? What if India herself was? Rud immediately reassured himself by turning his work-force into children – 'They are all willing enough but, in addition to their natural incapacity to understand, so ghastly careless and casual' – and he added to Margaret that he had been forced to call Ram Dass not just 'a child' but a 'child's child', a speaker of 'baby talk'.[5]

The next day, 17 December, Rud's ire switched to the Bengali clerk with a 'native B.A.' who was in charge of *Quartette*'s accounts. After being berated and fined for his incompetence, the clerk had the temerity to remind Rud of his university education. Rud's infuriation boiled over: 'Knows fractions and decimals – can't keep the register of two hundred orders correctly or neatly – Remembers the *Deserted Village* and mislays an account book. – Thirdly and lastly – Lies – Like a Bengali – to get out of the mess.' What could be done with someone like this, he wondered aloud to his cousin, someone married with three children and only twenty-one? What hope was there for someone 'of that stamp . . . broken down – used up – played out – before they are men and through the very weakness of their physical nature morally rotten and untrustworthy'? At which point, characteristically, Rud paused, suddenly aware of how he must sound; and finished by sending himself up: 'A-a-a-Men. I'm becoming a regular preacher in my old age.'[6]

It was an illuminating cameo. The Bengali clerk, unlike Ram Dass, was an educated man with a degree – and as such, represented a type that was more of a threat to English rule, being better informed, speaking better English, more on a par and therefore less easy to infantalise. Anglo-Indians labelled such educated Indians 'Babus', and to vilify them was standard practice. Hence, in fulminating about the clerk, Rud was trotting out a stock response, demonstrating his grasp of the Anglo-Indian script. However, there was something else (besides perhaps a certain sexual envy) fuelling the invective: Rud's own lack of a university education. 'I'd give something to be in the Sixth at Harrow as he is with a University Education to follow,' he had confessed to Aunt Edie the previous year about his cousin Stanley Baldwin.[7] The Bengali clerk with the BA offered a direct, personal threat to Rud's position, a threat which his Anglo-Indian stance did not entirely enable him to assuage.

Later that day Rud went home at seven, leaving Chalmers, the Scottish foreman, with a bottle of brandy, his blessing and 'forty odd men' to finish off. During the night, however, he became anxious, got out of bed, crept out of the house and returned to the office. There he found his men 'on the verge of mutiny'. Once more he resorted to a combination of cajolery and praise, supplemented by 'about *twelve pounds*' of local tobacco for the coolies, whom he worked in half-hour shifts. Momentarily relaxing, Rud had a chance to survey the scene in 'the big hall': the presses 'faintly lit by scores of candle ends', the 'bobbing shadows and reflections', the 'mob of white and red and green turbans tossing round the raised platform in the centre of the room'. Something went wrong with 'the two colour title page', but he was able to fix it. He corrected proofs for the advertisements. And he went round from shift to shift, 'keeping 'em in good temper and chaffing the men who were smoking and patting the children – for that's all they are in their tempers – on the back and telling 'em how such a work was never before produced in India and how the Calcutta printers would think shame of themselves when they heard that Panjabis worked all night like elephants'. Finally, at five in the morning, *Quartette* was 'born'. Rud and his men 'laid her aside reverently and departed into the dark each our several ways . . . And we felt mighty proud and sleepy.'[8]

As a result of the night's adventures, he was very late for breakfast. Once more it all turned into a game. ' "My boy", said the Pater eyeing my weary eyes and disheveled locks: "If you would only get up in the mornings and do your work you'd be ever so much better." I hid my head behind a coffee cup and chuckled.'[9] Not only had Rud got the job done, but to cap it all he had *fooled his father*. Beneath the bluster, the man's talk, the pressure of responsibility, the display of knowing the right racial and psychological buttons to push, he was a nineteen-year-old who had just pulled off a wizard jape.

On 11 January, Rud proudly announced to Margaret that *Quartette* had been 'a thundering success', both critically and financially. The *Bombay Gazette* had compared him to 'Wilkie Collins for having written the strange ride of Morrowbie Jukes!', and the proprietors of his own paper had again raised his salary. Then, at the very end of his marathon letter, came a final twist. Seemingly as an afterthought, he asked his cousin to do him a favour: would she go to the Slade Art School and look out for 'a maiden there of the name of Garrard – Flo Garrard'. He added: 'I want you as quietly and as unobtrusively as possible to learn all you can about this girl.' Typically, he gave no explanation for this mysterious assignment, but begged his cousin's help 'for old sake's sake'.[10] This sudden and desperate request – Rud clinging on to a fantasy of Flo – yet further underlined the precarious, improvised nature of his new Anglo-Indian attitudes. It was only with the greatest difficulty that he could keep the mask in place.

Rud's continuing obsession with Flo also left its mark on *Quartette*. Of the Christmas supplement's sixteen pieces, he contributed half: three stories and five poems. All but one of the latter were no more than exercises in Anglo-Indian light verse, but 'The Second Wooing' was pitched in a quite different key. In long, lingering couplets, a woman described being visited by 'One at midnight, on golden pinions', who declared that he was Love itself, bringing her 'a passion back from the dead'. The woman and her ghostly lover raked over the embers of the past and from its ashes tried to resurrect a new love. Here, once again, Rud was recycling old material. He had originally written the poem at school under the title 'A Visitation' and included it in *Sundry Phansies*, the collection he presented to Flo before leaving for India. He now changed the title and provided a new ending:

> And then, when the dawn was approaching, He paled in the coming
>   light;
> And e'en as He faded from me so Love passed out of my right.[11]

His motive for exhuming, recasting and publishing this piece of Pre-Raphaelite juvenilia was revenge. 'A Visitation' had left Flo and himself with a possible future, but with a vindictive twist the revised version cancelled that possibility. The obvious rhyme for 'light' in the final couplet was 'sight' – whereas 'right' not only undercut the predictably bland conclusion, but entirely altered the point of the original poem. With that single word, Rud turned 'The Second Wooing' into a re-enactment of his dismissal the previous year – with the tables turned. It was now Flo who was rejected, left with the knowledge that she had forfeited both the right to Rud's love and – the real pay-off – the right to *Love* itself.[12]

The very title 'The Second Wooing' also indicated that this was a revenge poem. In June 1886, Rud would belatedly tell Margaret of his '*jawâb*', which he described as 'the natural and most lawful ending of a boy and girl attachment'.[13] Here he was again playing one of his cryptic epistolary games. The Hindi word *jawâb* means 'a refusal to a proposal of marriage' – and what he was therefore telling his cousin (though again in terms she was unlikely to understand) was that two years earlier, in 1884, he had asked Flo to marry him and she had turned him down. Granted that, as far as Rud was concerned, he and Flo had been engaged for a couple of years by the summer of 1884, this offer of marriage was in effect 'a second wooing', and her refusal a final and absolute rejection. The fact that, a year after his dismissal, he should have published a revenge poem against Flo, while at the same time asking his cousin to spy on her, perfectly reflected his conflicting emotions – not to mention his capacity for locking up his feelings in separate compartments.

The possibility that the dead deliberately haunt the living would pre-occupy Rud for the rest of his life, inspiring some of his most powerful fiction. In the period following his *jawâb*, he became fixated with the idea, two of his three stories in *Quartette* also containing ghostly lovers. In 'The Unlimited "Draw" of "Tick" Boileau', the motif was treated as grim farce, an unpopular subaltern hoaxing the Mess into believing that his lady love had accepted his proposal of marriage *a few minutes after* she died of a heart attack. In the second, 'The Phantom 'Rickshaw', a similar haunting was presented in earnest.

The narrator, Jack Pansay, was about to die. He was condemned to death, he insisted, by 'the Powers of Darkness' and by the ghost of the woman he had rejected. He began his tale with his return from leave in England in 1882. On board ship he had a romance with Agnes Keith-Wessington, 'wife of an officer on the Bombay side'. The affair continued that season in Simla until in August, 'sick of her presence', he cast her off. Despite his callous treatment, Agnes remained devotedly in love, pursu-ing him in her black-and-white-liveried rickshaw, pleading, 'I'm sure it's all a mistake – a hideous mistake. We shall be as good friends some day, Jack, as we ever were.' The following two seasons in Simla they met again, she repeating 'the same appeals', he curtly repulsing her, until in 1884 he fell in love with another woman, and Agnes died of a broken heart. The next year, on the day that he and his new love, Kitty, went to buy an engagement-ring, the ghost of Agnes reappeared in her familiar rickshaw. (The rickshaw too was a phantom, having been destroyed when Agnes's coolies died of cholera.) The haunting began. In his crazed state, Pansay disclosed his previous affair to Kitty and she called off the engagement. Soon, despite the assistance of a friendly doctor who tried to cure him of his 'delusions', all Pansay had left were his walks and talks with the ghostly Agnes, and increasingly these came to seem more real than the living world around him. 'It was a ghastly and yet in some indefinable sort of a way a marvellously dear experience,' he recalled. 'Could it be possible, I wondered, that I was in this life to woo a second time the woman I had killed with my own neglect and cruelty?'[14] Pansay's narrative broke off in the summer of 1885 with him terrified by what, or who, might await him after death. He, like the woman in 'The Second Wooing', had been visited by 'a passion back from the dead', and for him too Love had passed out of his right.

Rud's interest in 'The Phantom 'Rickshaw' did not end with its appearance in *Quartette*. In 1888 he republished an expanded version, in which a lengthy preamble further emphasised the supernatural element and wryly commented on Pansay's 'blood-and-thunder magazine diction'.[15] He also gave the story particular prominence in his autobiography, identifying it as the earliest product of his personal, literary daemon and claiming that it was his 'first serious attempt to think in another man's skin'.[16] He did not feel so detached at the time of writing. Pansay related that he rejected Agnes in August 1882; that Agnes died in the summer of 1884; and that he himself was being haunted to death by Agnes the following summer. For Rud, each date had a real-life charge. August 1882 – engagement to Flo; summer 1884 – dismissal by Flo; summer 1885 – composition of the story, haunted by Flo. If into Agnes he transposed his feelings of abandonment, into Pansay he poured his sense of being haunted.

Rud's other story in *Quartette*, 'The Strange Ride of Morrowbie Jukes', was a further slice of Anglo-Indian Gothic, though there the narrator found himself trapped among not ghosts but the living dead. A civil engineer, Jukes was working in the desert with a gang of coolies. One night, light-headed with fever, he galloped out from his camp chasing wild dogs and plunged headlong into a valley. This valley, he discovered, was shut in on three sides by steep slopes and on the fourth by quicksand and a river (patrolled by a gun-boat). The only inhabitants were a few dozen natives, cholera victims who, recovering on the point of being burnt on a funeral pyre, had been condemned to see out their days in this 'village of the dead' (as Rud originally thought of calling the story). To his surprise, Jukes recognised Gunga Dass, a Government official whom he had previously known and mistreated. Dass gloatingly explained to Jukes the nature of the valley, the impossibility of escape, and tried to make him act as his servant. Dass also let slip that Jukes was not the first Englishman to be trapped in the valley and that his predecessor made a map, showing a safe route over the quicksand. (Dass, it emerged, murdered the Englishman before he could escape and concealed his body, but failed to locate the map.) Burying the dead Englishman, Jukes found the map, and he and Dass planned to escape together. That night, on the edge of the quicksand, Dass knocked Jukes unconscious, took the map and disappeared. Jukes was eventually rescued by his servant, Dunnoo, who had tracked his master across the desert and hauled him to safety.

It was presumably the tale's atmosphere of claustrophobic horror that reminded the reviewer for the *Bombay Gazette* of Wilkie Collins; more recent critics have detected the influence of Dante and Poe, both of whom Rud had read avidly at school. No literary influence, however, adequately accounted for the particular nature of the predicament that threatened to overwhelm Jukes: his growing sense of powerlessness as he gradually became aware that in the valley his customary authority as a sahib had neither meaning nor effect. His first intimation of this was when the other inhabitants emerged from their burrows and, on seeing him, were consumed with laughter: 'They cackled, yelled, whistled, and howled as I rode into their midst; some of them literally throwing themselves down on the ground in convulsions of unholy mirth.'

Dass, relishing the chance to get his own back for his earlier mistreatment by the engineer, took every opportunity to demonstrate to Jukes that everyone in the valley existed on an equal footing. 'We are now Republic, Mister Jukes, and you are entitled to a fair share of the beast,' he jeeringly pointed out when Jukes's horse was killed and divided up to be eaten, 'If you like, we will pass a vote of thanks. Shall I propose?' But Jukes himself increasingly realised that he only maintained a temporary equality with Dass and the others because of his greater physical strength, and even this was no reliable safeguard. The reality of his situation was that he was 'a Sahib, a representative of the dominant race, helpless as a child and completely at the mercy of his native neighbours'.[17] Such moments of self-recognition turned 'The Strange Ride of Morrowbie Jukes' into more than a piece of Gothic horror that happened to be set in India. However, the story was not *quite* an allegory of the Anglo-Indians' worst nightmare – being powerless and surrounded by natives – for the plot had a reassuring conclusion. Jukes was allowed to escape: not by the use of his superior English wits and know-how, but because his Indian servant, Dunnoo, remained faithful and rescued him.

Yet the most telling moment in Jukes's story came when, tormented by Dass, he described himself as 'helpless as a child'. Here Rud was identifying with his character's plight not so much as a fellow Anglo-Indian, but as the abandoned child at Lorne Lodge at the mercy of rather different native neighbours, Mrs Holloway and her son. At last, he was beginning to find ways of transmuting the Southsea legacy into imaginative gain.

6

Boundary-Crossing

Now twenty, Rud had been back in India for just over three years. Already he had established something of a name for himself as a journalist, and his poems and short stories were beginning to attract attention. The next two years, with the publication of *Departmental Ditties* and *Plain Tales from the Hills*, saw the birth of 'Kipling' as an identifiable literary personality.

Even before this transformation, Lockwood was worrying that success might be coming too easily. 'The temptations to vulgar smartness, to overemphasis and other vices are tremendous,' he confided in a letter to Margaret Burne-Jones in January 1886. 'One test of success here is frequent quotation by other papers. And the boy is much quoted – also it is not always his best work that goes the round.' Personally, Lockwood said, he had been against *Quartette* as a venture and had hoped that someone would rap Rud's knuckles 'for the unwholesomeness of the phantom 'ricksha & the coarseness of the Tragedy of teeth'. Instead the reviewers had showered the Christmas Annual with praise. Might Margaret or her mother be prepared to send some tougher criticism, since anything from either of them 'would sink deep'? On a lighter note, the family had been greatly entertained by Rud's falling in love. For the last few Sundays he had been riding five miles to morning service at Mian Mir to gaze at the daughter of the military chaplain, but was so 'vastly funny about it' that Lockwood could not decide whether Rud was serious or not.[1]

This infatuation with the chaplain's daughter was probably little more than a joke played out for the family's benefit. Rud found nothing funny, however, about two other bits of gossip that soon afterwards came his way. In early February, Dunsterville, now a subaltern, paid a brief visit en route to Rawalpindi. The two friends had not seen each other since USC and talked over old times. Rud was shocked to learn from Dunsterville that their housemaster, Pugh, had suspected him of having sex with other boys in his dormitory. 'Rabidly furious', he poured out his indignation in a lengthy tirade to Crofts:

> You will not recollect that he [Pugh] once changed my dormitory – just before I left – and insisted upon the change with an unreasoning vehemence that astonished me. Thereafter followed a row I think. I objected to be transferred because my little room was a snug one, had no prefect, and allowed me room to spread my books and kit. I took to reporting my dormitory – the new one – making life a burden to M.H.P. [Pugh] and, finally, in one big row, falling upon the members of the new dormitory with a small pen knife at least three quarters of an inch long in the blade. About this time M.H.P. – who must be a very Stead in his moral and virtuous knowledge of impurity and bestiality – transferred me to my old room; clearing out the other two boys who occupied it. It never struck me that the step was anything beyond an averagely lunatic one on the part of M.H.P. – I was not innocent, in some respects, as the fish girls of Appledore could have testified had they chosen – but I certainly didn't suspect anything. Dunsterville told me on Wednesday, in the plain ungarnished tongue of youth, the why and the wherefore of my removal according to M.H.P. and by the light of later knowledge I see very clearly what that moral but absolutely tactless Malthusian must have suspected. It's childish and ludicrous I know but, at the present moment, I am conscious of a deep and personal hatred against the man which I would give a good deal to satisfy.[2]

The vehemence of Rud's reaction has led a recent biographer to speculate that he was homosexual.[3] Rud's anger implies suppressed or concealed homosexual feelings, runs the argument; otherwise why all the fuss? But, given the contemporary stigma against homosexuality – and in the absence of hard evidence as opposed to conjecture – there is no reason not to believe that Rud's outrage was perfectly genuine. Again, the fact that he urged Crofts to have the whole matter out with Pugh *could* be high-handed bluff – or, less sensationally, an attempt to put the record straight.

On 30 April Rud was writing to a fellow journalist, Kay Robinson, about a rumour of a different kind: that he put his literary work before his duties in the office. He was again incensed. 'The whole settlement and routine of the old rag,' he told Robinson, 'from the end of the leader to the beginning of the advertisements is in my hands and mine only.' Robinson, who admired Rud's poems, had been encouraging him to leave India and try his luck as a writer in London. Rud, now the fully fledged Anglo-Indian, insisted that India was his home and was where he saw his future. Besides the debt he owed his employers, he said, 'I am deeply interested in the queer ways and works of the people of the land . . . I'm in love with the country and would sooner write about her than anything else.'[4]

Mother Maturin, now 350 pages long and still growing, was one outlet for this growing fascination with Indian life. Another was the new work he was publishing in the newspapers. The previous October the *Calcutta Review* had taken 'The Vision of Hamid Ali', a piece of Browningesque blank verse, describing a young Mohammedan's *ganja*-induced dream of the imminent and bloody collapse of Islam, Buddhism and Christianity. On the same day as his letter to Robinson, Rud published 'Section 420 I.P.C.' in the CMG. Better known as 'In the House of Suddhoo', the story showed Rud drawing inspiration from the tensions and contradictions of the Anglo-Indian situation as he had done in 'The Strange Ride of Morrowbie Jukes'. 'Section 420 I.P.C.' marked the début of the cocky journalist-narrator in his fiction and, like Jukes's tale, portrayed a sahib trapped among the natives.

This time the setting was not a remote valley in the desert but the backstreets of Lahore, and in place of the living dead the narrator was embroiled with a representative cross-section of ordinary Indian life: a grocer, a seal-cutter, two prostitutes, and old Suddhoo himself. The ending spelt out the complicated mess into which he had stumbled:

I cannot inform the Police. What witnesses would support my state-

ments? Janoo refuses flatly, and Azizun is a veiled woman somewhere near Bareilly – lost in this big India of ours. I dare not again
take the law into my own hands, and speak to the seal-cutter; for
certain am I that, not only would Suddhoo disbelieve me, but this
step would end in the poisoning of Janoo, who is bound hand and
foot by her debt to the *bunnia* . . . Suddhoo is completely under the
influence of the seal-cutter, by whose advice he regulates the affairs
of his life. Janoo watches daily the money that she hoped to wheedle
out of Suddhoo taken by the seal-cutter, and becomes daily more
furious and sullen.

She will never tell, because she dare not; but, unless something
happens to prevent her, I am afraid that the seal-cutter will die of
cholera – the white arsenic kind – about the middle of May. And
then I shall be privy to a murder in the House of Suddhoo.[5]

On the face of it, the narrator's position bore a close resemblance to Jukes's
(with the added twist that he was left without any reassuring means of
escape). But there the similarity ended. 'In the House of Suddhoo' was
anything but a nightmare vision of becoming entangled in Indian life; it
was not even a warning against the dangers of such an entanglement. The
narrator plainly relished every second of his final predicament and could
not wait to unpeel every last nuance. Instead of being punished or turned
into an exemplary symbol, he was rewarded for his curiosity about native
life by being placed in such an interesting situation. Rud had told Margaret
in one of his long letters the previous year that 'immediately outside of our
own English life, is the dark and crooked and fantastic, and wicked, and
awe inspiring life of the "native"'.[6] 'In the House of Suddhoo' was a
testament to the intense excitement he felt at all that other life going on
around him – just as 'The Strange Ride of Morrowbie Jukes' was a
reflection of how threatening and disturbing he sometimes found it.
Rather than one story being an urban replica of the other, the two were in
fact complementary, different sides of the same coin.

Alongside his deepening preoccupation with native life, Rud was also
exploring ways of depicting 'our own English life' in India. One abortive
attempt was 'Bungalow Ballads', a series of six would-be humorous poems
that appeared anonymously in the *Pioneer* in August and September
1885. Not even Rud's ingenuity with ludicrous names like Rattleton

Traplegh, Mrs Saphira Wallabie Smith and Jane Austen Beecher Stowe De Rouse could rescue these snippets of Anglo-Indian domestic life from the oblivion they deserved. But six months later he produced a new set of poems, which quickly established him as the foremost poet of Anglo-India. This unsigned series, called 'Departmental Ditties', ran in the CMG from February to April 1886. The poems proved so popular that by early June he had rushed out a volume bearing the same title. Within a month the first edition of 500 copies had sold out.

Part of the initial appeal of *Departmental Ditties* was its playful format. Kipling later described it as 'a lean oblong docket, wire-stitched, to imitate a D.O. Government envelope, printed on one side only, bound in brown paper, and secured with red tape. It was addressed to all heads of departments and all Government officials, and among a pile of papers would have deceived a clerk of twenty years' service.'[7] As part of the spoof, a facsimile of Rud's signature appeared on the front wrapper above his self-styled position as 'Assistant – Department of Public Journalism, Lahore District'. For a readership daily immersed in bureaucratic red tape, such a joke could hardly fail to succeed, particularly as the poems fulfilled the promise of the cover. Rud rightly gauged that what his audience most wanted to read about was themselves. So, as Anglo-Indian poets had done for the previous hundred years, he stuck to perennial subjects – lack of promotion, local scandals, loneliness, nostalgia for 'Home', administrative cock-ups and love tangles. His first readers were delighted by the deftness, the spirit of cheeky gusto, with which he handled this familiar material. As Rud told Aunt Edie in a letter at the end of the year, 'the little booklet just hit the taste of the Anglo-Indian public for it told them about what they knew'.[8]

At least one of the 'ditties' may have been another collaborative effort with his sister. Trix later claimed that she and Rud made up 'My Rival' extempore line for line on the Mall in Simla in the summer of 1885.[9] In the poem, a seventeen-year-old girl vented her frustration at her forty-nine-year-old rival's success with young men. Since the ages of speaker and rival exactly corresponded to those of Trix and her mother, the verses were probably intended as a family tease at Alice's expense:

> The young men come, the young men go,
>   Each pink and white and neat,

She's older than their mothers, but
　　They grovel at Her feet.
They walk beside Her 'rickshaw-wheels –
　　None ever walk by mine;
And that's because I'm seventeen
　　And She is forty-nine.[10]

Much of the humour in *Departmental Ditties* was pitched at this level of high-spiritedness. Occasionally Rud struck a more sardonic note, as in 'The Story of Uriah'. He took the title from the episode in 2 Samuel where King David, lusting after Bathsheba, sent her husband, Uriah the Hittite, to his death in the front-line. Rud's poem presented an Anglo-Indian equivalent, with Jack Barrett being transferred by his wife's high-placed lover from a safe billet in Simla to die in fever-ridden Quetta. According to Kay Robinson, the poem was a thinly disguised version of a topical scandal and 'those who had known the real "Jack Barrett", good fellow that he was, and the vile superior and faithless wife who sent him "on duty" to his death, felt the heat of the spirit which inspired Kipling's verse in a way that gave those few lines an imperishable force'.[11]

To Aunt Edie, Rud was characteristically dismissive about the 'ditties', describing them as 'bad rhymes and cheaply cynical'.[12] Nonetheless the collection marked a definite advance in his poetic apprenticeship, particularly in his experimentation with rhythm. Those experiments went far beyond the simple requirements of the form, and at times gave the poems a subtlety and technical interest unusual in verse of this type. In 'Public Waste', Exeter Battleby Tring, an expert railway-surveyor, was the obvious candidate to manage 'the Railways of State'. But since he did not come from the right social bracket, 'the Little Tin Gods on the Mountain Side' pensioned him off at great expense and appointed 'a Colonel from Chatham' in his place. Such a scam was likely to strike a chord with readers who were themselves regularly frustrated by a system of snobbish preferment. Rud gave extra force to his satire by dislocating the rhythm of the lines so that the act of reading them was itself frustrating.

By the Laws of the Family Circle 'tis written in letters of brass
That only a Colonel from Chatham can manage the Railways of State,

Because of the gold on his breeks, and the subjects wherein he must
    pass;
Because in all matters that deal not with Railways his knowledge is
    great.[13]

By rhyming the anapaestic lines alternately, Rud displaced the natural movement of the verse, just as the Little Tin Gods had displaced what should have been the natural administrative order.

It was such effects that Lord Dufferin had in mind when he complimented Lockwood on his son's ' "infallible" ear for rhythm and cadence' and 'uncommon combination of satire with grace and delicacy'.[14] Dufferin had succeeded Ripon as Viceroy at the end of 1884, and Rud's first major assignment as a 'special' had been to cover Dufferin's meeting with the Amir of Afghanistan. (Between 24 March and 14 April 1885, he produced no fewer than thirteen articles on the event, amounting to a staggering 30,000 words.) Dufferin was an old-style aristocrat, rich, cultured and widely travelled. He and his wife were no snobs and welcomed the acquaintance of the lively and the intelligent. They quickly took to the Kiplings, and by the summer of 1886 the two families were on such easy terms that Dufferin would casually drop in at their Simla quarters for cultural chats with Lockwood and to enjoy Alice's wit. 'Dullness and Mrs Kipling cannot exist in the same room' quickly became one of his favourite sayings.[15] The Kiplings were also regularly invited to the small, select dinner parties that Lady Dufferin held for their inner circle of friends. After twenty years in India, Lockwood and Alice had finally made it into the highest echelons of Anglo-Indian society. Not surprisingly, there was some resentment at their newly enhanced social standing and at their intimacy with the Dufferins, but those who showed it got short shrift from Alice. To one woman friend who enviously commented that she had been having a 'very long conversation . . . with his Excellency', Alice retorted tartly: 'Yes, my dear, and it was as broad as it was long.'[16]

Trix too shared in her parents' social success. Now in her second season, she was regarded as one of the local beauties and from an aloofness (which probably masked youthful shyness) had acquired the nickname 'The Ice Maiden'. Among other admirers, she attracted the attentions of the Viceroy's son, Lord Clandeboye. These attentions eventually became so pronounced that Dufferin suggested that Alice should take her daughter to a different hill-station. On the contrary, Alice replied, he should send his son home. It says much for the parents' friendship that not only was it Lord Clandeboye who left and Trix who stayed, but that the contretemps in no way damaged the Dufferins' liking for the Kiplings.

In 1885, covering the season, Rud had been able to spend most of the summer in Simla. This year he was not due holiday leave until September, but a breakdown through overwork in late June meant that he rejoined his family in the hills a month earlier than expected. To Margaret in a May–June letter, he bemoaned the 'desolate freedom' of the bachelor life that he and his father were forced to lead in Lahore after Alice and Trix had left. He had, he told his cousin, been particularly upset by the experience of reporting on the deaths of three boys, killed when the roof of the local high school fell in. The sight of 'the three swathed figures on the cots' and 'the death smell of carbolic acid' had haunted him all night. His eyes too had been playing up again and for several days he had been enduring what he called 'hemi crania' or 'half head ache'. The way he described this peculiar condition almost made it sound like an account of the Romantic imagination – one side suffering, the other observing: 'One half of my head in a mathematical line from the top of my skull to the cleft of my jaw, throbs and hammers and sizzles and bangs and swears while the other half – calm and collected – takes note of the agonies next door.'[17] Outside office hours he had been visiting the troops at Fort Lahore, observing the debilitatingly hot conditions in which they lived, and distracting himself by ratting with Vic, his new fox-terrier. Eventually the strain proved too great, and he left for a much-needed rest in Simla.

The day of his arrival, 6 July, happened to be Lockwood's forty-ninth birthday, and Rud marked the occasion with a celebratory sonnet. Dashing the lines off at high speed, he passed the results across the dining-room table to his father, who was in the middle of a letter:

> For us Life's wheel runs backward. Other nests
> Are stripped of all their fledglings when our Fate
> Pitying may be, a childhood desolate,
> Brings home deferred, – unparted each one rests

> Beneath one roof.
>   But the year's fitful span
> Brings change & growth & half displeased you say
> Musing upon the babes of yesterday:
> 'Behold, she is a woman; He a man.'
> Yet, spite of all, the childish wonder clings
>   About our spirits when we hear him say –
>   Our Father – 'Children I was born to-day.'
> And we return to nursery wonderings
>   Back comes the childish question to the tongue
>   Father a child! – Was Father ever young?[18]

Lockwood promptly copied the poem into his letter to Edith Plowden. 'Pretty, isn't it?' he told her with his usual blend of paternal defensiveness and pride, '– wanting a little polish and finish perhaps, as first draughts [sic] of verses are apt to do.' The letter also offered a glimpse of Kipling family banter. Lockwood described to Edith how he had pointed out to Rud that the sonnet was 'scarcely perfect as a compliment', since 'Why shouldn't I have been once young like other people?'[19] He made no mention of the poem's one chilling phrase: 'a childhood desolate' (Rud's first surviving reference to the 'House of Desolation'). This suggests that Lockwood and Alice were probably still unaware of just how devastating the years at Lorne Lodge had been.

After a couple of days with his family, Rud again shifted in with the Walkers at Kelvin Grove and immersed himself in the usual social round of riding and dancing, dining and paying calls. His network of contacts and acquaintances in Simla was already extensive, but his parents' friendship with the Dufferins now gave him an entrée to even more exclusive circles, and he made mental notes of what he saw and heard. Besides doing some occasional pieces for the *Pioneer*, he also engaged in some important literary business. Before going up to the hills, he had despatched review copies of *Departmental Ditties* to various literary periodicals in England and had written to the Calcutta firm Thacker Spink & Co. about a second edition. He wrote again to the firm several times from Kelvin Grove and eventually agreed to a deal whereby he bore the printing costs of the new edition in return for 75 per cent of any profits. Initially he assumed that the publishers would retain the docket-format of the original cover, but when they demurred, he reluctantly accepted something more conventional. Back in sweltering Lahore in early August, he was soon correcting proofs, and not long afterwards the second edition, now clearly bearing his name, was on sale for the price of 1.8 rupees (about 2s 8d in contemporary English money).

Rud's efforts to get noticed at 'Home' also paid off. *Vanity Fair* reviewed the poems briefly in September, and the following month Andrew Lang, one of the leading critics of the day, gave the collection an entire column in *Longman's Magazine*. Lang was positive if a little condescending in his praise, calling the book a 'quaint and amusing example' of 'a special variety of English *Vers de Société*, namely the Anglo-Indian species'. Although he found the more satirical pieces 'melancholy', he was very taken with the nostalgic 'In Spring Time' and quoted the poem in full. Lang also commended 'Giffen's Debt', describing it as 'worthy of Bret Harte'. Rud, a great admirer of Harte's humorous-pathetic verse and tales of Californian mining life, eagerly passed on this last nugget of praise to Aunt Edie. He did not mention the one major drawback to Lang's review: the famous critic had failed to grasp the point of the facsimile signature on the cover and had informed his readers that 'the modest author does not give his name'.[20]

Coinciding with the success of *Departmental Ditties* came another major change in Rud's fortunes. Wheeler retired from the CMG, and Kay Robinson took over as editor. The two young men already liked each other and soon became close friends. Ten years later, when Kipling was world-famous, Robinson would recall their working life in the office. Rud's usual attire was 'white cotton trousers and thin vest' and by the end of the day he resembled 'a Dalmatian dog' from 'his habit of dipping his pen frequently and deep into the ink-pot, and as all his movements were abrupt, almost jerky, the ink used to fly'. In addition, Rud was 'always the best of good company, bubbling over with delightful humour, which found vent in every detail of our day's work together'. Robinson remembered Rud's extraordinary sensitivity, his 'marvellous faculty for assimilating local colour without apparent effort' and how 'no half-note in the wide gamut of native ideas and custom was unfamiliar to him', just as he 'left no phase of white life in India unexplored'. Contrary to the rumours of Rud's dilatoriness, Robinson emphasised how hard his assistant had worked. 'If you want to find a man who will cheerfully do the office work of three men,' he claimed, 'you should catch a young genius.'[21] Rud was equally enthusiastic about his new boss, telling Aunt Edie at the time that it was 'a pleasant *interregnum* this work with a man in every way congenial and bright and witty, with unlimited powers of work and a shameful levity of disposition'.[22]

Together Robinson and Rud set about putting some 'sparkle into the paper'.[23] One of their innovations, adapted from Robinson's time on the *Globe* in London, was to institute regular 'turn-overs', 2,000-word pieces of local, topical interest which began on the front page and turned over to the next. These were Rud's special responsibility and after a few misfires in August and September, he hit his stride. The result was a series of thirty-nine unsigned stories called *Plain Tales from the Hills*, which appeared over a seven-and-a-half-month period from November 1886 to June 1887.

Again the idea originated in the Kiplings' penchant for literary games. Although in his autobiography Rud referred only to a family council over the overall title, his sister was certainly a contributor, and it seems likely that the series was initially envisaged as another joint effort, like *Echoes*. Of the thirty-nine 'Plain Tales' printed in the CMG, Rud later repudiated seven (including the opening two), and an eighth, 'A Scrap of Letter', has never been accepted as his. These stories – though the evidence is not conclusive – were probably Trix's work. One, 'A Pinchbeck Goddess', was definitely hers, and it is hard to imagine who else could have written the others.

Like the 'Departmental Ditties' series, 'Plain Tales from the Hills' was immediately popular and by early 1887 Rud was seriously contemplating a solo collection. On 3 February he wrote to Thacker Spink, asking them their terms for publishing 'a prose book . . . made up of twelve stories of native and twelve of English life in India; the whole to be called "Punjab people Brown & White"'.[24] The firm offered him two options: either a fifty–fifty share in the profits after production costs had been met and a 25 per cent commission from sales had been deducted, or the same deal as for *Departmental Ditties*. By May, Rud and his publishers were still negotiating, but by now he had decided on a larger, more diverse collection, wisely reverting to *Plain Tales from the Hills* as the title. On 17 June, after the completion of the series in the CMG, he finally agreed to the 'half profits share' option. Over a year later he was still complaining about the publishers' 25 per cent sales commission and trying to persuade them to waive it, which suggests that there may never have been a signed contract for the book, merely a gentleman's agreement.

Throughout his negotiations with Thacker Spink over both *Departmental Ditties* and *Plain Tales*, Rud did his best to maintain an air of brisk professionalism. But for all his reminders that he was in the business himself and not to be trifled with, the publishers had things very much their own way. During the second half of 1887, there were frustrating delays (partly Rud's fault, since he insisted on rewriting a good deal at proof stage), and *Plain Tales* did not come out until January 1888. At one point it was to have carried an epigraph in Persian, which roughly translated meant 'Come what may, we have cast our ship upon the waters.'[25] By the time the volume actually appeared, Rud had substituted: 'To The Wittiest Woman In India/I Dedicate This Book'.

The original *Plain Tales* series in the CMG depicted four worlds – Simla, the Station, the Army, and Indian life – with Simla and the Station predominating. For the book, Rud discarded the eight stories conjecturally by his sister and two others, which he presumably considered lightweight. To fill out the volume and provide a more even balance, he added three of his earlier Indian stories ('The Gate of the Hundred Sorrows', 'In the House of Suddhoo' and 'The Story of Muhammad Din') and eight newer, unpublished pieces – making forty stories in all. He also composed verse epigraphs and proverbs to head each tale and arranged the collection to maximise their contrast and variety.

Many of the stories, particularly those set in Simla, shared the high spirits of *Departmental Ditties*. Simla was Rud's Illyria, a place where everyone fell in love, usually inappropriately; where identities were mistaken; where tricks were played on the self-regarding and the unwary; and where there were occasional glimpses of a darker undertow. A number of these stories featured the machinations of the witty widow, Mrs Hauksbee. Based partly on his own mother and partly on a Mrs Isabella Burton, she was an early example of Rud's lifelong fascination with strong, self-determining, older women and would soon become one of his best-known characters. 'Kidnapped' contained an admiring résumé of Mrs Hauksbee's powers, describing her as 'the most wonderful woman in India' with 'the wisdom of the Serpent, the logical coherence of the Man, the fearlessness of the Child, and the triple intuition of the Woman'.[26] (Simla must have had its fair share of would-be Mrs Hauksbees, and Rud's first readers no doubt enjoyed the tease of trying to guess her true identity.)

The stories of Station life were less light-hearted and depicted a wider range of types and situations. In one, a man drove his colleagues to distraction with his humanist theories until he was suddenly struck down by aphasia. In another, a man who had married beneath him gained the promotion he needed to bring his wife out to India only after she had abandoned him and taken a new lover. Here the daily stresses of Anglo-Indian life were more pronounced, and the heat and tedious routine formed a constant backdrop.

By contrast, the tales of Army life tended towards the farcical – a put-upon subaltern dressed up in drag to get his own back; a contingent of British troops captured a Burmese village stark naked. Several of these stories involved the early exploits of three of Rud's most enduring characters, the Irish, Yorkshire and Cockney privates, Mulvaney, Learoyd and Ortheris. Rud clearly enjoyed the ventriloquist opportunities offered by his 'three musketeers' and in one bravura performance, jumping between dialects, even had the trio collectively tell the story. Occasionally the mood was grimmer. In 'Thrown Away', a pampered young subaltern, believing himself ruined, committed suicide. In 'The Madness of Private Ortheris', Ortheris, crazy with homesickness, was barely prevented from desertion.

Of all the stories in *Plain Tales*, those depicting Indian and Eurasian life consistently struck the deepest and most poignant note. In the volume's opener, 'Lispeth', a Himalayan hill-girl, brought up as a Christian, fell in love with an Englishman and was tricked into believing that he planned to return and marry her. When she discovered that she had been lied to, she angrily rejected Christianity and returned to her own people. In the previously unpublished 'Beyond the Pale', an Anglo-Indian carried on a dangerous liaison with a fifteen-year-old Indian widow. When her family discovered the affair, the girl's hands were cut off, and the Anglo-Indian, wounded in the groin, returned unhappily to the narrow confines of his former life.

What linked the stories (and made them anything but 'plain') was their highly distinctive voice – the same insouciant voice that Rud had first tried out in 'In the House of Suddhoo'. Sometimes located in the figure of an unnamed narrator, this voice (whether asserting or teasing) always demanded attention. The openings were instantly arresting and characteristic:

Some people say there is no romance in India. Those people are wrong. Our lives hold quite as much romance as is good for us. Sometimes more.

'Miss Youghal's Sais'

Mrs Hauksbee was sometimes nice to her own sex. Here is a story to prove this; and you can believe just as much as ever you please.

'The Rescue of Pfuffles'

When the Gravesend tender left the P. & O. steamer for Bombay and went back to catch the train to Town, there were many people in it crying. But the one who wept most, and most openly, was Miss Agnes Laiter. She had reason to cry, because the only man she ever loved – or ever could love, so she said – was going out to India; and India, as everyone knows, is divided equally between jungle, tigers, cobras, cholera, and sepoys.

'Yoked with an Unbeliever'

No man will ever know the exact truth of this story; though women may sometimes whisper it to one another after a dance, when they are putting up their hair for the night and comparing lists of victims. A man, of course, cannot assist at these functions. So the tale must be told from the outside – in the dark – all wrong.

'False Dawn'

We are a high-caste and enlightened race, and infant-marriage is very shocking, and the consequences are sometimes peculiar; but, nevertheless, the Hindu notion – which is the Continental notion, which is the aboriginal notion – of arranging marriages irrespective of the personal inclinations of the married, is sound. Think for a minute, and you will see that it must be so; unless, of course, you believe in 'affinities'. In which case you had better not read this tale.

'Kidnapped'[27]

In itself, each individual statement sounded straightforward enough: 'Mrs Hauksbee was sometimes nice to her own sex.' But as one succeeded the next, the effect quickly became equivocal: 'Here is a story to prove this; and you can believe just as much as ever you please.' The tone began to flicker with a range of ironic possibilities, so that it was often hard to determine quite where the irony was being directed. In a single sentence at the beginning of 'Yoked with an Unbeliever', Miss Agnes Laiter's grief shifted from the perfectly understandable ('She had reason to cry, because the only man she ever loved') to the melodramatic ('– or ever could love, so she said') to the mildly comic ('and India, as everyone knows, is divided equally between jungle, tigers, cobras, cholera, and sepoys'). And who was the intended target at the beginning of 'Kidnapped'? 'Us', the Anglo-Indians, archly described as 'a high-caste and enlightened race'? The Hindus, whose 'notion' of infant-marriage was called both 'very shocking' and 'sound'? Or the believers in 'affinities' who 'had better not read this tale'? In different ways all three were being mocked, but the consequence was that the irony hovered rather than becoming specific. And even when the stance within a specific story remained relatively stable, there was usually another story that appeared to endorse a contradictory point of view. In 'Lispeth', all the imaginative sympathy was reserved for the Himalayan hill-girl, while the missionary couple who lied to her were revealed as hypocrites. In 'Kidnapped', however, Miss Castries, being Eurasian, was never considered a possible partner for the Anglo-Indian Peythroppe.

The use of a knowing, ironic narrative voice was of course nothing new. Rud's version probably owed something to Byron, whom he had imitated in earlier poems, and to Thackeray and Jane Austen. ('On the Strength of a Likeness' opened in a distinctly Austenian manner: 'Next to a requited attachment, one of the most convenient things that a young man can carry about with him at the beginning of his career, is an unrequited attachment.'[28]) But if on one level the stories' equivocal tone was a literary game Rud was playing with his audience, it was also an expression of the anxieties inherent in his Anglo-Indian stance.

In his letters to Margaret in 1885–6, in which he had identified himself as an Anglo-Indian, a recurrent anxiety had been the conflict between his enthusiasm for the rich complexity of Indian life and his need to present himself as a useful Anglo-Indian. The protracted saga of how his intimate knowledge of native proverbs and customs had helped to get *Quartette* printed was one way he had tried to convince his cousin (and himself) that his knowledge had a practical value. The same anxiety re-emerged as an underlying preoccupation in *Plain Tales*. In the Anglo-Indian worlds of Simla, the Station and the Army, inside knowledge was a definite asset: because Mrs Hauksbee knew the bargaining power of confidential documents, she was able to assist Tarrion to a job; because Nafferton knew how to work the administrative system, he was able to take revenge on Pinecoffin. Though luck might play a part, it favoured those 'in the know'. For the characters who knew how to cross the boundary into native life, however, their knowledge was almost always problematical. To possess such knowledge was seen as potentially or actually dangerous; it had practical value only in exceptional circumstances and was often associated with powerlessness.

Take the example of the policeman, Strickland. At the beginning of 'Miss Youghal's Sais', he was built up as an expert on Indians, a master of disguise, 'feared and respected by the natives from Ghor Kathri to the Jamma Musjid'. Even when not working under cover, his main pleasure in life was to disguise himself as a native and disappear for weeks on end. Predictably, his 'outlandish custom of prying into native life' had done Strickland's reputation no good among respectable Anglo-Indians, and when he and Miss Youghal fell in love, her parents snobbishly forbade the match. Strickland took three months' leave and he and Miss Youghal secretly arranged for him to be taken on, in disguise, as her new groom (*sais*). His leave was almost up and matters no nearer resolution when, unable to bear listening to an elderly General flirt with Miss Youghal, Strickland gave himself away by threatening the General 'in most fluent English'. Fortunately the General was vastly amused at the idea of a white man dressing up as an Indian groom and agreed to intercede for the young couple with Miss Youghal's parents. At which point it appeared that in a roundabout way Strickland's native know-how had proved of advantage after all. However, he had to pay a heavy price for his happiness. The Youghals made it a condition of their consent that he drop 'his old ways' and become respectable. Strickland, now married, was left at the end of the story a diminished figure, already 'forgetting the slang, and the beggar's cant, and the marks, and the signs, and the drift of the undercurrents', but filling in 'his Departmental returns beautifully'.[29] The cost of his Anglo-Indian happiness was the loss of his Indian knowledge.

While Strickland was still a practising boundary-crosser, this activity was ambivalently portrayed. Although the phrase 'his outlandish custom of prying into native life' was obviously ironic (directed at those who disapproved of Strickland), what immediately followed was much more ambiguous: 'When a man once acquires a taste for this particular amusement, it abides with him all his days. It is the most fascinating thing in the world – Love not excepted.'[30] Strickland's outlandish custom was made to sound like a form of addiction, attractive but dangerous. 'Miss Youghal's Sais' was not the only story in *Plain Tales* to hint at the addictive aspects of boundary-crossing. The idea was tacitly present in 'The Gate of the Hundred Sorrows', in which the Eurasian opium-eater, Gabral Misquitta, gave up the outside world for the life and death of the 'Black Smoke'; and it was implicit in the previously unpublished 'To be Filed for Reference', the remarkable story that closed the volume.

Here the narrator made friends with another addict, the alcoholic loafer McIntosh Jellaludin, once a Classics Fellow at Oxford. From the start McIntosh was invested with considerable Romantic/Pre-Raphaelite allure. When the narrator first encountered him, he was singing Rossetti's 'The Song of the Bower' and on another occasion recited the whole of Swinburne's *Atalanta in Calydon*, 'beating time to the swing of the verse with a bedstead-leg'. His most prized possession was the manuscript of his book about his Indian experiences, which he bequeathed to the narrator on his death-bed. The reader was given scattered hints that McIntosh's seven years among the natives were an attempt to forget or expiate some former disgrace. But there was also a wariness, a parodic element even, in the depiction of McIntosh as the doomed artist. His desperate attempts to present himself and his drunkenness in a heroic light. ('I am as the Gods, knowing good and evil, but untouched by either. Is this enviable or is it not?') and the narrator's jaunty scepticism ('When a man has lost the warning of "next morning's head" he must be in a bad state') prevented the reader from taking McIntosh entirely seriously.[31]

It was implied, though never explicitly stated, that McIntosh's addiction to the 'bottles of excessively filthy country-liquors', which eventually killed him, was a metaphor for his seven-year addiction to native life. Whether these joint addictions had proved worthwhile was left open to doubt; and it was equally questionable whether his 'classical and literary knowledge', his devoted Indian wife and his book were adequate 'consolations' for the last seven years. McIntosh himself hoped that his book, the only useful product of his knowledge and suffering, would ultimately justify him and the life he had led: this 'monument, more enduring than brass, which I have built up in the seven years of my degradation', as he Horatianly put it. However, after his death, the fate of his book, and even its intrinsic value, remained doubtful. Strickland, who helped to sort out the loafer's papers, thought him 'either an extreme liar or a most wonderful person. He thought the former.' The narrator briskly claimed that the manuscript had already 'needed much expurgation and was full of Greek nonsense at the head of the chapters, which has all been cut out'. And the tale ended on a note of irresolution as Rud deliberately turned the question of the book's real authorship into a literary game:

> If the thing is ever published, some one may perhaps remember this story, now printed as a safeguard to prove that McIntosh Jellaludin and not myself wrote the Book of Mother Maturin.
>   I don't want the Giant's Robe [a contemporary novel about a man passing off a friend's book as his own] to come true in my case.[32]

That McIntosh was the most romanticised of the boundary-crossers in Plain Tales was not surprising. As the surrogate author of Mother Maturin, the novel that Rud still hoped to publish, he was a displaced self-portrait of Rud himself. The uncertainty about the usefulness of his knowledge was a dramatisation of Rud's own anxieties about how much could be known about Indian life and whether it was worth knowing. That the novel was never to appear, despite this attempted piece of advance publicity, gave McIntosh's fate an extra, unintended irony.

Strickland and McIntosh embodied Rud's central dilemma as an Anglo-Indian. He could know Indian life, but could never fully enter it. It was a dilemma he could only hope to resolve in fiction.

7

Out of India

By the time *Plain Tales* appeared, Rud had been promoted to the staff of the *Pioneer* and had shifted to Allahabad, 900 miles to the south-east. There had been talk of transferring him before, but up to now he had preferred to remain in Lahore within the Family Square. During 1887, as his name became increasingly well known, his proprietors must have stepped up their efforts, and by the autumn Rud too felt ready for a change. He may even have seen the move as a first step towards quitting India altogether. Before leaving Lahore in November, he sold the copyright of the third (and succeeding) editions of *Departmental Ditties* to Thacker Spink & Co. for 500 rupees (about £238). This suggests that he was trying to build up some capital, and the following January in a letter to his cousin Margaret he was mooting the idea of a visit to England in the foreseeable future. By May 1888 he had definitely made up his mind to go. An experience, en route to Allahabad, almost certainly played an important part in his decision.

The *Pioneer* commissioned him, on his way to taking up his new job, to write a series of travel pieces about the Native States of Rajputana, south of Delhi on the edge of the Bikaner Desert. (The Native States were self-administering territories, officially independent, but recognising the supreme authority of the British Government in India.) Rud spent a month in the area, producing nineteen unsigned articles, which ran in the *Pioneer* from 14 December 1887 to 28 February 1888. 'Letters of Marque', the overall title he gave the series, indicated the spirit in which he undertook the assignment. He saw himself as a kind of journalistic privateer, licensed to raid foreign lands for newspaper booty. An account to Margaret later conveyed the same breezy air of adventure: 'Oh it was a good and clean life and I saw and heard all sorts and conditions of men and they told me the stories of their lives, black and white and brown alike, and I filled three note books and walked "with death and morning on the silver horns" and knew what it was to endure hunger and thirst.'[1]

The Letters themselves were for the most part equally jaunty. Referring to himself throughout as 'the Englishman', Rud combined evocative passages of natural description with facetious commentary on the people and situations he encountered. The headnotes suggested the characteristic tone: 'Of the Beginning of Things. Of the Taj and the Globe-trotter. The Young Man from Manchester and Certain Moral Reflections' and 'Does not in Any Sort Describe the Dead City of Amber, but gives Detailed Information about a Cotton-Press'. The exception was the account of his visit to the old, ruined city of Chitor, described in Letters X and XI. Letter X provided a potted history of the city, its rulers and its three sackings; Letter XI, more memorably, recounted the eventful day he spent sightseeing among the ruins.

After a strenuous journey uphill on the back of an elephant, Rud passed through Ram Pol, the main gate, and entered Chitor itself. He decided to climb one of the city's surviving towers and clambered up a succession of winding, mazelike staircases, filled with revulsion at 'the slippery sliminess of the walls . . . worn smooth by naked men'.[2] But by the time he reached the top, physical disgust had given way to aesthetic awe. He found his imagination deeply stirred by thoughts of a culture that was sophisticated long before the British set foot in India. He began to think himself into the mind of the tower's architect:

The Englishman fancied presumptuously that he had, in a way, grasped the builder's idea; and when he came to the top story and sat among the pigeons his theory was this: To attain power, wrote the builder of old, in sentences of fine stone, it is necessary to pass through all sorts of close-packed horrors, treacheries, battles, and insults, in darkness and without knowledge whether the road leads upwards or into a hopeless *cul-de-sac*.

He imagined how Kumbha Rana, who ordered the building of the tower, 'must have swelled with pride – fine insolent pride of life and rule and power', looking down on 'a boundless view fit for kings'. He then wondered 'what Lord Dufferin, who is the nearest approach to a king in this India, must have thought when aide-de-camps clanked after him up the narrow steps'.[3] It was a jolting moment. Meditating on the tower's rich indigenous history, Rud had again allowed the Anglo-Indian mask to slip and seen the Viceroy and his clanking entourage as diminished figures, brash intruders in this relic of an heroic Indian past.

Descending from the tower, Rud slithered his way down a rock-slope like 'a great snail-track' to visit the Gau-Mukh, 'which is nothing more terrible than a little spring, falling on to a reservoir, in the side of the hill'. Or so he briefly pretended. In fact, he found his encounter with the Gau-Mukh nothing short of terrifying:

In a slabbed-in recess, water was pouring through a shapeless stone gargoyle, into a trough; which trough again dripped into the tank. Almost under the little trickle of water, was the loathsome Emblem of Creation, and there were flowers and rice around it. Water was trickling from a score of places in the cut face of the hill; oozing between the edges of the steps and welling up between the stone slabs of the terrace. Trees sprouted in the sides of the tank and hid its surroundings. It seemed as though the descent had led the Englishman, firstly, two thousand years away from his own century, and secondly, into a trap, and that he would fall off the polished stones into the stinking tank, or that the Gau-Mukh would continue to pour water until the tank rose up and swamped him, or that some of the stone slabs would fall forward and crush him flat.

Then he was conscious of remembering, with peculiar and unnecessary distinctness, that, from the Gau-Mukh, a passage led to the subterranean chambers in which the fair Pudmini [described in 'Letter X' as 'the Helen of Chitor'] and her handmaids had slain themselves. And, that Tod [author of an early nineteenth-century history of the area] had written and the Stationmaster at Chitor had said, that some sort of devil, or ghoul, or Something, stood at the entrance of that approach. All of which was a nightmare bred in full day and folly to boot; but it was the fault of the Genius of the Place, who made the Englishman feel that he had done a great wrong in trespassing into the very heart and soul of all Chitor. And, behind him, the Gau-Mukh guggled and choked like a man in his death-throe. The Englishman endured as long as he could – about two minutes. Then it came upon him that he must go quickly out of this place of years and blood – must get back to the afternoon sunshine, and Gerowlia [the elephant he had ridden up on], and the dak-bungalow with the French bedstead. He desired no archaeological information, he wished to take no notes, and, above all, he did not care to look behind him, where stood the reminder that he was no better than the beasts that perish. But he had to cross the smooth, worn rocks, and he felt their sliminess through his boot-soles. It was as though he were treading on the soft, oiled skin of a Hindu. As soon as the steps gave refuge, he floundered up them, and so came out of the Gau-Mukh, bedewed with that perspiration which follows alike on honest toil or – childish fear.[4]

Rud's earlier writing about India had no equivalent to the experience described in this passage. For all his attempts to distance and minimise his reaction ('some sort of devil, or ghoul, or Something', 'folly to boot', 'it was the fault of the Genius of the Place'), he was overwhelmed. He felt 'two thousand years away from his own century', that he had 'done a great wrong in trespassing into the very heart and soul of Chitor', that he was 'no better than the beasts that perish'.

This moment of existential panic anticipated the defining episode in E M Forster's *A Passage to India*, in which the two English visitors, Mrs Moore and Adela Quested, were overcome by the echo in the Marabar Caves. In each case the overwhelming panic took place in a primordial Indian setting and was accompanied by acute feelings of entrapment, engulfment and psychological panic. Indeed the parallels are close enough to suggest that Rud's account of the Gau-Mukh might even have provided a source for the episode in Forster's novel, published nearly forty years later. Forster knew Kipling's work well, and could easily have read 'The Letters of Marque', when the series was collected in *From Sea to Sea* (1900).

For Rud, who had prided himself on being 'the man who knows', the effect of the experience was profound. Faced by the Gau-Mukh, his knowledge had proved useless, his stance as an Anglo-Indian no defence. Although other factors also determined his decision to leave India, the Gau-Mukh marked a turning-point. From then on, his commitment to staying began to erode, and he started to look for alternatives.

Mrs Edmonia Hill, known to her family and friends as 'Ted', was a dark-haired, strong-faced American from Beaver, Pennsylvania, where her father was President of the Beaver College for women. At the time Rud met her, shortly after reaching Allahabad, she was twenty-nine and the wife of an Ulsterman, Alec Hill, Professor of Physical Science at the Muir College in Allahabad. The first meeting took place at a dinner-party, probably in late December 1887. The 'Letters of Marque', which had begun to appear, unsigned, in the *Pioneer*, provided the initial catalyst:

> We were all wondering as to their author, evidently from the Punjab. When we were seated at the table and conversation was in full swing, my partner called my attention to a short, dark-haired and moustached man of uncertain age, wearing very thick glasses. He said, 'That is Rudyard Kipling, who has just come from Lahore to be on the staff of the *Pi*. He is the writer of those charming sketches of the native states.' Of course I was at once interested.[5]

Rud noticed her interest, introduced himself after the meal and eagerly quizzed her about her homeland. Mrs Hill was intrigued and sent him an invitation to a tennis and badminton party. Rud replied in his most boyishly charming manner. He asked her whether she could imagine him 'bounding round in a badminton net' and, in a flagrant play for her attention, claimed that 'American – and more particularly the tongue of Pennsylvania – is the *one* language I have long and ardently desired to learn.'[6] After the party Mrs Hill told her family that he had talked a lot about his schooldays and had joked that 'if life here was to be tempered with Allahabadminton he would begin to take comfort'.[7] This meeting cemented the friendship.

It is easy to guess why they took to each other so readily. Besides being impressed by his literary talent, Mrs Hill found Rud lively and amusing. His enthusiasm for America was flattering, as was his openness about himself. He for his part saw in her another potential confidante. A married woman, she could be flirted with safely, while doubling as a possible mother-substitute for this insecure twenty-two-year-old. Furthermore Mrs Hill was an American, which was a decided advantage. Rud's extensive knowledge of American writing provided an immediate bond – and, more importantly, she was a natural outsider in the world of Anglo-India. With her, he could discuss his literary future and his personal life without any of the constraints he would have felt with an Englishwoman.

In April 1888, to escape the worst of the hot weather, Mrs Hill left Allahabad for Mussoorie, a hill-station near Simla. At once Rud began a voluminous and almost daily correspondence. His letters over the next three months used every possible ploy to sustain her interest and attention. He made constant references to 'your people' and 'your country', quoted apposite lines from American poets and paraded his knowledge of American colloquialisms. Two years before, he had declared to Kay Robinson that he was looking forward to nothing beyond a journalist's career in India. Now, with thoughts of a very different future in mind, he even cast himself as a surrogate American, telling Mrs Hill that he had long been an American in his reading and training.

Another tactic to engage her attention was to enlist her help with stories he was writing. He had recently started *The Story of the Gadsbys*, a novella, entirely in dialogue, about an Anglo-Indian couple's courtship and marriage. The first episode, 'Poor Dear Mama', contained 'a *causerie intime* between two girls at Simla', which was giving him trouble. He asked Mrs Hill to check and countersign a proof copy and, when she replied with suggested emendations, Rud was suitably grateful. Subsequent episodes were also despatched to her for vetting. For Rud, an invitation to literary play was always an expression of his desire for intimacy – while establishing, on his own terms, a safe area within which that intimacy could readily flourish. His collaboration with Mrs Hill repeated, in a more elaborate form, the pattern of earlier collaborations with his sister and his parents. Rud also allowed his new friend a privileged glimpse into his working methods. He gave her a detailed description, spread over two letters, of how he had 'pumped' David Beames, a young officer in the Lancers, about his infatuation with a Miss Ethel

Temple, and had made a note of 'some of his more excruciating sentences for future use'.[8]

In May, Rud was sent to Lahore as acting editor of the CMG while Kay Robinson took a holiday. His letters now became more directly confessional. For a month Mrs Hill was deluged with reports of the ups and downs (mostly downs) of his long-distance love affair with a woman referred to simply as 'My Lady'. In his biography C E Carrington conjectured that this mysterious person never existed, but was 'a projection, perhaps, of Mrs Hill herself, to whom he must not declare his devotion'.[9] The highly artificial manner in which Rud wrote about the affair supports this idea. He may even have half-consciously recycled aspects of his relationship with Flo, a phantom he was still able to conjure up almost at will. The pseudo-courtly language he used about 'My Lady' and the frantic (but not quite convincing) analyses of his feelings both strongly recalled his schoolboy letters about Flo to Mrs Perry, and later to Margaret. The picture he presented of himself, powerless in a hopeless entanglement, was also reminiscent of earlier attempts to solicit other correspondents' sympathy:

> I don't wait for her letters. I get one and go on till I get the next, my nose to the grindstone for fear of thinking. When a horrible Sunday comes and I am thrown back upon myself I know how long I have waited and then I get all the arrears of suspense in one gloomy lump . . . But the drawback of that sweet soul's letters is that they are in no sense keepable. I'd as soon think of filing them in my box as I would of putting a seraph under a bell-glass. Therefore, when they are gotten by heart they are reverently burned. . . . I can't imagine a man deliberately keeping sacred letters. If it all died, they would hurt more than any woe. If it lived he would have the reality and the memory. That is if he could repeat the letters off by heart as I can. You will see from this that My Lady does not favour me with any lengthy outpourings . . .

Even if the affair was not altogether a fiction, its timing and dénouement were highly convenient. The 'break-up' occurred shortly before Rud, en route for a month's leave in Simla, was due to spend a week at Mussoorie with the Hills. That said, Mrs Hill herself accepted that the affair was real. She later noted on one of his letters from this period: 'About RK's love affair – which he got bravely over. The girl was not worthy – she wouldn't marry such an "ineligible".'[10] Real or imaginary, 'My Lady's' main value for Rud was in providing another means of arousing Mrs Hill's interest and concern, a gambit that was entirely successful.

The Mussoorie visit passed off pleasantly. Rud was full of ideas for further stories about Privates Mulvaney, Learoyd and Ortheris and showed Mrs Hill a draft of 'Private Learoyd's Story', which she found incomprehensible due to the Yorkshire dialect. She recalled Rud as being very partial to girls and talking endlessly about 'a golden-haired beauty' he had glimpsed walking up the road; so presumably he continued to play up the callow image of himself as someone who was always falling in love and in need of constant commiseration.[11]

Leaving Mussoorie on 21 June, Rud reached Simla the following day. Lockwood was in England on business; so he joined Alice and Trix in lodgings they had taken for the season. As soon as he arrived, all three sensed that – over and above Lockwood's absence – a major change had taken place in the Family Square:

> It is owned [Rud told Mrs Hill punningly] that I am no longer own-able and only a visitor in the land. The Mother says that is so and the Sister too and their eyes see far. 'You belong to yourself' says the Mother and the Maiden says: – 'You don't belong to us at any rate . . .'[12]

Simla too seemed different. Although he was now moving in the top echelons, the place that had once appeared the acme of sophistication and intrigue had lost its appeal. Lord Dufferin, whose thoughts Rud had tried to imagine at the tower in Chitor, he now considered 'beastly affable in his dim shortsighted way'; the gossip he had once delighted in sounded tired and stale. Nevertheless he scraped together a few snippets for Mrs Hill's amusement and repeated some of the cattier nicknames currently going the rounds: 'the Vulgarian Mendacity', the Virgin Mary, Sis Cow, Alphonso the Page, Alonzo and the Fair Imogene, the Shadow and the Substance. He also reported the gist of a conversation between his sister and a Miss Lambert, whom he claimed had designs on him. Miss Lambert had asked Trix how she would like her as a sister-in-law; to which Trix had replied, 'Very much indeed if I had a lot of brothers – to spare.'[13]

Soon after Rud's arrival there was a staffing emergency on the *Pioneer*, and he had to take over the writing of the 'Simla Letters'. This extra chore further confirmed his desire for a new life. 'I am more than ever set in my determination,' he told Mrs Hill on 27 June, 'to go home and quit the *Pi*. (But this is still a confidence most particular.) The leading paper in India is an excellent thing but there are many things better in this world and I must strike out and find 'em.'[14]

At the end of the month Rud, Alice and Trix spent a few days at The Retreat, the country house of Sir Edward Buck, the Secretary to the Government of India. The most notable moment of the visit came on a raspberry-picking expedition with his sister when she confided to him her misery over Jack Fleming. The previous year Trix and Fleming, a Captain in the Scottish Borderers who had been seconded to the Survey of India Department, had become engaged; but she had broken off the engagement 'on the grounds of incompatibility of temper'.[15] Fleming had, however, been allowed to continue writing to Trix. This year the two had met again at Simla, and Fleming had pleaded to be allowed to see her – hence Trix's present unhappiness.

Rud's description of the scene to Mrs Hill carried an even stronger sense of the Family Square falling apart. He was of course genuinely sorry for his sister, but the persistently arch tone of his letter reveals an unwillingness to enter fully into her feelings and an uneasy awareness that he was breaking a family confidence:

The objectionable cuss with whom she had broken, had another last-despairing interview with her yesterday morn, and very naturally with his appeals and protestations had shaken the poor darling grievously though she persists and persisted in her original intent. She talked to me and told me as much about it as a woman would ever tell a man and at last the blessed tears came to her relief and she cried all among the pine-needles while I lacked words that could give her any comfort. Then she pointed out, half crying and half laughing, the uselessness of the beauty of the forest, in which point I heartily agreed with her till she turned upon me with: – 'Who else would you like to walk with except me you bad boy?' So we agreed that never since the world

began was there any sorrow like to her sorrow and hunted for rasp-
berries till the tears were dried and our fingers blue-red, and we began
to steal from each other's vines and throw pine-cones at each other's
heads as it was in the very early days. But somehow the fooling was
not amusing and when Trix collapsed on a rock and said: – 'Oh how
miserable I am!' I felt that we could not play at being babies any
more. Wherefore we came home solemnly to tea and announced that
we had had a riotously jovial afternoon. Ay de mi!'[16]

Back at Simla, Trix decided that she was in love with Fleming after all
and, with her mother's support, persuaded Rud to act as a reluctant emis-
sary. The engagement was renewed within a few weeks.

Lockwood, over in England, was dismayed when he heard the news.
He had been against the match from the start and expressed his fears to
Edith Plowden:

I can only hope with all my heart the child is right and that she will
not one day when it is too late find her Fleming but a thin pasture
and sigh for other fields . . . He is in the Survey & his record is good
– a model young man; Scotch and possessing all the virtues; but to
me somewhat austere; not caring for books nor for many things for
which our Trix cares intensely.[17]

Lockwood's anxiety proved prophetic. The wedding took place the following year, but although the couple remained married until Fleming's
death in 1942, the relationship does not seem to have brought either of
them much happiness.

Besides turning Rud's leave in Simla into a busman's holiday, the
staffing emergency on the *Pioneer* had a further consequence. Before his
stint in Lahore, he had been living in Allahabad with his proprietor,
George Allen. His rooms there were now required for another colleague,
and it looked as though Rud would have to put up at the club. Outlining
the problem to Mrs Hill on 27 June, he must have hoped that she and her
husband would offer to take him into their house, Belvedere. The offer
was duly made and accepted, and for his remaining nine months in India
Belvedere became Rud's home and base.

*

A major component of Rud's job when he joined the *Pioneer* was the editing of a weekly supplement called the *Week's News*, intended, as he later put it, 'for Home consumption'.[18] In addition to rehashing recent news and views, he was expected to contribute, for no extra pay, regular stories of 3,000–4,000 words. And so he did, often writing and publishing as many as four or five substantial tales per month until he gave up his editorship in September. Given his extraordinary output during this period, it is hardly surprising that the quality of the work was mixed, especially as he was also producing poems and further travel pieces. Towards the end of the year he collected most of his *Week's News* stories, with a few earlier pieces and some new tales written at Belvedere, into six slim volumes: *Under the Deodars*, *The Phantom 'Rickshaw*, *Wee Willie Winkie*, *Soldiers Three*, *The Story of the Gadsbys* and *In Black and White*. These were published in December by A H Wheeler in the Indian Railway Library Series and, paving the way for his eventual arrival in England, Rud sent copies for review to London literary magazines.

As one would expect with their greater length, the stories Rud wrote during 1888 were markedly different from those in *Plain Tales*. There his model had been the vignette or extended anecdote. Restricted space had determined that characterisation and narrative complexity be kept to a minimum and that variety was largely provided by the setting and type of situation described. Now he began to experiment.

In *The Story of the Gadsbys*, Rud attempted a novella made up of linked episodes. Each episode was complete in itself, but showed the development of the couple's relationship from first meeting to marriage and on to Gadsby's decision to quit the Army and retire with his wife and son to England. Six of the seven stories that eventually comprised *Soldiers Three* were also linked. Here, however, Rud was not trying for the sequential movement of the novella but for something closer to a narrative collage, in which each separate tale added to an overall picture of the sometimes comic, sometimes tragic lives led by the British troops in India. This altogether looser structure was given unity by concentrating on the same three characters, Mulvaney, Learoyd and Ortheris, and by using Mulvaney as the principal narrator.

A further refinement was Rud's development of a 'frame' to the central narrative, a technique that was to become a hallmark of his later fiction. In 'With the Main Guard', the 'frame' described a stiflingly hot June night in the barracks, with the heat so oppressive that the burly Learoyd was terrified of dying of apoplexy, and Ortheris desperately throwing buckets of water over him. Things were getting out of hand when Mulvaney was persuaded to tell them one of his stories. He launched into a dramatic account of a battle in which he and the other two had taken part. This instantly caught Learoyd's and Ortheris's attention, and by the time Mulvaney had finished, dawn was breaking and the three were ready to endure another day.

These formal experiments were accompanied by an extension of Rud's literary ventriloquism. The presiding voice in *Plain Tales* had been that of the anonymous narrator, brash, ironic, evasive. Rud now increased his range. In several dramatic monologues by Indian characters ('Dray Wara Yow Dee', 'At Howli Thana', 'In Flood Time', 'Gemini') he evolved an elaborately ornate English intended to convey the richly allusive, ritualistic texture of the vernacular. In a number of stories with Anglo-Indian children as the protagonists ('Wee Willie Winkie', 'His Majesty the King', 'Baa Baa Black Sheep'), he tried out a phonetic rendering of children's speech. If neither of those particular experiments was entirely successful (his Indian characters tended to emerge as exotic primitives, his children as overly sentimentalised), his development of Mulvaney's Irish brogue, of Learoyd's Yorkshire dialect and of the clipped tones of his Anglo-Indian civilians was an impressive achievement.

Rud's subject matter was also widening. *Soldiers Three* examined the vicissitudes of the private soldier's life. *The Story of the Gadsbys* investigated the contrary demands of love and duty. *Wee Willie Winkie* explored the bewilderment of children caught up in adult worlds they found incomprehensible – and, in one case, terrifying. *In Black and White* probed the complexities of Indian life beyond the confines of British law. In 'Only a Subaltern' (from *Under the Deodars*), Rud created the first of his exemplary young Army officers, Bobby Wicks, who died from fever after saving the Company drunk. More ambitiously, 'A Wayside Comedy' from the same collection presented an entire social world – the Kashima station – in miniature.

Another dimension of several of these 1888 stories was their concealed literariness. Rud's use of hidden literary references was no doubt partly for his own private satisfaction, a game he was playing with himself. As he later remarked, his Anglo-Indian readers 'wanted accuracy and interest, but first of all accuracy'. They 'were not concerned with my dreams'.[19] Such an audience was hardly likely to pick up the Tennyson echo at the end of 'With the Main Guard', where Mulvaney suddenly revealed the depth of his own despair. 'I've blandandhered thim through the night somehow,' he commented wearily to the anonymous narrator, 'but can thim that helps others help themselves? Answer me that, Sorr!' The sentence that followed and concluded the story – 'And over the bastions of Fort Amara broke the pitiless day' – was an adaptation of a line from Tennyson's *In Memoriam*: 'On the bald street breaks the blank day.'[20] This marvellously judged climax, which invested Mulvaney with the imaginative intensity of a figure from lyric poetry, was hardly one that Rud could have expected his Anglo-Indian audience to appreciate. By now, however, he was writing with not just an Anglo-Indian audience in mind. The *Week's News* was intended for the 'Home' market, and these purely literary moments were intended for a more sophisticated, English readership, readers like Andrew Lang who had reviewed *Departmental Ditties* two years before.

When the Indian Railway Library Series began to appear a few months later, with covers designed by Lockwood, several of the volumes contained new stories, including 'The Man Who Would Be King' and 'Baa Baa Black Sheep'. These new tales suggested that Rud was winding up his account.

'The Man Who Would Be King' derived its peculiar resonance from Rud's insertion of high tragedy into the late nineteenth-century English adventure yarn. Typically in such yarns the heroes disappeared into the wilds in search of fortune and fame. They endured physical hardship and danger and, by their daring, superior know-how and weaponry won success. Often, as in H Rider Haggard's *King Solomon's Mines* (1886) and G A Henty novels like *Under Drake's Flag* (1883) and *With Clive in India* (1884), an implicit myth of colonial conquest underwrote the swashbuckling and derring-do. Rud's adaptation of the formula was simple but radical: he gave it a tragic framework. The reader knew from the start of Peachey's account that Dravott was dead, and that Peachey himself was dying; consequently each stage of the triumphal progress by these 'loafers' took them a step nearer catastrophe. Once they achieved their dream and became kings – of Kafiristan, a remote district at the top of Afghanistan – tragedy inevitably followed. Dravott succumbed to hubris, overreached himself and precipitated their fall.

The implied analogy between 'The Man Who Would Be King' and the Anglo-Indian situation was underlined in two main ways. First, within the story itself, Peachey's and Dravott's exploits paralleled the history of the British take-over of India, particularly in their playing off of one tribe against another and their establishment of small, native armies. Second, to hint at its allegorical implications, Rud placed the story in *The Phantom 'Rickshaw* volume immediately after an expanded version of 'The Strange Ride of Morrowbie Jukes'. Jukes's tale, for all its obvious horror, was a fundamentally reassuring version of the Anglo-Indian position. Though his superiority as a sahib was threatened by the equality of life in the valley, it was finally reaffirmed when Jukes was rescued by his Indian servant. No such rescue awaited Peachey and Dravott. They too asserted their superiority, and by acting as gods they carried their sahibhood to its logical conclusion. But when they were revealed as equal (that is, human), the natives destroyed them. This double-bind closely mirrored the one that faced the British in India: having conquered, they had to govern; to govern, they had to act as gods; to act as gods was ultimately impossible. Rud could hardly have presented a more devastating critique of the Anglo-Indian dilemma.

This representation of imperial success as really tragic failure reflected a profound, if temporary, shift in Rud's sense of himself as an Anglo-Indian – a shift triggered by his experience at Gau-Mukh, then intensified by his friendship with Mrs Hill and by the certainty that he was about to leave. The critical perspective towards the colonial situation that he reached in 'The Man Who Would Be King' fleetingly suggested that even at this stage the gap between Rud and his liberal connections in England was not yet unbridgeable. We can even, with an effort, imagine him not as the ardent imperialist he actually became, but as a forerunner of George Orwell, arriving in England to expose the impracticability of the system of which he had been a part.

Rud's disaffection with being an Anglo-Indian was symptomatic of his growing disaffection with his audience. Previously he had written with two sets of readers in mind: the Family Square and his Anglo-Indian public. Now he was distanced, literally and emotionally, from the first and had become bored with the second. The readership he now wanted was over in England; in the meantime, he was increasingly writing for himself and, to a lesser extent, for Mrs Hill. This widening gap between

Rud and his local audience was reflected in his search for a new rationale for his work. Three years earlier, practical usefulness had provided him with one kind of justification: 'I'm death on Drains and watersupply' as he had proudly told Margaret in September 1885.[21] Later, with *Departmental Ditties* and *Plain Tales*, he had seen himself as offering his readers snapshots of their lives, telling them 'about what they knew'. The gift of storytelling might help others; but, Rud now wondered, could it help the storyteller? 'Baa Baa Black Sheep', in which Rud told himself the story of his childhood with the Holloways, offered an equivocal answer.

Apart from omitting the visit by his grandmother and aunts, and his Christmas escapes to the Burne-Joneses at The Grange, Rud stuck closely to his memory of what had happened. Punch (Rud) and Judy (Trix) were removed from their happy, indulged life in India and left by their parents with Uncle Harry, Aunty Rosa and Harry (the Holloways) at Downe Lodge (Lorne Lodge) in Rocklington (Southsea). Punch and Aunty Rosa disliked each other on sight, and she persecuted him, both physically and religiously. Uncle Harry, ex-Navy like Captain Holloway, allowed Punch to play with a model of the *Brisk*, took the boy for walks and was generally kind until his death. Judy became Aunty Rosa's pet. Punch discovered the solace of reading, but, exposed as a liar, was dubbed the 'Black Sheep' and tormented by Harry. After further humiliation and suffering, Punch's eyes gave way and he had some sort of breakdown. Finally the children's mother appeared and whisked the children away.

Re-creating these painful, personal events as fiction did no doubt afford Rud some therapeutic release from the remembered misery of the past; and were it not for the ending, one might assume that his primary motive for writing the story was as a form of imaginative exorcism. In the final scene Punch and Judy were joyously reunited with their mother, and Punch was telling Judy that 'It's all different now, and we are just as much Mother's as if she had never gone.' But just as it seemed that a harmonious resolution was in prospect, the voice of the narrator ominously intervened with 'not altogether, O Punch, for when young lips have drunk of the bitter waters of Hate, Suspicion, and Despair, all the Love in the world will not wholly take away that knowledge; though it may turn darkened eyes for a while to the light, and teach Faith where no Faith was'.[22] Punch might believe that he had been saved and that a happy future awaited him, but the narrator (his older self) knew better: Punch had, in fact, been emotionally damaged for life.

This sinister conclusion forces a radical reappraisal of the story and of Rud's motives for writing it. A clue was provided, appropriately, by Mrs Hill. In her diary entry for December 1888, after giving a summary of the story, she commented:

> It was pitiful to see Kipling living over the experience, pouring out his soul in the story, as the drab life was worse than he could possibly describe it. His eyesight was permanently impaired, and, as he had heretofore only known love and tenderness, his faith in people was sorely tried. When he was writing this he was a sorry guest, as he was in a towering rage at the recollection of those days. His summing up in the closing words shows the influence on his whole life . . .[23]

Throughout the year Rud had been soliciting Mrs Hill's interest and sympathy. He had co-opted her as a collaborator in his work, made her his personal confidante, revealed intimate family secrets. To tell the tale of his persecuted childhood was yet another of these gambits, and to judge by her reaction he again achieved his object. Mrs Hill's description of Rud as 'in a towering rage at the recollection of those days' suggests a further motive – revenge. In the process of 'pouring out his soul', Rud rediscovered not only his hatred of Mrs Holloway and her son, but his buried resentment towards his parents for abandoning him and towards his sister for her defection. 'Baa Baa Black Sheep' was intended to make his family feel guilty. Why did he choose this particular moment to repay old scores? Because at the time he was writing the story he was literally 'living over' crucial features of his childhood experience. He was again on the point of leaving India. He was again separated from his parents. His sister, now engaged to Jack Fleming, had again defected. He was again lodging with a substitute family. Though in more positive form, it must have seemed as if history was repeating itself.

The personal parallels between 1871 and 1888 are unlikely to have escaped Rud, and they help to explain the games he was playing in the story. Lorne Lodge was the place where he had first developed imaginative play as a means of survival. The point of the elaborate rituals he had acted out in the Holloways' basement had been to create a self-contained world that he could control, a secret community of insiders and outsiders. His writing, including his collaborations, had evolved as an extension of these private games. Now representing that period of his life as fiction, he underlined the suffering he had endured by travestying figures associated with a conventionally happy childhood. With the pseudonyms Punch and Judy, he implied that he and his sister had been no more than puppets, manipulated by the adults. He further reinforced the helplessness and isolation of his surrogate Punch by his parody of the familiar nursery rhyme that gave the story its title and epigraph:

Baa Baa, Black Sheep,
Have you any wool?
Yes, Sir, yes, Sir, three bags full.
One for the Master, one for the Dame –
None for the Little Boy that cries down the lane.[24]

Mimicking the three stages of the epigraph, Rud divided the story into three sections. 'The First Bag' began happily in India and ended with Punch's abandonment at Downe Lodge. 'The Second Bag', during which Punch became the 'Black Sheep', ended with Uncle Harry's death. 'The Third Bag' ended with Punch's rescue, but the loss of his future echoed the fate of the 'Little Boy' of the epigraph who received no 'bag' and 'cries down the lane'. These deliberate distortions of familiar childhood emblems are profoundly disturbing even now. With the implication that his childhood had been blighted at the root, how much more distressing these distortions must have been for Rud's family, though no record exists of their response.

As he had done in his basement games at Lorne Lodge, Rud in 'Baa Baa Black Sheep' was once more readjusting the world, expelling his parents and Trix from their central position and installing Mrs Hill in their place. He was also creating his own version of the Romantic myth of the artist's damaged childhood. None of this in any way invalidated the story as autobiography; it merely underlined the truism that the motives behind any autobiographical writing are always mixed and often unacknowledged. If 'Baa Baa Black Sheep' was unusual, it was only because Rud's motives could be identified with some certainty, as could the private audience he had in mind.

*

Rud now had his sights set firmly on England, and his proprietors on the *Pioneer* were probably not displeased to see him go. For all his local success and obvious talent, he had become something of a liability, voicing his discontent at Anglo-India a little too openly. In September 1888, using his own initials, he had published 'A Job Lot', a poem accusing Sir Frederick Roberts, Commander-in-Chief of the British Army in India, of making nepotistic appointments. In December, in another of his Browningesque monologues, 'One Viceroy Resigns', he had Lord Dufferin explain to his successor the futility of the task he was inheriting:

> You'll never plumb the Oriental mind,
> And if you did, it isn't worth the toil.
> Think of a sleek French priest in Canada;
> Divide by twenty half-breeds. Multiply
> By twice the Sphinx's silence. There's your East,
> And you're as wise as ever. So am I.[25]

Even more dramatically, an article of Rud's on the Indian National Congress led to a personal assault on the editor of the *Pioneer* and an exchange of lawsuits.[26]

Whether it was his proprietors, eager to remove an embarrassment, or Rud, in need of funds, who proposed that he should write a set of travel pieces in return for a trip abroad, an agreement was reached, and his plans began to take more definite shape. When Mrs Hill, convalescing from meningitis, decided with her husband to visit her relatives in Beaver, travelling by way of the Far East, Rud begged to be allowed to accompany them. In February 1889, he said his farewells to his family in Lahore. On 9 March he and the Hills embarked from Calcutta on the SS *Madura*. Apart from a flying visit three years later, Rud had seen the last of India.

8

Charting the Orient

The first leg of their journey took Rud and the Hills as far as Japan. En route they stopped at Rangoon, Penang, Singapore and Hong Kong, and Rud had his first glimpse of the Far East. Released from all the tensions of India, he quickly relaxed, and his initial Letters to the *Pioneer* luxuriated in a sense of holiday. 'There is no such place as India; there never was a daily paper called the *Pioneer*' ended the first Letter, in typically insouciant fashion. 'It was all a weary dream. The only real things in the world are crystal seas, clean-swept decks, soft rugs, warm sunshine, the smell of salt in the air, and fathomless, futile indolence.'[1]

Rangoon, reached on 14 March, briefly evoked elegiac thoughts of dead acquaintances – 'policemen, subalterns, young civilians, employés of big trading firms, and adventurers' – who had gone to Burma and never returned. More light-heartedly, he enthused over the colours and strangeness of it all and lamented in mock despair that he 'could not at once secure a full, complete, and accurate idea of everything that was to be seen.'[2] A trip across the bay to Moulmein later provided the raw material for 'Mandalay', one of his most popular poems, in which a private soldier nostalgically recalled his Burmese days and the Burmese girl he left behind, 'By the old Moulmein Pagoda, lookin' lazy at the sea'.

In real life both girl and pagoda played a rather different role – as comic copy to be served up for Rud's readers back in India. 'I should better remember what that pagoda was like had I not fallen deeply and irrevocably in love with a Burmese girl at the foot of the first flight of steps,' he told them. 'Only the fact of the steamer starting next noon prevented me from staying at Moulmein forever and owning a pair of elephants.'[3] The Burmese girl was the first of a succession of interchangeable girls with whom Rud claimed to fall hopelessly in love on his travels. None of these encounters meant anything of course. They were a game played for the benefit of his public back in India.

At the same time the lack of any reference to Mrs Hill in the Letters was revealing. While he gave Alec Hill a substantial role as 'the Professor' – part foil, part older, wiser *alter ego* – he left Mrs Hill out entirely. This reticence about those who meant most to him was to become a characteristic feature of his autobiographical writing. Mrs Hill's marked absence strongly suggested how much she mattered to him. Emotionally tied to her, he could pretend to lose his heart as often as he liked to anyone else. If there was a link between Kipling and the speaker of 'Mandalay', it was in his remembered feelings for Mrs Hill and his nostalgia for the trip as a whole, rather than in any momentary crush he might have had on the Burmese girl.

Penang reminded Rud of Palmiste Island in Walter Besant's *My Little Girl* and *So They Were Married*. A walk in drowsy heat up to a waterfall brought to mind Tennyson's 'The Lotos-Eaters' and, more surprisingly, Zola's 'description of a conservatory' in 'the very worst' of his novels. Penang also produced the first signs of the sinophobia that became increasingly pronounced as he travelled further East. 'Was it not De Quincey that had a horror of the Chinese – of their inhumaneness and their inscrutability?' he asked jauntily in Letter IV, before launching into some laboured banter about Chinese looks, gods, customs, cuisine and secret societies:

Certainly the [Chinese] people in Penang are not nice; they are even terrible to behold. They work hard, which in this climate is manifestly wicked, and their eyes are just like the eyes of their own pet dragons . . . what can you do with a people who revel in D. T. [delirium tremens] monsters and crown their roof-ridges with flames of fire, or waves of the sea? They swarmed everywhere, and wherever three or four met, there they ate things without name – the insides of ducks for choice.[4]

That Rud should have relayed such views back to his Anglo-Indian audience was not in itself remarkable; after all, a range of ties, including xenophobia and straight racism, united the British abroad. But again the uneasy phrasing and tone suggested that he did not entirely believe in the opinions he was voicing. The (not entirely accurate) allusion to De Quincey, for example, was an obvious attempt to justify his own and his readers' racism by a piece of literary name-dropping. At the same time the calculated way he so casually slipped in the name ('Was it not De Quincey . . .?') suggested that being flagrantly racist, sounding like a caricature of the Anglo-Indian abroad, was part of a role he had decided to play on the trip. The role was doubly attractive: he already knew the lines, and it allowed him to express objectionable views that he personally found congenial.

That said, Rud's sinophobia at times became so extreme that it simply ran away with him. For instance, he adored babies and children and despised those who mocked them. Yet here he allowed himself to talk about Chinese babies with a repellently gruesome jocularity: 'I saw cold boiled babies on a plate being carried through the heart of the town. They said it was only sucking-pig, but I knew better. Dead sucking-pigs don't grin with their eyes open.'[5]

On 24 March they arrived at Singapore, 'another Calcutta, but much more so'. After recommending Raffles Hotel as the place to eat but not to stay, Rud embarked on an extended imperial daydream. He imagined a future in which a federation of self-governing British colonies, 'too vast a hornet's nest for any combination of Powers to disturb', would through mutual trade come together 'in one great iron band girdling the earth'.[6] Hitherto he had given little thought to the British Empire as a whole; India, where he had been living and working, and England, where his literary ambitions were centred, had occupied most of his attention. Now, on the move, something of the size and potential of the Empire began to come home to him. Only a few months before, he had been writing a disaffected story like 'The Man Who Would Be King'. Once on board ship, his reservations quickly receded, and he busily reasserted his Anglo-Indian allegiance, spinning a new myth of the British Empire, a union of states, autonomous and treaty-bound, interdependent and tariff-free.

A few misty days at Hong Kong, including a trip ninety miles upriver to Canton, brought back Rud's sinophobia with renewed force. In a number of Letters, using the Professor as his foil, he conducted a kind of spoof debate about the perplexing nature of the Chinese. Soon after his arrival in Hong Kong, he claimed to be bewildered by the 'horrible contradiction' that the Chinese looked like devils and yet created such exquisite works of art; upon which he had the Professor calmly observe, 'They will overwhelm the world.' Shifting to the imperial plane, he then offered a distinction between the Chinese and the Indians:

> If we had control over as many Chinamen as we have natives of India, and had given them one tithe of the cosseting, the painful pushing forward, and studious, even nervous, regard of their interests and aspirations as we have given to India, we should long ago have been expelled from, or have reaped the rewards of, the richest land on the face of the earth.

Or more simply 'Let us annex China', the poker-faced line with which he closed the letter.[7]

The trip to Canton – Goblin Market, as Rud called it, after the Christina Rossetti poem – was again written up in the half-joking manner that he reserved for subjects that disturbed or frightened him: 'Do you know those horrible sponges full of worms that grow in warm seas? You break off a piece of it and the worms break too. Canton was that sponge.' Returning by steamer to Hong Kong, the Professor asked him for his impressions of Canton. Acknowledging the disjunction between his own subjective response and the Professor's calm rationality, Rud replied:

> A big blue sink of a city full of tunnels, all dark and inhabited by yellow devils, a city that Doré ought to have seen. I'm devoutly thankful that I'm never going back there. The Mongol will begin to march in his own good time. I intend to wait until he marches up to me. Let us go away to Japan by the next boat.
>
> The Professor says that I have completely spoilt the foregoing account by what he calls 'intemperate libels on a hard-working nation'. He did not see Canton as I saw it – through the medium of a fevered imagination.[8]

That Rud was indeed seeing things 'through the medium of a fevered imagination' is supported by the surviving fragment of a letter to Mrs Hill early the following year. 'My head has given out,' he wrote from London, 'and I am forbidden work and I am to go away somewhere. This is the third time it has happened – last time was on the Honam on the Canton river but this time is the completest.'[9] The idea that he had some sort of temporary breakdown around this point of the trip makes sense. It was almost inevitable that he would experience a counterswing to his initial feelings of escape. His sense of release may even have induced a kind of psychic agoraphobia, as he began to realise just how large and alien the world really was. For all the grinding frustrations of much of his life in India, he had after all created a place and a role for himself. Now here he was in limbo between the known civil and military world he had left behind and the unknown London literary world that lay ahead.

Back in Hong Kong, Rud's stay also included 'seeing Life' in the company of a young American. This comprised a night investigating the 'unmitigated horror' of various local brothels, drinking syrupy champagne and talking to a succession of English prostitutes, an experience that left him profoundly shocked. One prostitute, jumpy with drink but 'gay, *toujours* gay', he found particularly appalling and pathetic. He ended his account with a sententious self-denunciation. Although he had been genuinely moved by the 'woman half crazed with drink and fear', he also enjoyed making a meal of his guilt:

... mine was the greater sin. I was driven by no gust of passion, but went in cold blood to make my account of this Inferno, and to measure the measureless miseries of life. For the wholly insignificant sum of thirty dollars I had purchased information and disgust more than I required, and the right to look after a woman half crazed with drink and fear the third part of a terrible night. Mine was the greater sin.

When we stepped back into the world I was glad that the fog stood between myself and the heaven above.[10]

Rud and the Hills reached Nagasaki on 15 April. The voyage, a rough one, dispelled the horrors of Canton and Hong Kong, and he soon regained his holiday mood. For the next month the trio made a leisurely exploration of Japan, using a combination of boat, train, rickshaw and tram to visit most of the main tourist spots. They pottered about temples and shrines, strolled round gardens and lakes, admired Mount Fuji, roasted in the thermal area of Owakidani, ate in tea-houses, bathed in mixed bath-houses, investigated factories, watched a cherry-blossom dance, attended the Japanese theatre and, everywhere they went, enthused over the landscape.

Rud's sense of release was reflected throughout the twelve Letters on Japan he sent back to the *Pioneer*. These celebrated a Japan untouched by modernity and progress: small, exquisite, static and safe. Accordingly his descriptions made constant reference to the delicate refinement of the traditional architecture and lovingly detailed the dolls' house neatness of the buildings. He took a keen interest in the manufacture of porcelain, *cloisonné* and lacquerware and paid enthusiastic attention to the work of painters like 'the great Kano', who on the walls of the temple of Chion-in 'drew numbed pheasants huddled together on the snow-covered bough of a pine . . . a riot of chrysanthemums poured out of a vase . . . a hunting scene at the foot of Fujiyama'. The engine of the train that carried the trio from Kobe to Osaka became 'a lapis-lazuli coloured locomotive'; even the tramway driver who conveyed them from Miyanoshita to Yokohama was 'artistic' because 'his blue jerkin' was inscribed with three white 'rail-heads in a circle', and 'on the skirts' there were 'as many tram-wheels conventionalised'.[11]

But although he was excited by what he called Japan's 'otherness', Rud refused to be impressed by the country's recent moves towards democratisation and modernisation. He continually ridiculed its new German-based Constitution and poured scorn on attempts to adopt a Western style of dress. Barely had he stepped off the boat at Nagasaki than he encountered a figure whom he instantly turned into a symbol of everything he despised about modern Japan:

He was a Japanese customs official. Had our stay been longer, I would have wept over him because he was a hybrid – partly French, partly German, and partly American – a tribute to civilisation. All the Japanese officials from police upwards seem to be clad in Europe [sic] clothes, and never do those clothes fit. I think the Mikado [the Emperor] made them at the same time as the Constitution.

A few days later Rud found the passengers on the train from Kobe to Osaka equally absurd. They wore 'little tweed suits with fawn-coloured overcoats', with 'white cotton gloves' on 'their wee-wee hands', and in all 'resembled nothing more than Tenniel's picture of the White Rabbit on the first page of *Alice in Wonderland*'.[12]

Yet as he knocked out these verbal cartoons, Rud was usually having it both ways, careful while he sent up the Europeanised Japanese to point out his own ignorance and presumption. Here he wound up his bantering account with a mock-sententious remark of the Professor's: 'If you think you can understand Japan from watching it at a railway station you are much mistaken.' Adding to Rud's sense of being on holiday was his conviction that Japan posed no threat as a military power. 'The Japanese makes a trim little blue-jacket,' he remarked complacently at one point, 'but he does not understand soldiering.'[13] And later, a morning watching the imperial cavalry being put through its paces left him chortling over what he described as 'a wild dream of equitation'.[14] There was no danger to British influence from this quarter.

Feeling at ease, Rud allowed himself to entertain possibilities that he would normally have found too awkward or unsettling. He mused, for instance, about the idea of sahibhood. Walking around Nagasaki soon after his arrival, he was captivated by the cleanness and smallness of everything – particularly 'soothing', he commented, 'for a small man', a rare reference to his height. Then, with this outsized sense of himself, he passed into a tiny shop selling curiosities and felt 'for the first time that I was a barbarian, and no true Sahib'. Although he claimed to find the sensation a discomfiting one, the passage as a whole suggests that he also found the experience – and the admission – liberating. The British, he confided to the Professor soon afterwards, 'are not the only people in the world. I began to realise it at Hong-Kong . . . I shouldn't be surprised if we turned out to be ordinary human beings, after all.'[15]

This partial relaxation of the Anglo-Indian code with its rigid, racial hierarchy permitted Rud, wandering with the Professor in Kobe, to return to 'the Chinese question', which had so bothered him in Penang and Canton:

As in Nagasaki, the town was full of babies, and as in Nagasaki, every one smiled except the Chinaman. I do not like Chinamen.

They stand high above the crowd and they swagger, unconsciously parting the crowd before them as an Englishman parts the crowd in a native city. There was something in their faces which I could not understand, though it was familiar enough.

'The Chinaman's a native, 'Fessor,' I said. 'That's the look on a native's face, but the Japanese isn't a native, and he isn't a *sahib* either. What is it?' The Professor considered the surging street for a while.

'The Chinaman's an old man when he's young, just as a native is; but the Japanese is a child all his life. Think how grown-up people look upon children. That's the look that's puzzling you.'

I dare not say that the Professor is right, but to my eyes it seemed he spoke sooth. As the knowledge of good and evil sets its mark upon the face of a grown man of our people, so something I did not understand had marked the faces of the Chinamen. They had no kinship with the crowd beyond that which a man has to children.

'They are the superior race,' said the Professor, ethnologically.

'They can't be. They don't know how to enjoy life,' I answered immorally. 'And anyway, their art isn't human.'

'What does it matter?' said the Professor. 'Here's a shop full of the wrecks of old Japan. Let's go in and look.' We went in, but I want somebody to solve the Chinese question for me. It's too large to handle alone.[16]

What Rud found disturbing about the Chinese in Japan was their manner and bearing, which were uncomfortably close to those of Anglo-Indians in India. He also found the sheer antiquity of Chinese civilisation uncanny; it suggested the awkward possibility that the Chinese had pre-empted the civilising mission of British imperialism.

The entire passage revealed the kind of crazy, bigoted muddle that Rud (in his dual identity as himself and the Professor) had got himself into. From an Anglo-Indian perspective, *both* the Chinese and the Japanese ought to have been 'natives', identifiable by their look. But while the Japanese, though paradoxically neither 'native' nor sahib, could be safely infantilised, the Chinaman, whom Rud called a 'native', could not really be one because he looked at the Japanese like 'grown-up people look upon children' – in other words, like a sahib. Rud could hardly have demonstrated more damningly the absurdity of the Anglo-Indian stance on what did and did not constitute a sahib. He had argued himself into a position in which he virtually admitted that if the term 'sahib' meant anything at all, then the Chinese had to be accepted as sahibs. But such a notion, unfortunately, demolished the whole point of belonging to the Anglo-Indian club.

A passage from Letter V encapsulated his response to Japan. He began with a restatement of his delight in Japanese artistry, qualified this (while pretending not to) by giving thanks for a defect in the Japanese character and concluded with a very arch piece of British humility, which hardly bothered to conceal the implicit boasting:

Verily Japan is a great people. Her masons play with stone, her carpenters with wood, her smiths with iron, and her artists with life, death, and all the eye can take in. Mercifully she has been denied the last touch of firmness in her character which would enable her to play with the whole round world. We possess that – we, the nation of the glass flower-shade, the pink worsted mat, the red and green china puppy dog, and the poisonous Brussels carpet. It is our compensation . . .[17]

9

Knocking about the States

Even before Rud and the Hills left Yokohama for San Francisco, he had fired off a sighting broadside against the States. The cause was what should have been a pleasant visit to a bookshop, looking for reading matter for the voyage. Handed a list of the Seaside Library, a series of pirated editions put out by George Munro of New York and stocked by the shop, he was told that he would find everything he wanted:

> Apart from the mighty dead [he told his *Pioneer* readers] who are all the world's property, because they still compete with the living author, I found the names of all the lesser lights who twinkle from the tops of one, two or three columns today. Besant, Braddon, Inglesant, Haggard, Stevenson, Hall Caine, Anstey, 'Q', Farjeon, Ouida, Farrar, George Moore and others whom the pen holds not in remembrance were all on the list, and their works did follow their names orderly.

Among the pirated publications of these 'lesser lights', he came across some of his own work: 'Anglo-Indian stories not altogether unknown to me', as he put it.[1] (The United States did not observe international copyright; as a result, American pirated editions of foreign authors were relatively common, and widely distributed.)

He left the shop furious and empty-handed, vowing in his next Letter to 'pronounce a curse on the American people'.[2] And so he did, even though – in his eagerness to vent his feelings – he transposed the incident to the account he was currently writing of his earlier stop in Yokohama. His indignant protestations, however, failed to disguise that for him the only thing worse than being pirated was not being pirated. 'Anglo-Indian stories not altogether unknown to me': the coyness was transparent, the underlying gratification to his literary vanity all too palpable. The curse itself set a pattern that would be repeated throughout his trip across the States. By casting Americans as lawless barbarians, he bolstered his self-image (and by extension that of his Anglo-Indian audience), as representative of an older, more mature civilisation.

After a rough voyage involving some harmless flirtation by Rud with a 'sweet maiden from South Carolina', the *City of Peking* docked in San Francisco on 28 May.[3] Within a couple of days the Hills were on a train east, to stay with her family in Beaver, Pennsylvania. Rud remained in San Francisco for a further fortnight or so, pursuing family and other contacts and leading a hectic social life. He decided more or less on landing that San Francisco and its inhabitants, however exciting in some respects, were essentially uncouth and provincial. 'They spit even as in the time of Dickens,' he told Aunt Georgie after three days, 'and their speech is not sweet to listen to – 'specially the women's.'[4] In his first Letter from San Francisco, he transformed the spittoon into an icon of local vulgarity:

> In a vast marble-paved hall under the glare of an electric light sat forty or fifty men; and for their use and amusement were provided spittoons of infinite capacity and generous gape. Most of the men wore frock-coats and top-hats, – the things that we in India put on at a wedding breakfast if we possessed them, – but they all spat. They spat on principle. The spittoons were on the staircases, in each bedroom – yea, and in chambers even more sacred than these. They chased one into retirement, but they blossomed in chiefest splendour round the Bar, and they were all used, every reeking one of 'em.

Nor were San Franciscans much more prepossessing when they used their mouths to speak:

They delude themselves into the belief that they talk English, – *the* English – and I have already been pitied for speaking with 'an English accent.' The man who pitied me spoke, so far as I was concerned, the language of thieves. And they all do . . . Again and again I loitered at the heels of a couple of resplendent beings, only to overhear, when I expected the level voice of culture, the *staccato* 'Sez he', 'Sez I,' that is the mark of the white servant-girl all the world over.

Rud even claimed that 'the American has no language', that instead 'he is dialect, slang, provincialism, accent, and so forth'.[5]

Most Anglo-Indians of the 1880s would probably have felt contempt for the raw brashness of California, but Rud's volley of sneers served a more particular purpose. To emphasise the provincialism of San Francisco was surely a way of deflecting his concern about how, as a colonial, he himself might shortly appear in London. Dickens's *American Notes* some fifty years earlier had been characterised by its attacks on the vulgarity and incorrectness of American English; and taking a similar tack, as with the spittoons, Rud was – consciously or not – placing himself in the position of the great English author touring the provinces. It was a point tacitly acknowledged by the publishers of the pirated edition of his Letters, which were likewise called *American Notes*.

This stance also required Rud to rearrange his literary pantheon. He now discovered that 'all the beauty of Bret Harte' was 'ruined' because 'through the roll of his rhythmical prose' one could catch 'the cadence of his peculiar fatherland'. In effect, he had it both ways. While wittily puncturing the benign image of San Francisco presented in Harte's celebrated poem about that city, Rud endorsed in his own account of his stay there the frontier image of California popularised by Harte's fiction. No sooner had he stepped off the boat than he witnessed the stabbing of a Chinaman. A sortie to a gambling den in Chinatown produced a dead Mexican, shot before his eyes over a poker game. In another equally unverifiable episode, a 'bunco-steerer' (card-sharp) tried – unsuccessfully of course – to get him drunk and fleece him.[6] Rud arrived wanting San Francisco to be reckless and roaring, lawless and uncouth; and that was how he presented it to himself and his *Pioneer* readers.

For whatever reason, the unattractively patronising tone rarely faltered throughout his three Letters from San Francisco. The local journalists were a particular target:

> 'Have you got reporters anything like our reporters on Indian news-papers?' 'We have not,' I said, and suppressed the 'thank God' rising to my lips. 'Why haven't you?' said he. 'Because they would die,' I said. It was exactly like talking to a child – a very rude little child. He would begin almost every sentence with: 'Now tell me some-thing about India,' and would turn aimlessly from one question to another without the least continuity. I was not angry, but keenly interested. The man was a revelation to me. To his questions I returned answers mendacious and evasive. After all, it really did not matter what I said. He could not understand.

Indeed, before encountering these infantile hacks, not even the experience of steaming through the Golden Gate had removed his sneer, as Rud 'saw with great joy that the block-house which guarded the mouth of the "finest harbour in the world, Sir," could be silenced by two gun-boats from Hong-Kong with safety, comfort, and despatch'. There was also his predictable refusal to be deceived by the 'freedom' of American democracy, which he presented as merely a sham, sustained by corruption and self-interest. The two political parties were equally beneath con-tempt: 'Sometimes he [the Democrat] says one thing and sometimes another, in order to contradict the Republican, who is always contradict-ing himself.' And, at his most aggressively English, Rud poured scorn on the way the democratic process was perpetually at the mercy of the largest cheque-book:

> Boss Buckley, by tact and deep knowledge of the seamy side of the city, won himself a following of voters. He sought no office himself, or rarely: but as his following increased he sold their services to the highest bidder, himself taking toll of the revenues of every office. He controlled the Democratic party in the city of San Francisco. The people appoint their own judges. Boss Buckley's people appointed judges. These judges naturally were Boss Buckley's property.[7]

During his three weeks in San Francisco, Rud spent a good deal of time at

the local Bohemian Club, to which before leaving Allahabad he had been
given an introduction and which now granted him honorary membership.
Its emblem was the owl, and Rud knocked off some lively stanzas, reflecting how he was genuinely flattered by this honour:

> Men said, but here I know they lied,
>   The owl was of a sullen clan
> Whose voice upon the lone hillside
>   Forboded ill to mouse and man –
> A terror noiseless in the flight,
> A hooknosed hoodlum of the night.
>
> But I have found another breed,
>   An owl of fine artistic feelings,
> A connoisseur of wine and weed
>   Who flutters under frescoed ceilings
> Nor scorns to bid the passing guest
> Abide a season in his nest . . .[8]

Yet even here, Rud's far from effortless superiority soon resurfaced. The
occasion was a banquet at the club in honour of Lieutenant Carlin, the
naval hero of a recent cyclone off Samoa, and Rud wrote it up as a
grotesque display of patriotic 'blatherumskite':

It was my first introduction to the American Eagle screaming for all
it was worth. The Lieutenant's heroism served as a peg from which
those silver-tongued ones turned themselves loose and kicked. They
ransacked the clouds of sunset, the thunderbolts of Heaven, the
deeps of Hell, and the splendours of the Resurrection, for tropes and
metaphors, and hurled the result at the head of the guest of the
evening. Never since the morning stars sang together for joy, I
learned, had an amazed creation witnessed such superhuman brav-
ery as that displayed by the American navy in the Samoa cyclone. . . .
Then, according to rule, they produced their dead, and across the
snowy table-cloths dragged the corpse of every man slain in the
Civil War, and hurled defiance at 'our natural enemy' (England, so
please you!) 'with her chain of fortresses across the world'.

For the United States to be cocking a snook at British power must indeed have seemed the final absurdity. Yet the fun of debunking American pretensions was tempered for Rud by an awareness that, for the sake of good copy, he was betraying his position as an honorary club member. Consequently, his account of the banquet wound up with a few semi-conciliatory gestures designed to take some of the sting out of his attack. He reiterated his praise of Carlin, in what was to become a characteristic term of approval ('He was a man'); he agreed with the richest local businessman that the United States's 'desire to chaw up England' was really 'a sort of family affair'; and he concluded that America was 'a very great country', even if it was 'not yet Heaven with electric lights and plush fittings, as the speakers professed to believe'.[9] These placatory gestures proved futile. One member, subsequently reading Rud's comments on San Francisco, was so incensed that he ripped the poem about the owl out of the club album. Presumably its 'fine artistic feelings' had also been hurt.

On 16 June, in carefree mood, he took the train to Portland, Oregon, spending much of the journey (he told Mrs Hill) 'in the smoker swapping stories' with the secretary to a life insurance company and a 'small millionaire'. He christened the insurance man 'Portland' and the millionaire 'California', while they nicknamed him 'England' or 'Johnny Bull'. Rud particularly took to 'California' – 'a white-headed langur [long-tailed monkey] who chews tobacco owns cattle-ranches and ships and tells the wildest and most improbable anecdotes in the voice of a slightly tired archangel' – and on a steamboat from Portland up the Columbia River to the Dalles was enchanted by his river know-how.[10] The three became such bosom pals that they even had a day's fishing together in the Clackamas. An ecstatic Rud landed his very first salmon:

My hands were cut and bleeding. I was dripping with sweat, spangled like [a] harlequin with scales, wet from the waist down, nose-peeled by the sun, but utterly, supremely, and consummately happy. He, the beauty, the darling, the daisy, my Salmon Bahadur, weighed twelve pounds; and I had been seven-and-thirty minutes bringing him to bank! He had been lightly hooked on the angle of the right jaw, and the hook had not wearied him. That hour I sat among princes and crowned heads – greater than them all.

Next day, after an evening's reminiscences 'of fierce warfare with the Indians' from the old farmer with whom they stayed the night, he and 'California' travelled on to Tacoma (at the head of Puget Sound), which Rud quickly wrote off as another raw, money-mad town of overweening pretensions. The hotel stationery and local newspapers might claim that it 'bore on its face all the advantages of the highest civilisation', but for him its most notable features were 'the foundations in brick and stone of a gigantic opera house and the blackened stumps of the pines'.[11] Not to mention, he told Mrs Hill, the local mosquitoes: 'When you have killed one on your manly brow you feel as if you had upset a bottle of claret there.'[12]

After saying goodbye to 'California', Rud took the steamer up the Sound to Vancouver. On the way they passed the charred remains of Seattle, which had burnt down a few weeks earlier. Where the business quarters had stood, Rud recorded, 'there was a horrible black smudge, as though a Hand had come down and rubbed the place smooth'. Vancouver – itself rebuilt after a devastating fire three years earlier – lacked the frenetic bustle, the boasting and, not least, the spitting that Rud had found so repugnant across the border. Indeed, not only was Canada unAmerican, it was positively English, 'full of Englishmen who speak the English tongue correctly and with clearness, avoiding more blasphemy than is necessary, and taking a respectable length of time to getting outside their drinks'. Rud was so taken with Canada during his few days there that he even purchased two lots in the Mount Pleasant area of Vancouver, comprising, as he jauntily put it, 'some four hundred well-developed pines, a few thousand tons of granite scattered in blocks at the roots of the pines, and a sprinkling of earth'. More seriously, he pointed out Vancouver's potential military importance as 'the head-end of a big railway', should the Suez Canal ever be out of action and Britain need 'to throw actual fighting troops into the East' to combat the Russian threat. All that was required was 'a fat earthwork fort upon a hill . . . a selection of big guns, a couple of regiments of infantry, and later on a big arsenal'.[13]

There followed a long, numbingly dull train journey to Livingston, gateway to Yellowstone Park, arriving on 2 July. His boredom compounded by a growing contempt for his fellow travellers' frontier tales of gun-toting lawlessness, it was only while crossing the Rockies through the two-mile Stampede Tunnel, lit by electric lights, that his interest suddenly quickened:

> Black darkness would be preferable, for the lamps just reveal the
> rough cutting of the rocks, and that is very rough indeed. The train
> crawls through, brakes down, and you can hear the water and little
> bits of stone falling on the roof of the car. Then you pray, pray fer-
> vently, and the air gets stiller and stiller, and you dare not take your
> unwilling eyes off the timber shoring lest a prop should fall, for lack
> of your moral support.

After a night in Livingston, 'a grubby little hamlet full of men without
clean collars and perfectly unable to get through one sentence unadorned
by three oaths', Rud pushed on by train towards Yellowstone Park itself,
where his plan was to make a five-day round trip. The celebrated tourist
attractions – the geysers, the mud-pools, the hot springs – were all duly
noted and described; but for a writer always happy to drop scenery for
soldiery, the mileage for his Letters came from conversations with various
US Army troopers in the park. Reassuringly, these encounters left Rud
convinced of the British Army's inherent superiority. 'There's not half
the discipline here that there is in the Queen's service,' he was told, while
according to a Cockney ex-Fusilier, 'this service isn't a patch on the Old
Country's service'. Safe in that knowledge, Rud could afford to relax a
little, allowing an ex-Cape Mounted Rifles to observe that British troops
were poor shots and, patting his revolver pouch, to remark that 'all our
men know that up to a hundred yards they are absolutely safe behind this
old thing'. Even so, the same soldier was then quoted adding: 'Just now it
seems that the English supply all the men to the American Army. That's
what makes them so good perhaps.'[14]

From Yellowstone Park he travelled to Salt Lake City, home of
Mormonism, 'that amazing creed and fantastic jumble of Mahometanism,
the Mosaical law, and imperfectly comprehended fragments of Free-
masonry'. Did this particular brand of fundamentalism remind Rud of the
hours he had been forced to spend at the Holloways learning the Collect
and the Scriptures? At the end of his stay he climbed to the top of the
garrison post and looked down over 'the City of the Saints as it lay in the
circle of its forbidding hills'. From this vantage point he imagined 'the

mass of human misery . . . the hills have seen' and was profoundly relieved that 'fate did not order me to be a brick in the up-building of the Mormon Church, that has so aptly established herself by the borders of a lake bitter, salt, and hopeless'.[15] For once in these travel letters, it was a moment of neither posturing nor genre description, but real and unmistakable feeling.

On he went to the Rockies, a train journey inspiring a sudden panegyric on the American people. They might be 'bleeding-raw at the edges, almost more conceited than the English, vulgar with a massive vulgarity . . . lawless and as casual as they are cocksure'; but 'for all that, they be the biggest, finest, and best people on the surface of the globe!' – and he loved them. He even offered an excited snapshot of 'the Anglo-American-German-Jew', who in a hundred years' time would be 'the finest writer, poet, and dramatist, 'specially dramatist, that the world as it recollects itself has ever seen'. Indeed, he would 'by virtue of his Jew blood – just a little, little drop – . . . be a musician and a painter too'. In the future, he prophesied, America would 'sway the world with one foot as a man tilts a see-saw plank!' The passage was a reminder of how, when his defences were lowered, Rud was still capable, as in India, of being exhilarated by the prospect of boundary-crossing, of racial mixture. Yet it was equally characteristic that the same Letter included a tirade against American 'versatility', as he grew increasingly nervous about the possibly disastrous consequences of slipshod workmanship on the railway line. He identified the American tendency to put 'the thing through somehow', a 'dangerous casualness' resulting from a jack-of-all-trades mentality.[16]

Rud had two memorable encounters during the long ride from Utah. The first was with a recently bereaved biscuit salesman, whom he privately dubbed 'the Man with the Sorrow'. In the dusty heat of the desert, Rud quizzed him about his Baptist faith and its consolations with a fine mixture of compassion and irony:

'You must experience religion,' he repeated, his mouth twitching and his eyes black-ringed with his recent loss. 'You must experience religion. You can't tell when you're goin' to get, or haow; but it will come – it will come, Sir, like a lightning stroke, an' you will wrestle with yourself before you receive full conviction and assurance.'
'How long does that take?' I asked reverently.

138

'It may take hours. It may take days. I knew a man in San Jo who lay under conviction for a month an' then he got the sperrit – as you *must* git it.'

Rud's sympathy for 'that poor human soul, broken and bowed by its loss' was genuine, tempering his usual suspicion of the evangelical spirit's capacity for 'nerving itself against each new pang of pain with the iterated assurance that it was safe against the pains of Hell'.[17]

That night, unable to fall asleep in his anxiety over the state of the track, he left his sleeper for a 'common car'. There he fell in with 'the stranded, broken-down, husband-abandoned actress of a fourth-rate, stranded, broken-down, manager-bereft company'. Although 'muzzy with beer', she related to him 'the history of a life so wild, so mixed, so desperately improbable, and yet so simply probable, and above all so quick – not fast – in its kaleidoscope changes that the *Pioneer* would reject any summary of it'. Unfaithful, alcoholic husband; dead baby; 'barn-stormings, insults, shooting-scrapes, and pitiful collapses of poor companies' – it was not, as Rud confided to his readers, 'a cheerful tale to listen to'. He could not but contrast her with a 'real actress' on the same train (but in the Pullman) who was travelling 'sumptuously with a maid and dressing-case'. At one point the thought occurred to the failed actress of appealing to the successful one for help; but, defeated by an awareness of the gulf between them, she 'broke down after several attempts to walk into the car jauntily as befitted a sister in the profession'.[18]

Rud's Letter dealing with this leg of his trip ended in a remarkable blend of caricature, sentiment and surreal humour. Reintroducing the Baptist commercial traveller (or 'drummer'), he summoned a final glimpse of himself and his three travelling companions. Falling asleep at last, the broken-down actress:

> became almost beautiful and quite kissable; while the Man with the Sorrow stood at the door between actress and actress and preached grim sermons on the certain end of each if they did not mend their ways and find regeneration through the miracle of the Baptist creed. Yes, we were a queer company coming up to the Rockies together. I was the luckiest, because when a break-down occurred, and we were delayed for twelve hours, I ate all the Baptist's sample-biscuits. They

were various in composition, but nourishing. Always travel with a 'drummer'.[19]

Finally, it was across the Great Divide and, with barely a glance at Denver, on to Omaha and Chicago. In Omaha, the melting-pot America that he had briefly celebrated became in Rud's eyes the nightmare vision of a city 'populated entirely by Germans, Poles, Slavs, Hungarians, Croats, Magyars, and all the scum of the Eastern European States'. The embodiment of this multi-ethnic nightmare was an undertaker called Gring, whose practice was to embalm the corpse and place it in a coffin with 'a plate-glass window in front', thereby revealing the upper half of the body. Consequently, he had only to dress the corpse from the waist up, leaving the rest covered by 'terrible cheap black cloth that falls down over the stark feet'. Simultaneously amused, appalled and fascinated, Rud watched closely Gring's thrifty provisions:

> He took up the body of a high-necked dinner-dress in subdued lilac, slashed and puffed and bedevilled with black, but, like the dress-suit, backless, and below the waist turning to shroud. 'That's for an old maid. But for young girls we give white with imitation pearls round the neck. That looks very pretty through the window of the casket – you see there's a cushion for the head – with flowers banked all round.'

Rud's attempts to impress upon Gring 'the grotesquerie – the giggling horror of it all' met with predictably scant success.[20]

Arriving in Chicago, the city that epitomised thrusting American capitalism, Rud's focus shifted from the undertaker's to the abattoir. The Chicago stock-yards, almost as soon as he saw them, became his governing metaphor for the squalid materialism of the American obsession with money:

> I climbed to the beginning of things and, perched upon a narrow beam, overlooked very nearly all the pigs ever bred in Wisconsin. They had just been shot out of the mouth of the viaduct and huddled together in a large pen. Thence they were flicked persuasively, a few at a time, into a smaller chamber, and there a man fixed tackle

to their hinder legs so that they rose in the air suspended from the railway of death. Oh! it was then they shrieked and called on their mothers and made promises of amendment, till the tackle-man punted them in their backs, and they slid head-down into a brick-floored passage, very like a big kitchen sink that was blood-red. There awaited them a red man with a knife which he passed jauntily through their throats, and the full-voiced shriek became a sputter, and then a fall as of heavy tropical rain.

The Dantesque Inferno then became complete for Rud when he saw a woman visiting the stock-yards for entertainment. This shocking blood-red vision came, in his mind, to stand not only for Chicago, but for a whole, pernicious civilisation:

And there entered that vermilion hall a young woman of large mould, with brilliantly scarlet lips, and heavy eyebrows, and dark hair that came in a 'widow's peak' on the forehead. She was well and healthy and alive, and she was dressed in flaming red and black, and her feet were cased in red leather shoes. She stood in a patch of sun-light, the red blood under her shoes, the vivid carcasses stacked round her, a bullock bleeding its life away not six feet away from her, and the death-factory roaring all round her. She looked curi-ously, with hard, bold eyes, and was not ashamed.

Then said I: 'This is a special Sending. I have seen the City of Chicago.' And I went away to get peace and rest.[21]

'Peace and rest' he found in Pennsylvania with Mrs Hill and her family. Her father, the Reverend Taylor, was President of Beaver College for women, a Methodist foundation, and it was there that Rud stayed with the Hills during the two fortnight-long visits he made between late July and early September. He spent most of his time happily on a couch 'smoking, reading, and meditating, but not doing much writing', Mrs Hill noted.[22] Rud also met her younger sister, Caroline. The three of them with various other Taylor relations were to sail together to Liverpool on 25 September, and Mrs Hill and Caroline were then to go on to India to join Alec. 'How is Miss Carrie's badminton?' Rud asked Mrs Hill in a letter in August, and there is no evidence that at this stage there was anything more than flirtatious banter between them.[23] Instead, he concentrated on providing his Anglo-Indian readers with a coda to his American travels. It was, after all that had gone before, a remarkably tactful effort. He began, in deliberately moderate terms, with some reservations about the future of the United States, anticipating overcrowding, overuse of natural resources and racial tension. Then – in a complete volte-face after the derision he had previously poured on US nationalism – he claimed that what the English could learn from the American people was 'patriotism':

> They believe in their land and its future, and its honour, and its glory, and they are not ashamed to say so. From the largest to the least runs this same proud, passionate conviction to which I take off my hat and for which I love them.

Whereupon, working himself up into a lather of nationalistic fervour and pride – as well as perhaps glimpsing a future literary self – he proclaimed the necessity for 'a poet who shall give the English *the* song of their own, own country – which is to say, of about half the world'. And from there he galloped on, even more grandiosely, imagining the need for the composition of:

> the greatest song of all – The Saga of the Anglo-Saxon all round the earth . . . For We, even We who share the earth between us as no gods have ever shared it, we also are mortal in the matter of our single selves. Will any one take the contract?

After 'these rambling notions', he switched abruptly to 'the infinite peace of the tiny township of Musquash', his code name for Beaver, set in 'a rolling, wooded, English landscape'. Its people 'went straightest to this heart', asserted Rud, because – a benign wave to ancestors on both sides of his family – 'they were Methody folk for the most part – ay, Methody as ever trod a Yorkshire Moor, or drove on a Sunday to some chapel of the Faith in the Dales'. Celebrating this 'absolutely fresh, wholesome, sweet life that paid due reverence to the things of the next world, but took good care to get enough tennis in the cool of the evening', he overlaid the rural Yorkshire scene with a small-town America drawn explicitly from Louisa

May Alcott. 'Meg and Joe [sic] and Beth and Amy': he claimed to have met them all. The ensuing eulogy on 'the American maiden' included a tribute skilfully designed to cover both Mrs Hill and her younger sister (and perhaps Rud's own ideal for a wife):

> She is a companion, in the fullest sense of the word, of the man she weds, zealous for the interest of the firm, to be consulted in time of stress and to be called upon for help and sympathy in time of danger.

Only in the Letter's final paragraph was there anything remotely critical or even ironic about his hosts' home-ground, as he took leave by imagining with wry bonhomie the future life of the meek young men of Musquash: 'They will make good citizens and possess the earth, and eventually wed one of the nice white muslin dresses. There are worse things in this world than being "one of the boys" in Musquash.'[24]

At the last, the tone was less Louisa May Alcott than Mark Twain, whom Rud had interviewed in Elmira, New York, probably between his two visits to Beaver. Their talk, which Rud naturally wrote up as a scoop interview, ranged widely. On copyright, Twain laid down that a writer should have 'as complete a control over his copyright as he would over his real estate'. Did Rud tell his story about the Yokohama bookshop? If so, he did not mention it. But when Twain posited a sequel to *Tom Sawyer* that contained two endings (in one Tom becoming a member of Congress, in the other being hanged), Rud objected like a true fan, declaring that the character 'isn't your property any more. He belongs to us.' Autobiography called forth a characteristic paradox from Twain – 'in genuine autobiography . . . it is impossible for a man to tell the truth about himself or to avoid impressing the reader with the truth about himself'. Rud left, he says, with one especially useful piece of advice from the master (or 'Mark', as he was calling him by the end of the piece): '"Get your facts first, and" – the voice dies away to an almost inaudible drone – "then you can distort 'em as much as you please."'[25]

The trip across America, with all those hours spent on trains, had been a time for personal reflection, as well as for absorbing his impressions of a new country. Nostalgia for the harsh certainties of his old life jostled with speculation about his literary future in England. Rud also knew that, if things worked out, this sequence of Letters would be the last writing he would specifically address to his Anglo-Indian audience. A sense of guilt at abandoning that particular mission in life pervaded the heartfelt, if mawkish, final flourish to the Letter describing the journey to Yellowstone Park:

> O excellent and toil-worn public of mine – men of the brotherhood, griffins new joined from the February troopers, and gentlemen waiting for your off-reckonings – take care of yourselves and keep well! It hurts so when any die. There are so few of Us, and we know one another too intimately.[26]

Yet, if one part of his mind was looking back elegiacally to India, another was looking forward just as eagerly to England. 'The Spectator,' he informed Mrs Hill soon afterwards, 'has given me a "splendid review" of Soldiers Three.'[27] And, before sailing, he found that another London weekly, the St James's Gazette, was promising to keep 'our eye on that young man'.[28] Rud was nervous, ready, and not yet twenty-four.

10

London and Fame

The crossing to Liverpool took ten days. During the voyage Kipling concealed whatever apprehensions he may have felt about the future by playing court jester to Mrs Hill and her party. A limerick, with the note '9:35.
Had a good hand at Euchre', suggests a mood of noisy fun:

> There once were four people at Euchre
> Who played for mere Love – not for Lucre –
> But the row that they made
> O'er each diamond & spade
> Was suggestive of warfare not Euchre.[1]

The note was dated 30 September, the midpoint of the voyage. By then
the second line probably held an additional significance for Kipling and
Caroline Taylor, and on 9 October, five days after the boat docked, Mrs
Hill recorded in her diary: 'Carrie engaged to R.K.'[2]

Not much is known about Caroline – and, according to Trix, who met her
briefly a few months later, there was not much to know. In old age, Trix
recalled her as 'plump and plain and on the surface with none of her
sister's charm', and dubbed her 'the snub-nosed girl with the cottage-loaf
figure'.[3] Trix's recollections of the women in her brother's life were usually
crushing, but in any case Caroline's real attributes (or lack of them) were

145

beside the point. Her appeal to Kipling was that she was the sister of the unavailable Mrs Hill. The contrast between his letters to Caroline and those he wrote to Mrs Hill (both before and during the engagement) made it clear that his feelings for Caroline were mostly a willed fiction. Part of Mrs Hill's attraction was that she *was* unavailable, and though Kipling was often flagrant in his demands for her attention, affection and interest, he did in some sense love her. As for Caroline, whatever shine he took to her wore off almost as soon as she and Mrs Hill sailed for India on 25 October. A week later, in his first letter to Caroline as an engaged man, he was already scraping the barrel of epistolary love-talk:

> I am an ass. Perhaps you didn't know that before but I am. There lie in my waste paper basket the torn fragments of three long letters to you. Excellent letters they were but I destroyed 'em because I was afraid of the coldly critical eye that would read 'em. Heart o' mine you, as well as I, must have discovered by this time that the writing of love letters is no easy thing.[4]

That her older sister's clever, amusing friend was paying his attentions to her was perhaps enough to explain the engagement on Caroline's side; and shipboard intimacy and her relationship to Mrs Hill may have been enough to explain Kipling's proposal. But the engagement also had other things to offer him, not least an undemanding form of emotional insurance. While Caroline continued on to India, he could be confident that at least his love life was under control – and not only under control, but indefinitely deferred. In fact, he was repeating the pattern of seven years before. Then, off to India and an uncertain future, he had left considering himself engaged to the absent Flo Garrard; now, returning to England and an equally uncertain future, he got engaged to the equally absent Caroline.

The major uncertainty facing Kipling was his literary future. Would English editors and publishers want his work or, now that he was on the spot, would they put him down as just another colonial? Should he build on the positive reviews of his Indian and Anglo-Indian output or try a new direction? Prose or verse? Short stories or novels? Was he going to fit into the London literary world?

His first letter to Caroline after her departure outlined his short-term objectives with a revealing mixture of vagueness and determination:

> I did not come to England to write myself out at first starting – not by a very long sight. This seemeth to me the more perfect way. To go slowly and only do sufficient magazine work to enable me to rub along comfortably while I turn my attention to the novels and the books. A man can fritter himself away on piece work and be only but a very little the richer for it . . . Catch me putting my head into that old noose again – and me hardly recovered from the constant surprises of seven years' journalism.[5]

Ironically, one of his first moves was to follow up an introduction to Mowbray Morris, editor of the prestigious *Macmillan's Magazine*, who also acted as an overseas art critic for the *Pioneer*. With Morris, Kipling arranged to furnish a regular supply of short stories and verse for *Macmillan's*, much as he had done for the CMG and the *Pi*. But it is plain from his letter that he was only 'putting my head into that old noose again' for the security of Morris's £300 a year retainer, which would free him to work on 'the novels and the books' with which he really hoped to make his name.

Mowbray Morris, who would have come across Kipling's work via the *Pioneer*, was taken with Rud's lively personal charm, and promptly welcomed him into the Macmillan stable. 'I hope you read the ballad of the King's Mercy in my last number and thought it good,' Morris was soon writing enthusiastically to another young writer, A V Baillie. 'The writer is a young fellow by name of Rudyard Kipling – queer name is it not? . . . He is a most amusing companion, full of life and fun, very shrewd withal, and I think not likely to be spoiled.'[6] Published in *Macmillan's* in November 1889, 'The Ballad of the King's Jest' marked the beginning of a spate of Kipling's poems and short stories to appear in the magazine over the following year, including: 'The Ballad of East and West', 'The Head of the District', 'The Courting of Dinah Shadd', 'Without Benefit of Clergy' and 'On Greenhow Hill'.

Another enthusiastic London editor was Sidney Low, for whose *St James's Gazette* Kipling's old boss, Stephen Wheeler, was now working. Low approached Kipling through Wheeler and tried unsuccessfully to persuade him to an arrangement similar to the one with *Macmillan's*. Kipling refused, but Low was happy to help him 'keep his pot boiling' by taking anything Rud might offer. Even before they met, Low had been singing the praises of 'this marvellous youth who had dawned upon the Eastern horizon', whom he declared to be potentially 'greater than Dickens'. And when they did meet, he was magnetised by the 'short, dark, young man' who walked into his office 'with a bowler hat, a rather shabby tweed overcoat, an emphatic voice, a charming smile, and behind his spectacles a pair of the brightest eyes I had ever seen'.[7]

Another literary nabob whom Kipling bowled over was Coulson Kernahan, the English editor of *Lippincott's Magazine*. They bumped into each other the following year outside Edmund Gosse's house:

> His words were few – 'Sorry, sir. My fault' – but had I, long years after, chanced upon him again, and without knowing who he was, I should, on hearing his voice, have told myself: 'He and I once rubbed shoulders on the doorstep of 29 Delamere Terrace.' I have never heard another voice with any resemblance to Kipling's, for, like himself, it was charged with personality . . . It was suave and silky . . . it had a pleasant and polished persuasiveness . . . it was never raised, even if he had cause to raise it.[8]

Even someone as hard to impress as Twain was to remark that Kipling's talk 'might be likened to footprints, so strong and definite was the impression it left behind'.[9]

Indeed, Kipling's conversational powers played as significant a part in his easy conquest of the London literary scene as his existing publications. If Low had been initially struck by Kipling's charming smile and bright eyes, over lunch the same day in the grill-room of Sweeting's Restaurant in Fleet Street he was even more taken with his 'frank and communicative' manner. In fact, 'he talked in those days with the same abandon and energy as he wrote'.[10] The short stories 'The Comet of the Season', 'The Limitations of Pambé Serang' and 'The Battle of Rupert Square' each appeared in the pages of the *St James's Gazette* (or 'the Jimmy' as Kipling liked to call it) during the closing weeks of 1889.

Low later claimed that 'The Comet of the Season', unsigned and never collected by Kipling, was his first publication after returning to England.

1. The Father and the Mother, Lockwood and Alice Kipling, taken around the time of their marriage in 1865.

2. Rud as a baby on Alice's knee, 1866.

3. Rud as a toddler: the 'Little Friend of all the world'.

4. Rud as a small child: 'rather noisy and spoilt'.

5. Rud, nearly six, about the time he entered 'The House of Desolation'.

6. Lorne Lodge, 'The House of Desolation', as it looks today.

7. Rud as a sixteen-year-old schoolboy and in love with Flo.

8. Schoolboy Rud amongst his peers, 1882.

9 & 10. Rud and Trix: the authors of *Echoes*.

11. Mrs Hill and her husband at Belvedere, Allahabad.

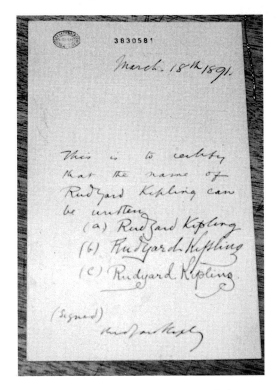

12. The newly famous Kipling replying to an autograph-hunter, 18 March 1891.

13. Kipling's 'brother' Wolcott Balestier who had the capacity to make others feel special.

14. Caroline Balestier before her marriage to Kipling; 'an admirable wife for a genius'.

In itself just a 'turnover', it was interesting as an early example of how Kipling used his art as a form of natural magic to try to forestall Fate. With publishers and editors falling at his feet, the idea that he might be merely another 'comet of the season' obviously preyed on his mind. By imagining the possibility in fiction, he tried to prevent it happening in reality – a literary equivalent to knocking on wood. He would repeat variations of this superstitious gambit throughout his life.

Before their departure Caroline and Mrs Hill had settled Kipling into rooms in Embankment Chambers on Villiers Street behind Charing Cross Station, and with the rent taken care of by his deals with Morris and Low, Kipling was free to explore the literary world. One of his first steps was to approach Andrew Lang, who had reviewed him so favourably. By late October Kipling was already on sufficiently friendly terms to send Lang a comic verse letter in which, in the character of Bret Harte's Truthful James, he imagined Lang and Rider Haggard on a lecture tour of the USA promoting their collaborative romance *The World's Desire*.

Lang's response to this literary calling card was a long, appreciative, unsigned review of *Plain Tales from the Hills* in the *Daily News* on 2 November. Only the second British reviewer of the collection, he was once again positive and discriminating. While welcoming 'a talent so fresh, facile and spontaneous' and picking out 'False Dawn', 'In the House of Suddhoo', 'Beyond the Pale' and 'The Gate of the Hundred Sorrows' for particular praise, Lang shrewdly put his finger on a 'fault' that was to recur throughout Kipling's writing, namely 'a certain knowingness and familiarity, as of one telling a story in a smoking-room rather late in the evening'. He was also the first to observe that the stories' appeal was not simply literary. Lang felt the thrill of Empire, the allure of the imperial mission: 'It may safely be said that *Plain Tales from the Hills* will teach more of India, of our task there, of the various peoples whom we try to rule, than many Blue Books. Here is an unbroken field of actual romance, here are incidents as strange as befall in any city of dream, any Kôr or Zu-Vendis, and the incidents are true.'[11] Not surprisingly, over thirty years later Kipling would remember Lang, 'who was immensely good to me when I was a youngster'.[12]

Simultaneously he made the acquaintance of the other major turnstile for aspiring young writers – the critic Edmund Gosse, who by the end of

1889 was declaring that Kipling was 'going to be one of the greatest writers of the day'.[13] Gosse tried to take him under his wing, and a couple of years later, in October 1891, did much to consolidate Kipling's reputation by publishing a long, perceptive appreciation of his early work. Together Gosse and Lang gave Kipling an automatic entrée to the inner circles of literary London. In a starry-eyed letter, as early as 1 November 1889, he told Caroline and Mrs Hill how he had dined at the Savile Club, the haunt of such literary notables as Stevenson, Henley, Hardy, Haggard, Besant and Saintsbury; and he noted with wonder that 'everyone seems to know me'.[14] In short, he had become a phenomenon.

The approach made by John Addington Symonds exemplified the stir Kipling created. Although nothing ultimately came of this connection, and Kipling was soon describing him as 'a sugary gushing sort of a Johnnie', Symonds's overtures illustrate the wide range of expectations that Kipling aroused among the literati, even before his arrival in London.[15] The episode, furthermore, offers a forcible reminder of how little Kipling's early work had established his allegiances in the minds of his contemporaries.

Symonds – essayist, poet, Renaissance historian, and discreet campaigner for homosexual law reform – felt, as his biographer Phyllis Grosskurth remarks, 'a sense of personal triumph when he found a painting, a poem, or a novel which seemed to glow with masculine love'. And she quotes a letter of 22 June 1891 to Gosse in which Symonds exclaimed: 'What a number of Urnings [homosexuals] are being portrayed in novels now! . . . I stumble on them casually & find the same note.'[16] Perhaps inevitably, reading *Soldiers Three* in the summer of 1889, Symonds thought he had made another discovery. On 23 June he wrote to his friend Horatio Forbes Brown in the first flush of excitement:

The 'Soldiers Three' has arrived. I mean to get more of this man's books – and perhaps to write to him. I cannot quite understand the Envoy. When first I read it I *felt* the lover in it; and then I got confused because it seemed to be the artist in a mysteriously religious mood. It is singularly touching – especially these lines,

'Because I wrought them for Thy sake,

And breathed in them mine agonies.'

What does that mean with reference to so humorous and remark-ably realistic a sketch of character?[17]

In fact, Symonds appears already to have written the letter in question (now lost) earlier that same month, though Kipling did not receive it until he reached London in early October.

Reading between the lines of Kipling's reply on 15 October, it sounds as though Symonds had cautiously sounded out the young author's atti-tudes to homosexual love. Whether Kipling realised this is a moot point. His friendly and deferential answer was either suitably guarded or (more probably) rather naïve. After thanking Symonds for his 'generous praise' of 'an unknown manufacturer of books – a savage from among savages', he continued:

In regard to my three friends [Mulvaney, Learoyd and Ortheris] whatever merit lies in my work comes from the fact that I loved 'em – very much, I take it, as you loved a man called Benevenuto [sic] Cellini and in your translation [of Cellini's *Autobiography*] showed that love – so that he became alive and swaggered and brawled and beat his way across the pages.[18]

It would be interesting to know quite what Symonds made of that 'very much, I take it, as you loved a man called Benevenuto Cellini': as encour-agement or ingenuousness?

His subsequent comments about Kipling suggest a mixture of responses in which literary and personal judgement became more and more inter-twined. To Horatio Brown on 18 November he described how he had now actually met the 'author of "Soldiers Three"', but all one can reliably deduce from the letter is that, like everyone else who encountered Kipling at this time, he was enormously impressed: 'It seems to me that he is going to make a name in England. The Savile Club was all on the *qui vive* about him, when I lunched there once with Gosse.' To Gosse on 8 December Symonds tried to be more specific, but though still fascinated seemed unable to make up his mind:

I wonder what it is that you find fetching in Kipling. I do not think I could define my own feeling about him. But I believe it is the keen appreciation which the man has of raw native humanity. I am sorry to be brought gradually to the conviction that, for literary purposes, he cooks this raw humanity & makes clever salines out of it. But the underlying sentiment is strong.

Thereafter Symonds lost interest in Kipling as a potential 'Urning' and became disappointed in him as a writer. A year later he had decided that as Kipling 'multiplied', so 'the weak side of his work became more apparent, while the stuff dwindled for a want of aliment' – and that, finally and damningly, what he lacked was 'Distinction'. Kipling had gone 'up like a rocket & come down like a stick': the comet of the season.[19]

By the time of this verdict, the end of 1890, Kipling's own attitude had already gone through some dramatic shifts. His instant social and literary success in clubs like the Savile soon lost its appeal as he became increasingly uncertain about his position in England and his status as an 'English' writer. These anxieties began to develop almost as soon as he stepped off the boat. His description of himself to Symonds as 'a savage from among savages' was not merely polite self-deprecation; it revealed a deepening ambivalence about how he now saw himself. In the United States, he had happily cast himself as 'the Englishman', as 'Johnny Bull' horrified by American provincialism and vulgarity. Now, barely had he landed in England than he began to wonder whether 'Home' itself was a foreign country. 'Moved by my small success,' he continued to Symonds, 'I am come to London to start that queer experience known as a literary career. At present the tide goes with me and I hope to bring the three men to the notice of the Englishman. But there is no light in this place, and the people are savages living in black houses and ignorant of everything beyond the Channel.'[20]

These feelings of alienation found eloquent expression in some verses called 'In Partibus', which he wrote on 11 November and promptly despatched to the CMG:

> The 'buses run to Battersea,
> The 'buses run to Bow,

London and Fame

The 'buses run to Westbourne Grove,
   And Notting Hill also;
But I am sick of London Town,
   From Shepherd's Bush to Bow . . .

The sky, a greasy soup-tureen,
   Shuts down atop my brow.
Yes, I have sighed for London Town
   And I have got it now:
And half of it is fog and filth,
   And half is fog and row . . .

But I consort with long-haired things
   In velvet collar-rolls,
Who talk about the Aims of Art,
   And 'theories' and 'goals',
And moo and coo with womenfolk
   About their blessed souls . . .

It's Oh to meet an Army man,
   Set up, and trimmed and taut,
Who does not spout hashed libraries
   Or think the next man's thought,
And walks as though he owned himself,
   And hogs his bristles short.

Hear now a voice across the seas
   To kin beyond my ken,
If ye have ever filled an hour
   With stories from my pen,
For pity's sake send some one here
   To bring me news of men! . . .[21]

Perhaps the very ease with which he won acceptance among London's literary coteries fuelled Kipling's sudden distaste for the Mother Country. He certainly seems to have felt that these literary clubs, so eager to solicit his membership, could hardly represent the Parnassian heights of which he had dreamt less than nine months before in India. Instead he found himself forging a renewed bond with his Anglo-Indian compatriots, the 'kin beyond my ken' as he now called them. The phrase was revealing: literally, they were 'kin' who were beyond his *immediate* 'ken'; but, at another level, he was acknowledging that they were 'kin' in a way he had never previously understood, or fully valued.

Re-emerging in Kipling's disenchanted vision of England was the same distaste for 'effeminate' Englishmen (in contrast to the robust guardians of Empire), which he had expounded back in the mid-1880s in letters to his cousin Margaret. The 'long-haired things/In velvet collar-rolls' who 'talk about the Aims of Art' and 'moo and coo with womenfolk/About their blessed souls' were the direct descendants of the 'Young Man of the present day' that Kipling had castigated to his cousin for his 'diseased vanity', his 'rotten little brains', and his 'fenced in, railway ticket, kind of life at home'. But what had then been a straw-man set up to put his cousin right about India was now his daily dining partner. Another letter of early November 1889, to Mrs Hill, revealed the mixture of aggression and defensiveness he soon felt towards these flattering, but increasingly unwelcome, attentions:

> London is a vile place and Anstey and Haggard and Lang and Co. are pressing on me the wisdom of identifying myself with some 'set', while the long-haired literati of the Savile Club are swearing that I 'invented' my soldier talk in Soldiers Three. Seeing that not one of these critters has been within earshot of a barrack, I am naturally wrath.[22]

And there were further disillusionments. Meredith, previously deployed by Kipling as one of his cultural counters in his American Letters, proved in person 'full to a painful overflowing of elaborated epigrammatic speech which on the first fizz strikes one as deuced good' – but 'five minutes later one cannot remember what on earth it was all about'. Then, six weeks later, at an 'awful dinner' with George Macmillan, he encountered the high priest of aestheticism, Walter Pater, who 'moaned and frothed and yammered over Blake's poems'. Unfortunately, Kipling crisply informed Mrs Hill: 'Pater's remarkably like a gorilla – no, a *langur*.'[23]

By stark contrast that same month, December 1889, Kipling found relief in harking back to the India he had left behind, as he published one of his most famous panegyrics of raw masculine courage on the borders of Empire, 'The Ballad of East and West'. The opening line, 'Oh, East is East, and West is West, and never the twain shall meet', has of course become proverbial, almost infamous, because of its dogmatic assertion of an unbridgeable racial gulf between peoples. Ironically, the poem itself went on to tell the story of how 'there is neither East nor West, Border, nor Breed, nor Birth,/When two strong men stand face to face, though they come from the ends of the earth!' and imagined a friendship based on a mutual recognition of honour and courage that crossed racial boundaries.[24] The poem was a remarkable testament to how, away from the day-to-day pressures of Anglo-India, Kipling was able to re-imagine the East as the place where borders could cease to operate. In India, he had been consistently drawn to tales energised by the illicit excitement of cultural 'boundary-crossing', but had been unable to envisage anything other than a tragic resolution to these situations. Now, at one remove, he could for the first time conceive of this crossing of cultures as a meeting of equals. East and Anglo-Indian West were 'two strong men', both infinitely preferable to the sickly aesthetes of London, and through the bonding of Kamal and the Colonel's son, Kipling was able to re-create, without anxiety, his enthusiasm for going out of bounds. Yet, it was not entirely inappropriate that, over the years, the opening line should have become divorced from its context. Kipling archly noted this phenomenon in his autobiography:

> Long ago I stated that 'East was East and West was West and never the twain should meet.' It seemed right, for I had checked it by the card, but I was careful to point out circumstances under which cardinal points ceased to exist. Forty years rolled on, and for a fair half of them the excellent and uplifted of all lands would write me, apropos of each new piece of broad-minded folly in India, Egypt, or Ceylon, that East and West *had* met – as, in their muddled minds, I suppose they had.[25]

Ironically, although he was complaining here about persistent misreadings of the line, by the time he came to write this passage he himself had come to accept the absolute separation of East and West, with no trace of his former excitement for the exceptional moments when these boundaries could cease to exist.

If the Savile was proving uncomfortable, two places he could feel sure of a 'welcome as warm as the food' were the homes of his aunts, Georgie Burne-Jones and Aggie Poynter. In his first few weeks he was a regular visitor to both households, occasionally moving on from tea in one to dinner in the other. He found himself getting on particularly well with his cousin Ambrose Poynter, Aunt Aggie's elder son, who – though only a year or so younger than himself – at once adopted Kipling as a mentor. Ambo, son of the Academician painter Sir Edward Poynter, was experiencing the not unusual problem of being the son of a famous father. He also had literary ambitions, and after dinner at the Poynters on 13 November the already experienced author had a 'M.S. volume of poems and A FIVE ACT TRAGEDY IN BLANK VERSE!' thrust into his hands. Unfortunately, Kipling added to Mrs Hill, the tragedy suffered from over-immersion in Shelley and Shakespeare, while Ambo 'estimates all his poems *not* by the thing actually put down in black and white but by all the glorious inchoate fancies that flashed through his brain when his pen was in his hand'. The blame lay, Kipling portentously concluded, in Ambo's 'over-selfconsciousness' and 'morbid condition of the nerves', the characteristic sins of 'the young man of the Nineteenth century'.[26] Neither family link nor friendship prevented him eighteen months later from using Ambo and his confessions as a model for Charlie Mears, the talentless young bank clerk with literary aspirations, in 'The Finest Story in the World'.

As for Kipling's other male cousin of his own age, Phil Burne-Jones, at this time a promising painter in his own right, he had apparently got himself entangled with a 'rascally firm of publishers' of 'a mean little rag which professed to publish the lives of "Eminent Workers"'; and on 14 November, writing to Mrs Hill, Kipling was able to congratulate himself on having extricated the 'phool Phil' from their clutches. Phil's sister Margaret was by this time married to the classical scholar J W Mackail, and Kipling spent an evening with the young couple in 'their funny little-old house in Kensington'. If, with Phil and Ambo, he could see himself as the worldly-wise older brother, 'the delight and comfort' of Margaret's 'quiet little *ménage*' reminded him that, while engaged, he was also a young and lonely bachelor.[27]

Although Kipling clearly enjoyed re-establishing contact with his family, he was also determined to make his way without leaning too heavily on their assistance. 'People who asked for money, however justifiably, have it remembered against them,' he would recall in his autobiography. 'My rent was paid; I had my dress-suit; I had nothing to pawn save a collection of unmarked shirts picked up in all the ports; so I made shift to manage on what small cash I had in pocket.' His decision to live in Villiers Street, 'above an establishment of Harris the Sausage King, who, for tuppence, gave as much sausage and mash as would carry one from breakfast to dinner', was a declaration of independence – from his family, and equally from the fashionable world of the literati:

> My rooms were small, not over-clean or well-kept, but from my desk I could look out of my window through the fanlight of Gatti's Music-Hall entrance, across the street, almost on to its stage. The Charing Cross trains rumbled through my dreams on one side, the boom of the Strand on the other, while, before my windows, Father Thames under the Shot Tower walked up and down with his traffic.[28]

Sitting at his large roll-top desk, pipe in hand, Kipling would work from ten till four, banging out stories and poems. His desk bore the inscription, gouged with a Gurkha kukri in letters six inches high, 'Oft was I weary when I sat at thee', testament to the frustrations of keeping the pot boiling.[29]

Kipling shared the prevailing opinion that the short story, however good, was inherently inferior to the novel; his main goal, as he told Caroline, was to move on to 'the novels and the books'. A P Watt, the literary agent with whom the novelist Walter Besant had put him in touch, was telling him to 'Hurry up your novel . . . and become rich', and he knew that if he was to be more than a nine days' wonder, he had to get his novel under way as soon as possible. (Kipling later said of Watt, while recommending him to the South African writer Olive Schreiner, 'he is very kind and nice and does everything for you except – writing your book. That we have all to do by ourselves isn't it?'[30]) Not surprisingly, his thoughts turned to the unfinished manuscript of *Mother Maturin*, which he asked his parents in mid-November to forward to him from India. But even before it arrived, he had decided that it would not do.

Although the flow of stories and poems never dried up, Kipling became increasingly anxious as he cast around for the big work that would consolidate his reputation. A mysterious project entitled *The Book of the Forty-Five Mornings*, which was probably a collection of journalistic pieces and stories, was repeatedly advertised during 1890, but never published. As his travel letters for the *Pioneer* started to turn up in London, Kipling read them with nervous embarrassment, worried about how they might affect his standing. 'I wish the Pioneer would hurry up with those things and get them over,' he complained to Mrs Hill on 11 November. 'They hurt.'[31]

In early 1890 Kipling suffered some sort of breakdown. Whether there was a particular event or circumstance that triggered it, one can only guess from the scrappy evidence that survives. In an unsigned pencilled letter, postmarked 24 January, all he could say was: 'Can't write you anything this week. I'm better but my head is all queer and I am going to have it mended some day. Keep better than me.'[32] According to Mrs Hill, this poignantly cryptic note was addressed to her husband and was, she noted, 'the last thing that R.K. wrote when he went into that extreme illness in 1890 – and thought he had lost his mind – claiming that "drugs did it".'[33] A letter to her, or part of one, in early February offered a little more:

> you do well to say that the half year has begun. It has and I have broken up. My head has given out and I am forbidden work and I am to go away somewhere. This is the third time it has happened – last time was on the Honam on the Canton river but this time is the completest. I do not want, even if I deserved, your pity. I must go on alone now till the end of my time. I can do nothing to save myself from breaking up now and again.
>
> I hope you are keeping well. I am physically in perfect health but I can neither work nor think nor read and have been in this state for – since the 20th of January – alone. You and the doctors always laughed but I knew that the smash would come some day. It's nobody's fault but my own. Thank Alick for his letter and tell him I'm not well.

Between these two fragments was a longer letter from Kipling to the poet and editor W E Henley. For the most part this was another of his reverential bows to a literary notable, but it also mentioned, almost in passing, that the writer had been 'ordered off for a month's idleness now 'cause of my head'; and, thanking Henley for a copy of his *A Book of Verses*, the letter made one statement that reverberates very oddly: 'Since we be only islands shouting misunderstandings to each other across seas of speech or writing I am going to say nothing.'[34] The deliberately mixed metaphors – and distorted echoes of Donne and Matthew Arnold – convey a sense of bewildered despair about the impossibility of connecting or communicating with anyone else.

Had he received a telegram from Caroline breaking off their engagement? This might explain why he had made a point of describing himself to Mrs Hill as 'alone'. Caroline may have felt forced to end the relationship because of a letter Kipling wrote to her on 9 December in which he outlined his religious beliefs. She seems to have got the idea from Professor Hill that Kipling might be 'a veiled adherent of the Church of Rome', and he was writing to reassure her:

Chiefly I believe in the existence of a personal God to whom we are personally responsible for wrong doing – that it is our duty to follow and our peril to disobey the ten ethical laws laid down for us by Him or His prophets. I disbelieve directly in eternal punishment for reasons that would take too long to put down on paper. On the same grounds I disbelieve in an eternal reward. As regards the mystery of the Trinity and the Doctrine of Redemption I regard them most reverently but cannot give them implicit belief, accepting them rather as dogmas of the Church than as matters that rush to the heart. I would give much to believe in them absolutely . . . Summarised it comes to *I believe in God the Father Almighty maker of Heaven and Earth and in one filled with His spirit who did voluntarily die in the belief that the human race would be spiritually bettered thereby.*

I believe after having seen and studied eight or nine creeds in Justification by work rather than faith, and most assuredly do I believe in retribution both here and hereafter for wrong doing as I believe in a reward, here and hereafter for obedience to the Law.[35]

This was one of Kipling's few direct statements of faith and was particularly notable for its implicit rejection, in what he said about 'eternal punishment' and 'eternal reward', of Mrs Holloway's Evangelicalism. If Caroline (the daughter of a Methodist minister) was herself devout, one could imagine her being genuinely scandalised by her fiancé's declaration of 'disbelief' and by his assertion of Jesus's humanity rather than his divinity.

If Caroline did break off the engagement, Kipling, already under enormous strain, would have felt that the emotional safety-net he had so carefully constructed had suddenly disintegrated and that he was indeed 'alone'. Just as plausibly, however, one could imagine that it was he who ended the engagement as a result of his disturbed mental state. What we *do* know is that sometime during this period, probably in February, Kipling met Flo Garrard again. 'He met Flo again by chance, as in "The Light that Failed", and was instantly her slave again,' our only source, Trix, recalled. 'She refused him more than once – his love took a deal of killing – and I think she half accepted him, or he thought she did.'[36] Did he feel free to become Flo's slave because Caroline had broken their engagement? Or did he realise that he could not marry Caroline because of his unresolved feelings for Flo and end things himself? Equally uncertain is whether Kipling's breakdown was caused by, or a cause of, his passion for Flo. Whatever the actual sequence of events, the fragmentary evidence from these two months presents a picture of a very confused and unhappy time.

Characteristically, there is no reference to this traumatic period in Kipling's autobiography, unless it is obliquely transposed into his nightmarish account of seeing from his rooms in Villiers Street a man commit suicide:

> Once I faced the reflection of my own face in the jet-black mirror of the window-panes for five days. When the fog thinned, I looked out and saw a man standing opposite the pub where the barmaid lived. Of a sudden his breast turned dull red like a robin's, and he crumpled, having cut his throat. In a few minutes – seconds it seemed – a hand-ambulance arrived and took up the body. A pot-boy with a bucket of steaming water sluiced the blood off into the gutter, and what little crowd had collected went its way.[37]

The abrupt transition from five days of staring at his own reflection to this remarkably public suicide – of which there was no reference in his surviving letters – invites a psychological reading. Certainly if we came across such a passage in one of Kipling's own stories, we would connect the observer's state of mind with the incident on the street.

As usual, when he was up against it, Kipling was capable of creatively rearranging his life in order to overcome or displace a crisis. This time his way out was to join the 'Henley regatta' – Max Beerbohm's term for the diverse group of young writers and critics (including Stevenson, Yeats, Barrie, Grahame and Wells) whom Henley published in a succession of literary weeklies and monthlies between 1888 and 1897.

Henley was a rumbustious, domineering character, a literary bullock looking for a china shop, who inspired either strong affection or strong antipathy. Like Ezra Pound, with whom he had a certain amount in common, he had a passion for nicknames, and those who stayed for any time within his compass were likely to receive at least one. Kipling became interchangeably 'The Kipperling' or 'The Kip'. Henley's own name was synonymous with the Edinburgh-based *Scots Observer* (1888–90), then with its London successor, the *National Observer* (1890–4), and finally with the *New Review* (1894–7). Kipling would remember him as 'a jewel of an editor, with the gift of fetching the very best out of his cattle, with words that would astonish oxen', while Yeats recalled how Henley made young writers like himself 'feel always our importance, and no man among us could do good work, or show the promise of it, and lack his praise'.[38] When Henley gave up the editorship of the *National Observer*, Beerbohm paid him and the paper he had moulded a memorably witty tribute: 'The paper was rowdy, venomous, and insincere. There was libel in every line of it. It roared with the lambs and bleated with the lions. It was a disgrace to journalism and a glory to literature.'[39]

Kipling, then, was in no danger of being smothered with effete theorising on the 'Aims of Art'. Moreover, Henley's imperialist nationalism provided him with a way of bypassing the problems of national and personal identity with which he had been struggling since his arrival in England. If he could not happily be an English writer, he could begin to see himself as the Bard of Empire, capable of the 'Saga of the Anglo-Saxon', which he had foretold in America. Henley's populist sympathies and stance as a Tory permanently in opposition to the status quo were similarly congenial to someone always more comfortable on the margins than at the centre. If Kipling could not happily address himself to the English literati, he could make himself into a writer who would not only portray the life of the average Tommy, but whose works the average Tommy would know by heart.

Under Henley's auspices, and within weeks of his breakdown, he now found the voice that Twain would call 'Kipling's far-reaching bugle note'.[40] On 22 February he published 'Danny Deever', the first of the *Barrack-Room Ballads*, to be followed over the next five months by a dozen more, including 'Tommy', 'Fuzzy-Wuzzy', 'The Widow at Windsor', 'Gunga Din' and 'Mandalay'. Henley was ecstatic. 'Tell me what you think of the Kiplings,' he wrote from his Edinburgh base to Robbie Ross. 'Up here we all mashed on 'em.'[41]

Besides showing Kipling's sympathy for Tommy Atkins, the ordinary private soldier, what these new poems shared was the common touch. In form, content and idiom, they were genuinely populist and quickly proved popular as songs and recitation-pieces. He had struck the vein that was to become Kiplingesque. Written in a rough Cockney dialect, the ballads captured with vigorous humour and sometimes sentimental pathos the hardships and camaraderie of life in the Widow's service. What appealed to the soldiers themselves was Kipling's genuine understanding of their lot, including the odd shrewd dig at the pompous indifference of the stay-at-home civilian:

For it's Tommy this, an' Tommy that, an' 'Chuck him out, the brute!'
But it's 'Saviour of 'is country' when the guns begin to shoot;
An' it's Tommy this, an' Tommy that, an' anything you please;
An' Tommy ain't a bloomin' fool – you bet that Tommy sees!

Occasionally the poems even turned their irony on the imperial enterprise itself. 'The Widow at Windsor' went beyond 'Tommy's' sharp observation of complacent civilian attitudes, to anticipate by nearly thirty years Sassoon's satirical swipe at those who 'speed glum heroes up the line to death':

Walk wide o' the Widow at Windsor,
    For 'alf o' Creation she owns:

162

We 'ave bought 'er the same with the sword an' the flame,
An' we've salted it down with our bones.
(Poor beggars! – it's blue with our bones!) . . .[42]

Nor were these ballads merely populist. 'Danny Deever', a chilling account of a regimental hanging, may soon have been set to music and become a popular standard of the time; yet when it first appeared in the *Scots Observer*, Professor Masson of Edinburgh University strode into class, brandishing a copy and exclaiming, 'Here's Literature! Here's Literature at last!'[43] Fifty years later, T S Eliot would single out the poem as 'technically (as well as in context) remarkable' with its perfect 'combination of heavy beat and variation of pace'.[44]

Nevertheless for all their undeniable literary qualities, Kipling primarily intended these 'Barrack-Room Ballads' as his bid to become the kind of poet he had envisaged only a few weeks after reaching London. In mid-November 1889, after an evening in Gatti's Music Hall across the street, he had mused to Mrs Hill that 'surely the people of London require a poet of the Music Halls'.[45] The next morning he had knocked off 'My Great and Only', a turnover in which he imagined himself listening to the first triumphant performance of his own music-hall hit, entitled 'That's what the Girl told the Soldier'. Although the story made good copy, he was not then ready to assume this new literary identity in real life; consequently, he did not offer 'My Great and Only' to 'the Jimmy' or *Longman's*, but instead sent it off to the safe distance of the CMG. Then, sometime in the New Year, the idea that he really might become such a poet took hold. And when the ballads quickly proved a success, he must have felt that the hunch that had led him to 'primitive and passionate' Villiers Street, rather than to stay with his uncles and aunts or borrow the money for a smarter address, had amply paid off.[46]

Whatever Kipling's personal crises, the early months of 1890, with the publication of the soldier ballads, the regular appearance of new stories in magazines and the reprinting of his earlier volumes of stories quickly confirmed him as the hottest new literary talent in England and soon afterwards in America. 'Just now the man most talked of in literature here is Rudyard Kipling,' the Irish politician Justin McCarthy wrote to a friend on Easter Sunday.[47] Soon afterwards Hardy was jotting down in his notebook plot summaries of his favourite stories from *Plain Tales from the Hills* and lines from a new (fourth) edition of *Departmental Ditties*, commenting that Kipling 'adroitly mixes two tones, the gay & the bitter'.[48] Across the Atlantic, in late April, James Russell Lowell was replying to an enquiry from the London literary hostess (and admirer of Kipling) Mrs W K Clifford: 'Yes, I have read Kipling's stories, and with real pleasure. I read them while I was still in bed and under the spell of opium, and so was adopted into their Orientalism.' Looking ahead to his next book, however, the urbane Lowell expressed the hope that 'he will drop his Hindostanee [sic] pedantry'.[49]

A resounding public affirmation of this mounting popular appeal was the appearance on 25 March of a long, unsigned piece in *The Times*. Written by Mrs Humphrey Ward's husband, T H Ward, this mostly concentrated on the recently reprinted Indian work, complimenting Kipling on 'having tapped a new vein' and worked it out 'with real originality'. In particular, he was praised for his stories of 'native life' ('they appear to lift the veil from a state of society so immeasurably distant from our own and to offer us glimpses of unknown depths and gulfs of human existence') and for his 'studies' of Mulvaney, Learoyd and Ortheris ('The comedy, the dull hard work, and the not unfrequent tragedy of life in the ranks are admirably given in the stories which concern these three soldiers'). Even so, despite this generous praise, Kipling could not be placed 'in the first rank of contemporary writers' since he had not yet attempted 'the long distance race' – in other words, a novel. The article ended by flashing an unmistakable warning light: 'it is to be hoped he will not write himself out. Modern magazines and their eager editors are a dangerous snare in the way of a bright, clever, and versatile writer, who knows that he has caught the public taste.'[50]

It was in many ways a boom that had come looking for him, rather than the other way round. Lockwood Kipling, with his usual astuteness, observed to Edith Plowden in the autumn of 1890 that his son's meteoric rise to fame would not have been possible in any previous epoch:

His Mother is putting in a book the press notices of his work & it is growing an amazing volume. The Americans think much more of him than the English & that is saying a great deal. And an odd thing is happening: – Owing to the recent developments & organising of

journalism, syndicates & what not, each new boom is more porten-
tous, more wide-spread and more voluminous in print than the last
and it will be literally true that in one year this youngster will have
had more said about his work, over a wider extent of the world's surface than some of the greatest of England's writers in their whole
lives. Much of this, of course, is merely mechanical, the result of the
wholesale spread of journalism and the centralising tendencies of
it.[51]

Addressing a huge popular audience at the dawn of mass communication,
the twenty-four-year-old Kipling resembled nothing so much as
Browning's Bishop Blougram 'nicking the moment with a happy tact'.

Kipling's parents, on leave for eighteen months, had arrived in May. He
went down to Plymouth to meet them and with his father soon afterwards
paid a visit to his old school, where Uncle Crom was still headmaster. In
honour of his visit, the boys were given a half-day's holiday – a further
sign of his burgeoning fame. Lockwood and Alice took lodgings in
Kensington, providing Kipling with a second base. This reconstruction of
three sides of the Family Square gave him some much-needed stability in
all the turmoil of his 'notoriety', as he later sardonically called it.
Although his claim in *Something of Myself* that his parents formed 'the
only public for whom . . . I had any regard whatever till their deaths'
rather overdid the filial piety, having their unreserved approval, support
and criticism was undoubtedly of the first importance to him. The constructive banter of the family group and the changing emphasis of his literary ambitions around this time were both reflected in his reminiscence
of the reunion:

> Their arrival simplified things, and 'set' in my head a notion that
> had been rising at the back of it. It seemed easy enough to 'knock
> 'em' [the public] – but to what end beyond the heat of the exercise?
> . . . I had been at work on the rough of a set of verses called later
> 'The English Flag' and had boggled at a line which had to be a key-
> line but persisted in going 'soft'. As was the custom between us, I
> asked into the air: 'What am I trying to get *at*?' Instantly the
> Mother, with her quick flutter of the hands: 'You're *trying* to say:

"What do they know of England who only England know."' The
Father confirmed . . .

In the talks that followed, I exposed my notion of trying to tell to
the English something of the world outside England – not directly
but by implication.[52]

Kipling's parents, long-time Anglo-Indians, could easily sympathise with
his emerging role as a spokesman for a wider England; nor would they
quarrel with his desire to point out that, beneath its smug assumption of
superiority, London sophistication was really just another form of provincialism.

The degree to which the presence of Lockwood and Alice worked to
boost Kipling's confidence after the emotional turmoil of January and
February was perhaps suggested by the romantic excursion he undertook
from 24 to 28 May to visit Flo Garrard in her Parisian studio. As with all
his dealings with Flo, little is known for certain about this quixotic interlude. Although their relationship undoubtedly provided the springboard
for the tortured romance of Dick and Maisie in The Light that Failed, written the following year, no details from the novel can be reliably extracted
as evidence of what happened in real life. What The Light that Failed
betrayed was Kipling's attitude towards his final failure to forge a relationship with Flo. The novel worked hard to solicit the reader's sympathies
for its protagonist Dick, leaving the selfish, unreasonable and capricious
Maisie to regret, too late, the emotional frigidity that spoilt their chance
of happiness.

The Light that Failed told the story of Dick Heldar, a successful young
war-artist who made his name with sketches of British troops serving in
far-flung corners of the Empire. Returning to London and fame, he met
up with his childhood sweetheart, Maisie, an ambitious but untalented
painter. Dick, his old passion instantly rekindled, became Maisie's artistic
mentor as well as her devoted admirer, but she refused to respond to his
romantic advances. Maisie shared lodgings in London and Vitry-sur-
Marne with a 'red-haired impressionist girl' who promptly fell in love
with Dick, but suffered in the knowledge that her love would never be
returned.[53]

In May 1890, Flo was living in Paris with her friend Mabel Price in the
Avenue de Jena near the Étoile. It is possible the two women were lovers,

which may explain Mabel's transformation into the predatory redhead of the novel. Trix, furthermore, claimed that Flo 'was simply not attracted' by anything that her brother 'had to offer'.[54] The two fictional characters, Maisie and the redhead, were at least sufficiently recognisable for Flo and Mabel to acknowledge the likeness, though both repudiated specific aspects of the novel. In particular, personal testimony was given to Kipling's official biographer that Mabel Price had not made advances to 'Rudyard-Dick' on her own account.[55]

'Blue Roses', the verse epigraph to chapter 7, encapsulated Kipling's self-approving version of the relationship between Dick and Maisie in suitable Nineties' quatrains:

> Roses red and roses white
> Plucked I for my love's delight.
> She would none of all my poses –
> Bade me gather her blue roses.
>
> Half the world I wandered through,
> Seeking where such flowers grew;
> Half the world unto my quest
> Answered but with laugh and jest.
>
> It may be beyond the grave
> She shall find what she would have.
> Oh, 'twas but an idle quest –
> Roses white and red are best![56]

Thirty-six years later, on the fly-leaf of a 1927 printing of *The Light that Failed*, Flo Garrard replied to the novel, and specifically to these verses. Her acerbic, private rejoinder is her only known comment on her relationship with Kipling:

If you happen to read this singular, if somewhat murky little story you are very likely to rather wonder if real people could be quite so stupid and objectionable as this crowd.

Of course its difficult to see oneself as others see you, still m'thinks there's something somewhat distorted about it all; and that the story does not run throughout its whole length on lines quite parallel with Truth.

It looks to me rather like its image reflected in a Distorting Mirror appearing all distorted, and grotesque.

For instance in the case of the 'Blue Roses' (I didn't refuse any other colour) but as a matter of fact, Dick, with his obliquity of vision failed to observe, that I wasn't exacting them of him, but *he* of me. A trifle obvious enough, but somehow overlooked.

In fact the only time I ever seemed to see eye to eye with him was when he said

'It may be beyond the grave'
'She shall find what she would have.'
'Oh! t'was but an idle quest, –'
'Roses white and red are best!'

Maisie[57]

The evident, if awkward, passion that infused Kipling's novel does suggest that he went to Paris with some hope that his reunion with Flo would rekindle past passions, genuine or imagined. In reality, following these few days, she disappeared for ever from Kipling's life. Still, the visit had served a purpose. Almost eight uneasy months after returning to England and stepping into 'a sort of waking dream', in which he could not but take 'the fantastic cards that Fate was pleased to deal me',[58] he had solved his problem of a subject for the novel that both critics and public were so urgently and oppressively demanding.

11

An American Wife

The title of *The Light that Failed* could be taken in at least two ways. Literally, it referred to Dick's failing eyesight, the consequence of a sword-cut to the head, which eventually led to his total blindness. Metaphorically, it alluded to the extinguishing of his artistic talent. Like a number of Victorian novels, *The Light that Failed* was published in two versions. The magazine version, which appeared in January 1891 in *Lippincott's*, ended happily with Maisie hearing of Dick's affliction and returning from her studio in France to marry him. The book version, published two months later, ended unhappily with Maisie abandoning the blind Dick, who sought and found death on the battlefield. A cryptic one-sentence preface to the book version read: 'This is the story of *The Light that Failed* as it was originally conceived by the Writer.'[1]

Kipling wrote the novel, or most of it, in a concentrated burst after returning from his abortive trip to Paris in May 1890, completing it sometime that August. Predictably, given that he was in part rewriting his failed relationship with Flo, the love scenes contained large doses of self-pity, with the reader's sympathy for Dick constantly solicited – and Maisie's frigid perversity in refusing him constantly underlined. This need to score points against Flo meant that Maisie never developed into a credible heroine. Not only was Dick's caring warmth continually contrasted to Maisie's emotional chilliness, but his preoccupation with his art was never questioned, whereas her single-minded determination to devote herself to her painting was presented as merely selfish stupidity. Considered as a romance, the novel was callowly adolescent – at times laughably so.

More engrossingly, two episodes revealed Kipling's interest in bargaining with Fate. When Dick returned to London to make his name, he, like his author, was temporarily short of funds. Refusing to call on his friends for financial aid, he too survived for a month on sausages and mashed potatoes. His explanation to his journalist friend, Torpenhow, echoed Kipling's own rationale:

'Why in the world didn't you come to me?'
'Couldn't; I owe you too much already, old man. Besides, I had a sort of superstition that this temporary starvation – that's what it was, and it hurt – would bring me more luck later.'

Another such bargain occurred in the scene where, as a placatory sacrifice, Dick threw a keepsake from Maisie into the Thames:

Dick made his prayer to Fate disjointedly after the manner of the heathen as he threw the piece of silver into the river. If any evil were to befall, let him bear the burden and let Maisie go unscathed, since the threepenny piece was dearest to him of all his possessions. It was a small coin in itself, but Maisie had given it, and the Thames held it, and surely the Fates would be bribed for this once.[2]

Indeed, arguably, the novel itself was a piece of propitiatory magic, offering up a surrogate Kipling as a sacrifice to the Gods of the Literary Marketplace.

Similarly, there was a strong autobiographical resonance to the treatment of Dick's unhappy upbringing as an orphan raised and persecuted by a Mrs Jennett. Here Kipling again revisited the torments of his Southsea years, firmly restating his case against Mrs Holloway and her Evangelical cruelty:

At such times as she herself was not personally displeased with Dick, she left him to understand that he had a heavy account to settle with his Creator; wherefore Dick learned to loathe his God as intensely as he loathed Mrs Jennett; and this is not a wholesome frame of mind for the young. Since she chose to regard him as a hopeless liar, when dread of pain drove him to his first untruth, he naturally developed into a liar . . .

What was new in *The Light that Failed*, going beyond 'Baa Baa Black Sheep', was Kipling's recognition that aspects of his artistic creed derived from Mrs Holloway's Evangelical teachings. Explaining to Maisie the tough and self-denying discipline of the true artist's life, Dick sounded the recognisable Kiplingesque note. The artist's creative powers, he told her, were subject to 'the law – just the same as it was at Mrs Jennett's'.[3]

The particular commandment that Dick was expounding at this point was that listening to praise, or painting with one eye on the gallery, vitiated one's artistic powers. But the various passages in which Dick outlined his aesthetic theories to Maisie made it clear that Kipling's sense of the artist's necessary subservence to 'the law' went far beyond this one instance. In particular, Dick insisted on the impersonal nature of the artist's gift: 'Don't you understand, darling?' he tried to explain to her. 'Good work has nothing to do with – doesn't belong to – the person who does it. It's put into him or her from outside.'[4] Kipling might, at a conscious level, have rejected much of Mrs Holloway's religious instruction; yet, as he half-acknowledged in Dick's insistence on the artist's passive dependence on an external force, her theology had reappeared transmogrified in this aesthetic creed. Years later, he would sum up his view of the artist's function in a famous remark to Rider Haggard. 'We are,' he claimed, 'only telephone wires.'[5]

This did not stop Kipling from hoping that *The Light that Failed* would impress the Savile Club as serious art. If 'In Partibus' had scoffed at 'long-haired things' wittering on about the 'Aims of Art,/And "theories" and "goals"', his novel wittered with the best. The brief account of Dick's war experience and a smattering of music-hall and other songs were, strikingly, the only concessions made to the kind of popular audience imagined for the 'Barrack-Room Ballads'. Instead, Kipling for the most part was keener to show off his literariness, as he planted a wide range of allusions in both the plot and the verbal detail. Elizabeth Barrett Browning's *Aurora Leigh* (with its blind hero, artistic theme and recurrent images of light, blindness and failure) was the most obvious archetype, though there were also echoes of *Jane Eyre* and *Westward Ho!*; while in the text itself Kipling referred to such diverse works as 'To His Coy Mistress', 'The City of Dreadful Night', Juvenal's *Satires*, 'The Song of Hiawatha', 'Nightpiece to Julia' and 'Annabel Lee'.

Kipling's hopes of impressing the literati did not last long. Barrie, in the March 1891 *Contemporary Review*, objected that Maisie was 'utterly uninteresting' and 'colourless' – in fact, a 'nonentity' – and claimed that 'despite its vigour and picturesqueness, the story would probably have attracted little notice had it been [by] an unknown man, and such as it might have got would have been won by its almost brutal cynicism'. Prophetically, he advised the would-be novelist to write 'of what he knows best' and to 'lay his scene in India'. Gosse, later that year, was even tougher. He disliked the two protagonists and the best he could say was that *The Light that Failed* had 'oases of admirable detail in a desert of the undesirable'. The novel, he confessed, had wakened him 'to the fact that there are limits to this dazzling new talent, the éclat of which had almost lifted us off our critical feet'.[6] Above all, though confining himself to private rumbles of criticism, there was Henry James: 'The talent enormous, but the brutality even deeper-seated,' he gravely informed Gosse. 'It comes out so abnormally in *The Light that Failed*. And then the talent has sometimes failed.'[7] The fastidious James no doubt had in mind the scene in which, during a battle in the Sudan, Torpenhow thumbed out an Arab's eye and then got up, 'wiping his thumb on his trousers'.[8]

'Dead tired and frabjous an' muzzy about the head' was how Kipling described himself in August 1890 shortly after finishing his novel. 'Likewise polumneas and metheoligastical which are serious diseases.'[9] More matter-of-factly, he told other correspondents that he was not well and under doctors' orders to have a holiday. His extraordinary productivity over the spring and summer probably brought on this nervous relapse, but worry about his novel's imminent reception may also have played a part. The standard prescription was a sea-voyage, for those who could afford it, and he duly spent most of October either on board ship or staying with Lord Dufferin (now Ambassador to Italy) at his villa near Naples.

Ironically, while he sweated over his novel, it was his shorter pieces that were providing the strongest evidence of his developing literary power. Between finishing the manuscript of *The Light that Failed* in the summer of 1890 and the novel's appearance in book form in England the following spring, two collections of his short stories were published in America. The first of these, *The Courting of Dinah Shadd and Other Stories*, with an introduction by Lang, was a quasi-pirated collection published by *Harper's* that autumn. There followed in March 1891 an authorised collection called *Mine Own People*, with an introduction by James. Few, reading these volumes alongside *The Light that Failed*, would have disputed Barrie's assertion that the short story was where Kipling's genius lay.

Kipling's success with these stories stemmed in part from his confident reworking of familiar material, as he gave his readers more of what they had already found so appealing. Even before reaching London, Kipling was aware that his three musketeers, Mulvaney, Ortheris and Learoyd, had touched a nerve with his growing public. Among the first stories he wrote on his arrival was 'The Courting of Dinah Shadd', in which he further developed the comic and tragic potential of Mulvaney. Sitting round the campfire after a hard day on manoeuvres, Mulvaney told the story's narrator how, as a handsome and ambitious young corporal, he won the hand of Dinah Shadd, the Sergeant's daughter. On the very day she consented to marry him, driven by high spirits and the exuberant recklessness that would keep him 'reduced' to the rank of private, Mulvaney flirted with Judy Sheehy, the slatternly daughter of the canteen-sergeant. Insisting that Mulvaney had offered to marry Judy, 'Ould Mother Sheehy', 'far gone in dhrink', confronted him at the Shadds and, when Dinah stood faithfully by her man, she delivered 'The Black Curse of the Shielygh' on the two of them – prophesying all the disasters that would subsequently plague Mulvaney's life. 'The Courting of Dinah Shadd', for all its melodrama, was genuinely moving, almost justifying the tragic if strained grandeur of its conclusion: 'When I woke I saw Mulvaney, the night-dew gemming his moustache, leaning on his rifle at picket, lonely as Prometheus on his rock, with I know not what vultures tearing his liver.'[10]

A later story, 'On Greenhow Hill', written and first published in magazine form during the summer of 1890, showed the rapid development of Kipling's narrative technique. In the frame, the three soldiers lay in ambush waiting to shoot an Indian deserter who had been disturbing the camp. The Himalayan landscape reminded Learoyd of Greenhow Hill in

Yorkshire, where he was raised. As they waited, Learoyd told of his love as a young man for the consumptive Liza Rountree, daughter of a Methodist minister, and how her death prompted him to enlist. The story's pathos was generated by the multiple contrasts between frame and inset: the familiar Yorkshire landscape and the exotic Himalayan foothills, the passion of youth and the wry detachment of maturity, the open-endedness of civilian life and the narrowed options of life in the regiment. Above all, there was the disconcerting juxtaposition of the intensity of Learoyd's remembered romance and the coolly dispassionate professionalism with which the three soldiers set out to silence the deserter. This juxtaposition constantly reminded the reader of the emotional costs of army life for the individual trooper. Although never invited to pity the deserter, the reader was allowed, even encouraged, to feel disturbed by the soldiers' clinical approach to the assassination. The story's intimation that Learoyd could have become a quite different person in civilian life underscored the diminished human sympathies that he and his friends had had to acquire in order to survive in the army. 'On Greenhow Hill' ended on a note of heavily compromised triumph, as Ortheris expertly disposed of the deserter and was left 'staring across the valley, with the smile of the artist who looks on the completed work'.[11] The impersonal nature of the artist's gift, which Dick in The Light that Failed had vaunted as an heroic dedication to aesthetic integrity, was here presented as a ruthless – and potentially inhuman – devotion to the task in hand.

Also first published that hectic summer was 'Without Benefit of Clergy'. It was Kipling's most radical story of racial boundary-crossing, reflecting how, for all his renewed identification of himself as an Anglo-Indian, he was at the same time growing further away from the lived complexities of colonial life. In the story, Holden set up house with Ameera in a secret, de facto marriage, which was cemented by the birth of their son Tota. The imaginative sympathy here was unequivocally on the side of the lovers, and the details and delights of their life together were fully imagined – a private life obviously more attractive and rewarding than the dutiful routine of Holden's public life as a Government official. Consequently, when Tota died of 'the seasonal autumn fever' and Ameera of cholera, and Holden was left with nothing but a blank future, the effect was very moving. Bleakly romantic, 'Without Benefit of Clergy' offered a persuasive picture of how things were in India: Nature audited her accounts 'with a big red pencil'; love was no defence; no one was safe; nothing could be relied upon.[12]

In stories like 'Without Benefit of Clergy', 'On Greenhow Hill' and 'The Courting of Dinah Shadd', all written within a few months of *The Light that Failed*, Kipling achieved the subtlety of characterisation and depth of feeling that his novel notably lacked. If the novel over which he had taken such pains marked a backward step in his literary development, the stories he was simultaneously knocking out showed his art developing by leaps and bounds.

Shortly before he left for Italy on his recuperative sea-voyage, Kipling found himself in the midst of another copyright row. His agent, Watt, had sold Harper and Brothers the American serial rights of the cream of his new stories ('The Courting of Dinah Shadd', 'The Man Who Was', 'A Conference of the Powers', 'Without Benefit of Clergy' and 'On Greenhow Hill'), and these had been appearing regularly in the firm's magazines. Then Harper brought out *The Courting of Dinah Shadd and Other Stories*, an unauthorised collection of those five stories plus 'The Incarnation of Krishna Mulvaney' (for which they sent Kipling a £10 'honorarium', which he tersely returned). What really riled him, he told Henley, was that he had been planning to publish a volume of the best of his new work, properly revised and prefaced, in his own good time; but Harper had pre-empted him by this 'grotesque Yahoodom of nipping pieces off a half-presented foetus and slamming it into the market'.[13] It also rankled that, as a relative unknown, he had approached Harper in the States the year before on his way to England, and they had turned down the opportunity to republish early collections like *Plain Tales from the Hills*.

Now tired, edgy but famous, Kipling decided to make a fuss. Before setting off for Italy, he went to the *Athenaeum*, London's most prestigious literary review, and told his story. On 4 October its Literary Gossip column outlined his dealings with Harper, tartly concluding that 'When an author is unknown to fame, they, it would seem, content themselves with insulting him; when he is celebrated, they insult and rob him.' Harper attempted to justify itself on 1 November by blurring the boundary between serial production (for which Kipling had given permission) and book production (for which he had not). Kipling returned to the attack the following week, explaining exactly how Harper had appropriated his work, but conceding that the real problem was not this or that publisher, but rather that 'the high seas of literature' were 'unprotected', and that 'those who traffic on them must run their chance of being plundered'.[14]

Nor was that the end. On 22 November the *Athenaeum* printed a letter by the novelists Walter Besant, William Black and Thomas Hardy. They avoided commenting on the specifics of Kipling's case, but objected to his 'sweeping condemnation' of Harper, who 'in the matter of book-production' had always been 'willing and desirous to do what is possible for the foreign author, whose interests the American law not only fails to protect, but entirely ignores'. Kipling hit back in the *Athenaeum* on 6 December with 'The Rhyme of the Three Captains'. The ballad, continuing the naval vein of his earlier complaints, neatly allegorised his version of the story, with Black as 'Admiral of the North from Solway Firth to Skye', Hardy as 'Lord of the Wessex coast and all the lands thereby' and Besant as 'Master of the Thames from Limehouse to Blackwall'. In case anyone missed the point, he identified the three novelists near the end with a punning play on their names: 'the bezant is hard, ay and black'. Kipling cast himself as the skipper of a 'trading-brig', who had been tricked and robbed of cargo and crew by an American 'privateer'. His list of the stolen goods was particularly ingenious, cryptically alluding to 'The Courting of Dinah Shadd' ('shaddock-frails'), to the unrevised state of the stories ('green unripened pine') and to their Indian subject matter ('my bale of dammer and spice', 'my grinning heathen gods'). He even hinted that it was his forthcoming novel ('the failing light') and recent breakdown ('a rough beam-sea beside') which had prevented him from taking appropriate action against the Yankee pirate:

> He has taken my little parrakeets that nest beneath the Line,
> He has stripped my rails of the shaddock-frails and the green
>   unripened pine;
> He has taken my bale of dammer and spice I won beyond the seas,
> He has taken my grinning heathen gods – and what should he want o'
>   these? . . .
> I could not fight for the failing light and a rough beam-sea beside,
> But I hulled him once for a clumsy crimp and twice because he lied.[15]

Thanking Gosse, who had written to compliment him on 'The Rhyme of the Three Captains' (and to point out some syntactical problems), Kipling explained that he began the ballad 'personally and too personally and then got interested in it for its own sake'.[16] He might also have added that the poem included some advance publicity that he would soon be back on the literary high seas, bigger and more unassailable than before as a novelist. Or, as he put it in the idiom of the poem: 'We'll make no sport in an English court till we come as a ship o' the Line'.[17]

Ironically the person who probably gave him most support during his copyright war with Harper was an American. Wolcott Balestier was the London agent of another New York publishing firm and, like Mrs Holloway and Flo Garrard, was one of those shadowy figures in Kipling's life about whom little is known, but much has been speculated. One biographer, Angus Wilson, has thought it 'likely that Kipling was much in love with Wolcott', while adding that Kipling would not have allowed himself 'to glimpse anything that was unorthodox in his feelings for his friend'.[18] Another biographer, Martin Seymour-Smith, has gone much further, conjecturing that Kipling and Wolcott were lovers. The probability is more prosaic.

Wolcott's career before he arrived in London in 1888 as Lovell's representative had been patchy. Born in 1861, he had two younger sisters, Carrie and Josephine, and a younger brother, Beatty. Their father died early, but the children were brought up in comfortable circumstances in Rochester, New York State, spending their summers at Beechwood, their maternal grandmother's large house in Brattleboro, Vermont. Briefly a student at Cornell, Wolcott then worked as a journalist in Rochester and as a librarian in New York, as well as making a couple of trips out West, which made a deep impression. Two early ambitions shaped his future life: to be the friend of writers and to be a writer himself. By the time he left for England, he had published three short novels and gained the friendship of a well-known American novelist, W D Howells.

Wolcott's self-appointed mission on coming to London was to get around the lack of international copyright arrangements by securing for English authors a simultaneous publication with his American firm, thus establishing some sort of American copyright and, he hoped, the loyalty of those authors for future American editions. From his two-room office at

2 Dean's Yard, Westminster, Wolcott quickly established himself as a prime mover in literary London. His success owed something to his ambition, self-belief and hard work, but just as much to his personal charisma. Evelyn Waugh's father, Arthur Waugh, who began his publishing career as Wolcott's dogsbody, would never forget his first encounter with the young American:

> There was one young man in the company [at one of Gosse's celebrated 'At Homes'] whom no one could help noticing . . . He was tall, pale, very thin, with quick, flashing eyes which seemed to take in everyone at a glance; he had a rather sharp voice, with a marked American accent, and he was not afraid of expressing his opinion against anyone's at the table. I thought him alarming, but at the same time master of a curious kind of charm that I had never encountered before; and, when he began to talk to me, his capacity for expressing interest in his fellow guest set me speedily at ease.[19]

A capacity for making others feel special, allied to the chameleon quality of taking on something of the nature of those he talked to: no wonder Wolcott charmed the writers whom he so assiduously courted. Henry James was particularly smitten by the young entrepreneur, constantly lauding him in letters to friends as the 'wondrous Balestier', 'the admirably acute and intelligent young Balestier' or 'the precious Balestier'. It was through the promptings of Gosse, however, that Kipling was first brought to Wolcott's attention in the autumn of 1889. Gosse had been reading *Soldiers Three* and enthusiastically recommended the author. Even so, as Waugh would recall, by early the following June, Wolcott was still in negotiation with Kipling:

> I was sent to Embankment Chambers, Villiers Street, over against the old Gatti's Music Hall, with an urgent note, begging that Balestier might have a glimpse of an unfinished story called, I think, *The Book of the Hundred Mornings* [presumably *The Book of Forty-Five Mornings*, which never appeared] upon which some literary gossiper had reported Mr Kipling to be engaged. I was shown into a dark room, where the author of *Soldiers Three* was seated on a bed, covered with sheets of manuscript. His reception was kindly, but a

little querulous. 'Extraordinarily importunate person, this Mr Balestier,' he exclaimed (or words to that effect), 'tell him that *The Book of a Hundred Mornings* is all over my bed, and may never get finished. Tell him to inquire again in six months.'[20]

Soon afterwards the friendship between Wolcott and Kipling had begun to ripen, though leaving frustratingly few traces.

On 12 July 1890, however, Wolcott was writing to W D Howells: 'Lately I have been seeing more of Kipling with whom I am writing a story in collaboration. The scene is to be partly far Western American (W.B.) and partly Indian (R.K.).'[21] Their working methods, according to one report, were for Wolcott to sit hammering away at the typewriter and Kipling to pace about the room while both kept up a constant volley of lines, suggestions and criticism.[22] The resultant collaboration, *The Naulahka*, turned out to be a full-length adventure novel – sprawling from Colorado to Rajputana and recounting the romance of Tarvin, a thrusting but idealistic American engineer, and Kate, a proto-feminist made to see the errors of her ways. It was a novel very much in the ripping-yarn line of *King Solomon's Mines* and *The Black Arrow*, and Kipling's and Wolcott's references to the work confirm that they had no pretensions beyond the limits of the genre. Between summer 1890 and the following spring they had immense fun – reflected in the novel's jaunty melodramatics – putting it together. In Wolcott, it is not fanciful to suggest, Kipling had found a replacement for his old collaborator, the now-married and unavailable Trix.

Indeed, 'brother' was how both Kipling and Wolcott referred to each other: Wolcott in the only surviving fragment of their correspondence, Kipling in his dedicatory poem to *Barrack-Room Ballads*. A letter from Wolcott's sister Josephine suggests that the Balestier family saw the relationship in a similar light. 'After the authors' dinner the other night,' she wrote to their mother as early as June 1890, 'Wolcott and young Kipling talked until four in the morning. They are growing fast friends; they are very congenial, dove-tail finely. I think it rather picturesque that the two London literary infants should play so prettily together.'[23] Quite apart from his personal charm, Wolcott appealed to Kipling in various ways: as a confidant, with that role vacant in the absence of Trix, cousin Margaret and Mrs Hill; as an American, capable of sharing Kipling's own sense of 'foreignness'; as someone intimate with the English literary scene, yet not constrained by its archaic gentility; and as a doer, above all revealed through his campaign against the American publishing pirates.

The only *direct* evidence of the character of their friendship is preserved in a fragment of a letter, part typed and part handwritten, from Wolcott to Kipling. It was discovered in a bank box in Brattleboro, Vermont in May 1992. The opening remarks referred to a story that Wolcott was currently writing:

> It isn't as good as Reffey, but there is a rather funny scene in which they talk over their rival sheets together. I wish it were in a state to send you, but I will post it to the next station and you can cable me a title. The name of the paper I repeat is 'The Rustler Telepheme'. Observe my rubbing in my invented name.
>
> Make a good job of it, this time old man; and return only when copper-fastened, double-rivetted and warranted not to fade, tear or unravel! Carrie bears up like the grave child she is. She counts the days; but she is strong. And it will really be a short cut, in the end, to do it right while you are at it. I want you back most hideously; but not enough to want you till the job's done.
>
> Heaven be with you! God bless you!
>
> Always and Ever
>
> Your brother,
>
> Wolcott[24]

The word 'telepheme' was a private joke. Writing in 1890 to an editor, Kipling had already mentioned the invention by 'my friend Mr Wolcott Balestier' of the word 'telepheme' to mean telephonic despatch.[25] Slender evidence perhaps, but this mutual enjoyment of verbal play recalls the games Rud and Trix used to enjoy – speaking only in lines from Shakespeare, making up parodies of their favourite poets, or the 'Wop of Albion' and 'Wop of Asia' titles that he and Margaret had given each other. This kind of easy banter might seem inconsequential from the outside, yet a shared sense of the ridiculous can both spark and sustain a friendship.

Wolcott's letter, from internal evidence, was written between late August and early December 1891 while Kipling was travelling in the Southern Hemisphere. The reference to Carrie, Wolcott's sister Caroline, shows that by this time there was already an accepted understanding between her and Kipling. The organiser in the family, Carrie had taken charge of the household in Kensington, of Wolcott's cottage on the Isle of Wight, and of his office at Dean's Yard shortly after her arrival in early summer 1890, with her mother and her two other siblings, Josephine and Beatty. Thomas Hardy met this 'attractive and thoughtful young woman' at Gosse's in May and was struck by her description of England as 'so reposeful', whereas in America, she told Hardy, 'you feel at night, "I must be quick and sleep; there is not much time to give to it." '[26] Kipling probably first met Carrie not long afterwards when she arrived at Dean's Yard one day to consult Wolcott, carrying the housekeeping books under her arm.

'That woman is going to marry our Ruddy,' was Alice Kipling's unenthusiastic prophecy when she set eyes on Carrie Balestier; while Lockwood, enigmatically, described her as 'a good man spoiled'.[27] Little evidence about the courtship's progress survives. Hilton Brown, an early biographer who had considerable help from Trix, claimed that Kipling was actually engaged to Carrie before June 1891, though the engagement was temporarily broken off that month; and according to him, Kipling's sudden trip to New York in June to see his dying uncle Henry was prompted more by the emotional turmoil of the broken engagement than by nepotic solicitude. The trip itself was futile (Kipling being besieged by reporters in New York, where he found that his uncle was already dead), but on his return he and Carrie, according to Brown's Trix-inspired account, renewed their engagement.

Whatever the circumstances of his love life, Kipling was under considerable strain – which, once again, his doctors put down to overwork. In July 1891, back in London, he wrote to a friend of his parents:

Now the brutes of doctors are trying to chase me out of England again on another sea voyage. I wish to goodness they'd give a man a rest sometimes. Mother's out of town, the Father is going north and I am getting back to the country this afternoon to further educate my arm in the playing of golf. The trouble is that all work of any kind is forbidden; and so I can't tell quite what to do with myself or how to do it.[28]

On 22 August, Kipling boarded the SS *Mexican* bound for the Cape. He was planning to visit Britain's southern dominions (South Africa, Australia and New Zealand), and to continue on to see Robert Louis Stevenson in Samoa before spending Christmas with his parents in Lahore. The fragment of Wolcott's letter lends support to Brown's claim that Kipling left England an engaged, or re-engaged, man. As with Flo on his departure for India, and with Caroline Taylor on his return to England, Kipling found it easier to propose when separation was imminent – and emotionally reassuring to be engaged when he was venturing into the unknown.

Kipling set out for the colonies with a worldwide reputation based principally upon the stories in *Soldiers Three* and his other earlier collections. *The Light that Failed* was certainly known, but what had done more to cement his reputation was the recent publication in America of *Mine Own People* and in England of *Life's Handicap*, both collections of newer (and older) short stories. *Mine Own People*, published by Lovell (no doubt through Wolcott's efforts) was almost certainly a response to Harper's pirated volume, *The Courting of Dinah Shadd and Other Stories*. In addition to some stories not included in that edition, Kipling and Wolcott arranged for the extra attraction of an introduction by Henry James.

James's introduction, written in his hypnotically magisterial style, is a reminder that even at this stage Kipling had not yet fully become 'Kipling'. Although duly praising the stories for their 'freshness' and 'prodigious facility', James dampeningly compared their author's 'performance' to 'a tremendous walk before breakfast, making one welcome the idea of the meal, but consider with some alarm the hours still to be traversed'. What would lie ahead? James eagerly anticipated the emergence of a quite different writer from this 'singularly robust little literary character', when to Kipling's other strengths was added 'the voice, as it were, of the civilised man':

> It is a part of the satisfaction the author gives us that he can make us speculate as to whether he will be able to complete his picture altogether (this is as far as we presume to go in meddling with the question of his future) without bringing in the complicated soul. On the day he does so, if he handles it with anything like the cleverness he has already shown, the expectation of his friends will take a great

bound. Meanwhile, at any rate, we have Mulvaney, and Mulvaney is after all tolerably complicated.[29]

James would subsequently recall that the Kipling he had hoped to see emerge was nothing less than an 'English Balzac'.[30] That hope would be disappointed, but in 1891 James's introduction was a gratifying endorsement from the emerging doyen of Anglo-American letters – the high-water mark, as it turned out, of Kipling's approval from the intelligentsia.

Despite his burgeoning fame, Kipling's southern voyage in 1891 was his last chance to travel with something of the independence of his Indian and American excursions. Although he was treated as a celebrity in each port of call, outside the main centres he was left mostly to his own devices. The voyage to Cape Town and a fortnight spent in South Africa, from 10 to 25 September, provided him with a new friend, Captain Bayly, who introduced him to the Navy Club in Simonstown, the start of an enduring fascination with the Royal Navy. There was also a brief encounter with Olive Schreiner, author of *The Story of an African Farm*, to whom Kipling recommended his London agent, A P Watt; and, at lunch in an Adderley Street restaurant, a first glimpse of Cecil Rhodes.

In Wellington, New Zealand, Kipling was given celebrity treatment from the moment he arrived on 18 October, which may account for the warmth of his recollections:

Wellington opened another world of kindly people . . . large, long-eyelashed, and extraordinarily good-looking. Maybe I was prejudiced, because no less than ten beautiful maidens took me for a row in a big canoe by moonlight on the still waters of Wellington Harbour, and every one generally put aside everything for my behoof, instruction, amusement, and comfort.[31]

Kipling told eager journalists that he was on his way to visit Stevenson and had 'only come for a loaf and to see pretty things'.[32] After four days he travelled up the North Island to the thermal district around Wairakei just beyond Lake Taupo. His brief stay among the mud-spouts and hot pools provided him with the setting for the one story he is known to have written during this whole trip. A lively 'turnover' for the *New Zealand Herald*, 'One Lady at Wairakei' showed Kipling confidently predicting, as he had in America, the emergence of a distinctive identity for another of the younger Anglo-Saxon countries. Significantly, it was the possibilities of the literary rather than the imperial future of New Zealand ('a new land teeming with new stories') which most intrigued him. With some prescience he anticipated that women writers would play a determining role and hinted that a truly national literature could only develop once the country ('one big encumbered estate') became economically independent.[33]

After a few days in Auckland ('Last, loneliest, loveliest, exquisite, apart') and forced to abandon his trip to Samoa because of problems with sailing times, he took the boat down to Christchurch. There he saw one of his old Classics masters from USC, F W C Haslam, and on 6 November after a short stop in Dunedin he sailed for Australia on the SS *Talune*. Also on board was General Booth of the Salvation Army, whom Kipling watched 'beat a tambourine in the face of the singing, weeping, praying crowd who had come to see him off'.[34] Melbourne, reached on 18 November, put Kipling in mind of America. He told local journalists it was 'second-hand American, there is an American tone on the top of things, but it is not real. Daresay, by and by, you will get a tone of your own. Still, I like these American memories playing around your streets.' Still in tactless mood, he added prophetically: 'I like America. When I am there I am railing at the country, but out of it, I want to get back there.'[35] From Melbourne he went to Sydney, where two days left him with the impression of 'leisured multitudes all in their shirt-sleeves and all picnicking all the day'.[36]

On 25 November, now at Adelaide, he boarded the SS *Valetta* bound for Colombo. General Booth was again a fellow passenger, and during the voyage Kipling conceived a 'great respect and admiration for this man with the head of Isaiah and the fire of the Prophet' – though not before his ingrained suspicion of religious enthusiasts had led him to take Booth to task: 'Like the young ass I was, I expressed my distaste at his appearance on Invercargill wharf. "Young feller," he replied, bending great brows at me, "if I thought I could win *one* more soul to the Lord by walking on my head and playing a tambourine with my toes, I'd – I'd learn how."'[37] From Colombo, Kipling crossed to India on 12 December and over the next several days travelled north by train to Lahore. There he met up with his parents, who had recently returned from their leave in England and had brought back Aunt Edie for a visit. Almost as soon as he arrived, he was making his plans for the trip back to England.

'WOLCOTT DEAD. COME BACK TO ME.'[38] Wolcott Balestier had died on 6 December, in Dresden, and Carrie's cable to Lahore implored Kipling's speedy return. We know nothing of his immediate reaction to the news, but on or about Christmas Eve he left Lahore for England. A brief visit to his old *ayah* in Bombay did not prevent him from reaching London on 10 January 1892, a remarkably rapid journey. He had had his 'last look round the only real home I had yet known.'[39]

Wolcott had suffered from poor health during the summer, some of which he had spent at his place on the Isle of Wight with his family and Kipling, before the latter's trip overseas. Back in London, in addition to his work for Lovell, he pushed ahead with the new firm he had set up with William Heinemann and their plans to bring out a series of cheap reprints modelled on the Tauchnitz Collection of British and American Authors. In mid-November, probably already ill with the typhoid that was to kill him, Wolcott travelled to Dresden in connection with this scheme.

At the end of that month a mutual friend persuaded Carrie, Josephine and their mother to come and attend to the dying Wolcott. Carrie's capacity to organise the family came to the fore in this crisis. Both in Wolcott's final illness, and through the ensuing funeral, she proved the mainstay. One of her first acts was to contact Henry James in London and call him to his friend's death-bed. He arrived only in time for the funeral on 10 December, and that day wrote a vivid description to Gosse. Not otherwise a huge admirer of Carrie, this time James was full of praise:

> The mother and sister are altogether wonderful, and so absolutely composed – that is, Mrs B. and Josephine – that there is scarcely any *visible* tragedy in it. By far the most interesting is poor little concentrated, passionate Carrie, with whom I came back from the cemetery alone in one of the big black and silver coaches, with its black and silver footmen perched behind (she wanted to talk to me), and who is remarkable in her force, acuteness, capacity and courage – and in the intense – almost manly – nature of her emotion. She is a worthy sister of poor dear big-spirited, only-by-death-quenchable Wolcott

... What is clear, at any rate, is that she can do and face and more than face and do, for all three of them, anything and everything that they will have to meet now.[40]

Exactly one month after the funeral, Kipling arrived in London. Carrie was waiting for him. Eight days later, and already arranging 'a year's wandering round the world from Mexico and Texas to Honolulu, Japan and India', they were married by special licence at All Souls', Langham Place. Wolcott's death, and the sense of loss and incompleteness that must have accompanied it for both of them, was surely the catalyst for this precipitate marriage and flight from their friends and families; but Kipling's surviving letters announcing the event betrayed little of these emotions:

Dear Aunt Louie

By this light prepare yourself for that which is coming in your family! I am, for rare and singular merits which I cannot at this present moment realise or detail, to be married tomorrow to the sister of the man with whom I wrote the *Naulakha*, now running in the *Century*. The affair has been going on for rather more months than I care to think about in that they were sheer waste of God's good life but – unless Miss Balestier or myself go down with the influenza before tomorrow noon – we are launched on the threshold of things from All Soul's Church. That I am penetrated with the solemnity of things in general is true. That I am riotously happy is yet more true and I pray that out of your own great store of happiness you will bless us, because we have gone through deep waters together.

To Margaret he described himself as 'idiotically happy' and to his Uncle Crom he wrote jokingly of his 'sinful joy'.[41]

The congregation at All Souls' was sparse – due in part to the influenza epidemic sweeping London, but in part also to the hurried wedding arrangements. Henry James, taking Wolcott's place, gave the bride away; Gosse, by his own account, 'supported the bridegroom'. Otherwise present were Gosse's young son and daughter, Kipling's cousin Ambo, Wolcott's business partner Heinemann, the clergyman, the clerk and the pew-opener. 'At 2.8,' noted Gosse, 'the cortège entered the church and at 2.20 left it, the sharpest thing of modern times.'[42]

12

An American Home

The fortnight following the wedding passed in a flurry of visits and dinners and packing as the newly-weds hastily made arrangements for a round-the-world honeymoon. Amid this bustle, all briefly noted in the diary that Carrie now began to keep, Kipling still found time to tidy up a few literary loose ends and to establish new contacts.[1] Now that he was a celebrity, *The Times* wanted the rights to a series of travel Letters, and were prepared to pay £25 a column. These pieces duly appeared over the succeeding months and were syndicated in the New York *Sun* and, a hint of old loyalties, in the CMG.

Kipling also despatched *Barrack-Room Ballads* to his agent, Watt. This, his first 'English' collection of poems, came out in March 1892, sold 7,000 copies in its first year, and went into dozens of editions during his lifetime. The volume was made up of the soldier ballads, like 'Danny Deever' and 'Gunga Din', which had cemented his reputation two years before, together with other poems from the same period like 'The Ballad of East and West', 'The Ballad of the King's Jest', 'The English Flag' and 'The Rhyme of the Three Captains'. Kipling gave the collection a valedictory twist by dedicating it to Wolcott and prefacing it with a sub-Swinburnian elegy for his dead friend:

Beyond the loom of the last lone star, through open darkness hurled.
Further than rebel comet dared or hiving star-swarm swirled,

Sits he with those that praise our God for that they served His
world.

Closing the volume was an envoi, later entitled 'The Long Trail'. In an
earlier manuscript version, the poem had invited Wolcott ('dear lad') to
'Ha' done with the Tents of Shem' (the rat-race) and set off with Kipling
'on the Long Trail – the trail that is always new'; now, in the published
version, with minimum alteration ('dear lass' for 'dear lad'), the poem
invited Carrie to play the gipsy.[2]

'Tomlinson' and 'The Ballad of the *Bolivar*' were two late additions to
the collection. 'Tomlinson' was another of Kipling's cultural swipes. It
told how the dead Tomlinson's spirit was refused entry to Heaven and
Hell because he had lived his life second-hand through books, and how
he was sent back to Earth to try again. Heading for a wider, more vital
world, Kipling was once more distancing himself from the London
literati. More speculatively, Tomlinson represented the timid, bookish
side of Kipling himself, a side with which he periodically felt uneasy and
needed to put down.

Sidney Low, editor of the *St James's Gazette*, would recall the composition of 'The Ballad of the *Bolivar*':

We had been writing strongly in support of a bill, then before
Parliament, intended to prevent unscrupulous ship-owners from
risking the lives of sailors by sending ships to sea in a dangerous condition.

One morning Kipling strode into my office and began at once
with breezy vehemence, 'I say, you know, I like those screeds of
yours on the coffin-ships. Do you want a poem about them?'

I assured him I did.

'All right,' he replied; 'give me some paper, something to smoke,
and something to drink, and you shall have it.'

I supplied his simple needs, put him in a room by himself, and left
him in what the novelists of the period would have called 'the
throes of composition'. They were easy throes for Rudyard Kipling
anno aetat. 26.

In about half an hour, or a little more, I went in to see how he was
getting on. 'Here's your poem,' he said. 'Would you care to hear it?'

And then, in his rich, sonorous voice, he rolled out the resounding lines:

> Seven men from all the world back to Docks again,
> Rolling down the Ratcliffe Road, drunk and raising Cain.
> Give the girls another treat 'fore we sign away;
> We that brought the *Bolivar* out across the Bay!

And so on for twelve stanzas. That was the first time 'The Ballad of the Bolivar' ever fell upon human ears. I wonder how many thousands of ears have been thrilled (and occasionally tortured) by its subsequent recitation.

Kipling handed me the copy of the poem. It was written, in his exquisite neat and tiny handwriting, on one side of a single sheet of paper, without a correction or erasure. I sent the MS. to the printers, with instructions that it was not to be cut or in any way defaced, and returned to me.[3]

This feat of poetic spontaneity soon became part of office lore at 'The Jimmy', and visitors and new employees would be reverently shown the very desk where the young genius had dashed off the lines.

What really happened was less romantic. While Carrie's diary confirms both the visit to Low (on 28 January) and the writing of 'The Ballad of the *Bolivar*' at his desk, it also reveals that her husband had been working on the poem the previous day. So much for spontaneous creativity. When Low later remembered how he left Kipling 'in what the novelists of the period would have called "the throes of composition"', his use of the handy literary cliché was even more apt than he realised. Kipling had been acting a part for Low's benefit, the stereotypical part of the inspired young writer pouring out his genius; and had evidently given a convincing performance. It was precisely the sort of hoax he enjoyed writing about; what was unusual was to find Kipling attempting such a stunt in real life. In a state of post-marital high spirits, he wanted to show off to Carrie, to show her that he had literary London taped; but he also wanted the two of them to 'play', and one can see the hoodwinking of Low as a foretaste of the kind of fun he hoped they were going to have together as a married couple.

*

The following week, 3 February, Kipling, Carrie, her mother and her sister Josephine sailed from Liverpool on the SS *Teutonic*. They eventually, after a few days in New York, reached Brattleboro, Vermont on the 16th in order to pay a brief visit to the rest of the Balestier family. Carrie's surviving brother Beatty – 'a walrus sitting on a woolsack . . . in his sleigh', as Kipling jovially described him – met the travellers at midnight. Wrapping them up in 'buffalo robes and blankets' against the freezing cold, he drove them through the snow to 'Maplewood', his seventy-acre farm a couple of miles outside town and a mile from Beechwood, where Carrie's and Beatty's grandmother, old Madam Balestier, resided.[4]

Kipling was at once charmed by Beatty, his wife Mai and baby Marjorie and thought everything delightful. His sense of release was evident throughout his first Letter, parts of which fell into an almost Wordsworthian cadence:

> But for the jingle of the sleigh-bells the ride might have taken place in a dream, for there was no sound of hoofs upon the snow, the runners sighed a little now and again as they glided over an inequality, and all the sheeted hills round about were as dumb as death.

In the days that followed, he found himself recalling his recent trip to New Zealand and again began to 'read' the unfamiliar landscape. He imagined the remote, cyclical, 'iron-bound life' lived by the inhabitants, the farm talk, the gossip, the hard, monotonous lot of the women, and what he called 'some finished chapters of pitiful stories', represented near the Green Mountains by 'a few score abandoned farms, started in a lean land, held fiercely so long as there was any one to work them, and then left on the hill-sides'. Mount Monadnock provided a more personal link, though typically still a literary one. Kipling had long known of the mountain from the Emerson poem and associated it with 'everything that was helpful, healing, and full of quiet'. Now he gazed at the peak itself in the distance, 'like a gigantic thumbnail pointing heavenward'.[5]

Always superstitious, Kipling took the background presence of Monadnock as a good omen, a sign that here was a place he might settle down. That, together with the other local ties and associations, made him eager to take up Beatty's and Mai's offer of a ten-acre plot of land – though not without some family wrangling. Carrie wanted to exchange her future share of the Balestier estate for Beatty's farm and to keep on a retainer her usually hard-up brother. Beatty refused, but eventually agreed to sell (rather than give) his new in-laws the ten-acre plot for $750; this they raised with an advance on *The Naulahka* from Macmillan.

By 26 March, when the couple left on the next leg of their honeymoon, Kipling was already writing to an American friend about their becoming 'settled down citizens of the United States'.[6] But while one part of him was starting to imagine being an American, another part was as busily reasserting the superior stance he had adopted on his previous visit. He dismissed New York as loftily as he had done San Francisco three years before. The city's 'management', he told his London readers, was 'the shiftless outcome of squalid barbarism and reckless extravagance'; its 'government' was 'a despotism of the alien by the alien for the alien, tempered with occasional insurrections of the decent folk'; its inhabitants were noisy, boastful children.[7]

This inner tug-of-war, and the corresponding impulse to let it all go, left their mark on 'The Gipsy Trail', another new poem addressed to Carrie. By the last quatrain one can almost feel him tugging at her sleeve in his impatience to be off:

> The heart of a man to the heart of a maid, –
> Light of my tents, be fleet.
> Morning waits at the end of the world,
> And the world is all at our feet![8]

A week's travel took them to Vancouver via Chicago, St Paul, Dakota and Winnipeg. From the vantage point of his train window, Kipling continued to seesaw between enthusiastic praise for the orderliness and generosity of small-town, rural America and haughty disparagement of the lawlessness and greed of the States as a whole, 'a land rotten before it was ripe'. Canada, on the other hand, gave him the chance to have a dig at England's lack of imperial responsibility: 'the Mother of Colonies has a wonderful gift for alienating the affections of her own household by neglect'. By the time they reached Vancouver, however, it was spring, and waiting to take them to Japan lay the *Empress of India*. 'What more auspicious name,' Kipling perkily concluded his second Letter, 'could you wish to find at the end of one of the strong chains of empire?'[9]

*

The *Empress of India* reached Japan after a fortnight's run. This was the first concentrated period that the couple had spent on their own. In a rare, personal remark Carrie confided to her diary that her husband was 'sweet to live with'.[10] Kipling for his part found it all a bit claustrophobic. 'If you'll take my advice,' he warned the Australian novelist Guy Boothby a few years later, 'you will *not* start on a sea tour, of cabins and decks and the like, immediately after you are wed. Get to know each other a little ere you deliberately face the cooping up of shipboard and all the attendant evils.'[11] It was probably during the voyage while they were 'cabin'd, cribbed, confin'd' that Carrie became pregnant.

They docked in Yokohama on 20 April. Writing up this second visit to Japan, Kipling was soon aestheticising the country and its inhabitants, turning both into a work of art as eagerly as he had done on his earlier trip with the Hills:

> We ... sit in a garden that is not ours, but belongs to a gentleman in slate-coloured silk, who, solely for the sake of the picture, conde-scends to work as a gardener, in which employ he is sweeping deli-cately a welt of fallen cherry blossoms from under an azalea aching to burst into bloom.

There were also more pungent reminders that he was back in Asia. In relaxed mood, with his imperialist guard lowered, he waxed lyrical about the 'Smell of the East', celebrating it as something which 'railways, telegraphs, docks, and gunboats cannot banish' and which 'will endure till the railways are dead'. But while he was eagerly savouring his own reunion with the East, he could not resist having a go at the groups of mere tourists, shaking his head knowingly at the 'globe-trotting million-aires', anxiously buying up ready-made curios in case old Japan should dis-appear under the increasing encroachment of Western civilisation.[12]

Having already 'done' Japan with the Hills, Kipling felt little inclina-tion to do it again; so for the next few months he and Carrie stayed in and around Yokohama, making only a couple of excursions to Tokyo and Nikko. This explains why instead of the exotic, scenic writing they might reasonably have expected, readers of *The Times* were treated in one Letter to a barrage of details about Japanese crop-yields and land-taxes, in another to an extended meditation on the 'Outside Men' – Kipling's term for Englishmen working abroad in business and trade. Reflecting on the clubs around the world where the Outside Men gathered, Kipling put his stay-at-Home London audience firmly in its place with the kind of observation that was already hardening into a refrain:

> There is no provincialism like the provincialism of London . . . Look back upon her from ten thousand miles, when the mail is just in at the Overseas Club, and she is wondrous tiny. Nine-tenths of her news – so vital, so epoch-making over there – loses its significance, and the rest is the scuffling of ghosts in a back-attic.[13]

To point out that, from a sufficient distance, even London looked provincial was justified, but, as with his more aggressive put-downs of America, Kipling was also revealing his own anxieties. He would not have harped on quite so persistently about London's, or anywhere else's, provincialism, had he not felt uncomfortable about his own.

The couple's general plan had been to stay in Japan until mid-June, then wander south and, after stopping over in New Zealand, visit Stevenson in Samoa. (Henry James in a March letter to Stevenson had been mentally rubbing his hands at 'the concussion' of Kipling's 'extraordinary personality with your own . . . We devoutly hope that this time he will really be washed upon your shore.'[14]) But on 9 June, the day after a severe earthquake, Kipling's bank, the New Oriental Banking Corporation, went bust. To readers of his fourth Letter, describing the failure of the bank and the tight-lipped post-mortem that evening at the Yokohama Club, it would not have been clear that Kipling himself had been a major loser. But the truth was that he had lost his entire savings (nearly £2,000), leaving him and his now-pregnant wife with the £10 he had taken out from the NOBC that morning and $100 in a New York bank. Years afterwards, he offered a slightly more expansive version of the calamity and the practical way in which he and Carrie responded to it:

> I returned with my news to my bride of three months and a child to be born. Except for what I had drawn that morning . . . and the unexpended Cook vouchers, and our personal possessions in our trunks, we have nothing whatever. There was an instant Committee

of Ways and Means, which advanced our understanding of each other more than a cycle of solvent matrimony. Retreat – flight, if you like – was indicated. What would Cook return for the tickets, not including the price of lost dreams? 'Every pound you've paid, of course,' said Cook of Yokohama. 'These things are all luck and – here's your refund.'[15]

At the time, the sudden collapse of their fortunes was no doubt rather more hair-raising. Even so – and one imagines Carrie chairing the Committee of Ways and Means, with Kipling as secretary – there was, in truth, no real cash crisis once they knew that Thomas Cook would give them a refund. (As for the lost money, Kipling's proposal at an NOBC creditors' meeting on 24 June that they should accept preference shares from the bank against lost deposits met with general approval, and eventually all the creditors got their money back.) For the young couple the longer-term prospects were hardly a problem in any case: more royalty cheques would soon be coming in, and any occasional work of Kipling's would always command a healthy price. In the medium term, with publishers' advances, they could probably have rustled up the money needed to continue the trip if they had really wanted to – which, perhaps, with Carrie newly pregnant, they no longer did. Instead, on 27 June, they turned their backs on Asia and, heading for Vancouver, began to retrace their steps; the 'gipsy trail' had quickly petered out.

A month later the newly-weds were back in Brattleboro and showing every intention of settling down in earnest. Madam Balestier had offered them Bliss Cottage, a farm-worker's house on her estate, at a monthly rent of $10, and they moved in on 10 August. 'The Blizzard', as they affectionately nicknamed the cottage, became their home for their first year in Brattleboro. Kipling later recalled this happy period with evident nostalgia:

We furnished it with a simplicity that fore-ran the hire-purchase system. We bought, second or third hand, a huge, hot-air stove which we installed in the cellar. We cut generous holes in our thin floors for its eight-inch tin pipes (why we were not burned in our beds each week of the winter I never can understand) and we were extraordinarily and self-centredly content.[16]

In 1892 itself, he was not quite so blasé. 'It has been an awful job,' he told a friend, 'though amusing in places. I don't think Heaven made me to put up bedsteads.'[17] Nor were they quite as hard-up as he later made out or, if they were, this can only have been for a few months at most. In late November Carrie's diary mentioned the arrival of a royalty cheque for $3,888 besides a steady trickle of smaller sums like the $260 received on 20 September for a new story, 'The Potted Princess'.

This now almost forgotten, charmingly slight tale (of Punch and Judy, Rud's and Trix's fictional counterparts in 'Baa Baa Black Sheep', being told a tale by their *ayah*) was crisscrossed with personal references which, together with the story's sunny mood, reflected Kipling's happiness as husband and father-to-be. The most striking indication of this was the radical rewriting of the children's history. In 'Baa Baa Black Sheep', Punch and Judy had been packed off to England at the ages of five and three; now, in 'The Potted Princess', aged seven and five, they were still living in Bombay, surrounded by adoring servants and devoted parents. It was as though the traumatic years at Rocklington (Southsea) had never happened or had been miraculously cancelled out. Moreover, the inset tale that the *ayah* told Punch and Judy had personal relevance in the light of Kipling himself being recently married and also the son of a potter.

Put simply, he projected two positive versions of himself into the story and had Punch, his happily 'adjusted' child self, listen to the tale – appropriately transformed – of how as an adult he got happily married. He could not have expected anyone (except perhaps his immediate family) to grasp such an intricate set of personal associations, or to see how the final 'Punchline' ('A pot is a pot, and I am the son of a potter!') so neatly clinched his double identity as successful suitor and restored child.[18] However, Carrie, as 'the potted princess', would have understood at least some of this; and for Kipling that was what mattered most. The story was a private thank-you to her, and its appearance in print, exactly a year after their marriage, a form of secret anniversary present.

By then, a 'potted princess' of a rather different kind had entered their lives – their daughter Josephine, born in the early evening of 29 December 1892. 'I *do* wish she hadn't had the bad taste to be born on

Gladstone's birthday,' Kipling grumbled to Henley a few days later, adding, 'That reconciles me to her being a girl.' However, his real delight and fatherly pride spilled out in a letter to his cousin Margaret three weeks later:

> She has a chin ear and nose which is a ridiculous plagiarism from her father – specially the chin but I can't understand how her hair comes to be downy fluff. She's to be called Josephine but Joss suits her better now seeing as she is the image of a Burmese idol and I'm afraid The Joss she'll remain till late in life. Carrie is walking through new worlds, wild with happiness and though I can't pretend to know The Joss intimately or to talk to her she is more than very dear to me. We can be very hoity-toity before a baby comes but once there, boy or girl, we're all too glad for what we've got to discuss it.[19]

From then on, Kipling's correspondence to family and close friends invariably contained the latest besotted bulletin on the progress and accomplishments of 'The Joss'.

Coinciding with relief at his daughter's birth was a relief about his father. Lockwood had written in August, saying that he had finally had enough of India and wanted to retire, but was worried that due to a technicality he might not be eligible for his full Government of India service pension. A couple of months later there were concerns about his health, and Kipling, now seriously alarmed, solicited the support of Lord and Lady Dufferin. His appeal was successful and, on full pension, Lockwood and Alice duly quit India on 17 April after twenty-eight years.

Kipling remained as industrious a correspondent as ever during this first winter in the States. When Uncle Alfred, an MP, solicited his views on the Indian opium question – then a hot topic in Parliament – he replied that opium was 'an excellent thing in itself and in moderation about as harmful as tobacco'. To Heinemann, he wrote mainly about publishing matters, but also remembered their absent Wolcott. And with Henley, he stuck mostly to imperialism and literature, including a subplot on the question of who should become Poet Laureate following Tennyson's death in 1892. Sir Theodore Martin, more translator than poet, was one of those being bruited, and Kipling not unmaliciously imagined the reactions of the disappointed candidates (Swinburne, Gosse *et al.*) should Martin get the post. In the event, the laureateship remained vacant until 1896, when Alfred Austin – not much more of a poet than Martin – was appointed; in the meantime, Kipling himself had been sounded out, but had declared himself 'not interested'.[20]

It was to Henley that Kipling siphoned off his anti-American views:

> Dickens never did better work than his American Notes and the more I get to know the land, the more do I stand 'astounded at my own moderation' . . . The moral dry rot of it all is having no law that need be obeyed: no line to toe: no trace to kick over and no compulsion to do anything. By consequence, a certain defect runs through everything – workmanship, roads, bridges, contracts, barter and sale and so forth – all inaccurate, all slovenly, all out of plumb and untrue. So far the immense natural wealth of the land holds this ineptitude up; and the slovenly plenty hides their sins unless you look for them. *Au fond* it's barbarism – barbarism plus telephone, electric light, rail and suffrage but all the more terrible for that very reason.[21]

Although this passage sounds like a repetition of his earlier anti-American invective (barbarism, lawlessness, etc.), there was a subtle difference. Previously, in 1889 and in January–February 1892, Kipling had played the part of the visiting English literary celebrity who refused to be impressed. Now his stance of English superiority was inevitably complicated. Not only was he married to an American, but he had opted for the present to become an American resident. The bracing diatribe to Henley was probably intended to reassure himself, as much as his imperialist chum, that 'the Kipperling' was not going native.

In fact, Kipling was soon putting down a few American roots. In October 1893, he joined the Association of American Authors, a semi-formal acknowledgement of his new literary affiliations. More casually, a spring trip to New York with Carrie earlier the same year allowed him to further his acquaintance with Mark Twain and to meet Wolcott's old friend, the novelist W D Howells. On the same trip he also made a point of getting to know less well-known writers like the rural novelist Hamlin Garland and the dialect poet James Riley. Garland would recall Kipling as 'colonial in accent, quick-spoken and humorous' and as a hypnotic talker, who after their dinner regaled Riley and himself with stories of 'cobras, typhoons, tropic heat, windless oceans, tiger-haunted jungles, and elephants, especially elephants'. He remembered too Kipling's enthusiastic 'By the Lord, *that's* American literature!' after Riley's recitation of his poem 'That Young 'Un'.[22] No doubt, as Garland suggested, he and Riley were sought out because they neatly fitted their host's image of the 'real' American writer – rural subjects, vernacular idiom – but Kipling's admiration for Riley's work at least was genuine. In 1890 he had written a poem, 'To James Whitcomb Riley', in which he had warmly praised the latter's *Rhymes of Childhood*; and after the New York meeting he was equally warm about more recent collections like *Poems Here at Home*. 'Your blamed verses,' he told Riley, '. . . are the only ones I know that can make me gulp.'[23]

To an apprentice writer of the same stamp, Frederick Cowles, who had sent him a short story for comment, Kipling responded with encouragement and practical advice. The title 'Jim', he pointed out, was bland and overused, and in its place he suggested a number of alternatives, including 'The Female of his Species', which, slightly altered, he was to use himself for a notable poem nearly twenty years later. He also offered Cowles some sound tips on dialect: 'The dialect [in 'Jim'] is unnecessarily misspelled. All you have to do is to give the reader a notion of the dialect. If he knows it he will read in the rest. If he does not no amount of commas and elisions will help him.'[24] By this time Kipling's own use of dialect had become increasingly subtle and daring. At the climax of a new story, 'Love-o'-Women' (collected in *Many Inventions* in June 1893), he had imagined the syphilitic gentleman-ranker, Larry Tighe, on the point of death quoting Antony's line to Cleopatra, 'I'm dying, Egypt, dying.' However, since Larry's tale was told by the Irishman Mulvaney, the famous line had become 'I'm dyin', Aigypt – dyin'', a distortion which ironically mirrored Larry's distorted myth of himself as a tragic hero, some latter-day Antony.[25]

But the most important of Kipling's new American ties, next to the birth of Josephine, was Naulakha, the house he and Carrie built on the plot of land they had bought from Beatty. Attentive to every last feature of the design and construction, the couple tried to create their ideal home. In a letter to Margaret in early 1893, with the house still six months from completion, Kipling took his cousin on a guided tour:

Josephine will spend her summer to come I hope in a hammock in the covered verandah at the south end of the house. You will see from the picture that her nursery – the bay window in the second story and running back the whole depth of the house – gives on to a second piazza where she can nearly always get out. My work room is the room below; next on the right is Carrie's. Next (the big open window thing) is a loggia which can be entirely opened: next is the dining room, and then a little overhung verandah to play in.

The kitchen is the last room at the north. Above it are the servants' quarters: next going S. a guest room: then the bathroom (that is what I am most interested in. I never had a bathroom to meet my views yet) next our room and then the nursery. Overhead there will be a clear run of 70 feet of attic that we can use for the most delightful rooms as we want them. All the foundation is in place – grey stone with moss on it that you can't distinguish from the lichened rocks of the pasture behind.[26]

A house designed for work and play, 'riding on its hillside like a little boat on the flank of a far wave' as Kipling later remembered it in his autobiography, Naulakha also memorialised the dead.[27] Kipling's and Carrie's choice of name (the spelling of the title now corrected) recalled the adventure yarn he had co-written with Wolcott and reaffirmed the continuing bond between the three. On a more mundane level, the name commemorated the fact that it was an advance on the novel that had allowed the couple to buy the land in the first place.

They moved into Naulakha on 12 August – or, to be exact, Carrie and Josephine moved in. Kipling and his father, who had arrived in June for an extended stay, were away on a trip to Canada. Carrie's diary implied that the trip was a case of strategic male withdrawal, rather than a father-and-son holiday cheerfully endorsed by Carrie herself. For her, the whole move was a nightmare. Not only was her husband away, but she had a contretemps with their two servants over dress codes. They promptly gave notice, leaving her to pack up The Blizzard and shift to Naulakha on her own. Predictably, none of this domestic disruption appears in Kipling's letter of 27 August to Margaret, merely the relieved comment that 'Carrie has been working like a demon to bring the new house into order and now it runs silently.' It is obvious, however, that he was thrilled with the new place, especially the loggia. 'The joy of the house,' he told Margaret, 'is the loggia with the ten foot window that slides up bodily and lets all the woods and mountains in upon you in a flood.'[28] Although Naulakha ended up costing $11,175 ($4,000 more than the original estimate), it and the surrounding area were to remain a constant delight.

'Rud tells me at night of the return of a feeling of great strength such as he had when he first went to London and met the men he was pitted against,' Carrie noted three months after the move.[29] Some of this resurgence of literary self-confidence was surely attributable to the security of being at last installed in his own home. Soon afterwards, in December, he wrote buoyantly to another new American literary friend, Edward White, telling him that although he had been 'scandalously neglecting' his duties to the Muse of lyric poetry, he was now once again 'experimenting with divers metres and various rhymes'. The spur on this occasion was a recent re-reading of Donne, 'Browning's great-great grandfather', and other early seventeenth-century poets like Michael Drayton, William Drummond and Phineas Fletcher. Kipling then treated White to a vigorously insouciant defence of his current political position:

> As for the Tory spirit – what would you have? It's a question of raising and training again. All I've been taught to see is that carelessness in administration, sloppiness of speech, vague appeals to the sentiments of great multitudes and tampering with the Decalogue, because a lot of people don't like to play consequences logically, ends in sending up the murder statistics and murder is no good thing. There's nothing in the People and the talk about the people a jot more to be reverenced than in Kings and the Divine right of the same.

He swept on to a nicely self-deflating warning about the problems of writing with a moral – a warning that says a good deal about his own practice. 'Remember,' he told White, 'it is evil to do one's work baldheaded for the sake of a Purpose. Purposes are good things but they are apt to make writing stodgy – same as this last page and a quarter. Let the Purpose come in accidental like, obliquely, from afar, casually and do not drive it too hard.'[30]

In the early years of their marriage, Kipling would usually add a brief annual coda to his wife's diary. On 31 December 1893 he wrote: 'Another perfect year ended. The Lord has been very good to us. All well in this House. Amen.'[31]

13

The Trouble with Beatty

The year of 1894 was one of trips: a week in New York in January, three weeks in Bermuda in February–March, most of a particularly wet summer in England. All of which must have cost a good deal. By now, however, the Kiplings were comparatively well-off. Carrie's diary continued to record the regular arrival of substantial drafts from his agent, Watt, and publisher, Macmillan: $485 on 23 January, $1,004 on 5 February, $1,456 on 15 February, and so on throughout the year, so that by the end of it Kipling had earned about $25,000 or £5,000. A tidy sum, worth perhaps £200,000 in present-day values.

When the Kiplings docked at Southampton on 10 April, it was over two years since they had set off on the gipsy trail, and a lot had happened since then. For a start there was Josephine. One reason for the visit was to show off 'Baby Jo' (or 'Flat Curls' or 'Bips' as she was also called) to Alice, who, with Lockwood, was now ensconced in Tisbury, Wiltshire and settling down to a busy retirement. The couple had already been accepted by the local country-house set, and Alice had booked nearby Arundell House (belonging to the Arundells at Wardour Castle) for her visitors' use. Although Kipling mock-grumbled about the lousy weather, the proximity to his parents – and the prescribed limits of his stay – prompted another of his astonishing bursts of creativity. Over the next three months or so, he and his father blocked out the plan of the *Just So Stories* and Kipling started 'How the Camel got his Hump'. He worked on 'How Fear Came', 'The Miracle of Purun Bhagat' and 'The Undertakers', which would subsequently appear in *The Second Jungle Book*. He wrote or recast 'The Song of the Banjo', 'The Miracles', 'An American', and 'The Three-Decker', his valedictory tribute to the comforting pleasures of the Victorian three-volume novel:

> Full thirty foot she towered from waterline to rail.
> It took a watch to steer her, and a week to shorten sail;
> But, spite all modern notions, I've found her first and best –
> The only certain packet for the Islands of the Blest.[1]

In addition he produced 'My Sunday at Home', a good-natured farce which he sent off to Robert Barr, the editor of the *Idler*, with jottings of other ideas for stories in 'the complicated absurdity line'. They were, Kipling observed, 'all full of purely male horse-play and schoolboy rot that womenfolk bless 'em find it so hard to understand.'[2] In another letter he mischievously encouraged Barr to run a series of 'Imaginary Interviews' and proposed, among other pairings, the promising mismatch of Emile Zola and Henry James.

Kipling also wanted, for all his reservations about the London literati, to keep in touch with the English literary scene. On their arrival he, Carrie and Josephine took lodgings for a fortnight at 84 Ebury St, Pimlico, and from there he made sorties into the old familiar world. Two days after landing, he was lunching at the Savile; the next day he was seeing Henley. The following week 'Spy' was doing his cartoon for *Vanity Fair*, and so – interspersed with breaks in Wiltshire – it went on throughout his stay. One evening in early May, he was attending the Royal Academy banquet; on another, at a dinner given by Lord George Hamilton, he was sitting next to his military hero Lord Roberts, or 'Bobs'; two days later, he was dining with Lord Arundell at Wardour Castle. One evening in June it was dinner with Sir Walter Besant, the next with the London Scottish. Far from being forgotten, he found himself an established literary lion, fêted and honoured wherever he went. In his own correspondence, of course, Kipling did not present himself as the returning hero: proper modesty and his superstitious streak would never have allowed that. Instead he struck a suitably blasé pose. 'News in town is small,' he wrote to an

American friend. 'Coming back as one does after two years' absence, is like entering a theatre in the middle of the second act. You see all sorts of situations and hear a deal of vastly fine dialogue but not being privy to the events that led up to all the row, you are only a little amazed and more than a little bored.'[3]

It was not only Kipling who arrived in April 1894, but also *The Yellow Book*, that short-lived literary and art journal whose name still instantly evokes the Decadence Movement of the 1890s. Indeed, it achieved immediate notoriety, thanks largely to Aubrey Beardsley's provocative cover, title-page and drawings. Kipling saw a copy as soon as it came out, for Carrie's diary for 27 April mentions him doing some drawings in Beardsley's style. (He was already something of a Beardsley fan, having made a point of calling on the artist in New York in 1893.) The first issue contained other material to interest Kipling – not least the opening story, 'The Death of a Lion', one of Henry James's cautionary tales about the dangers of popular and social success. In addition, following contributions by such friends and acquaintances as Saintsbury, Gosse and Arthur Waugh, there was a brief, resonant entry on the page advertising recent books published by William Heinemann:

> BENEFITS FORGOT. A Posthumous Novel. By WOLCOTT BALESTIER, Author of 'The Average Woman' and 'The Naulahka' (with Rudyard Kipling). In 3 vols.

Kipling's only surviving comment on *The Yellow Book* came in a letter in late July to the American writer Brander Matthews:

> As for the *Yellow Book*, let us remember what Pudd'nhead Wilson did *not* say: – 'When you see a man standing on his head in the streets don't interfere with him. He won't walk far that way but the chances are he'll have learned a great deal about the centre of gravity by the time he is through.' The thing's so mixed – any way.[4]

The air of casual detachment was probably assumed: the implied preference here for Twain's *Pudd'nhead Wilson*, which had just finished its serial run and was the *dernier cri* in America, almost suggests one American author writing to another. Nor was this an impression Kipling cultivated only in letters. The *Philadelphia Ledger* noted that 'English people who have met Rudyard Kipling during his visit home are reported to be pained at what they regard as the Americanisation of his manners.'[5]

Rivalling *The Yellow Book* as the literary event of the summer was the publication of *The Jungle Book* on 24 May. The individual stories had been appearing in *St Nicholas Magazine* and other journals over the previous nine months, and Kipling had been alerting friends that a 'book of children's beast-tales' was on the way. When the book appeared, he felt he had again flummoxed the critics. 'The reviews are rather funny,' he told an American friend. 'They don't know how or at which end to pick the thing up.'[6] In fact, the reviews could not have been more positive. On 16 June *Punch* carried an appreciative notice by 'Baron De Book-Worms', which dubbed him 'Sir RUDYARD KIPLINGO, the Laureate of The Jungle-Jingle and the Bard of the Bandar-dog', with an accompanying cartoon of a turbaned, banjo-strumming Kipling, surrounded by his animal characters. The same day, at the other end of the scale, the *Athenaeum* gave him two laudatory columns, concluding with 'our sincere thanks to Mr Kipling for the hour of pure and unadulterated enjoyment which he has given us, and many another reader, by this inimitable "Jungle Book"'.

Among the chorus of public praise, Henry James was a strong, though private, dissenter:

> He sends me too [James told Gosse] his jungle book which I have read with extreme admiration. But *how* it closes his doors & sets his limit! The rise to 'higher types' that one hoped for – I mean the care for life in a finer way – is the rise to the mongoose & the care for the wolf. The *violence* of it all, the almost exclusive preoccupation with fighting & killing, is also singularly characteristic.[7]

Was there an element of envy in James's disenchantment? During the first half of the 1890s James was desperately hungry for popular success – while decrying it in a story like 'The Death of the Lion' – and it must have been exasperating to witness the continual rise of the wilfully unrefined Kipling. There was perhaps too a residual jealousy about that friendship with Wolcott.

Kipling's own delight at what he had achieved in this new book flashed out in a letter to an old Anglo-Indian friend, Eric Robertson: 'I'm glad you like the *Jungle Book*. I hoped it would go well for the reason that I got more pleasure out of writing it than anything I've done for a long time.'[8] He was to recall that pleasure all his life and to leave over forty years later a memorable snapshot of it:

> My workroom in the Bliss Cottage was seven feet by eight, and from December to April the snow lay level with the window-sill. It chanced that I had written a tale about Indian Forestry work ['In the Rukh', *Many Inventions*] which included a boy who had been brought up by wolves. In the stillness, and suspense, of the winter of '92 some memory of the Masonic Lions of my childhood's magazine [*King Lion* in the *Boy's Own Paper*], and a phrase in Haggard's *Nada the Lily*, combined with the echo of that tale. After blocking out the main idea in my head, the pen took charge, and I watched it begin to write stories about Mowgli and animals, which later grew into the *Jungle Books*.[9]

He personally acknowledged one of these debts closer to the time. 'It was a chance sentence of yours in *Nada the Lily* that started me off on a track that ended in my writing a lot of wolf stories,' he confessed to Rider Haggard in October 1895. 'You remember in your tale where the wolves leaped up at the feet of a dead man sitting on a rock? Somewhere on that page [page 103] I got the notion. It's curious how things come back again, isn't it?'[10]

'It's curious how things come back again, isn't it?' And not just the memory of the page in Haggard's book but, as the passage in his auto-biography suggests, the associated childhood memories that the page from *Nada the Lily* stirred up. What is most striking about Mowgli's story, from a biographical point of view – as it unfolds in 'Mowgli's Brothers', 'Kaa's Hunting' and 'Tiger! Tiger!' – is watching Kipling once more rewriting aspects of his own childhood. The pattern of abandonment was repeated no fewer than three times: twice in 'Mowgli's Brothers', which opened with him losing his human parents and closed with him being cast out by the wolf-pack; and again at the end of 'Tiger! Tiger!', when he was rejected by the village. Mowgli became, in effect, a super-orphan. But while the abandonment motif was magnified, so too were the emotional compensations. Kipling provided Mowgli at each successive abandonment with a queue of would-be foster-parents, falling over each other to look after him: Father and Mother Wolf, Akela the Lone Wolf, Baloo the Bear, Bagheera the Black Panther and Kaa the Python. Not only were all these wild animals eager to care for Mowgli, but they competed with each other for his affection and acknowledged his power over them, a situation that has appealed to generations of child readers.

Equally gratifying for Kipling was Mowgli's eventual outwitting and destruction of Shere Khan the Lame Tiger, the malevolent would-be foster-parent who, like the giant or witch in the fairy story, wanted to eat the hero. Shere Khan stood for Mrs Holloway, and his sidekick, Tabaqui the Jackal, for her son. There were, however, distinct traces of her Evangelical influence, suitably 'improved', in the obsession with rules that ran through the stories and was encoded in the 'law of the jungle'. While these rules emphasised obedience and knowing your place, they also established ties with others and – one of Kipling's favourite paradoxes – conferred the freedom to move between different worlds. It was Baloo's teaching that helped to save Mowgli when he was kidnapped by the *Bandar-log* in 'Kaa's Hunting', in the process allowing him to become another of Kipling's 'boundary-crossers'.

The non-Mowgli stories in the volume offered variations on the main themes. 'Rikki-Tikki-Tavi', for instance, replayed the basic pattern of abandonment, fosterage and victory, but here the orphaned hero, the quick-witted mongoose, found loving human foster-parents; and, unlike Mowgli, he was personally allowed to kill his enemies, the cobras Nag and Nagaina and their offspring. In most of the tales the British presence in India was either minimal or simply not an issue; only at the end of the last story, 'Her Majesty's Servants', did Kipling bring in a deliberately imperialist note as a native officer explained to an Afghan chief the chain of hierarchic obedience that stretched from camp-animals to Empress:

'Would it were so in Afghanistan!' said the chief; 'for there we obey only our own wills.'

'And for that reason,' said the native officer, twirling his moustache, 'your Amir whom you do not obey must come here and take orders from our Viceroy.'[11]

Marriage and fatherhood provided the conditions for this positive revision of his childhood; so too did living in America. There Kipling had the advantage of both belonging (marriage and being a householder) and not belonging (upbringing and imperialist affiliation). He could thus lead a kind of double life, part American, part English, which did not lock him into either. There was always, to adapt Philip Larkin's phrase, 'an else-where to underwrite his existence'. Living in America also meant that the strains he had felt as a self-professed Anglo-Indian in India in the 1880s and later in England were automatically allayed. In America he could, if he chose, see himself as a writer and Carrie's husband first, and an Englishman or Anglo-Indian second. In England, as on the 1894 trip, he could see himself as Ruddy staying with his family, or as the famous ex-patriate writer in transit, or even as a visiting American. This chameleon tendency was reflected in *The Jungle Book* in Mowgli's ability to adapt suc-cessfully to different environments (jungle, village) and was enshrined in his amphibious name, 'Mowgli the Frog'. As for Kipling's relocation to Vermont, elements of this were reconfigured in 'The White Seal', where the young outsider, Kotick, led his mate and the other seals from the killing-grounds of their 'home' nurseries to a safe haven 'in that sea where no man comes'.[12] *The Jungle Book* could not have been conceived without the Southsea 'orphanhood', but it was living in America that allowed Kipling imaginatively to revisit those years and convert loss into gain.

By late July Kipling was eager to get back to his other life in the States. He told Barr:

> There's one Britisher at least homesick for a section of your depraved old land, and he's going, please Allah, the first week in August by the Kaiser Wilhelm and won't New York be hot just! There's a smell of horse-piss, Italian fruit-vendor, nickel-cigars, sour lager and warm car-conductor drifting down Carmine Street at this minute from Sixth Ave, which I can smell with the naked eye as I sit here.[13]

The Kiplings duly left for New York on 5 August on the *Kaiser Wilhelm II*. Ten days later, after a wretched passage, they reached Naulakha, dashing around the house in their happiness to be home.

This did not, however, prevent a few more excursions during the autumn and early winter: trips to Gloucester, to New York, to Cambridge. There were also visitors to Naulakha, including Conan Doyle, who was on a lecture tour of the States and came for a couple of days at the end of November with his brother and his golf-clubs. He would later recall giving Kipling 'lessons in a field while the New England rustics watched us from afar, wondering what on earth we were at'; and Kipling rather took to golf, playing with red-painted balls when the ground was covered in snow.[14] Doyle's reminiscences also afford a rare glimpse of Kipling reading his work. Earlier in the year, he had written 'McAndrew's Hymn', a Browningesque dramatic monologue in which an ageing Scottish engineer reviewed his life at sea and his discovery of the idiosyncratic faith that had sustained him:

> Lord, Thou has made this world below the shadow of a dream,
> An', taught by time, I tak' it so – exceptin' always Steam.
> From coupler-flange to spindle-guide I see Thy Hand, O God –
> Predestination in the stride o' yon connectin'-rod.
> John Calvin might ha' forged the same – enormous, certain, slow –
> Ay, wrought it in the furnace-flame – my 'Institutio'.

McAndrew revealed that, tempted by the East in his wild youth, he gave way to the Sin 'against the Holy Ghost': the despair that leads to suicide. He was saved, he confessed – 'An', by Thy Grace, I had the Light to see my duty plain./Light on the engine-room'. In other words his salvation, a typically Kiplingesque one, was through work and being 'o' service to my kind'.[15] Kipling's performance of the poem sounds impressive. He 'surprised me,' Doyle remembered, 'by his dramatic power which enabled him to sustain the Glasgow accent throughout, so that the angular Scottish greaser simply walked the room'.[16] Kipling in his turn was a fan of Doyle's, enjoying both his Sherlock Holmes stories and historical romances like *Sir Nigel*. The two writers also shared a deep interest in the paranormal, a link reflected in Kipling's 'The House Surgeon' (1909), a psychic detective story about a house aptly named Holmescroft.

In September an Englishman, Matthew Howard, joined the Naulakha establishment as the Kiplings' new coachman. He was taken on as a married but childless man; in fact, he had eight children who by degrees came to live with him, some working in various capacities for the Kiplings. Five foot six, exactly the same height as Kipling, he 'wore top-boots and cord breeches even when cleaning out the stable'.[17] Part dutiful handyman, part rascal – always a favourite combination with Kipling – Howard's qualities as a coachman were soon tested. In late October one of the carriage horses 'got his leg over the pole', and as the coachman was 'pulling them away from a hill the off hind wheel of the trap gave way – spilling C., Armstrong and Baby'. Fortunately, Carrie, Josephine and her nanny were unhurt, and Kipling's letter recounting the incident to Aunt Louie was full of praise for Howard's nerve and skill. Always superstitious, he was sending, he added, a 'little thank-offering to a children's home in New York' to mark the escape.[18]

Even before the accident, horses had been on Kipling's mind. He had been writing a satire on American labour politics called 'In the Back Pasture' (later retitled 'A Walking Delegate'), in which a socialist 'yellow horse' from Kansas tried to incite a group of Vermont horses to overthrow (and kill) their human owners. The *Century*, which published the tale in December, paid him $135 per 1,000 words, a new high in his rates. In addition to its political thrust – and calling one of the horses 'Tedda Gabler', cheekily described as having 'a reputation for vice which was really the result of bad driving' – 'A Walking Delegate' showed Kipling extending his ventriloquist range and experimenting with different kinds of American vernacular.[19] The story itself was admired in its day, not least by the New England realist Sarah Jewett. To encourage the 'American' Kipling, she sent him volumes of recent local work, including a copy of her own *A Native of Winby and Other Tales* and Rowland Robinson's *Danvis Folks*. Kipling's letter of thanks reflected his desire to do more in this line and his reservations about his home-grown qualifications. *Danvis Folks*, he told Jewett, 'is a mine which I purpose to work . . . What a mass of material there is to work at in this land! But it must – woe is me – be done by an inhabitant and that makes me rage like the heathen.'[20] He also informed Jewett that he was busy revising a new edition of some of his old Indian stories. Watt had just bought back for £1,200 the copyright of his six Indian Railway Library collections, and Kipling reissued these in two volumes with Macmillan.

He was busy too writing up 'An Error in the Fourth Dimension', one of the notions he had sent to Barr in the summer. By fourth dimension he meant, as he later explained to a correspondent, the dimension in every country 'in which no one except a lawful native of the land can move without violent collisions'.[21] In the story Wilton Sargent, the son of a railway magnate, bored with his American lifestyle, went to live in England with the aim of being 'just a little more English than the English'.[22] As Kipling told his correspondent, Sargent 'knew his three dimensions perfectly. It was only when he tried to put a thing through in a hurry on hereditary lines that he came to grief.'[23] Sargent's 'error' was to flag down a train passing through his property when he wanted to get up to London quickly, and his failure to understand that such cavalier behaviour was unacceptable in England. Complementing this portrait of American naïvety was 'The "Mary Gloster"', another of Kipling's digs at 'Young England'. This companion piece to 'McAndrew's Hymn' was a kind of mercantile homage to Browning's 'The Bishop Orders His Tomb', in which a venal, self-made shipowner issued death-bed instructions to his decadent *flâneur* of a son.

This further flurry of creative activity was interrupted in December by the news of Robert Louis Stevenson's death. Although the two never met, Kipling was more in sympathy with Stevenson than with any other of his literary contemporaries. Stevenson's flair for the exotic and the demotic, his blend of literariness, humour and romance, made him very much Kipling's sort of writer; and there had been the added bond that both were expatriates and had American wives. Kipling was so cut up by the news that for a time he was simply unable to write. He did, however, sound off caustically to Charles Norton as personal reminiscences began to appear and plans were announced to publish Stevenson's letters. This idea Kipling found particularly repellent:

I suppose selling chunks of dead friends is all right . . . They are digging out all R.L.S.'s letters and nailing every chance word to the public barn door and I am very sick of it . . . It's rather like the Pest-cart of old with the bell and candle and the cry: – 'Bring out your dead'. We have added the book but I think I should prefer being shot feet first out of the tumbril with half a pound of quicklime into the common ditch.[24]

The pattern of 1895, Kipling's last full year in the States, followed that of 1894: trips, intensive work and the appearance of a second *Jungle Book*.

Although a planned visit to India failed to come off, there was again a trip to England: this time only for a month, from mid-July to mid-August, presumably to avoid the rigours of another English June. After the triumphs of the previous year, it was an altogether quieter affair, mostly centred around the usual family and friends: Lockwood and Alice, the Poynters, the Burne-Joneses, 'Crom' Price and Henry James, though there was also a call on the three old ladies with whom Kipling had spent his holidays as a schoolboy.

A more memorable trip had been the one to Washington for six weeks in the spring. Details of this brief stroll in the American halls of power remained with Kipling for the rest of his life. President Cleveland and his entourage at the White House disgusted him. 'A colossal agglomeration of reeking bounders – awful; inexpressible; incredible,' he noted in Carrie's diary.[25] Otherwise, he was to remember with affection these 'great and spacious and friendly days in Washington which – politics apart – Allah had not altogether deprived of a sense of humour; and the food was a thing to dream of'. Much of this friendliness and humour came from the circle surrounding the historian and later autobiographer, Henry Adams, a former shipboard companion. Kipling quickly became firm friends with two members of that set: the diplomat and writer, John Hay, and a Washington lawyer, William Hallett Phillips. It was Hay who would give him the key to American perceptions of England: 'When a man comes up out of the sea, we say to him: "See that big bully over there in the East? He's England! Hate him, and you're a good American." '[26] As for Phillips, it was to him that Kipling turned in May when he was trying to establish what was more or less a personal post office at the nearby Waite farm. Phillips duly fixed it for him. The following year when he was doing research for his boys' novel *Captains Courageous* and needed charts of the Newfoundland fishing banks, Phillips was again equally helpful.

It was through the Adams circle that, on this Washington trip, Kipling met and made friends with Theodore Roosevelt, the American statesman he most came to admire. Over the years the two enjoyed a series of good-natured jousts about Anglo-American relations. Kipling was to combine a memory of these amicable tussles with a sharp dig at American imperial self-righteousness in one carefully weighted paragraph in his autobiography:

The Smithsonian [Institution], specially on the ethnological side, was a pleasant place to browse in. Every nation, like every individual, walks in a vain show – else it could not live with itself – but I never got over the wonder of a people who, having extirpated the aboriginals of their continent more completely than any modern race had ever done, honestly believed that they were a godly little New England community, setting examples to brutal mankind. This wonder I used to explain to Theodore Roosevelt, who made the glass cases of Indian relics shake with his rebuttals.[27]

Roosevelt, for his part, was to say that Kipling was one of the only two Englishmen he ever wished to hear from.

On the literary front, the main event in 1895 was the publication in November of *The Second Jungle Book*. If anything, the tales were consistently stronger and richer than those in the first volume. 'The Miracle of Purun Bhagat', about a wealthy Brahmin who renounced the world to become a *sanyasi* (a wandering holy man), has become one of Kipling's most highly praised stories. (As with *Kim*, an early version of which he had begun in the autumn of 1892, he drew heavily on his father's knowledge and expertise in writing it.) 'The Undertakers', in quite a different vein, has worn equally well. In it a jackal and an adjutant-crane sucked up to a huge crocodile, the 'blunt-nosed Mugger of Mugger-Ghaut', who expatiated on the banqueting highlights of his long and eventful life 'in a muddy voice that would have made you shudder'.[28]

All five new Mowgli tales were excellent, adding further chapters to his life in the jungle and bringing it to a fitting conclusion in 'Spring Running'. These additions made it clear that Kipling's model for the overall shape of the Mowgli story was appropriately mythic and had more in common with the structure of older heroic narratives than with the tighter sequential plotting of most nineteenth-century fiction. These older narratives traditionally began with the emergence of the hero and concluded with his death or disappearance, and in between there was a timeless zone in which a number of self-contained episodes took place. So 'How Fear Came' gave a version of the Fall, told by Hathi the Elephant to Mowgli and the other animals during a terrible drought. 'Letting in the Jungle' showed Mowgli saving the couple who were kind to him in 'Tiger! Tiger!' (his human foster-parents) and, with the help of Hathi and his sons, flattening the village. 'The King's Ankus' was a deliberate reworking of 'The Pardoner's Tale', with Mowgli learning a lesson about human greed and Death. 'Red Dog' recounted the epic battle that the boy and the wolf-pack waged against the invading 'dhole-pack', and how Akela the Lone Wolf fought his last fight. Finally, in 'Spring Running', Mowgli, now 'nearly seventeen years old' (Kipling's age when he left school), reluctantly left the Jungle and followed 'a new trail' in the human world.[29] The new book was an instant success, Lockwood proudly telling an Italian friend that it had sold 10,000 copies in England in its first week.[30]

The most notable adult stories Kipling wrote this year were 'The Brushwood Boy' and 'William the Conqueror', both collected in *The Day's Work* (1898). 'The Brushwood Boy', long by Kipling's standards at forty-five pages, was conceived and written in a sustained burst between 23 August and 8 September, and when he sold it to the *Century* he was able to charge $170 per thousand words, a further jump in his rates. If, in the Mowgli stories, he had imagined an improved childhood for himself, here he imagined an alternative childhood, adolescence and adulthood. Georgie Cottar, the 'Brushwood Boy', was Kipling's fantasy of himself as a model subaltern. The 'Youngest major in the army, and should have had the VC, sir', he came back to England on leave from India and married his 'dream girl' – quite literally, for she had been appearing in his dreams (and he in hers), since they were children. Georgie in the main was allowed an ordinary, happy, middle-class home life with both parents. What he had by way of a traumatic equivalent to Kipling's childhood experiences was an extremely complicated and disturbing dream life, involving the same landscape, and repeated, shared adventures with a girl called 'Annie*an*louise'. The dreams stopped when Georgie went to boarding school ('Ten years at an English public school,' we are told, 'do not encourage dreaming'), but resumed again on service in India, as Georgie with modest heroism pursued his brilliant career.[31]

The sentimental dénouement in which Georgie found Miriam, the girl of his dreams, was routine enough, as were the military scenes in India, but the childhood sections and dream sequences remain convincing and uncanny. So much so, that it is tempting to read Georgie's first discovery of his imaginative life as a sliver of autobiography:

A child of six was telling himself stories as he lay in bed. It was a new power, and he kept it a secret. A month before it had occurred to him to carry on a nursery tale left unfinished by his mother, and he was delighted to find the tale as it came out of his own head just as surprising as though he were listening to it 'all new from the beginning'. There was a prince in that tale, and he killed dragons, but only for one night. Ever afterwards Georgie dubbed himself prince, pasha, giant-killer, and all the rest (you see, he could not tell any one, for fear of being laughed at), and his tales faded gradually into dreamland, where adventures were so many that he could not recall the half of them.[32]

Shortly before publication, Kipling alerted 'Crom' Price to an altogether different aspect of the story. There were, he told him, 'some references in a yarn of mine that will appear in the Xmas *Century*, which may possibly remind you of old days at Westward Ho! Some time I think I'll write a boys book and pitch the scene there.'[33] Here, growing out of 'The Brushwood Boy', was the germ of the idea for *Stalky & Co.*

If Miriam represented one kind of ideal girl, the eponymous tomboy heroine of 'William the Conqueror' represented quite another. This two-part story (with epigraphs from Donne) charted the developing romance between Scott of the Irrigation Department and Miss Martyn, when the two worked together during a famine in southern India. Miss Martyn ('who answered indifferently to William or Bill') was portrayed as a practical, no-nonsense girl who shared her future husband's Anglo-Indian service ethic and was a working partner as much as a wife in the conventional, old-fashioned sense.[34] Carrie noted of the story: 'He has got the hang of quite a new sort of woman and she is turning out stunningly.'[35] The phrase 'a new sort of woman' suggests that William was Kipling's response to the idea of the 'New Woman' then much in the air, and usually taken to mean a woman who believed in women's suffrage and the eradication of the sexual double standard. Predictably, Kipling's version was a little different, consistent with his reply the previous August when he had been asked for his views on the 'New Woman'. She was, he had insisted then, 'shouting for a cause already won', claiming that 'A woman to-day can do exactly what her body and soul let her.'[36] For a 'new woman' of that kind he had of course a model at home, Carrie herself, whose 'masculine' qualities he much admired. 'Carrie behaved superbly,' he had told Aunt Louie after the carriage-accident, while at the start of 1895 he had witnessed her stoicism when she painfully burnt her face.[37] That William was also in part a tribute to his wife (the real girl as opposed to the ideal), and was accepted as such, is supported by Carrie's own evident enthusiasm for the character.

Not that life with Carrie was all happy camaraderie. In April, after congratulating his cousin Stanley Baldwin on the birth of his daughter Diana, Kipling passed on a couple of tips. The first, 'Don't believe a grandmother is infallible', suggested that Alice had probably been a bit of a trial the previous summer. The second strongly implied that after Josephine's birth Carrie had suffered quite badly from post-natal anxiety and that this had been a trying period: 'Let us know how the wife does and (this is worth knowing) you must be more than gentle with her these next months to come. A woman isn't well before her child comes bodily but it's her spirits and mind that are all on edge afterwards.'[38]

Kipling was always properly loyal and devoted to Carrie, and it is only in the occasional aside that one senses he ever found her difficult to live with. Others were less restrained. A particularly tough-minded account of the impression she made during this period was provided by the Kiplings' neighbour and frequent visitor, Mary Cabot:

Mrs Kipling prided herself on being practical. She was not, however, a natural housekeeper, provided only bare necessities and slender allowances for her life, made much of the difficulty of conducting a household like hers so far from the source of supplies, and kept the machinery of life always in evidence. An unexpected guest at luncheon would have been an impossibility. Nor did she know how to make a house attractive . . .

Although not given to hospitality herself, and averse to the prodigality of her husband's social instincts, Mrs Kipling was, in many respects, an admirable wife for a genius. She guarded his health, assumed the supervision of every detail of the routine of his daily life, published his works, was his business agent, and stood between him and any obstacles to the free and full development of his powers. I once went to the railroad station when they were starting for Lakewood, New Jersey. While Mrs Kipling was checking the baggage, I happened to ask Mr Kipling the name of the hotel where they were to be. He replied, 'Why, bless you, I don't know! I am no more than a cork on the water, when Carrie is with me.' . . .

He suffered from sightseers, lion-hunters and newspaper reporters, by whom he was so often misrepresented that he learned to crave protection from the unknown. To the large numbers in these classes his wife was the formidable dragoness who inhabited a small sewing-room between the entrance hall and library. No one could gain access to him in working hours without running the gauntlet of her authority.[39]

Stingy, complaining, vulgar, domineering, super-efficient and protective: not an appealing list of qualities. Mary Cabot's antipathy towards Carrie owed something to her admiration for Kipling himself, though much of what she said fits the account left by the Kiplings' second daughter, Elsie. Her mother, Elsie would recall, 'introduced into everything she did, and even permeated the life of her family with, a sense of strain and worry amounting sometimes to hysteria'.[40] Yet it is clear enough that Kipling himself came to terms with Carrie's nature and, at least most of the time, accepted unquestioningly the kind of marriage they had. There was no bitterness in his 'a cork on the water' metaphor to Mary Cabot; and in his autobiography, he wryly described their union as the 'Committee of Ways and Means'.

By the latter half of 1895, Kipling seemed to be settling ever more firmly into the rhythm of his American life. Following the successful establishment of the post office at Waite's farm, he tried to negotiate a flag and freight station at the same location. He was elected a member of the Century Club, and to his delight two new towns on the Michigan peninsula were named after him: Rudyard and Kipling – the 'Michigan twins' as he nicknamed them.[41] But already international and family events that would permanently uproot him were under way.

The international event was the sudden escalation of a long-term boundary disagreement between British Guiana and Venezuela. When gold was found in the hinterland of both countries, Britain and Venezuela vigorously pushed their respective border claims. The United States took a strong line on Venezuela's behalf against possible British intervention in the Americas, and by the closing weeks of 1895 there was, on both sides of the Atlantic, talk of war. 'It's the futilest piffle I've ever heard of and I wish to heaven I could write a set of verses chaffing the thing dead,' Kipling wrote to Phillips on 23 November, before things got really serious. A few weeks later came Cleveland's 'ultimatum', and Kipling described himself to Charles Norton as 'regularly upset and bewildered', as if he 'had been aimed at with a decanter across a friendly dinner table'.

Early in the New Year, two further anxieties were pushing the thirty-year-old Kipling over the edge into outright panic and hysteria: Carrie was about to give birth to their second child, and the German Kaiser had sent a much-publicised offer of support to the Boers in the Transvaal after the fiasco of the Jameson Raid. Surrendering to this concatenation of public and private fears, Kipling became so paranoid that for a time he convinced himself he was in serious personal danger:

> I seem to be [he told Norton on 8 January] between two barrels like a pheasant. If the American mine is sprung it means dirt and slush and ultimately death either across the Canada border or in some dis-embowelled gunboat off Cape Hatteras. If the German dynamite is exploded equally it means slaughter and most probably on the high seas. In both cases I am armed with nothing more efficient than a note-book, a stylographic pen and a pair of opera glasses . . . but whether it be peace or war [with America], this folly puts an end to my good wholesome life here: and to me that is the saddest part of it. We must begin again from the beginning elsewhere and pretend that we are only anxious to let the house for a year or two. It is hard enough God knows but I should be a fool if after full warning I risked my own peoples' happiness and comfort in a hostile country.[42]

As he often did, he managed to channel some of this galloping apprehension into verse. The poem 'Hymn before Action' had strong affinities with the later 'Recessional', though its imperial posturing, clearly a displacement of his own anxieties, was far more overt:

> The earth is full of anger,
>   The seas are dark with wrath,
> The Nations in their harness
>   Go up against our path:

> Ere yet we loose the legions –
> Ere yet we draw the blade,
> Jehovah of the Thunders,
> Lord God of Battles, aid![43]

The Times had recently put him on its 'free list', and he sent the verses off to the editor Moberly Bell, who wisely did not print them. By then, in any case, things were quietening down. Some of the heat had gone out of the American situation and, on 2 February, his second daughter, Elsie, was born without complications. At this point Kipling tried (not for the first time) to resume work on his novel *Kim*, but after a few days decided that he needed his father's assistance.

Instead he went ahead with his boys' novel, *Captains Courageous*, which – with help from his neighbour Dr Conland and various visits with him to the harbours at Gloucester and Boston – was finished during the summer. The plot was thin and the characterisation sketchy, but what made the book memorable was the wealth of detail about the boats, the fishing and the life at sea. This, and the collaborative friendship with Conland, stamped Kipling's account in *Something of Myself*:

> We assisted hospitable tug-masters to help haul three- and four-stick schooners of Pocahontas coal all round the harbour; we boarded every craft that looked as if she might be useful, and we delighted ourselves to the limit of delight . . . And Conland took large cod and the appropriate knives with which they are prepared for the hold, and demonstrated anatomically and surgically so that I could make no mistake about treating them in print. Old tales, too, he dug up, and the lists of dead and gone schooners whom he had loved, and I revelled in profligate abundance of detail – not necessarily for publication but for the joy of it.[44]

Viewed as Kipling's only sustained attempt to make fiction out of exclusively American material – to be an 'American' writer – it was symbolically apt that most of *Captains Courageous* took place offshore and that he never really 'landed'. The explanation perhaps lay in Kipling having a far more pressing matter on his mind while he was writing the book.

*

The whole history of the trouble with Beatty will probably never be known for certain. At first, relations between Kipling and Carrie and Beatty and his wife Mai were extremely friendly. The Kiplings' honeymoon visit when they stayed at Maplewood was a success, and when they returned after the bank crash, they were again welcomed with open arms. Beatty was big, open, sociable and generous: the kind of man Kipling took to on sight, and he was equally taken with the hospitable Mai. For the first two years or so, there was almost daily contact between the households and much mutual goodwill. Three things soured the relationship: the rekindling of early sibling conflict between Carrie and the younger Beatty; the eventual clash of values and lifestyle between Naulakha and Maplewood; and the resentments that arose from Beatty working for his sister and brother-in-law.

The main source for the sibling rivalry element was Mary Cabot, who confidently stated that it was 'a Balestier feud, beginning in childhood with a natural antagonism between the inconsequent characteristics of Beatty and the disciplinary temperament of his sister Caroline'. It is Mary too who gave a suggestive clue to Beatty's habitual relations with others, recalling how Wolcott told her that 'Beatty never cared for anything less than the best and the most expensive, but that the cost fell on some one else.'[45] Collision was almost inevitable between the impetuous, irresponsible, improvident brother and his colder, more calculating, rule-conscious sister, particularly if one adds that Beatty was a noted drinker in what was then a dry State.

When the Kiplings came back as the tenants of Bliss Cottage in the autumn of 1892, they were relatively hard-up. They had prospects, but little immediate cash. As such they posed no threat to Beatty; in fact, with his farm he was probably in the better financial position. With Kipling's literary earnings constantly rising, however, it was not long before this situation changed. Soon the Kiplings were carrying through the plans for their new house, and it was then that, to help Beatty, they employed him as a bailiff and works manager. Initially this arrangement suited everyone. The Kiplings felt they were assisting him and his family and, so Kipling later claimed, fulfilling Wolcott's wish that they should look after Beatty. Beatty, for his part, was receiving a steady income in addition to whatever he made through his farm.

Here Carrie's diary supplies a vital clue as to what went wrong. It shows that from October 1892 to June 1895 she, as the accountant and paymaster of the 'Committee of Ways and Means', was handing out money to Beatty, often on a daily basis. These payments included his wages as foreman and money for materials and labour on the house. What was striking about almost all these sums was that they were so small, usually ranging between three and twenty-five dollars. In other words, no large sums, for fear that Beatty would blow them on drink. Up to a point it was no doubt well-intentioned parsimony on Carrie's part, but the controlling, dependency aspect probably also had its appeal. By all accounts Beatty was not a malicious person, but nor was he a scrupulous one. Known to be 'backed' by his increasingly well-off relatives, he was able to command credit in Brattleboro and the neighbourhood; credit led to debt; debt eventually to filing for bankruptcy. Without anyone quite meaning it, goodwill turned to disgruntlement, then to resentment and open animosity. One flashpoint was Kipling offering to support Beatty's wife and daughter for a year, while Beatty went away and sorted out a new life. Another was a squabble over the mowing rights of a meadow that Carrie wanted to turn into a formal garden. Things were bad when the Kiplings went off to England in the summer of 1895. By that autumn the two families were no longer on speaking terms, and Carrie's diary for 10 October recorded bleakly: 'a glory of a day turned wrong by miserable Beatty complications'.[46]

Over the next six months (during the Venezuela crisis, the German threat and Elsie's birth), the row with Beatty remained in the background, corrosive and unresolved. Then, on the afternoon of Wednesday 6 May 1896, catastrophe. It took place in the woods called 'The Pines' on the road between the village and Naulakha and Maplewood. Beatty was driving his buckboard. Kipling was pushing his bicycle, which he had just fallen off. Beatty pulled up in a fury:

'See here, I want to speak to you.'

'If you have anything to say, say it to my lawyers.'

'By Jesus this is no case for lawyers. I want you to understand that you have got to retract those Goddammed lies you've been telling about me. You've got to do it inside a week or I'll punch the Goddammed soul out of you.'

'Let us get this straight. Do you mean personal violence?'

'Yes, I'll give you a week, and if you don't do it, I'll blow out your Goddammed brains.'

'You will have only yourself to blame for the consequences.'[47]

That at least is what Kipling claimed took place before his coachman came to his rescue, adding that he was also called a liar, a cheat and a coward. Beatty never denied the substance of Kipling's account, claiming only that he had threatened to beat up his brother-in-law, not to shoot him.

The upshot was that, after Kipling had gone to his lawyer, Beatty was arrested on Saturday 9 May and charged with 'assault and opprobrious and indecent epithets and threatening to kill'. When the question of Beatty's bail was raised, and it looked as though he might be unable to pay and have to stay in the lock-up, there was a half-comic, half-poignant moment when Kipling offered to stand bail for his brother-in-law, before Beatty was released on his own recognisance. The hearing was set for the following Tuesday.

It is possible to have some sympathy for both sides. Meeting Kipling on the road, Beatty might have been hoping for a man-to-man chat to clear the air. Had that happened, Kipling could have explained that the particular story that had upset Beatty had been misrepresented: that he had not told Colonel Goodhue that he 'had been holding Beatty up by the skirt of his trousers', but that, when the Colonel had asked him whether he was supporting Beatty, Kipling had replied that he was doing all he could for him.[48] One can see that as soon as Kipling mentioned lawyers, someone like Beatty, quite possibly drunk, would fly off the handle and say whatever came into his head. Similarly, one can imagine Kipling, confronted by his livid boor of a brother-in-law, thinking that Beatty in this state was capable of anything, even shooting him. There is too a certain bathetic quality about the encounter: short, timid aesthete pushing his bike faced by big, self-confident cowboy on his buckboard; or more archetypally, arty versus hearty; weedy Englishman versus macho American.

It is usually assumed that Carrie's influence was decisive in bringing the matter to court. This is quite possible, but ignores the impact of the previous six months on Kipling's state of mind. Beatty's violent threats against him were an almost exact counterpart of America's threats of war against England. Private and public had come to mirror each other, and someone who in January could believe himself in grave personal danger from an Anglo-American war would in May be likely to believe a furious brother-in-law who threatened to blow his brains out. Kipling probably did not need much encouragement from Carrie to call in the sheriff. This was the moment he made his 'error in the fourth dimension'. To have evoked the law against Beatty in England might have been an effective move; to evoke it in the States was asking for trouble.

Beatty's counsel, G B Hitt, gave Kipling, the only witness, a real grilling on the Tuesday. 'He did not remain in the same position more than a minute at a time, and his constant shifting betrayed intense nervousness' was how a local paper described Kipling's unease during his two-hour ordeal in the witness box. 'He would cross his legs, uncross them, crumple his soft hat into a ball, throw it upon the floor and then immediately stoop to pick it up and busy himself in straightening it out.'[49] Hitt even managed to get Kipling to contradict himself once or twice, producing laughter and cheering from the large audience in the town hall.

Kipling spoke in 'quick, hurried nervous sentences . . . evidently trying to conceal the great agitation which he felt'. Nevertheless, some of his reported replies were rather witty, given the ghastly circumstances. He claimed in his testimony that his decision to settle in Brattleboro had been in part to honour Wolcott's wish that he should look out for Beatty. When Hitt jocularly asked him whether 'looking out for Beatty was his main occupation', Kipling replied, 'Incidentally, I have written a thing or two.' Asked whether he was afraid of being shot, he answered, 'I have an objection to it.' And on Hitt's suggestion that he 'did not try to smooth out the trouble last Wednesday', Kipling retorted, 'This was the first time I had had my life threatened, and I did not know what the etiquette was in such cases.'[50]

The legal outcome at the end of a gruelling day was that Justice Newton placed Beatty under $400 bonds to keep the peace and a further $400 to appear at the county court in September. Kipling had won the battle – but already lost the war. Kipling, the literary celebrity, taking his farming brother-in-law to court was big news and received huge national and international coverage. The media forces – which only a few years before had syndicated him to worldwide fame – now exposed Kipling to ridicule and humiliation on the same scale. The irony of the creator of tough old sweats like Learoyd and Mulvaney calling in the sheriff to protect him against his own brother-in-law was lost on no one. The *Boston Post* included a cruel but funny parody of 'Danny Deever', which scored a number of easy hits:

'What makes the Kipling breathe so hard?' said the copper-ready-made.
'He's mighty scart, he's mighty scart,' the First Selectman said.
'What makes his wife look down so glum,' said the copper-ready-made.
'It's family pride, it's family pride,' the First Selectman said . . .[51]

Some old newspaper scores against Kipling were being settled. Here was a chance of revenge for all the swipes he had taken at America on his first visit in 1889 and again in 1892; revenge too for the scores of interviews he had refused to give after becoming a celebrity and making his home in Vermont. And no doubt there was also relish at the opportunity to cut down a tall poppy, particularly a British one, after the Venezuela crisis. For Kipling, it was a horror show; for Beatty, a triumph. He was the hero of the hour, the darling of the press, suddenly everybody's friend, his drinking and his debts conveniently forgotten. 'Brattleboro,' wrote Mary Cabot to her sister the day after the hearing, 'has never had such fun in all its eventful life as for the last few days.'[52] At least one close friend in England, Henry James, was following news reports of the story with an appalled fascination – though, writing to Edmund Gosse, he could not resist the inevitable pun on the town's name: 'I feel as if I were looking through poor Wolcott's horrified eyes at the events of Battleborough.'[53]

At first Kipling was shattered. Carrie's diary for Wednesday 13 May, the day after the court case, records simply: 'Rud a total wreck. Sleeps all the time. Dull, listless and weary. These are dark days for us.'[54] By the weekend he had pulled himself together enough to tell Rudolph Block of the New York *Journal*:

As to the 'nightmare' it is behind me; and I find myself slowly re-covering. Do you know 'apo-morphine'? It's a drug, a subcutaneous injection of which makes you heave up your immortal soul. I feel as though about a gallon and a half has been injected into *my* soul but that too will pass away.[55]

At the same time he must have been somewhat cheered to hear that both the *Century* and *McClure's Magazine* were offering $10,000 for the serial rights to *Captains Courageous*.

Over the next couple of months, trips to Gloucester with Conland, a short fishing holiday in Canada and a visit to the Nortons provided Kipling with some welcome distraction. There were a few spurts of work: he wrote 'Sestina of the Tramp-Royal' in a single day, added the final lines to 'The "Mary Gloster"' and corrected page proofs for his new collection of poems, *The Seven Seas*. He was also corresponding with a new American publishing friend, Frank Doubleday, about the Outward Bound Edition of his work. But for all these signs of returning normality, predictions after the hearing that he and Carrie would soon return to England proved to be accurate, and during the last week in August they were busy packing. Mary Cabot gives us a last glimpse of the American Kipling:

I went to say good-bye to the Kiplings. She was tearful, but he seemed frozen with misery. He said it was the hardest thing he had ever had to do, that he loved Naulakha. I spoke of the touch of Autumn already on the distant hills – as he put me in the carriage – which brought the tears to his eyes. His last word[s], in a tone of piercing sadness, were: 'Yes! 'tis the Fall! Good-bye, Miss Cabot!'[56]

14

Recessional

The Kiplings moved into Rock House, Maidencombe, near Torquay on 10 September 1896. The location was chosen with some care: by the sea; reasonably close, but not too close, to his parents at Tisbury; not in or around London. Kipling was wary after his years away, and wanted initially to preserve a certain distance from the literary, familial and other worlds to which he was returning.

The relative remoteness suited Carrie. 'Daily life is smooth with a polish unknown to us,' she told Mary Cabot, writing in December from her 'charming big house in this most beautiful part of England'. The contretemps with Beatty had not put them off cycling, for she added that 'we wheel [i.e. bicycle] daily on the perfect roads, with the sea always in sight one side, and the long blue line of Dartmoor on the other'.[1] Kipling from the first was less enthusiastic, calling Rock House 'our stone barrack . . . overlooking the sea'. Nor was he much impressed by the local ambience. 'Torquay,' he told Charles Norton, 'is such a place as I do desire acutely to upset – by dancing through it with nothing on but my spectacles. Villas, clipped hedges and shaved lawns; fat old ladies with respirators and obese landaus – the Almighty is a discursive and frivolous trifler compared with some of 'em.'[2]

But though he never took to the house, found Torquay stuffy and was already nostalgic for 'the keen sniff of an autumn morning' in Vermont, Kipling was soon re-establishing old contacts and making new ones.

During the months leading up to Christmas, there was a succession of visits by family and friends: Ambo Poynter in September, Alice and Lockwood for most of October, and Aunt Edie in December, followed by Uncle Crom. In late September, a sign of things to come, there was an invitation to Dartmouth. It was, he told Conland, 'to sleep in the Britannia – the old three decker training school for officers in our Navy'. There, Kipling had 'a great time among the naval cadets', and the day after his return from the *Britannia* his imagination was still all at sea. Mrs Humphry Ward had sent him an advance copy of her new novel, *Sir George Tressady*. His thank-you letter culminated in one of those extravagant compliments he liked to pay 'senior' writers, with Mrs Ward imagined as a large ocean-going liner and himself as a little trading coaster:

It will always be one of the darkest mysteries to me that any human being can make a beginning, end *and* middle to a really truly long story. I can think them by scores, but I have not the hand to work out the full frieze.

It is just the difference between the deep-sea steamer with twelve hundred people aboard, beside the poor beggars sweating and scorching in the stoke-hold, and the coastwise boat with a mixed cargo of 'notions'. And so when the liner sees fit to salute the coaster in passing that small boat is mightily encouraged.[3]

Behind the elaborate conceit, playing on the different senses of 'three-decker', one can feel Kipling's continuing frustration that he still had not written a proper novel, together with a certain pride at what he had achieved in his own line.

Appropriately, his 1894 poem 'The Three-Decker', in which he had affectionately farewelled Victorian novels like Mrs Ward's, was about to reappear in *The Seven Seas*. This volume, his first verse collection for four and a half years, offered a fresh series of 'barrack-room ballads' (though none as striking as the earlier ones), preceded by a varied mixture of other poems with titles that evoked the communal, oral tradition: 'The Song of the English', 'The Song of the Sons', 'The Song of the Banjo', 'The Rhyme of the Three Sealers', 'The Last Rhyme of True Thomas', 'Hymn Before Action', 'McAndrew's Hymn'. Testament to Kipling's instinct for the quotable quote, individual lines and phrases – like 'Romance brought up the nine-fifteen', 'the Colonel's Lady an' Judy O'Grady/Are sisters under the skin' and 'the God of Things as They Are' – were at once picked up and repeated around the English-speaking world.

The poems had been carefully selected and arranged. As the global title suggested, the readership at which Kipling was aiming was the 'Greater Britain' of emerging Empire nations rather than the literary world encompassed by, in Gosse's phrase, the 'three-mile radius of Charing Cross'.[4] It was specifically to this widely scattered, colonial audience that 'The Song of the Dead' was addressed:

> We were dreamers, dreaming greatly, in the man-stifled town;
> We yearned beyond the sky-line where the strange roads go down.
> Came the Whisper, came the Vision, came the Power with the Need,
> Till the Soul that is not man's soul was lent us to lead.[5]

The same audience was offered a different kind of gratification in 'The Song of the Cities', a whistle-stop tour of the Empire from Bombay to Auckland in fifteen complimentary quatrains, one per city. While encouraging the reader in Victoria, Cape Town or Sydney to feel part of a greater whole, this worldwide sweep was also intended to arouse the English reader's patriotic pride in Britain's overseas possessions.

A few poems showed an ambitious interweaving of low-brow and high-brow elements. Speaker, idiom and milieu were calculatedly working-class in 'McAndrew's Hymn', the engineer 'alone wi' God an' these/My engines'; yet the dramatic monologue form, with its artful construction of an apparently artless narrator, was literary and sophisticated. The poem imagined one kind of reader who would fuss over all the technical jargon, another who would see at once that McAndrew's wish for 'a man like Robbie Burns to sing the Song o' Steam!' was being granted even as they read. And so, rather neatly, Kipling was able to present himself as simultaneously the poetic heir of both Burns, provincial maverick, and Browning, English literary establishment. The other, more distant poetic ancestor he invoked in *The Seven Seas* was the tribal bard – an identification openly espoused in 'The Last Rhyme of True Thomas', 'The Story of Ung' and 'In the Neolithic Age'. The last of these 'primitive' utterances ended – a nice irony – with an unequivocal affirmation of cultural difference and artistic freedom:

Still the world is wondrous large, – seven seas from marge to marge, –
  And it holds a vast of various kinds of man;
And the wildest dreams of Kew are the facts of Khatmandu,
  And the crimes of Clapham chaste in Martaban.

Here's my wisdom for your use, as I learned it when the moose
  And the reindeer roared where Paris roars tonight: –
There are nine and sixty ways of constructing tribal lays,
  And every – single – one – of – them – is – right.[6]

By mid-November he was telling Conland that 'The cccccccc's', as he later jokingly referred to the collection, had 'sold mighty well this side the water and seems to have made a small splash'.[7]

The collection was also a hit in the States, with Charles Norton particularly fulsome in the *Atlantic Monthly*. Kipling, he claimed, could now take his place 'in the honorable body of those English poets who have done England service in strengthening the foundations of her influence and of her fame'. Norton singled out 'McAndrew's Hymn', in which Kipling had 'sung the song of the marine steam-engine' and thus fulfilled Wordsworth's prophecy that 'when the discoveries and applications of science shall become "familiarised to men . . . the Poet will lend his divine spirit to aid the transfiguration, and will welcome the Being thus produced as a dear and genuine inmate of the household of man"'.[8] Kipling reacted to Norton's praise with a mixture of proper modesty and superstitious unease, but in truth was enormously gratified by this piece of literary kingmaking. 'I felt,' he told Norton himself, 'about eighteen inches high when I began to read; then eighteen feet at the end and ten minutes later, on mature reflection – excessively small. I don't think even you who know me, will ever know what that review means to me.'[9]

W D Howells in *McClure's Magazine* was more temperate and more perceptive. Recognising the real audience at which *The Seven Seas* was directed, he crowned Kipling 'The Laureate of the Larger England'. Astutely, he linked the poems' intense patriotism with Kipling's own colonial background and, rather than the overblown 'Song of the English', chose 'The Flowers' as the pick of the bunch. In the latter poem, the new Empire nations lovingly offered old England their indigenous blooms, but, Howells argued, their offer was 'futile, because it is from the ardour of the younger world to the indifference of the elder, which must grow more and more with age'. The British Empire, Howells predicted, would 'die first at the heart'. He made two other challenging claims, both on the basis of the poem 'An American'. First, that whether Kipling liked it or not, he was 'in some sort American', having divined 'our actual average better than any American I can think of offhand'.[10] And second that, also in that poem, he wrote not as an imperialist but as a humanist. This unexpected claim by such a well-respected figure was another reminder that Kipling's image in the public mind – and his own – had not yet hardened into its later shape, and that readers trying to determine his politics and philosophy of life continued to find the signals intriguingly contradictory.

One strong dissenter from the chorus of praise that greeted *The Seven Seas* was the young Winston Churchill. In a letter of 7 January 1897 he gave the volume short shrift: 'Rudyard Kipling's new book is I think very inferior and not up to the standard of his other works. Few writers stand the test of success . . . I am afraid Kipling is killed.'[11] A more august critic, Henry James, was as usual impressed, in spite of himself. He read the collection at once and was soon hedging his plaudits to Gosse: 'I am still prostrate beneath the impression of *Rudyard*'s supreme deviltry . . . The talent, the art, the hellish cunning of this last volume (& all exercised in its amazing limitations, which only makes the phenomenon more rare,) have *quite* bowed me down with admiration.'[12]

Did Kipling ever read his old friend's correspondence, posthumously published in two volumes in 1920? Sadly, we do not know. Hardy was so annoyed by phrases like 'the good little Ts. Hy' and 'the great little Rudyard' that he transcribed them into his notebook and in retaliation labelled James 'the Polonius of novelists'.[13] Other than affectionate admiration, the most one gets from Kipling on James is the odd playful parenthesis, like the one to John Hay in October 1896: 'Henry James made a promise (with the usual Jamesidian reservations) to come down and stay with us awhile.' Not that Kipling was always pleasant about his literary contemporaries. 'The little runt' was his description of Alfred Austin, while he once portrayed Gosse – a friend – as a vulturous magpie 'with a piece of Carrion, flirting his tail and looking sideways as he hops along with it to the nearest bank'.[14]

That was to Norton in the wake of Stevenson's death, and it was also to Norton that Kipling from Rock House offered a notable epitaph on his

American period. 'I have been studying my fellow countrymen from the outside,' he told him. 'Those four years in America will be blessed unto me for all my life. We *are* a rummy breed.'[15] Despite the Venezuela crisis and the trouble with Beatty, he could see that his time in America had given him a valuable perspective on England and the English, reminding him that there were advantages to being a kind of resident alien. Even before the States was ceded the Philippines in 1898, and in Kipling's eyes became a potential co-worker in the great white imperial mission, the regularity of his letters to a wide range of American friends attested to his desire to keep the American channel open.

For Kipling, as for most of the rest of the English-speaking world, 1897 was dominated by Queen Victoria's Diamond Jubilee. It was from this point that the Kipling of popular imagination – all eyebrows and imperialist fervour – began to take hold. Carrie had feared just such a development, having told Mary Cabot during the Venezuela crisis that should the family return to England, her deepest anxiety was that her husband would 'become so much absorbed in the Imperial Federation and other questions of National importance' that he would 'sacrifice his literary career to them'.[16]

Again, as when he transformed himself into an Anglo-Indian, there was something willed and self-conscious about his adoption of a more strident imperialist stance – most strikingly in his preoccupation henceforth with 'White Men', 'the White Man's work' and the 'White Man's destiny'. Soon after the Jubilee, he attempted to explain to a Newfoundland correspondent what he meant by 'White Men'. They were 'the races speaking the English tongue, with a high birth rate and a low murder-rate, living quietly under Laws which are neither bought nor sold'. Or, as he informed an American correspondent the following year, 'the White Man's work' was 'the business of introducing a sane and orderly administration into the dark places of the earth' – a phrase that eerily anticipates Conrad's ironic story of colonial expansion, 'Heart of Darkness', published a few years later. In short, as Kipling told the American painter Charles Bacon at about the same time, 'It is the fate of our breed to do these things – or rather to have these things forced upon us.'[17] Put another way, there was no choice in the matter, and therefore no possible blame.

That, however, was all to come. Back in the spring of 1897 at Rock House, Kipling was still keeping himself aloof from the whole Jubilee phenomenon, due to culminate on 22 June with a thanksgiving service at St Paul's. 'I believe I'm the sole, solitary, single and only "poet" who isn't writing a Jubilee Ode this year,' he declared to his American friend Phillips in late March, predicting 'a ghastly crop of 'em'. Dinner with Cecil Rhodes in early April probably persuaded him that it was his duty to produce the fitting response, yet by 8 May, just before quitting Rock House for good, he was complaining to Moberly Bell of *The Times* that he was getting nowhere:

> As to the Jubilee, I loathe it. I've done a lot of costive disconnected bits of verse like macaroni, and I can't string 'em on one thread to save myself. After all, it's Austin's job [as Poet Laureate]. Like a fool I've used up my best notions of a scheme in 'a song of the English'. But I will try till the last minute.[18]

Most of the rest of May was spent socialising in London before, on 2 June, the family moved into North End House, the Burne-Joneses' place in Rottingdean on the Sussex coast. On 11 June he was briefly back in town for a 'Colonial lunch'. Here he met the premiers from the eleven self-governing English colonies (Canada, Cape Colony, Natal, Newfoundland, New Zealand, New South Wales, Queensland, South Australia, Western Australia, Victoria and Tasmania). They were 'the kind of men', he told the novelist Stanley Weyman, 'who drink whisky straight and believe in preferential tariffs'. This meeting led to him dashing off a breezy dialogue entitled 'Premiers at Play' in which the colonial heads discussed the pros and cons of Imperial Federation and agreed to come into 'The White Man's jack-pot'.[19] On 27 June he despatched the piece anonymously to the *St James's Gazette*, where it appeared on 8 July.

The 'Colonial lunch' also gave him a more productive lead for his 'Ode'. Four days later, on 15 June, he started a poem which at first looked as though it might be what he was after. Rather than portraying the Empire as 'The White Man's jack-pot', or promoting the pomp and circumstance of the Jubilee pageant, the verses highlighted responsibility and duty, even representing colonial rule as colonial servitude in disguise – a thankless, relentless task that someone had to do. The title phrase, repeated in the first line of each stanza, was to become notorious – and still instantly evokes a particular period and set of attitudes:

> Take up the White Man's burden –
>   Send forth the best ye breed –
> Go bind your sons in exile
>   To serve your captives' need;
> To wait in heavy harness
>   On fluttered folk and wild –
> Your new-caught, sullen peoples,
>   Half devil and half child.[20]

Approaching the height of the Jubilee celebrations, Kipling may well have thought such a tough challenge an appropriate bulletin from the tribal bard. There was, however, a rather obvious problem. Although Kipling felt that Britain had not yet shouldered the burden of its imperial responsibility, that would hardly have been the general – or indeed acceptable – perception in the midst of the Jubilee celebrations. Not surprisingly in the circumstances, Kipling put 'The White Man's Burden' aside.

Then, either on Jubilee Day itself or a few days later, inspiration did arrive, and he wrote a draft of a poem with the Hardyesque title 'After'. Carrington, Kipling's official biographer, confidently attributed the first draft of the poem to Jubilee Day. Certainly this creates a convincingly dramatic picture: London bursting with pageantry, pomp and hubris, while Kipling at his desk in Rottingdean desperately pleaded with Jehovah not to strike down his chosen people. Carrington, moreover, did see the original of Carrie's subsequently destroyed diary. His surviving note of her entry for 22 June was, however, ambiguous. It read: 'Jubilee Day. Dull and foggy morning. Rud does verses. We see bonfires. "Recessional".'[21] 'Recessional' here must be Carrington's interpolation, since the poem at that stage was still called 'After'. So either he assumed that the 'verses' must be 'Recessional' or he knew they were. One simply cannot tell. That Kipling actually wrote the poem in the immediate aftermath of the celebrations, rather than on the day itself, is supported by the earlier title and by a letter from the Kiplings' house-guest, Sally Norton, who was visiting England. On 17 July she specifically told her father that 'the Hymn was written just a few days after the Jubilee'.[22]

Whatever the date of its composition, the springboard seems to have been the phrase 'lest we forget', salvaged from the bits of 'macaroni' Kipling had mentioned so disparagingly to Moberly Bell. What often happened when he was writing verse was that a tune would come to mind, and he would hum away at it until he got the words to fit. The tune on this occasion was 'Eternal Father, strong to save' with its imploring refrain: 'O hear us when we cry to thee/for those in peril on the sea.' Having written seven stanzas, he laid the poem aside while he went off on manoeuvres with the Channel Fleet.

During his absence, Sally Norton came to keep Carrie company in North End House. On 15 July, the day after his return, Kipling read his 'Ode' to Sally and then later to Aunt Georgie.[23] Both approved, and the next day a neat copy of 'Recessional', as it was now called, was sent to Moberly Bell at *The Times*. On 17 July the poem appeared in the same column as the Queen's Jubilee letter to her people, and a leader praised both letter and poem for their 'moral responsibility', which 'rings out as clearly in the simple grandeur of the Queen's message as in Mr Kipling's soul-stirring verses'.

Recessional
God of our fathers, known of old,
    Lord of our far-flung battle-line,
Beneath whose awful Hand we hold
    Dominion over palm and pine –
Lord God of Hosts, be with us yet,
Lest we forget – lest we forget!

The tumult and the shouting dies;
    The Captains and the Kings depart:
Still stands Thine ancient sacrifice,
    An humble and a contrite heart.
Lord God of Hosts, be with us yet,
Lest we forget – lest we forget!

Far-called, our navies melt away;
    On dune and headland sinks the fire:
Lo, all our pomp of yesterday

Is one with Nineveh and Tyre!
Judge of the nations, spare us yet,
Lest we forget – lest we forget!

If, drunk with sight of power, we loose
   Wild tongues that have not Thee in awe,
Such boastings as the Gentiles use,
   Or lesser breeds without the Law –
Lord God of Hosts, be with us yet,
Lest we forget – lest we forget!

For heathen heart that puts her trust
   In reeking tube and iron shard,
All valiant dust that builds on dust,
   And guarding, calls not Thee to guard,
For frantic boast and foolish word –
Thy mercy on Thy People, Lord![24]

For two, or even three, generations, this was one of the most famous, or infamous, poems in the world. Kipling eventually claimed that he wrote it as 'a *nuzzur-wattu* (an averter of the Evil Eye)', because he was 'scared' by the mood of overwhelming national self-confidence that surrounded the Jubilee. Given his superstitious nature and his tribal view of the poet, that is plausible. He also stated in *Something of Myself* that he 'gave' the poem to *The Times* 'because for this kind of work I did not take payment'.[25] The idea that the poem was a 'gift' again fits in with other complicated deals he periodically tried to make with Fate and/or his personal daemon. His sister Trix would confirm after his death that he always refused payment for 'poems of a serious sort', adding that 'he certainly had very strong feelings about his Daemon and the possibility of a gift used unworthily being withdrawn'.[26]

To see 'Recessional' as an act of propitiation hints at another aspect of the poem: the far from humble emotions that lay just beneath the surface of the lines. Like 'The White Man's Burden', the poem sent out a double-signal. Ostensibly, it advocated humility ('An humble and a contrite heart') and pleaded for clemency ('Thy mercy on Thy people, Lord!'). Implicitly, it thrilled at the sense of divine mission ('Beneath whose awful

Hand we hold'), exulted at the size of the Empire ('Dominion over palm and pine'), and crowed over less-blessed imperial nations ('lesser breeds without the Law'). The problem with the poem, for all its apparent gestures of humility, was that it was simply not humble: the voice of England presumed to judge others while in the same breath begging for judgement in its own case to be suspended.[30] Ironically, with the Jubilee marking the British Empire's zenith, the poem turned out to be prophetic in a way Kipling never intended. Almost despite himself, his instinct to change the title to 'Recessional', a hymn sung by the clergy and choir while withdrawing to the vestry at the end of the service, was sound.

Part of the poem's fame lies in the story (deriving from Sally) that attaches to its composition. Kipling, on the morning of 16 July, was sorting papers at his desk and throwing out the rejects. Sally asked if she could go through the wastepaper basket, pulled out 'After', read it, and declared it had to be published. Kipling 'demurred' but referred the matter to Aunt Georgie, who sided with Sally. Whereupon Kipling cut the poem from seven stanzas to five and, on Sally's suggestion, used the concluding couplet of the first stanza ('Lord God of Hosts, be with us yet,/Lest we forget – lest we forget!') as a refrain in the second and fourth verses, even inscribing opposite the first insertion 'written with Sallie's pen – R.K.' The final line too was changed – to 'Thy mercy and forgiveness, Lord' – before being restored to its original form. Kipling then added the word 'Amen', signed it and wrote at the bottom: 'done in council at North End house, July 16, Aunt Georgie, Sallie, Carrie and me'.[27]

It makes an appealing story. There is the slight discrepancy over dates (Carrie has 15 July), but there could easily have been two 'council meetings' on successive days, with only the second one 'minuted'. And some at least of the details are obviously authentic, being in Kipling's own handwriting. All the same, it is unlikely that the survival and publication of his 'Jubilee Ode' was quite so dependent on chance intervention. Sally, in a letter to her father on the day the poem was published, made no reference to its rescue from the wastepaper basket, commenting only 'when I read it I begged R. to send it to The Times'.[28] Furthermore, nearly a week earlier, Kipling had obviously been giving serious thought to the poem's publication. A letter on 10 July to Rider Haggard strongly suggested that Kipling had sent the poem to his old friend, asking him if he thought it would do. Kipling's own reservation about what became 'Recessional' was that 'it may be quoted as an excuse for lying down abjectly at all times and seasons and taking what any other country may think fit to give us. What I wanted to say was: – "Don't gas but be ready to give people snuff" – and I only covered the first part of the notion.'[29] That Kipling already had publication in mind is implicit in his remark 'it may be quoted'. Perhaps he changed his mind and pitched the draft in the bin; but on balance, it is more likely that Sally's and Aunt Georgie's enthusiastic reception of the poem clinched the decision to publish.

The letter to Haggard also makes it clear that his only real objection to the poem was that it might be misconstrued as conciliatory. He was right to be concerned, for that was exactly how it was read by Jack Mackail, cousin Margaret's husband and politically a Liberal. 'I cannot tell you how glad I am of it,' he assured Kipling the day the poem appeared, 'or forbear writing to say so. There are all the signs of England saving up for the most tremendous smash ever recorded in history if she does not look to her goings.'[30] Kipling was quick to set him straight:

> Thank you very much but all the same seeing what manner of armed barbarians we are surrounded with, we're about the only power with a glimmer of civilisation in us. I've been round with the channel fleet for a fortnight and any other breed of white man, with such a weapon to their hand, would have been captivating the round Earth in their own interests long ago. This is no ideal world but a nest of burglars, alas, and we must protect ourselves against being burgled.

Just to make absolutely sure that the middle-class, pacifist Mackail understood the fundamental difference in their positions, he went on: 'The big smash is coming one of these days, sure enough, but I think we shall pull through not without credit. It will be the common people – the 3rd class carriages – that'll save us.'[31]

Kipling's letters to Haggard and Mackail are unequivocal. 'Recessional' was never intended as in any sense anti-imperialist or apolitical. But at the time liberals and imperialists alike felt the poem expressed their deepest feelings. Walter Besant put it best: 'I know of no poem in history so opportune, that so went home to all our hearts – that did its work and delivered its message with so much force.'[32] Such a unanimous reaction, seen in context, was hardly surprising. Kipling's popularity had mounted like a tidal wave during the 1890s and, following the phenomenal success of the two *Jungle Books* and *The Seven Seas*, was now at its height. When 'Recessional' appeared on 17 July, everyone discovered in it a reflection of their own feelings about the Jubilee and the state of the nation – and read the poem they most wanted to find.

At first the Kiplings' living arrangements in Rottingdean were temporary, but then Uncle Ned invited them to have the house until after the birth of their third child. They gratefully accepted, and it was in North End House on 17 August that John Kipling was born. 'It's a boy,' Kipling wrote to an American friend excitedly, '– a black haired boy who howls like a month-old baby.'[33] That communication was straightforward, unlike his rather grotesque announcement of the news to a chief engineer acquaintance, with Kipling succumbing to his recent penchant for converting everything into naval terms:

Ref: t.b.d. [torpedo-boat destroyer] trials. My attention is at present taken up by one small craft recently launched from my own works – weight (approx.) 8.957 lbs: h.p. (indicated) 2.0464, consumption of fuel unrecorded but fresh supplies needed every 2½ hrs. The vessel at present needs at least 15 yrs for full completion but at the end of that time may be an efficient addition to the Navy, for which service it is intended. Date of launch Aug. 17th, 1.50 a.m. No casualties. Christened John.[34]

A few weeks later, The Elms, just across the tiny green from North End House, fell vacant, and on 25 September father, mother, three children and domestic retinue moved in at a rent of three guineas a week. From Kipling's point of view it was ideal: he was out of London, on the coast, close to the South Downs, next door to the Beloved Uncle and Aunt.

Rambles on the Downs became a regular feature of Kipling's five years in Rottingdean, walks long remembered by those who accompanied him. That first summer the artist William Nicholson came down to do a portrait of Kipling for Henley's *New Review*. During one walk with Kipling and Josephine, they overheard a shepherd using the traditional shepherds' counting-system: een, teen, tethera, fethera, fib, hater, slater, quoter, diver, dig. To Nicholson, the numbers sounded like nothing so much as 'eena, meena, mina, mo', but Kipling assured him that the shepherd was using 'Saxon numerals'.[35] Nicholson was at work on his *An Almanac of Twelve Sports*, a sporting calender for 1898, and showed Kipling some of his woodcut prints. Kipling was intrigued, and the almanac soon turned into a collaboration, with Kipling supplying appropriate epigrammatic verses. In at least one case he produced different versions. The published text of 'Coaching' reads:

> The Pious Horse to church may trot,
> A maid may work a man's salvation . . .
> Four horses and a girl are not,
> However, roads to reformation.[36]

An alternative, unpublished version was considerably racier:

> Youth on the box and liquor in the boot,
> My Lord drives out with My Lord's prostitute.[37]

Often the expeditions on the Downs were more child-orientated and might involve storytelling. The novelist Angela Thirkell (Margaret and Jack Mackail's daughter) remembered how in the summers of 1897 and 1898 she and her 'bosom friend' Josephine Kipling, 'very fair-haired and blue-eyed', would be told early versions of the *Just So Stories*. The two girls would 'lie panting on the shady side of a haystack up on the downs . . . and hear his enchaining voice going on and on till . . . sleep descended on us; sleep from which one was probably roused by having the soles of one's feet tickled with straw by way of vengeance from a slighted story-teller'. One of Thirkell's most cherished possessions was a letter in Josephine's 'sprawly childish capitals'. For a moment its three simple sentences bring Josephine startlingly into focus, offering a glimpse into the intensity of her play-world and her father's central role in it: 'I will help you in the war against the Roundhead. He has a large army but we can beat him. He is a horrible man let us do all the mischief we can to him.'[38]

Another who gratefully recalled rambling on the Downs with Kipling and Josephine was the engineer Harry Ricardo, then in his last year at a local prep school. A chat about butterflies led to Kipling asking the young

Ricardo 'to take him for a walk on the Downs and to show him where certain species were to be seen':

> At that age I was very shy about expressing any opinions of my own to any but intimate friends or relations, but Kipling had the gift of drawing people out and, to my surprise, I found myself chatting freely about my hopes, my ambitions and airing my views on subjects about which I really knew very little. Before the walk was over I had told him all about the school, my hatred of the Matron and the Headmaster's 'Pi-jaws', about my crossbow pistol and about the technique of woodlice racing . . . On these walks Kipling would engage in conversation the farm-workers and shepherds and the occasional stranger we met, and by means of a few adroit questions, get them to talk freely about their affairs and interests.[39]

Ricardo never forgot Kipling's kindness or his charm, a quality that seems to have struck almost everyone. As Thackeray's daughter Anne Ritchie, who also met him at this time, put it, he was 'a Fascinator'.[40]

Ricardo's stories of boarding-school life struck a particular chord. Shortly before Christmas 1896, Kipling had begun a two-part story, 'Slaves of the Lamp', published in *Cosmopolis* in April and May 1897. Part 1, set at school, showed Stalky (Dunsterville), with his sidekicks M'Turk (Beresford) and Beetle (Kipling), getting back at an officious master, King (a composite of Crofts, Haslam and others). When King kicked the trio out of their study, Stalky tricked a drunken local into wrecking King's own study and making it uninhabitable. Stalky and his cohorts were not suspected, having apparently cast-iron alibis. Part II, set fifteen years later, showed how Stalky, now an army officer and besieged by two hill-tribes on the North-West Frontier, employed similar tactics to turn the tribes against each other while he and his men made their escape. The main point was clear: it was the lessons learnt at public school outside the classroom that trained one for later life, especially a life defending or extending the Empire.

'Slaves of the Lamp Part 1' – with its war between the three boys and King, and its slangy, irreverent tone – established a blue-print for a second wave of 'Stalky' stories. It comprised eight new stories, each published in magazines between August 1898 and April 1899: 'In Ambush',

'Stalky', 'An Unsavoury Interlude', 'The Impressionists', 'The Moral Reformers', 'A Little Prep', 'The Flag of their Country' and 'Last Term'. All, except 'Stalky', were collected in *Stalky & Co.* in October 1899.

As a rewriting of the past, *Stalky & Co.* was far less radical than *The Jungle Book* or 'The Potted Princess'. Kipling's memories of United Services College were mostly happy and self-enhancing; consequently there was no need for wholesale re-creation. He wanted to give a more or less realistic picture of school life as he remembered it. That said, *Stalky & Co.* contained all sorts of readjustments. A minor one was the length of time the trio spent at school. In real life, Kipling was at USC for four and a half years, arriving after Dunsterville and Beresford and leaving before them. In the fictional version, the trio arrived together, stayed at the school for seven years and left together. The point of the change was to accentuate the reader's sense of the boys' shared experience and of the bond between them. Similarly, as Dunsterville was later to insist, 'the incidents recorded in the books are of the nature of actual incidents, but cannot be regarded as history'.[41] The boys did built huts and hide-outs in the furze-bushes, like the one in 'In Ambush', where they read and smoked and hatched plots against their enemies; there was a local carrier whom they nicknamed 'Rabbits-Eggs'; Dunsterville was daring and resourceful. All the same, the retributive exploits of Stalky, M'Turk and Beetle are too good to be true. It is unlikely that, in real life, the trio tricked two masters who had accused them of trespass into getting caught themselves as trespassers, or that they stank out the dormitory of a master who had called them smelly.

More significant were two major shifts of emphasis. Price might recognise himself as the Head and record in his diary 'happily I am a respectable figure', but in fact the remote, all-wise, super-caning 'Prooshian Bates' of the stories bore little resemblance to the surviving accounts of Price himself.[42] To make the point on the most literal level: Price never beat Kipling, whereas Bates regularly dished out lickings to the rebellious trio. Besides his expertise with the cane, Bates displayed other tougher qualities not associated with tolerant, liberal Uncle Crom. Price became a trainer of imperialist colts more or less by accident; he was, as it were, an amateur. Bates, whom Kipling later likened to the centaur Chiron, instructor of heroes, was a professional. Godlike, he saw through Stalky's stratagems, understood and condoned the trio's constructive devilry, and maintained authority with beatings that, while flagrantly unfair, were not resented by the boys because they did not inhibit their extracurricular activities. The Prooshian Bates, as pupils and old boys agreed, was 'a downy bird'.

The other major transformation was Gigger-into-Beetle. At USC the bespectacled Kipling's main nickname was 'Gigger' – and as 'Gigger' the would-be aesthete, he was every bit as distinctive a figure as Dunsterville the soldier-to-be. However, as Beetle in the stories, he played second fiddle to Stalky; here the reader was in no doubt that the sword was mightier than the pen. This was a noticeably different kind of reinvention from the one in *The Jungle Book*, where Kipling 'promoted' himself through the figure of Mowgli, becoming the amphibious child-hero of his own rewritten script. Now, re-creating himself as Beetle, Kipling 'demoted' himself to a large bit-part, as a loyal member of Stalky's gang. This imaginative shift reflected Kipling's repositioning of himself once he returned to England. Consciously or not, his adolescence had to be made to fit, had to lead up to, the more stridently imperialist stance he was now adopting. Had Kipling's life after USC developed along other, more liberal, lines, one can imagine a *Stalky & Co.* in which the aesthete Beetle was in opposition to the warrior Stalky, rather than in cahoots.

Kipling's own most revealing comment on the stories came in a letter to Price on 4 January 1899 as the second wave of stories was appearing in magazines and already causing a stir:

> I'm going to dedicate the book to you and it will cover (incidentally) the whole question of modern education. Ordained headmasters and people of the Welldon and Farrar types will weep and howl at it: but we of the genuine congregation will approve. I get the wildest sort of letters from school-masters, denying or confirming my simple narratives.[43]

The Reverend J E C Welldon, headmaster of Harrow from 1885 to 1898, was the quintessential imperialist public-school headmaster of the period.[44] In May 1895, at the Royal Colonial Institute, he had delivered a famous paper on 'The Imperial Aspects of Education'. Public schools, Welldon maintained, had to turn out governors and generals, men who could run and hold an Empire. Games played a vital part in that process:

'The pluck, the energy, the perseverance, the good temper, the self-control, the discipline, the co-operation, the esprit de corps, which merit success in cricket or football, are the very qualities which win the day in peace or war . . .' In sum, he told his audience, 'the boys of today are the statesmen and administrators of tomorrow. In their hands is the future of the British Empire.' Kipling directly satirised Welldon in 'The Flag of their Country', in which Raymond Martin, impeccable Conservative and 'Jelly-bellied Flag-flapper', told the boys that 'they would grow up into men, because the boys of to-day made the men of to-morrow, and upon the men of to-morrow the fair fame of their glorious native land depended'.[45] Elsewhere in the stories Welldon and his brand of blatant imperialism were more generally reviled in the trio's repeated contempt for games and house matches held sacred by their housemaster Prout ('Heffy'). As for F W Farrar – Dean of Canterbury and the author of those mid-Victorian classics of school life, *Eric, or, Little by Little* and *St Winifred's; or The World of School*, written while he was master at Harrow – the trio's delighted mockery of his 'pure-minded' books became a running gag throughout the second wave of 'Stalky' stories.

What Kipling had against the Welldon and Farrar models of education was that both were designed to produce conformists. While he undoubtedly admired the dutiful subaltern, he preferred the maverick. Cricketing Christians might be all very well for running the Empire, but he believed that only imperial-minded adventurers – like Rajah Brooke of Sarawak, or Charles 'Peccavi' Napier of Sind, or indeed his old schoolfriend Dunsterville – had the imagination and resource to acquire that Empire in the first place.

Welldon's and Farrar's Harrow connection was probably also significant, given Kipling's conviction that smaller, newer, less traditional schools like USC were more effective than the grand old public schools at training imperialists. This viewpoint owed at least something to his envy of his cousin Stanley's Harrow education. 'I'd give something to be in the Sixth at Harrow as he is with a University Education to follow,' he had told Aunt Edie in 1884 as a cub reporter in Lahore.[46] Now, rewriting his own schooldays, he was able to perform a little retrospective redressing of the balance.

Almost as soon as *Stalky & Co.* was published in book form, Dean Farrar sent Kipling the expected letter of reproach. Beetle, accused of breaking the literary-moral rules, now faced his housemaster. Kipling's marvellously characteristic reply laced token regret, plausible self-justification and straightfaced cheek:

> I am in receipt of your letter and can only express my sincere regret that the schoolboy's comments on *Eric* and *St Winifred's* should have pained you so much. At the same time I would ask you remember that the two books are practically classics, that it would be impossible to write any sketch of schoolboy life of twenty years ago without in some way alluding to their influence; and also that there are boys – ignorant and vulgar minded it may be – who take less interest in the moral teachings of the two books than in their divergencies from the facts of school-life as boys know these today.
>
> I can assert honestly that it was no part of my intention to try to injure you with gratuitous insult. Your years and your position in the English Church alike forbid the thought of that.[47]

The year 1897 had been, Kipling noted in Carrie's diary, 'in all ways the richest to us two personally'.[48] The next year started just as positively. On 8 January 1898 the family, plus Lockwood, left Southampton for Cape Town. 'Little Josephine faces the prospect with great calm and serenity,' Kipling told Conland shortly before the voyage. 'She tells me that the best way of studying geography is "to go about in ships, Father, till you have seen them all" and frankly I am somewhat of her way of thinking.' Reaching Cape Town on the 25th, Kipling had, over the next ten weeks, what he described as 'a Royal Time – the best of good times'. Carrie meanwhile was less fortunate. While her husband was taking trains all over Southern Africa, she was left with the children at the Vineyard Hotel, a Newlands boarding house 'kept by three thoroughpaced female devils – one with a moustache and no figure – who . . . made things just as unpleasant all round for all the guests as the twelve hours of daylight would let 'em'.[49]

At first the sheer potential of South Africa quite took Kipling's breath away:

> I have seen Diamond mining at Kimberley where the diamonds come out by hundreds from the washed gravel . . . I have seen every

type and breed of native south of the Zambesi in the huge guarded
enclosures where the native labour is kept . . . Then I went a thousand miles north into Matabele land, over a new land railroad across
dry rivers, till I came to the city of Bulawayo, a town of 5,000 white
men. They treated me like a prince. Then I went on into the
Matappos – a wilderness of tumbled rocks, granite boulders and
caves where the white men fought the Matabele in '96. You never
dreamed of such a country.[50]

While this princely reception was due in part to Kipling's escalating fame,
part was no doubt due to Cecil Rhodes's good offices. The day after the
Kiplings' arrival in Cape Town they lunched with Rhodes, and this was
followed by other memorable meetings. Soon after docking, Kipling also
dined at Government House with the British High Commissioner, Alfred
Milner, who had recently been sent out by the Colonial Secretary Joseph
Chamberlain to try to resolve differences with the Boers. Rhodes and
Milner sought Kipling's acquaintance, as he sought theirs, primarily
because of a shared enthusiasm for the New Imperialism and the prospect
of federation between the Empire nations. South Africa, all three agreed,
represented the future.

The young Edgar Wallace, on the other hand, wanted to meet Kipling
because he was the brightest star in the literary firmament. Wallace, a private in the Medical Staff Corps, desperately wanted to be a writer.
Shortly before Kipling's arrival in Cape Town, he sent the *Cape Times* a
poem that was in every way calculated to catch his hero's attention.
'Welcome to Kipling' was the ultimate compliment: a real Tommy Atkins
welcoming the author of *Barrack-Room Ballads* in the very idiom of the
poems:

> You're *our* partic'lar author, you're our patron an' our friend.
> You're the poet of the cuss-word an' the swear,
> You're the poet of the people, where the red-mapped lands extend,
> You're the poet of the jungle an' the lair,
>   An' compare
> To the ever-speaking voice of everywhere . . .

The verses did the trick. 'Whoop!' wrote Wallace in his diary after he

245

received an invitation to dine with Kipling a few weeks later. The great event went well, as he told English friends: 'Kipling was exceedingly nice to me and not only gave me his autograph attached to a verse of the "Song of the Banjo" but wrote me a fine letter the following day, complimenting me on my "London Calls"', a poem by Wallace, just published in the *Cape Times*. Wallace confined to his diary, and omitted to tell his friends, Kipling's parting shot: 'For God's sake, don't take to literature as a profession. Literature is a splendid mistress, but a bad wife!'[51] The encounter was a reminder that in 1898 to be a self-avowed 'son of Rud' was still perfectly acceptable; in fact, a rather good career move. Kipling himself enjoyed the role of literary godfather, handing Wallace his London address and expressing his willingness to give any advice he could.

Six weeks after the Kiplings' return to England, Edward Burne-Jones died suddenly of a heart attack. 'He was more to me,' Kipling wrote to Charles Norton, 'than any man here.' Norton was a close friend of Burne-Jones, and Kipling described to him the burial service at the village church:

> The decency, the cleanliness and the sanity of it all were as he would have wished. I had had a horror in my mind of some bungling, hireling business with ropes and boards. All that thank God was done away with. Just at the end, I saw Uncle Crom – my Uncle Crom – near me – broken to pieces. You know how he and Ned had been together always. It was awful. I can tell you about Aunt Georgie when we meet. One doesn't want to write these things. She was standing with her eyes shut at the head of the grave and at the end she knelt for a minute or two; and then we came away . . . There was no mobbing; no jabber; no idiotic condolences; and the rest of us of his kin, walked about our garden for awhile till it was time to get the carriages and go back to town.

Kipling noticed about his own grief that, although he felt 'broke – broke – broke', he was unable to cry. 'I can't cry,' he told Norton, adding with an awkwardness that mirrored the unsuccessful effort: 'At least I don't seem able to have found out the way yet and I don't think it will come either. It's all a sort of clot in my head because one has to realise that the man won't come back.' And, in a final revealing connection, he linked his present state with that of two years earlier, following the Beatty trial: 'You know, things had rather broken me up before I left America and this thing has snapped something else inside me.'[52]

As usual at a crisis, Kipling threw himself into work and hardened his political line. It was no coincidence that within a few weeks of Uncle Ned's death, and with the imminent cession of the Philippines to America, he was banging on in letters about the white man's destiny and taking part in further naval manoeuvres. Nor that at the same time he returned to a concentrated burst on his Indian novel *Kim* in which the boy's loving discipleship to the Lama reflected aspects of his own relationship to Burne-Jones.

A new volume of stories, *The Day's Work*, appeared at the end of September, bringing together a dozen tales written during his American period. The collection opened in India with 'The Bridge-Builders', one of Kipling's most successful allegories about the collision between new Western technology and old Eastern spirituality. In one remarkable night-scene Findlayson, whose bridge across the Ganges was almost destroyed by floods, had an opium-induced vision of the Indian gods inconclusively debating whether their reign had ended. Complementing this at the end of the volume was the uneven 'Brushwood Boy', in which the hero again inhabited a double-reality and was able to move from the workaday world to the night-world of dream. Little of this boundary-crossing found its way into the rest of the collection. Several of the stories, like 'The Ship that Found Herself' and '.007', celebrated the importance of finding one's role, fulfilling one's function and doing one's job. Not everyone was enthralled. 'When you come to writing a story to show how all the parts of a ship, the rivets, stringers, garboard-strake, and heaven knows what else, have feelings to be considered and how each learns a common lesson – why then you are very apt to be a bore,' Stephen Gwynn, a professed admirer, wrote anonymously in *Macmillan's Magazine* of 'The Ship that Found Herself'. And, he went on, 'when you bring in the steam as a kind of guardian angel with a tendency to be facetious, you approach to being intolerable'.[53] It was not the first time Kipling had been criticised – but he had never before been called a bore.

November brought a return of family worries as Trix, now back in England, had a nervous breakdown. Sometimes she would sit in a kind of catatonic state; sometimes talk endless gibberish. Everyone in the extended family was immediately supportive, but found themselves having to tiptoe round Alice who refused (then and subsequently) to accept the possibility that her daughter might be mentally ill. 'The main point is not to flutter the mother,' Kipling told his Uncle Alfred.[54] Trix's condition was to remain unstable for most of the following year, and though she eventually rallied, a cycle of collapse and recovery had begun that was to continue well into middle age.

Uncle Ned dead, Trix out of her mind: Christmas 1898 was a gloomy affair, and one might have expected that after his royal time in South Africa, Kipling would have been eager to return that winter. Instead, on 25 January 1899, he, Carrie and the children left for a short visit to the States. When the decision was made is not known – nor quite why. Carrie wanted to see her mother and Kipling to pursue another of his copyright battles, but spring or summer would have been at least as convenient. Perhaps they were all genuinely homesick. Or perhaps it was a spur-of-the-moment decision. Kipling gave his mother the latter impression, to judge by Alice's letter to her sister Louisa: 'Rud and his nursery sail for America . . . they go for 6 weeks only & I believe regard crossing the Atlantic in the winter as a pleasant trip!'[55]

Things went wrong from the start. The crossing was rough and freezing, the children were sick, and Josephine and Elsie developed colds. They docked in New York on 2 February to be faced with an aggravating two-hour hold-up at customs and hordes of reporters outside. By the time they made it to their hotel, the Grenoble, the children were in a worrying state. Carrie's mother was there, so too was her sister Josephine and her husband Theo Dunham, a doctor. It was thought the children might have whooping-cough. The weather remained foul, cold and snowy. During the week Josephine got worse, and on 8 February Carrie also went down with fever. Conland's arrival from Brattleboro was a relief, though he brought alarming reports that Beatty was threatening to bring an action against Kipling for $50,000. Four days later Carrie's health had picked up, the children's was unaltered, Kipling seemed well.

For a week everything held. They socialised and saw Carrie's family. Kipling tried to make headway with his copyright problem, which involved trying to prevent Putnam from bringing out an unauthorised

Brushwood edition of his work as a rival to Scribner's authorised Outward Bound one. Then quite suddenly, on 20 February, Kipling himself fell ill. The next day his condition was serious, with inflammation in one lung. On 22 February, a day of doctors and delirium, Carrie noted: 'An anxious night and more anxious day. Rud so good and patient – sleeps much – good friends lend helping hands and I feel how everyone Rud has ever spoken to has loved him and is glad and happy to help do for him.'[56]

On the 23rd, though Kipling was 'sane and quiet', Josephine had relapsed, and Carrie took her to their friends the de Forests, with whom she left her. 'A moment of conscious agony!' she confided to her diary, her last entry until 5 March.[57] We can, however, follow the intervening period through the regular daily reports in *The Times*. On 26 February the doctors were admitting that Kipling had pneumonia: 'Both lungs are known to be involved, the fever runs high, delirium is frequent, and the patient's strength is ebbing fast, but Mr Kipling's courage is unfailing and his will power is unshaken . . . Public interest in every bulletin is unprecedented.' And not simply in America. News of Kipling's illness aroused enormous interest all over the world. It was for many people one of those defining moments. Years later, the theatre critic James Agate recalled how he made 'a solemn vow' that if Kipling died, 'I would wear a black tie for the rest of my life!'[58]

On 27 February the crisis continued. 'His breath is drawn in gasps, and his pulse and heart beat very faintly. Both lungs are now solidified, leaving but scant space for inhalation, and preventing the oxidising of the blood by the natural process. The free use of pure oxygen is, therefore, necessary.' But for the oxygen, he would already have died; there had been frequent delirium over the last forty-eight hours; there were now fears of heart failure. His delirious visions were, not surprisingly, full of a sense of anxiety and threat. At one point, he was to be put on trial for remarks he had made about a New York girl called either Miss Bailey or Miss Brady: a transposition of his past and present troubles with Beatty. At another point, there were echoes of Lorne Lodge: 'We sail away and reach, as I believe, England. Am kidnapped and taken to horrible house in a garden of weeping willows, rocks and running water . . .'[59]

Reports for 28 February oscillated between hope and fear. On 1 March it was the same story, with Dr Janeway, one of the rota of doctors now attending Kipling, only able to say that 'the next 24 hours will tell volumes of what we want to know'. Reading this in *The Times* the following day, Winston Churchill assumed the worst: 'Poor Rudyard Kipling is I fear at the point of death. It is a terrible loss to the English speaking world.'[60] But even while Churchill was writing him off, there were clear signs of improvement, so that by the same evening *The Times*'s correspondent in New York could declare: 'The doctors are almost certain of his recovery.'

By the 4th Kipling's recovery seemed sufficiently certain for *The Times*, instead of its usual bulletin, to run a column's appreciation of his work and significance. After praising him for 'his discovery of India as a field of poetry and romance' and, nearer to home, for 'the character of Mr Thomas Atkins', the article likened him to Tyrtaeus, the Greek elegiac poet whose poems inspired the Spartans to defeat their enemies. Kipling was praised for promoting, 'in ways which men of the world understand, duty, obedience, resignation, and self-denial, as if they were the cornerstones of Empire'. The panegyric read like a recast obituary, which perhaps it was. The *Daily Mail* was said to have had to scrap an edition carrying a full-page death notice, while W D Howells, after initially agreeing to write an advance obituary for *Literature*, found the task too 'insincere and histrionic' and withdrew.[61]

But as Kipling steadily moved out of danger, the six-year-old Josephine continued to decline. Carrie's diary entries were almost unbearably poignant. The entry for 5 March read: 'I saw Josephine 3 times today, morning, afternoon and at 10 pm for the last time. She was conscious for a moment and sent her love to "Daddy and all".' The entry for the 6th said simply: 'Josephine left us at 6.30 this morning.'[62]

It was decided that the news must be kept from Kipling until he was stronger. For a few days a strange conspiracy of silence prevailed, in which everyone knew of Josephine's death except her father. The strain on Carrie, having to be cheerful in front of her husband, must have been appalling. She may not always have been easy to live with in the ordinary run of events, but she was the person for a crisis, and her fortitude was widely and rightly admired.

Once her husband was known to be recovering, Carrie was inundated with letters and telegrams from all over the world from family, friends and well-wishers. Henry James's message of exuberant congratulation on 7 March was particularly unlucky. He wrote it unaware of Josephine's death and had at once to follow this 'jubilation so mistimed' with a letter of heartfelt condolence.[63] It was just the sort of ghastly, unintentional blunder which, under different circumstances, Kipling might well have found arresting. A telegram of congratulation from Kaiser Wilhelm of Germany might again ordinarily have raised a wry smile, especially as the German press insisted on referring to 'the American author Rudyard Kipling', predicting that the Emperor's telegram would usher in a new era of German-American relations.

But, of course, none of this would ever seem remotely quaint or amusing. When eventually Carrie and the doctors decided that Kipling was strong enough to bear the news, she told him. Sally Norton's letter to her father on 25 March gave some faint sense of how agonising the days of silence and the moment of disclosure must have been. Carrie, she wrote:

> told me a great deal about Ruddy's illness but she said very little about little Josephine. I could see it was all too painful in its detail, too heartbreaking for her to talk of now. She said the days between little Josephine's death and Ruddy's knowing of it, were 'dreadful', and that at last she *had* to tell him though the doctors said, perhaps she had better wait another day, 'and at first', she added, 'he was too ill to realise it quite, but now every day he feels it more.'[64]

Over forty years later, Trix would describe very succinctly to Josephine's surviving sister, Elsie, the impact on Kipling: 'After his almost fatal illness & Josephine's death – he was a sadder & a harder man.'[65]

15

Reputations

Had Kipling died in that New York hotel room in the spring of 1899, aged thirty-three, how would he have been remembered? How might we think of him now?

'About a dozen books – a book a year for the years of his activity – provide us with the scope of Mr Kipling's genius. If he wrote no more they were sufficient to establish his reputation as a man marking an epoch in English letters,' the popular novelist Neil Munro declared during Kipling's slow convalescence.[1] *Departmental Ditties, Plain Tales from the Hills, Soldiers Three and Other Stories, Wee Willie Winkie and Other Stories, Life's Handicap, The Light that Failed, Barrack-Room Ballads, Many Inventions, The Jungle Book, The Second Jungle Book, The Seven Seas, Captains Courageous* and *The Day's Work*; to this baker's dozen one can add *Stalky & Co.*, the two travel volumes of *From Sea to Sea*, and assorted poems (such as 'Recessional') and tales (including the earliest *Just So* stories), all of which would have been collected and published post-humously. It makes an impressive list. English Studies as it took off in the 1920s and 1930s might even have found an honourable position for such a Kipling: as an early modern precursor perhaps; as the inventor (for the West) of India as a literary subject; as the champion of the working-class Tommy Atkins; as an important Nineties' vernacular poet; as a major innovator in children's writing and school writing; as the leading exponent of the short story between Poe and Mansfield. F R Leavis might have given controversial lectures on him at Cambridge. Lytton Strachey or E M Forster might have delivered a paper at a Bloomsbury gathering on 'The Kipling That Everyone Read'. People would have argued about the direction that Kipling's work would have taken. *Kim*, rather than *Mother Maturin*, would have become the mysterious lost novel – Carrie having either destroyed the unfinished draft manuscript or placed it under some super-embargo in the British Museum. Provocatively, someone would have proposed that Kipling was, in fact, played out and would have stopped writing altogether.

The problem is that reservations – sometimes strong reservations – were already being expressed even before his near-fatal illness. The *locus classicus* was Henry James's crushing letter of Christmas Day 1897 to Grace Norton:

> His *Ballad* future may still be big. But my view of his prose future has much shrunken in the light of one's increasingly observing how little of life he can make use of. Almost nothing civilised save steam and patriotism – and the latter only in verse, where I *hate* it so, especially mixed up with God and goodness, that that half spoils my enjoyment of his great talent. Almost nothing of the complicated soul or of the female form or of any question of *shades* – which latter constitute, to my sense, the real formative literary discipline. In his earliest time I thought he perhaps contained the seeds of an English Balzac; but I have quite given that up in proportion as he has come steadily from the less simple in subject to the more simple, – from the Anglo-Indians to the natives, from the natives to the Tommies, from the Tommies to the quadrupeds, from the quadrupeds to the fish, and from the fish to the engines and screws. But he is a prodigious little success and an unqualified little happiness and a dear little chap.[2]

Yet, arguably, James was too old, too incorrigibly highbrow, to be an accurate barometer of current and future critical taste. The reactions of two younger, more middlebrow writers – Arnold Bennett and George Gissing – provide a more reliable guide.

Bennett was an exact contemporary of Kipling. Coming from the Potteries, he too was a provincial, though of a less exotic kind, and also moved to London in 1889 in hopes of a literary career. While Kipling almost instantly soared to fame, Bennett's fortunes moved much more slowly, his first novel not being published until 1898. The previous year in the course of an elaborate disquisition to a fellow writer George Sturt, Bennett managed to set up Kipling as a talented primitive in polar opposition to the conscious stylist that he was training himself to become:

> Kipling has the ideas; he has the poetic insight, the large *synthetic* view which enables him to see an Empire in one sweep, the poet's sympathy which illuminates all the dark corners of human experience; but having seen, felt, heard – as an artist would see, feel, hear, he is content. Forgetting that after all the art of literature consists in *writing*, he is content to do the supreme labour of all in a haphazard, rapid, careless fashion. True, his *expression* is nearly always vivid, but this is due to the triumphant vividness of his *seeing*, rather than to any care he may exercise as a writer. He succeeds not because of, but in spite of, his mode of expression. I fancy he would rather scorn 'mere' artistry, & when it was mentioned would begin to talk about fighting or famine or fakirs.[3]

But there was another, more hard-nosed dimension to Bennett's attitude. 'Kipling stands solitary and terrible, at £50 per thousand, £200 being his minimum for his shortest short story,' he ruefully noted in January 1898, surveying the magazine rates that leading writers could charge.[4] Kipling's rate was over four times that of Hardy or Wells and of course far outstripped Bennett's own. Later that year he reflected in his journal after reading reports of a triumphant verse-reading by Kipling on board HMS *Majestic*: 'This is my idea of fame . . . At the conclusion a body of subalterns swept him off the stage, and chaired him round the quarter-deck, while "For he's a jolly good fellow" was played by the massed bands of the Fleet and sung by 200 officers assembled.'[5] Bennett's defence mechanism against the Kipling phenomenon was to take the aesthetic high ground; yet for him Kipling remained the benchmark of success and fame.

Gissing, author of *New Grub Street*, offers an instructive contrast. Born in 1857, he had already published half a dozen well-received social realist novels before Kipling burst on the scene. During the first half of the

1890s, he became an avid Kiplingite. 'Kipling's book is tremendous,' he enthused in November 1896 after the appearance of *The Seven Seas*. 'I delight in the force & the glow of it. It is unmistakably the product of original genius; nothing of the kind existed in English literature before.'[6] A month later, he finished his most ambitious novel, *The Whirlpool*, in which Kipling and his influence played a significant part. The last chapter started with the hero, Harvey Rolfe, reading aloud to his friend Basil Morton:

It was a little book called 'Barrack-Room Ballads'. Harvey read in it here and there, with no stinted expression of delight, occasionally shouting his appreciation. Morton, pipe in mouth, listened with a smile, and joined more moderately in the reader's bursts of enthusiasm.

'Here's the strong man made articulate,' cried Rolfe at length. 'It's no use; he stamps down one's prejudice – what? It's the voice of the reaction. Millions of men, natural men, revolting against the softness and sweetness of civilisation; men all over the world; hardly knowing what they want and what they don't want; and here comes one who speaks for them – speaks with a vengeance.'

'Undeniable.'

'But—'

'I was waiting for the *but*,' said Morton, with a smile and a nod.

'The brute savagery of it! The very lingo – how appropriate it is! The tongue of Whitechapel blaring lust of life in the track of English guns! – He knows it; the man is a great artist; he smiles at the voice of his genius – It's a long time since the end of the Napoleonic wars. Since then Europe has seen only sputterings of temper. Mankind won't stand it much longer, this encroachment of the humane spirit. See the spread of athletics. We must look to our physique, and make ourselves ready. Those Lancastrian operatives, laming and killing each other at football, turning a game into a battle. For the milder of us there's golf – an epidemic. Women turn to cricket – tennis is too soft – and to-morrow they'll be bicycling by the thousand; – and they must breed a stouter race. We may reasonably hope, old man, to see our boys blown into small bits by the explosive that hasn't got its name yet.'

'Perhaps,' replied Morton meditatively. 'And yet there are considerable forces on the other side.'

'Pooh! The philosopher sitting on the safety-valve. He has breadth of beam, good sedentary man, but when the moment comes – The Empire; that's beginning to mean something. The average Englander has never grasped the fact that there was such a thing as a British Empire. He's beginning to learn it, and itches to kick somebody, to prove his Imperialism. The bully of the music-hall shouting "Jingo" had his special audience. Now comes a man of genius, and decent folk don't feel ashamed to listen this time. We begin to feel our position. We can't make money quite so easily as we used to; scoundrels in Germany and elsewhere have dared to learn the tricks of commerce. We feel sore, and it's a great relief to have our advantages pointed out to us. By God! we are the British Empire, and we'll just show 'em what *that* means.'[7]

Yet within months of the novel being published in spring 1897, Gissing's perspective on Kipling and imperialism had fundamentally changed. The decisive event was the Jubilee – and all the jingoism and demagogy that, to his mind, it represented. To correspondents over the next few years he insisted that Rolfe's tone had been bitterly ironic. And he described the recently published *Stalky & Co.* as 'the most vulgar & bestial production of our times', a book fit only to be 'burnt by the hangman!'[8] Kipling, in short, had become the enemy – the more so because Gissing had once so wholeheartedly admired him.

Such contradictory responses bring out the difficulty of gauging how Rudyard Kipling would have gone down in literary history. He might have joined those whom dying young invests with a kind of untouchable mythic status. Bennett's view could have accommodated that; he did after all think Kipling 'great'.[9] Alternatively, Gissing's rapid shift from approbation to abhorrence confirms that some reaction against Kipling was already under way; and that reaction would have continued, despite the drama and poignancy of his early death. All the same, he would never have become, in Edmund Wilson's adhesive phrase of the 1940s, 'The Kipling That Nobody Read'.

16

A Sadder and a Harder Man

Kipling's convalescence was slow. On 2 April 1899 he issued a short press statement from the Hotel Grenoble, gratefully acknowledging 'the wonderful sympathy, affection and kindness shown towards me during my recent illness, as well as . . . the unfailing courtesy that controlled its expression'.[1] Of the many friends who rallied round, the most indefatigable was Frank Doubleday, who had become Kipling's American publisher. Doubleday now turned into a close family friend, and Kipling took to calling him 'Effendi', a pun on his initials FND. It was Effendi who on 17 April moved the whole Kipling entourage by private railcar to Lakewood, a New Jersey resort, where Kipling took gentle exercise and put on some much-needed weight. On 9 May the invalid party proceeded, again by private railcar, to Morristown for a month with other American friends. There Kipling was visited by Conland, who pronounced his lung healed but urged a further six months' rest. Then there followed a week at Effendi's house on Long Island, before 13 June found them back in New York. Next day Kipling and his family (including his father, who had come over to add his reassuring presence) set off for England on the SS *Teutonic*.

Also on the boat was Edward Bok, editor of the *Ladies' Home Journal*. One day he tried to find out what Kipling *père* thought of Kipling *fils'* work. The exchange, perhaps a little touched up in Bok's memoirs, confirms the impression that one of Lockwood's favourite roles was that of the laconic, pipe-smoking Yorkshireman:

'You should feel pretty proud of your son,' remarked Bok.

'A good sort,' was the simple reply.

'I mean, rather, of his work. How does that strike you?' asked Bok.

'Which work?'

'His work as a whole,' explained Bok.

'Creditable,' was the succinct answer.

'No more than that?' asked Bok.

'Can there be more?' came from the father . . .

'But surely you must consider that Rud has done some great work?' persisted Bok.

'Creditable,' came once more.

'You think him capable of great work, do you not?' asked Bok. For a moment there was silence. Then:

'He has a certain grasp of the human instinct. That, some day, I think, will lead him to write a great work.'[2]

In similar tenor, Lockwood soon afterwards described Bok himself as 'not an altogether mediocre man'.[3]

By late June the Kiplings were back at The Elms. There, in the midst of familiar surroundings, the full force of Josephine's death hit home. Kipling confessed to his mother that he 'saw her when a door opened, when a space was vacant at table, – coming out of every green dark corner of the garden – radiant and – heartbreaking'. Carrie too was able to share her feelings with Alice.[4]

During his convalescence Kipling had heard again from Mrs Hill, their first communication in nearly ten years. A further note in July prompted him to resume the correspondence, and they soon re-established something of their old sympathy. 'I don't think it likely that I shall ever come back to America,' he confided to her on 30 July. 'My little Maid loved it dearly (she was almost entirely American in her ways of thinking and looking at things) and it was in New York that we lost her. Everybody was more than kind to us and to her but I don't think I could face the look of the city again without her.'[5]

Kipling never did visit America again. Although he kept in regular touch with some old friends there, one effect of Josephine's death was to reinforce his strong reservations about the States. Another – more damagingly – was an increased sense of distance even with those to whom he had been close. Angela Thirkell, half a lifetime later, still felt hurt about the 'barrier' that had suddenly gone up:

> I feel that I have never seen him as a real person since that year. There has been the same charm, the same gift of fascinating speech, the same way of making everyone with whom he talks show their most interesting side, but one was only allowed to see these things from the other side of a barrier . . .[6]

The main literary event in the first year of the rest of Kipling's life was the publication of *Stalky & Co.* on 6 October 1899. Henry James gave it a private, disapproving sniff – 'the misguided, the unfortunate Stalky' – but more significant was Andrew Lang's brusque non-review in *Longman's Magazine*: 'As my sympathies are not wholly engaged with *Stalky & Co.* in their long and successful combat with their masters, I prefer to say very little about these heroes. Whatever they may be they are not normal schoolboys.'[7] This was nothing, however, compared to the full-frontal attack mounted by the poet Robert Buchanan in the December 1899 issue of the *Contemporary Review*. In 'The Voice of the Hooligan' he saved his ripest invective for the 'deplorable' *Stalky*:

> The vulgarity, the brutality, the savagery, reeks on every page. It may be noted as a minor peculiarity that everything, according to our young Hooligans [Stalky, M'Turk and Beetle], is 'beastly', or 'giddy', or 'blooming'; adjectives of this sort cropping up everywhere in their conversation, as in that of the savages of the London slums. And the moral of the book – for, of course, like all such banalities, it professes to have a moral – is that out of materials like these is fashioned the humanity which is to ennoble and preserve our Anglo-Saxon empire!

Kipling – 'the spoiled child of an utterly brutalised public', in Buchanan's memorable phrase – was surprisingly sanguine about this onslaught from someone who almost thirty years earlier had infamously damned 'The Fleshly School of Poetry' being created by Rossetti and the other Pre-Raphaelites.[8] 'We must remember that there is bound to be a sharp and savage reaction against any man who has had the luck that I've had, and that there is no decency in our profession,' Kipling observed to Besant in the course of thanking him for coming to his defence. 'I'm sorry about Buchanan because he did write lovely verses. I expect something we know nothing of is bothering him. God help us all!'[9]

Away from the hothouse of the monthlies, *Stalky & Co.*, although set fifteen to twenty years earlier, was striking an immediate chord with its target reader, the contemporary public-school boy. In October 1900 the future royal secretary, Sir Alan Lascelles, then a thirteen-year-old at Marlborough College, informed his sister that he was chief storyteller in his dormitory. The night before he had told the story of Kipling's 'The Mark of the Beast'. 'It was much appreciated,' he assured his sister. 'They liked the "bloody chops with gristle".'[10] Fittingly, this was almost exactly what Beetle had done in 'The Impressionists', whispering scary bits from Mrs Oliphant's *Beleaguered City* in the twilight to a horrified audience.

What really mattered to Kipling in the winter of 1899–1900 was the Boer War. As soon as it was declared on 11 October he threw himself into the British cause, including getting involved locally with rifle-training and the setting up of a Volunteer Corps. He also, on the 16th, began a four-stanza poem that took just under a week to complete:

When you've shouted 'Rule Britannia,' when you've sung 'God Save
     the Queen,'
     When you've finished killing Kruger with your mouth,
Will you kindly drop a shilling in my little tambourine
     For a gentleman in khaki ordered South?
He's an absent-minded beggar, and his weaknesses are great –
     But we and Paul [Kruger] must take him as we find him –
He is out on active service, wiping something off a slate –
     And he's left a lot of little things behind him . . .[11]

'The Absent-Minded Beggar' was, in Lockwood's words, a 'rhymed invitation to subscribe to a Soldiers' wives & children fund', run under the populist auspices of the *Daily Mail*.[12] Arthur Sullivan produced the tune – described by Kipling as 'guaranteed to pull teeth out of barrel-organs', and on 13 November 'The Absent-Minded Beggar' had its first public performance at the Alhambra Theatre.[13] Daily recitals and recitations followed all over the country, as the initial enthusiasm for the war grew, and vast numbers of copies of the poem/song were sold. In the first three and a half months the fund raised £70,000 and eventually closed at a quarter of a million. Kipling himself took a realistic view of the verses' literary merits. When someone, not long after the song's appearance, asked him if they had the honour of meeting the author of 'The Absent-Minded Beggar', he replied: 'Yes, I have heard the piece played on a barrel-organ, and I would shoot the man who wrote it if it would not be suicide.'[14] At the same time he took a modest pride in his ability to raise money to help 'the 3rd class carriages', as he had called them to Jack Mackail. 'I've raked in a little cash for my men,' he told Charles Norton in January 1900. 'It's the first time I ever set out of malice aforethought to sell my name for every blessed cent it would fetch and the result so far as women and children are concerned is good.'[15]

In part the energy with which Kipling threw himself behind the British effort was a reaction to his devastation at the loss of his daughter. Acute personal stress followed by a hardening of his political stance: the by now familiar pattern. The outbreak of the war provided a ready-made occasion for this kind of emotional compensation, in which the private could be displaced into the public. Thus his almost parental attitude to the 'absent-minded beggars' who were being sent off to the Cape – 'my men', as he called them to Norton, when relating the success of the fund. Yet in the same letter there was a new, almost frightening harshness: 'The war is having a splendid effect on the land and all fires will burn more clearly for the fierce draft that has been blown through them.'[16]

Not all of Kipling's extended family shared his views about the war. The Burne-Joneses (Aunt Georgie, Phil, Margaret and her husband, Jack Mackail) were all strongly opposed, and remained so throughout. After a chat with Mackail, Lockwood told Sally Norton that Mackail's 'notions' on the subject were 'on so lofty and merely academic a plane that they have but little concern with any of the actualities of life and so don't count'. As for Lockwood himself, it was, he told Sally, an imperial issue, but one that had to be looked at pragmatically: 'Since we *have* an Empire, needs must we hold it. It is our existence that is at stake, – *rien que ça*. And it's too late in the day to attempt to persuade our public that empire ought to be thrown away.'[17] Inevitably, Lockwood's son was seen from the first as the unofficial spokesman for the British cause. 'The Old Issue', which had appeared in *The Times* on 29 September, was not one of his most accessible poems, but its main thrust was obvious enough:

Clamour over ocean of the harsh, pursuing Trumpets –
Trumpets of the Vanguard that have sworn no truce with Kings![18]

That unmistakably meant Boer repression of the Uitlanders in South Africa – with, by implication, German menace in the background. It was this sort of pronouncement that Joseph Conrad had in mind when he caustically observed a fortnight later: 'If I am to believe Kipling, this is a war undertaken for the cause of democracy. *C'est à crever de rire* [It's enough to make you die laughing].'[19]

Yet, despite all the exhortations, the early weeks and months of the war proved a military nightmare, culminating with reverses at Stormberg (10 December), Magersfontein (11 December) and Colenso (15 December). 'Black Week', as it quickly became known, led to Kipling's old hero 'Bobs' (Lord Roberts) taking over from Buller as Commander-in-Chief in South Africa, with Kitchener as his Chief of Staff. Ironically it was during Black Week that Kipling was offered a knighthood by the Prime Minister, Lord Salisbury. He declined, believing that (in Carrie's words) 'he can do his work better without it'. She added that 'we are much pleased to be offered it however'.[20] This was neither the first nor the last time that Kipling refused such an honour, usually giving the reason that he did not want his independence compromised. That was genuine, though he probably also refused on the same superstitious grounds that prevented him taking money from *The Times* for poems like 'Recessional' and 'The Old Issue' – tangible reward being a contravention of the private deal he had struck with his literary daemon and with the gods.

Kipling would probably have gone back to South Africa in any case. He had enjoyed his previous trip and had been advised after his illness to avoid English winters. Now the outbreak of war, the prospect of seeing for himself what was happening and the chance to be useful probably exerted a strong additional pull. The family left England on 20 January 1900, and on the boat Kipling talked to volunteers and recited 'The Song of the Banjo' at a ship's concert. Reaching Cape Town on 5 February, they put up at the Mount Nelson Hotel, and Kipling was soon conferring with the powerful and the influential: Roberts, Milner and Leo Amery, chief political correspondent for *The Times*. One morning over breakfast, discussing the crucial issue of military transport, Amery suggested that Kipling write a poem 'to celebrate the trek-ox as the pivot of all strategy in South Africa'. Within a few minutes, Kipling had jotted down a pungently apt epigram:

> The Trek-ox when alive can haul
>   Three-quarters of a ton per head.
> But he can shift you, camp and all,
>   Once he is dead.[21]

As a result of asking Roberts what he could do to help, Kipling – equipped with a travel pass and a chit for hospital supplies – embarked on a round of recitals and hospital visits. He modestly played down his Good Samaritan role during this and subsequent winters in the sub-continent, but there would survive various stories of his kindness to the troops. During a three-day train journey from the Orange River Station to Cape Town, for instance, he shared his food with the hospital cases and devoted 'his entire time to writing letters home for the more severely wounded and signing them himself'.[22] The stories that Kipling himself told in his autobiography tended to reflect the humour and stoicism of the Tommies. On one trip on a hospital-train, helping to pick up casualties, he tripped over someone in the dark by the railtrack, 'and filled my palms with gravel. He explained in an uneven voice that he was "fractured 'ip, sir. 'Ope you ain't 'urt yourself, sir." I never got at this unknown Philip Sidney's name.' More generally, Kipling added that they 'were wonderful even in the hour of death – these men and boys – lodge-keepers and ex-butlers of the Reserve and raw town-lads of twenty'.[23]

On 7 March there was lunch with Rhodes, who had been holed up in Kimberley during its 124-day siege and had only recently returned to Cape Town. Rhodes told the Kiplings that he planned to build a house on his property at Groote Schuur, just outside Cape Town, which would then be at their disposal whenever they wanted it. (The Woolsack, designed by Rhodes's architect, Herbert Baker, was ready by the following year and from then on became the Kiplings' home-from-home on their annual visits to South Africa.) The next day Kipling and Rhodes set off for a short trip to Stellenbosch and Paarl.

If Rajah Brooke of Sarawak was Alice Kipling's favourite real-life hero, Cecil Rhodes was undoubtedly her son's. Diamond magnate, multi-millionaire, past Prime Minister of Cape Colony, he was called by Mark Twain (no respecter of persons) 'the most imposing figure in the British Empire outside of England', with Twain adding that 'when he stands on the Cape of Good Hope, his shadow falls to the Zambesi'.[24] 'I don't think that anyone who did not actually come across Him with some intimacy of detail can ever realise what He was,' Kipling would remark to Herbert Baker many years later. 'It is his Presence that had the power.'[25] For most of his contemporaries, Rhodes's charisma derived almost entirely from the great power he wielded in Southern Africa. Kipling, by contrast, wanted to believe that this charisma was something innate. During Rhodes's lifetime, however, Kipling saw him less in quasi-religious terms, and more as a heroic throwback: one of the 'adventurers and captains courageous of old', like Drake or Sir Philip Sidney, Clive or Hastings, who 'have only changed their dress a little and altered their employment to suit the world in which they move', as he had put it in 1892.[26] Six years later, interviewed after his first extended visit to South Africa, Kipling described Rhodes as 'the greatest of living men'. He extolled his frugal lifestyle ('didn't spend more than £600 a year on himself'); his hospitality ('keeping free and easy open house'); his humanity ('Men – natives – formerly in his employment in the diamond mines . . . come long and trying and laborious journeys to be employed by him again'); and his idealism ('The best ideal is to spread civilisation, and make an empire in doing it').[27] Yet if Kipling, through Empire-tinted spectacles, saw only the Rhodes he wanted to see, he did not harbour any illusions about his own purpose in their relationship. 'My use to him,' he admitted in his autobiography, 'was mainly as a purveyor of words . . . After the idea had been presented – and one had to know his code for it – he would say: "What am I trying to express? Say it, *say* it." So I would say it, and if the phrase suited not, he would work it over, chin a little down, till it satisfied him.'[28]

It was also as a writer, not as a man of action, that Kipling set off for Bloemfontein in mid-March 1900. Roberts, on occupying the capital of the Orange Free State, had set up a troops' paper, *The Friend*, and he asked Kipling to be a guest journalist on it. 'Never again will there be such a paper – never such a staff – never such fine Larqs as we 'uns had,' Kipling enthused after a fortnight of sub-editing and proof-reading.[29] He also, as in his old journalistic days, contributed poems and short satirical prose. Their patriotism, however, easily outweighed their literary merit, and more interesting in this fortnight was Kipling's first experience of coming under fire. This was at the Battle of Karee Siding, really little more than a skirmish a few miles to the north of Bloemfontein. Kipling described it nonchalantly to Conland as 'about as merry a day as ever I spent'.[30] Nevertheless, over thirty years later, the details were still etched on his memory: what it felt like to be 'under aimed fire – being, as it were, required as a head'; how a pom-pom shell hitting a rock-face would 'yowl like a cat'; and the way 'a small piece of hanging woodland filled and fumed with our shrapnel much as a man's moustache fills with cigarette-smoke'.[31] What also struck him at the time was the absurd inappropriate-ness of the British tactics: 'The Boers hit us just as hard and just as often as they knew how; and we advanced against 'em as if they were street-rioters that we didn't want to hurt.'[32]

Returning to Cape Town on 3 April, he told Carrie that he had had 'the greatest of times' and, more gnomically, that he had 'joined up all his ideas with the others of many years ago'.[33] When the family embarked for England eight days later, he had a good deal to think about. During his two-month visit he had seen the way the war was being conducted, and misconducted, at first hand. He had picked up a mass of fresh impressions and raw material for new stories. And, more than ever before, Kipling was eager to try to influence public opinion and involve himself directly with public affairs.

Back in England, this involvement was immediate and across a broad front. He had several meetings with Chamberlain, the Colonial Secretary, and began to lobby journalists and editors with imperialist leanings. The best way, he informed Fabian Ware at the *Morning Post*, to increase the number of 'clean white men of colonial experience in S. Africa' was not to recruit the English – who soon became 'bored or fright-ened at the big spaces and fenceless farms' – but to get Australians or Canadians. He also cultivated John St Loe Strachey, editor of the *Spectator*, whose reservations about his hero's probity Kipling was eager to dispel. 'As to Rhodes you are dead wrong,' he told him. 'He isn't a politician. He's the political arena itself.' Later in the summer when there was disturbing talk of Milner being replaced as High Commissioner, Kipling wrote an 'open letter' in the *Daily Express* addressed to his Uncle Alfred, the MP for West Worcestershire. 'I do hope,' the letter concluded, 'you'll be able to make the people your way realise that this silent capable man worrying out his path alone, down South, in the face of all conceivable discouragements is not a steward to be got rid of on the threats or the wire-pulling of a rebel commando.'[34] Kipling even, in the 'Khaki Election' that October, made a speech on behalf of James Morrison, the Conservative candidate for his parents' constituency in Tisbury. Insignificant in itself, the fact of the speech was testament to a new, more public Kipling.

The *Daily Express* was also his forum for four newly written 'Stories of the War', published between 12 June and 4 July. The first two, 'Folly Bridge' and 'The Outsider', concentrated on the rule-bound inefficiency of the British Army in conditions that required energy, enterprise, and speed, while the final one, 'The Way that He Took', preached the value of proper scouting as a stuffy old-fashioned British colonel failed to listen to an intrepid young captain. Kipling did not overrate these stories, describing them as 'foolish yarns about the war which may or may not do some good'; and their general thinness suggests that in writing them, he was breaking one of his own literary rules and forcing his talent.[35] Tellingly, the most sympathetic character was a transplanted Scotsman, Allen, the protagonist of 'A Burgher of the Free State'. Among the blimp-ish British and breezy colonials, he was the only character allowed any degree of complexity, as he tried to live by his conscience while sorting out his conflicting allegiance between the Boers and the British. Even so, the stories did dramatise sharply Kipling's exasperation with upper-class British smugness and Old Boyism. This was pointedly contrasted with the enterprise and practicality of the various Australians, New Zealanders, Canadians, Anglo-Indians and British South Africans who were thwarted or hampered by the bumbling bureaucracy of Mother England.

Kipling was particularly struck by the Australian troops he came across in South Africa. A 'cleaner, simpler, saner, more adequate gang of men I've never met up with,' he later told Charles Norton.[36] In September 1900 he wrote 'The Young Queen', a poem that celebrated the coming federation of the six separate colonies of Australia to become a single independent dominion of the British Empire, a kind of imperial coming of age. Australia was portrayed as a young woman warrior leaving the battlefield for her coronation:

High on her red-splashed charger, beautiful, bold, and browned,
Bright-eyed out of the battle, the Young Queen rode to be crowned.[37]

The verses were printed in *The Times* on 4 October and prompted a terse reaction from the Sage of Box Hill. 'Are you swayed by the Kipling we see in the *Times*?' George Meredith asked a friend. 'We are in a dreary plight when Mob-orator puts on the Muse to move the country, and shows her as a slattern with a furious jingle, to suit the country's taste. And a *Times*' eulogistic Leading Article on such red spume!'[38]

Meredith's tart put-down encapsulated an increasingly prevalent view of Kipling. The mood of exhilaration after the relief of Mafeking the previous May – a relief fully felt by Kipling, who led the festivities in Rottingdean – was turning to one of frustration as it started to become clear that, although Britain was eventually going to win, the war itself seemed to be dragging on interminably. This shift of mood directly affected Kipling's standing. Some saw him as a pernicious reactionary. 'For progressive thought there has been no such dangerous influence in England for many years,' the poet and critic Richard le Gallienne observed the same year in his bluntly entitled *Rudyard Kipling: a criticism*.[39] For others, Kipling was becoming a bore. 'I'm getting just a wee bit tired of Mr Kipling,' Jerome K Jerome remarked even before the relief of Mafeking in his column in the *Sun*. 'Since this war began he appears to have dominated the universe to the exclusion of all other beliefs.'[40] It was all a far cry from that fortnight only a year or so previously, when the world had waited for the latest news of the genius at death's door.

In the eyes of the intelligentsia he was rapidly turning into a caricature of his former self – a transformation wittily caught in 1901 in C L Graves's and E V Lucas's *Lives of the 'Lustrious*:

KIPLING, RUDYARD, Poet Laureate and Recruiting Sergeant, was born all over the world, some eighteen years ago. After a lurid infancy at Westward Ho! in the company of Stalky & Co., he emigrated to India at the age of six and swallowed it whole. In the following year the British Empire was placed in his charge, and it is still there. A misgiving that England may have gone too far in the matter of self-esteem having struck him in 1897, he wrote 'The Recessional', but there are signs that he has since forgotten it . . . He lives in Cape Colony, which is a suburb of Rottingdean, and at intervals puts forth a fascinating book, or a moral essay in *The Times* . . .[41]

By so earnestly, and ostentatiously, aligning himself with the British cause in the war – and the set of attitudes that went with it – he had become a sitting target and a figure of fun. Though exceptions would usually be made for his writing for children and for *Kim* (published in 1901), some readers found it increasingly hard to take Kipling and his work quite seriously. He was in a wholly negative sense becoming Kiplingesque, evoking the cartoon image of a bald dwarf with glasses and eyebrows, energetically beating some sort of drum.

In unconscious harmony with that image, Kipling and his family departed in December 1900 for another winter in South Africa. On board ship he worked at a new two-part story, 'The Army of a Dream', a thinly veiled piece of propaganda on the need for wholesale army reform and a form of National Service. At the time the story meant a lot to him. Perhaps, like 'Recessional', he saw it as a *nuzzur-wattu*. In any case, he held off publication until June 1904 in the *Morning Post*. By the time *Traffics and Discoveries* came out later that year, he had persuaded himself that the collection 'was really done for the purpose of carrying one political pamphlet – *the Army of a Dream* . . . what I saw during the war of our arrangements and notions of work, scared me and I thought it might be good to try to train people before a real war came'.[42] The title reflected a typical blend of optimism and pessimism: Kipling's 'Army of a Dream' was both the army he dreamt of seeing formed and the army he knew was possible only in dreams.

They reached Cape Town on Christmas Day to find a message from Rhodes, saying that The Woolsack was ready for their use. 'A Dutch-model house in a garden of figs and loquats and grapes *and* oranges' was how Kipling described the place to Conland. 'From our verandah we look straight across to the mountains 30 miles away, over the whole flat of the Cape peninsula.'[43] The easy access to Groote Schuur meant regular talks and meetings with Rhodes. The slow progress of the war was a common topic; so too was Rhodes's pet scheme to establish annual scholarships to send students from the colonies, America and Germany to study in Oxford. Kipling would become one of the trustees of the fund to administer the scholarships, but he always emphasised that at their inception it was his wife's practical advice that was decisive: 'It was she who suggested that £250 a year was not enough for scholars who would have to carry themselves through the long intervals of an Oxford "year". So [Rhodes] made it three hundred.' It was also Carrie, armed with 'stout motorgloves, and the largest of babies' bottles', who took on the nursing of Sullivan, the lion-cub that joined their household. Kipling in his autobiography left a touching portrait: 'For three months he was at large among us, incessantly talking to himself as he wandered about the house or in the garden where he stalked butterflies. He dozed on the stoep, I noticed, due north and south, looking with slow eyes up the length of Africa – always a little aloof, but obedient to the children . . .'[44]

This time round, Kipling preferred to stay put at The Woolsack and get on with some writing. As usual he had a number of things on the go: a new *Just So* story, 'How the Leopard got his Spots'; a prose monologue, 'A Sahib's War', in which through the Sikh narrator he questioned the appropriateness of 'sahib' rules in the South African context; and a poem, 'The Lesson', eventually published in *The Times* on 29 July, which tried to draw positives from the British Army's continuing inability to combat the Boers' hit-and-run guerrilla tactics. The poem's message ('We have had an Imperial lesson. It may make us an Empire yet!') was one he hammered home at every opportunity.[45] Even a Democrat friend like Conland, who cannot have been that interested, was treated to little else. 'The Boers are doing it very well,' Kipling told him on 20 February. 'They keep in small parties, looting and riding away, and except where the carelessness of our infantry gives them the chance they take care not to attack.'

Kipling used letters like these to sort out his thoughts about the meaning of the war. Half the problem, as he explained to the patient Conland, was that the British were so gentlemanly about it all. But at least, he comforted himself, they might end up with an army: 'We ought to come out with 300,000 trained soldiers at the end of the game – men with from six months to a year's good experience behind 'em.' And he was convinced that the experience was uniting the Empire and reducing British snobbery about the colonies: 'I was talking to an Ontario man yesterday and he told me that at the start the regular regiments patronised the colonials. They're all brothers now and eat out of the same dish.'[46]

Back at The Elms in early May 1901, he was giving Charles Norton more of the same, emphasising the revitalising effects that the war was having on England. His letter demonstrated the double-bind in which Kipling now found himself as a result of his Larger Englandism. The basic problem was that England was the source, the centre, the *raison d'être*, of the Empire, but it did not care for the Empire in any deeply bonded sense. Consequently, Kipling had a narrow range of options. He could emigrate to one of the newer colonies; he could adjust his ideas about England; or he could try to make England adjust to his own ideas. Wintering in South Africa was a gesture towards the first option, but emigration was never really a serious possibility. The second option was a non-starter. That left, as his only real alternative, a programme to give England a political, social and psychic spring-cleaning. The strain involved in trying to sustain such a position, and believing that the Boer War was the necessary revolutionary agent, came through painfully in his shrill despatch to Norton:

We [the English] were bung-full of beastly unjustified spiritual pride as we were with material luxury and over much ease. We went about despising things and people and unconsciously turning our ideals to mean an easy life – virtuous maybe, perhaps even beneficent but at heart easy – soft-rubber-tyred. Now we are slowly coming back to the Primitives and realising that a lot of what we called civilisation was another name for shirking. The mere war, though that is fairly large, is the least part of the business. Every thing we have – church school and craft – has, so to speak, been challenged to show cause why it should continue on the old unthinking hidebound lines: has been asked explicitly by circumstance and necessity whether all the trappings with which the centuries have adorned it, do not cover the ordinary tendency of mankind to be – plain dog-gone idle. One can feel this in the air, and see it in people's faces. It makes for humility and common earnestness. Moreover the war has given us a new nation – Australia. We've seen a lot of them down south and a cleaner, simpler, saner, more adequate gang of men I've never met up with. Indeed, taking it all round, one may almost hope that England (by which I mean the Island) may almost, in time, learn to work and be less of a fatted snob than it is at present.[47]

He was, finally, beginning to sound like one of the parodies of himself that Max Beerbohm would soon be creating with so much relish.

That autumn *The Times* published his poem 'The Reformers'. It imagined a representative young upper-class Englishman who by fighting in the war not only redeemed his family's sins, but also emerged as the saviour of his country, averting Jehovah's wrath:

> *Who is his Nation's sacrifice*
> *To turn the judgement from his race.*[48]

Given the poem's imperial overloading, it was perhaps inevitable that something would sabotage its message. What happened was that, on the day it appeared, *The Times*'s leader-writer borrowed the line 'the fatted shows wherein he stood' to attack Rhodes for his attempts to influence the Liberals' policy on Egypt ten years before. (Rhodes had paid £5,000 into the party's funds.) Kipling, who had had his hero to tea only a few days earlier, was horrified. He remonstrated with Moberly Bell, on paper and in person, and earnestly assured Rhodes that no one had been fooled by *The Times*. Rhodes, the practical politician, was unfazed. 'It really does not matter,' he told Kipling, 'and I have forgotten about it.'[49]

More auspiciously, October 1901 saw the publication in book form of *Kim*, which Kipling had spent much of 1900, in the intervals of public life, completing. It marked, bar a couple of minor stories, his swansong to India and was a delighted celebration of cultural and racial difference – in the strongest contrast to his White Man bluster. As readers followed Kim and his master, the Lama, all over northern India, they were constantly made aware of life's multiplicity and interdependence. The Grand Trunk Road along which the pair travelled for much of the time ('such a river of life as nowhere else exists in the world') was both an alternative to, and simply another version of, the River of the Arrow, which was the object of their quest. At one point Kim and the Lama reached their resting-place for the night:

> By this time the sun was driving broad golden spokes through the lower branches of the mango-trees; the parakeets and doves were coming home in their hundreds; the chattering, grey-backed Seven Sisters, talking over the day's adventures, walked back and forth in twos and threes almost under the feet of the travellers; and shufflings and scufflings in the branches showed that the bats were ready to go out on the night-picket. Swiftly the light gathered itself together, painted for an instant the faces and the cart-wheels and the bul-locks' horns as red as blood. Then the night fell, changing the touch of the air, drawing a low, even haze, like a gossamer veil of blue, across the face of the country and bringing out, keen and distinct, the smell of wood-smoke and cattle and the good scent of wheaten cakes cooked on ashes. The evening patrol hurried out of the police-station with important coughings and reiterated orders; and a live charcoal ball in the cup of a wayside carter's hookah glowed red while Kim's eye mechanically watched the last flicker of the sun on the brass tweezers.
>
> The life of the *parao* [resting-place] was very like that of the Kashmir Serai on a small scale. Kim dived into the happy Asiatic disorder which, if you only allow time, will bring you everything that a simple man needs.[50]

When *Kim* was originally conceived nearly ten years before, Kipling was just married, eagerly anticipating his first child and relishing his new life in Vermont. It was a time of tremendous inner release, during which he revisited and re-imagined his two greatest subjects, childhood and India. Distanced in time and space, he could let himself off the Anglo-Indian leash, switch off the imperialist censor and enjoy (rather than feel threat-ened by) India's teeming diversity. These rather special conditions helped to create the novel's feeling of spaciousness and lack of constraint. We are told, for instance, that Kim 'dived into the happy Asiatic disorder' (a phrase that could stand for many Western readers' experience of the novel). Here Kipling was positively luxuriating in that disorder, whereas if he had been wearing his White Man's helmet, a description of the same disorder would have required anxious justifications of the British imperial mission. Strikingly, and perhaps surprisingly, he was aware of this anomaly. In early 1900, he described *Kim* as 'a long leisurely Asiatic yarn in which there are hardly any Englishmen. It has been a labour of great love and I think it is a bit more temperate and wise than much of my stuff.'[51]

This lack of White Man anxiety was evident in the portrayal of the Babu, Hurree Chunder Mookerjee, one of the spies with whom Kim worked in the Great Game. Hurree, a highly educated English-speaking Indian, was just the kind of figure whom Kipling had found threatening in India and usually depicted in his fiction and letters as a coward, a comic or a fake. In *Kim*, Hurree was presented sympathetically, even heroically, as he helped to outwit the Russian threat. The novel also displayed an acceptance of different ways of looking at and living in the world. Much of this openness was mediated through the quietism of the Lama, one of whose many admirable qualities, we are informed, was 'having nothing of the white man's impatience, but a great faith'.[52]

Even more than the *Jungle Books*, *Kim* was full of moments when the usual terms of the child/adult relationship were gratifyingly reversed. This was especially the case in the relationship between Kim and the Lama. On their travels the boy time and again proved more practical and effective than the old man. He understood how the train worked, knew the best ways to beg for food, sprang to defend the Lama when the Russian struck him. In one supreme reversal, Kim even acted as interpreter between three adults, the two regimental chaplains and the Lama, neither side being able to communicate with the other without him. He was also, like Mowgli, a boundary-crosser, equally at home in different worlds: as a sahib, as a half-caste or as any of a wide array of Indians. Kim reflected Kipling's own chameleon qualities, in particular his sympathetic knack of entering into other people's situations. The novelist H A Vachell would remember him 'marching up and down . . . talking about *my* work, hurling himself into *my* difficulties and perplexities. This was his God-given mission; he could race out of himself and become the man to whom he was talking.'[53]

Responses to *Kim* were positive from the start. Kipling was back on track, Andrew Lang announced even in the early stages of serialisation. He was 'once more the Mr Kipling who first won our hearts'. When the novel appeared in book form, the reviews were glowing. 'We despair of giving our readers any conception of the glorious variety of the feast here spread before them,' J H Millar gushed in *Blackwood's*.[54] *Kim* has never lost that early appeal, holding a special place for those born in India, like T H White, author of *The Once and Future King*. As White told a friend in 1941: 'Did you know that I was born in India and could speak Hindustani before I could speak English? You probably have to be like that to understand Kim properly: it is one of the books which is absolutely true to the feeling of a place.'[55]

At the time, even Henry James was impressed, hoping that Kipling the artist was indeed back on track:

> I find the boy himself a dazzling conception [he wrote to Kipling], but I find the Lama more yet – a thing damnably and splendidly *done* ... The way you make the general picture live and sound and shine, all by a myriad [of] touches that are like the thing itself pricking through with a little snap – that makes me want to say to you: 'Come, all else is folly – sell all you have and give it to the poor!' By which I mean chuck public affairs, which are an ignoble scene, and stick to your canvas and your paint-box. There are as good colours in the tubes as ever were laid on, and *there* is the only truth. The rest is base humbug. Ask the Lama.[56]

James's approval meant a lot to Kipling, who specifically mentioned it in a letter to Sarah Jewett. However, he remained deaf to the well-intentioned advice about abandoning public life. Confident that he had his finger on the pulse ('I don't know a dam [sic] about politics but I think I know something about public opinion,' he boasted to Rhodes), he convinced himself that the letters to the papers, the propagandist stories and poems, the electioneering speech were all an integral part of his work rather than a distraction from it.[57] For every member of the intelligentsia whom he alienated, there were – he knew – thousands all over the world for whom his patriotic and imperialist bulletins hit the spot.

Shortly before Christmas 1901, the family again left for South Africa. This year Carrie's health as well as Kipling's made them eager to get away. During the summer there had been talk of an operation (cause unknown), which had seriously depressed her. 'A night of mental agony leaves me down in the bottom of the pit and well nigh hopeless for the black future,' she noted in her diary on 6 August.[58] To her great relief, an operation was eventually ruled out, but a return to the sunlit peace of The Woolsack was a high priority.

The Kiplings reached Cape Town on 7 January 1902. He stepped off the boat to be surrounded by reporters wanting to ask him about 'The Islanders', which had appeared in *The Times* three days before. Kipling was indeed, as Twain so pertinently remarked, 'the only living person not head of a nation, whose voice is heard around the world the moment it drops a remark, the only such voice in existence that does not go by slow ship and rail but always travels first-class by cable'; 'The Islanders' itself confirmed that, far from chucking public affairs, he still intended to grab them with both hands.[59]

The prompt for the poem was a letter in early December from 'Bobs', urging Kipling to promote the issue of conscription. He got to work at once, and by the 16th told Moberly Bell that he had a poem ready, 'on the matter of compulsory service for home defence'. He added that 'it isn't precisely polite but it's rather good verse and, as politicians say, it "affirms the principle" and enunciates the doctrine etc. with a clarity that leaves little to be desired'. *The Times* could have the poem, he concluded – with the proviso that it was prepared to 'back the principle with a leader'.[60] This it did, though rather tentatively. 'The Islanders' was one of Kipling's most uncompromising attacks on English insularity and complacency, particularly that of the Tory Old Guard. From its opening lines, the thumping hexameters pulled no punches and announced their intention to say the unacceptable in an unacceptable way:

No doubt but ye are the People – your throne is above the King's.
Whoso speaks in your presence must say acceptable things:
Bowing the head in worship, bending the knee in fear –,
Bringing the word well smoothen – such as a King should hear.

The aristocracy was told in no uncertain terms that if it wanted to preserve its pampered life ('Ancient, effortless, ordered, cycle on cycle set') from the menace from overseas, then every native-born Englishman must be 'broke to the matter of war'. Some of the most stinging couplets developed the anti-games line that Kipling had pushed in *Stalky & Co.*:

Will ye pitch some white pavilion, and lustily even the odds,
With nets and hoops and mallets, with rackets and bats and rods?
Will the rabbit war with your foemen – the red deer horn them for
    hire?
Your kept cock-pheasant keep you – he is master of many a shire.

The most famous couplet was in the same vein, with an extra dig at country-house aesthetes:

Then ye returned to your trinkets; then ye contented your souls
With the flannelled fools at the wicket or the muddied oafs at the
    goals.[61]

(When, a few weeks later in Cape Town, a Scottish colonel suggested that he had been a bit tough on cricketers and footballers, Kipling retorted: 'Possibly, but if you don't exaggerate no one will take any notice . . . You have to hit an Englishman more than once on the jaw before he will take a thing seriously.'[62]) The poem ended with a ringing triplet, sarcastically affirming the main charges and laying the onus for the future where he felt it belonged:

No doubt but ye are the People – absolute, strong, and wise;
Whatever your heart has desired ye have not withheld from your eyes.
On your own heads, in your own hands, the sin and the saving lies![63]

'The Islanders', Kipling would recall in his autobiography, enjoyed 'a few days' newspaper correspondence', before being 'dismissed as violent, untimely, and untrue'.[64] Still, as he remarked three weeks after publication to H G Wells (an improbable correspondent, but one who shared Kipling's dislike of inherited wealth and privilege): 'not all the truth in the world saves a man who interferes with the noble English pastime of watching games. *"Which has made us what we are!"* '[65]

During this year's South African visit, Kipling again did his share of recitations in hospitals, for instance on 18 January reading a couple of new 'Service Songs', 'M.I.' and 'The Parting of the Columns', to 500 appreciative patients. He wrote two further *Just So* stories, 'The Cat that Walked by Himself' and 'The Butterfly that Stamped', and a poem,

'Sussex', which suggested that after nearly six years back in England he was starting to put down some roots. Lockwood joined the party in February, and there were calls from friends and admirers, including Edgar Wallace. Though the war was at last drawing to an end, Kipling's attention for once was elsewhere. Rhodes, after many years of heart problems, was dying. Kipling was a regular visitor at his friend's bedside as the latter sat up – a bloated, dropsical figure, his lungs congested, fighting to breathe. Rhodes died of heart failure on 26 March. 'So little done, so much to do.'

A fortnight later, Kipling told Mrs Hill that he felt as though 'half the horizon of my life had dropped away'.[66] It was an image conveying more powerfully what Rhodes had meant to him than anything in 'The Burial', the elegy he wrote for the private funeral service at Groote Schuur on 2 April. The elegy imagined Rhodes in the Matoppo Hills gazing from his grave 'Across the world he won' and, in a conclusion one might describe as 'imperial Wordsworth', saw him impelling the future as he had impelled the past:

> The immense and brooding Spirit still
>   Shall quicken and control.
> Living he was the land, and dead,
>   His soul shall be her soul![67]

Next day the official funeral took place in the cathedral at Cape Town. Kipling, in the same letter to Mrs Hill, called it 'the most marvellous thing I have ever seen – a whole city of 60,000 moved as one man with a common grief and reverence.' Inevitably his own sense of loss brought the greater misery of Josephine's death forcibly to mind. 'I think that that is the one grief that grows with the years,' he confessed to his old confidante. 'The others only stay still.'[68]

The Kiplings left Cape Town on 16 April and were back in England in early May. A few days before their departure peace had unofficially been declared, and on 31 May the Treaty of Vereeniging was signed. Though news of the peace brought the expected celebrations in England, the fact that the Orange Free State and the Transvaal had been forced to relinquish their political independence outraged Liberals like Aunt Georgie. From one of the windows of her house in Rottingdean she displayed a large blue cloth on which were stitched the words: 'We have killed and also taken possession.' This led to a local demonstration outside her house, and according to her granddaughter Angela Thirkell, 'for some time there was considerable personal danger to her from a populace in Mafeking mood'.[69] Luckily Kipling was at home in The Elms, and he quickly came across to pacify and disperse the angry crowd.

In fact, he was about to move. Two years earlier he and Carrie had tried but failed to purchase Bateman's, a Jacobean house in the East Sussex village of Burwash, some twenty-five miles from Rottingdean. They had kept their eye on the house, hoping it might again become available. Negotiations began soon after their return from the Cape, and on 10 June they were able to secure Bateman's and thirty-three acres for £9,300. Purchase was completed at the end of July, and on 3 September they moved in. Carrie's diary suggests a shambles: a drunk foreman, a cock-up about the electric lighting. 'Meet chaos and black night' as she tersely put it.[70] But this did not detract from their pleasure at what Kipling was to call 'The Very-Own House'.[71] He was soon giving Charles Norton a lovingly detailed description:

> Behold us the lawful owners of a grey stone lichened house – A.D. 1634 over the door – beamed, panelled, with old oak staircase all untouched and unfaked . . . It is a good and a peaceable place standing in terraced lawns nigh to a walled garden of old red brick and two fat-headed old oast-houses with red brick stomachs and an aged silver grey oak dovecot on top. There is what they call a river at the bottom of the lawn. It appears in all the maps and that, except after very heavy rain, is the only place where it puts in any appearance. Normally you hunt for it with a pole through alder bushes but in flood time (so we are told) it runs about all over the little valley. Its name is the Dudwell, and it is quite ten feet wide.
>
> But I think you'd like the inside of the house if you were here. There is a black and white tiled hall all panelled to the naked beamed ceiling and the doors out of it have stone heads and old oak frames – dark as teak. There is a deep window seat and a high leaded window with lots of old greeny-glass panes left and a flap-table of Queen Elizabeth's time (the worst of the place is that it simply will not endure modern furniture) and benches and a stone arched fire

place backed by old Sussex iron work. We burn wood in all the fires and the hall takes five foot logs.

But in reality the house is little – not a manor house or a 'place' – just the kind of house that a successful Sussex iron master builded himself two hundred and fifty years ago. It hasn't a lodge or any non-sense of that kind. You walk up to the porch over a stone-paved path laid down in the turf and the cartroad runs within fifty yards of the front door. The rest is all fields and farms and to the southward one glorious sweep of woods. We coveted the place for two and a half or three years and have loved it ever since our first sight of it.

Still only thirty-six, Kipling would live at Bateman's for the rest of his days. 'England is a wonderful land,' he told Norton in the same letter. 'It is the most marvellous of all foreign countries that I have ever been in.'[72]

17

Family and Foes

The best story about Kipling is also the best story about Henry James. It was told by the novelist Ford Madox Ford in his gossipy book of reminiscences *Return to Yesterday*. In October 1902 he came to visit James in Rye, and on 'the narrow cobbled street that led to the Master's house' passed Mr and Mrs Kipling 'hurrying down' in a perturbed state. Ford was admitted to the Master's presence, where James explained, at uniquely Jamesian length, the cause of the Kiplings' perturbation:

'A writer who unites – if I may use the phrase – in his own person an enviable popularity to – as I am told – considerable literary gifts and whom I may say I like because he treats me' – and here Mr James laid his hand over his heart, made the slightest of bows and, rather cruelly rolling his dark liquid eyes and moving his lower jaw as if he were rolling in his mouth a piquant tit-bit, Mr James continued, 'because he treats me – if again I may say any such thing – with proper respect' – and there would be an immense humorous gasp before the word 'respect' – . . . 'I refer of course to Mr Kipling . . . has just been to see me. And – such are the rewards of an enviable popularity! – a popularity such as I – or indeed you my young friend if you have any ambitions which I sometimes doubt – could dream of far less imagine to ourselves – such are the rewards of an enviable popularity that Mr Kipling is in possession of a magnificent one thousand two hundred guinea motor car. And, in the course of conversation as to characteristics of motor cars in general and those of the particular one thousand two hundred guinea motor car in the possession of our friend . . . But what do I say? . . . Of our cynosure! Mr Kipling uttered words which have for himself no doubt a particular significance but which to me at least convey almost literally nothing beyond their immediate sound . . . Mr Kipling said that the motor car was calculated to make the Englishman . . .' – and again came the humorous gasp and the roll of the eyes – 'was calculated to make the Englishman . . . think.' And Mr James abandoned himself for part of a second to low chuckling. 'And,' he continued, 'the conversation dissolved itself after digressions on the advantages attendant on the possession of such a vehicle, into what I believe are styled golden dreams – such as how the magnificent one thousand two hundred guinea motor car after having this evening conveyed its master and mistress to Batemans Burwash of which the proper pronunciation is Burridge would to-morrow devotedly return here and reaching here at twelve would convey me and my nephew Billiam to Burridge in time to lunch and having partaken of that repast to return here in time to give tea to my friend Lady Maud Warrender who is honouring that humble meal with her presence to-morrow under my roof . . . And we were still indulging in – what is it? – delightful anticipations and dilating on the agreeableness of rapid – but not for fear of the police and consideration for one's personal safety *too* rapid – speed over country roads and all, if I may use the expression, was gas and gingerbread when . . . There is a loud knocking on the door and *avec des yeux éffarés* . . .' and here Mr James really did make his prominent and noticeable eye almost stick out of his head . . . 'in rushes the chauffeur . . . And in short the chauffeur has omitted to lubricate the wheels of the magnificent one thousand two hundred guinea motor car with the result that its axles have become one piece of molten metal . . . The consequence is that its master and mistress will return to Burwash which should be pronounced Burridge by train, and the magnificent one thousand two hundred guinea motor car will *not* devotedly return here at noon and will *not* in time for lunch convey me and my nephew Billiam to Burwash and will *not* return here in time for me to give tea to my friend Lady Maud Warrender who is honouring that humble meal with her presence to-morrow beneath my roof or if the weather is fine in the garden . . .'

'Which,' concluded the Master after subdued 'ho, ho, ho's' of merriment, 'is calculated to make Mr Kipling think.'[1]

Ford was a notorious embellisher and recycler, often publishing different versions of his favourite anecdotes. So one might describe this version of the Kipling Car story as the 1931 *de luxe* model, the culmination of careful touching-up over the years, so that in effect the story had become two jokes in one: against Kipling for being so rich, brash and philistine; and against James for being so elephantinely orotund.

Kipling's own version of the story, relayed at the time to Charles Norton, offered one significant variation. He not only shared the joke, he even told it against himself:

We went down to see him [Henry James] in our new motor (Amelia is her name) some six weeks ago and because we swaggered and boasted about Amelia (she being a virgin) and told him how we would drive him all over Sussex in two hours, Amelia was took with cataleptic trance then and there – opposite a hotel – and she abode in Rye, stark and motionless till we wired to the place where she was born (it happened to be Birmingham) for an expert mechanician or obstetrician or whatever the name is and after two days Amelia came back to us. But Henry James's monologue over her immobile carcase – with all the machinery exposed and our engineer underneath growing progressively blacker – would have been cheap at the price of several wrecked cars.[2]

James's first delivery of the great monologue was actually made over Amelia's 'immobile carcase' – with Kipling a delighted spectator. That there was no place in Ford's story for a Kipling who enjoyed the joke is revealing: such a Kipling would have to be taken seriously and could not be dismissed as a philistine butt.

The Ford/James story was a direct product of the abrupt decline in Kipling's literary reputation in Britain in the decade or so before the First

World War. Even a hack like T W H Crosland now felt free to take a tilt at him. When *The Five Nations*, Kipling's collection of mostly Boer War poems, appeared in late 1903, Crosland rushed out a series of parodies called *The Five Notions*. The opening quatrain of the title poem adequately reflected the level of entertainment on offer:

> 'E 'ath Five Notions 'ath R.K.,
> For to put in 'is 'eavenly song,
> An' come to think of it, I say
> That every one of 'em is wrong.

It speaks volumes for the drop in Kipling's standing that the *Daily Telegraph* should have found these feeble parodies 'very clever and incisive . . . The wit is excellent, the barb is pointed, and Mr Kipling is fair game.'[3] Or take the opening number, two and a half years later, of *John Bull*, the populist weekly founded by the financier and Liberal MP Horatio Bottomley. Selected as 'Prisoner at the Bar', Kipling was convicted of 'wilful murder of the King's English' and transported for life to a Crown Colony. There, he was to be 'prevented, by force if need be, . . . from the unnatural habit of imperial thinking', taught basic grammar and 'kept in confinement until such time as you may be delivered of a less ridiculous muse'.[4] By the time the American poet Robert Frost came to England in 1912, Kipling was an established back-number. 'How slowly but surely Yeats has eclipsed Kipling,' he remarked the following year. 'I have seen it all happen with my own eyes.'[5] Roger Fry had recently put it more brusquely. 'So sorry I seem so snarkish just now,' he apologised to a friend. 'I've been seeing the French Post-Impressionist people whom you don't like; but they are nice people, only they will like Kipling.'[6]

Ironically, while Kipling's literary stock was plummeting in English artistic circles, it was steadily rising on the Continent. In 1902, according to the German dramatist Gerhart Hauptmann, Kipling was 'the most powerful poet of the time' and the 'idol' of the *Junker* class; and, as Roger Fry's remark suggests, he was even more popular in France, being regularly translated and interviewed throughout the Edwardian period.[7] Kipling himself relished this French connection, and was particularly appreciative of the way that French journalists, unlike their American counterparts, usually allowed him to have second thoughts before publication. When

Jules Huret interviewed him for *Le Figaro*, Kipling made some absurdly negative remarks about German science, technology and literature. When sent the proofs, he was grateful for the chance to modify his views. In science the Germans were 'leaders', he admitted to Huret. 'In literature I know that I owe much to Heine. So I have softened or cut down the interview in this regard.' Even when one early translator and interviewer, Vicomte Robert d'Humières, made a gaffe by publicly claiming that Kipling adored Offenbach, he was merely amused. 'I would rather be the "aggressive imperialist" of fiction,' Kipling told the Frenchman, 'than an adorer of Offenbach.'[8] Such was the French enthusiasm for his work that when the young Alain-Fournier, future author of *Le Grand Meaulnes*, visited London in 1905, he found himself bewildered by the English view of Kipling. 'Everybody laughs at me about Kipling,' he reported, 'maintaining his tales are either for "children" or "soldiers".'[9]

Equally ironically, while the English literati were busy relegating Kipling to such nether-regions, the academic honours and awards began to roll in. His big year was 1907, when honorary degrees in June from both Durham and Oxford were followed before Christmas by the Nobel Prize for Literature. The ceremony at Oxford gave a welcome opportunity to hobnob with Mark Twain, like himself receiving a D.Litt. As they processed through the streets, Kipling told his mother-in-law, he walked directly behind Twain. 'Whole detachments of Englishmen shouted: "good old Mark" and he took off his mortarboard and smiled and waved his hand and seemed perfectly happy. It was glorious.' While to his son John, now nearly ten, Kipling described how during the long wait for their turn he, Twain and a couple of other honourands sneaked out 'like naughty boys' for a smoke 'under a big archway'; and how, when at last his turn came, and he had been mumbled at inaudibly in Latin, an undergraduate shouted out: 'You'll tell us about it afterwards Rudyard.'[10]

Someone who was particularly riled by Kipling's doctorate was Max Beerbohm. 'The idols of the market-place need no wreaths from an university,' he objected in a piece written a few days later.[11] Beerbohm, like many others, had taken against Kipling during the Boer War and by this time had become one of his most savage critics. He attacked Kipling in reviews, reviled him in a series of wittily cruel caricatures, and produced what is still the best parody of his early manner, 'P.C., X. 36', in which a thuggish bobby arrests Santa Claus for burglary on Christmas Eve. It was an antipathy that became a lifelong obsession. 'Friends of his and mine,' Beerbohm would recall in his eighties, 'kept telling me that he was pained and shocked by what I wrote, but I couldn't stop. You know, I couldn't stop. As his publication increased, so did my derogation. He didn't stop; I *couldn't* stop. I meant to. I wanted to. But I couldn't.'[12]

What Beerbohm thought of Kipling being awarded the Nobel Prize is not recorded, but he probably felt as outraged as the leading Liberal journalist A G Gardiner, still fulminating the following year about the choice of Kipling as 'the first Englishman to be crowned in the Court of Literary Europe'. Noting that Meredith, Hardy and Swinburne were all still alive, he concluded that 'the goldsmiths are passed by and the literary blacksmith is exalted'.[13] Hardy, one of the passed-by, kept his sense of humour. It was 'odd', he mused, to associate Kipling with 'peace'.[14]

Kipling himself, with his usual superstitious distrust of good fortune, played down the prize. On the eve of his departure for Sweden, he told his Burwash friend Colonel Feilden that he had 'already been decimated by agile Swedish journalists demanding locks of my golden hair and the bulk of the continental press has written articles on my virtuous life!' The Swedish King, Oscar II, died during the Kiplings' crossing to Stockholm, and they arrived to find everyone in mourning and, as a mark of respect, the ceremonial side of the awards greatly reduced. Kipling described to his children how, on a winter afternoon, they drove through 'the dark shiny wet streets', where everyone 'seemed to be in black and the shops were full of black dresses'. Also for their benefit, he played up the more comic aspects of the ceremony itself: how he 'felt rather like a bad boy up to be caned'; and 'how difficult it is to shake hands gracefully when one arm is full of a large smooth leather book on top of which is [a] slippery slidy red leather box – like a huge Tiffany jewel case. Try, with a blotter and the case of my silver key and see what happens.' In retrospect, he would tell his sister-in-law Josephine, the whole experience of going to the Palace was rather like being in a certain kind of adventure novel:

I had to go to be presented to King Gustav V – Oscar his father lying dead in the great rambling city of a palace. I drove through vast squares of buildings hundreds of yards across, dived into a gallery of singularly unpleasant statues, climbed echoing empty stairs that always sprouted into smaller staircases, found myself before a shut door which allowed no sound to come through – opened it at a venture and tumbled slap into Rupert of Hentzau, Stevenson's Prince Otto and all the rest of them.[15]

A further irony of Kipling's Edwardian eclipse was that it coincided with the publication of some of his greatest work. The delightful *Just So Stories*, which appeared in September 1902, were quite unlike anything previously written for children. Most of the tales invited the child-listener to pretend that the world was being made up from scratch. What evolved was an elaborate and outrageous fantasy of how things did not happen: how the elephant did not get its trunk, how the leopard did not get its spots, how the camel did not get its hump. From the extravagant names (Taffimai Metallumai, the Little God Nqa) to the hypnotic catchphrases ('*Have* you forgotten the suspenders?', 'full of ''satiable curtiosity') and the punning signature of the ark (for RK) in some of Kipling's illustrations, the child knew that he or she was being invited to be co-conspirator in a game where the usual rules did not apply. In 'The Elephant's Child', the young elephant (the child in the story) entirely turned the tables on the grown-ups and ended up spanking them rather than being spanked. In addition, he was actually rewarded for his ''satiable curtiosity' and for being so enterprising as to go to 'the banks of the great grey-green, greasy Limpopo River, all set about with fever-trees, to find out what the Crocodile has for dinner'.[16] A further ingredient of this and the other stories' great charm was the way that the narrating voice focused so exclusively on the imagined child-listener, the 'Best Beloved', making her or him feel the absolute centre of attention. Angela Thirkell, one of the earliest listeners, would always insist that the stories were specifically designed to be told or read aloud; and she almost allows us to hear Kipling himself deliver them:

> The *Just So Stories* are a poor thing in print compared with the fun of hearing them told in Cousin Ruddy's deep unhesitating voice. There was a ritual about them, each phrase having its special intonation which had to be exactly the same each time and without which the stories are dried husks. There was an inimitable cadence, an emphasis of certain words, an exaggeration of certain phrases, a

kind of intoning here and there which made his telling unforgettable.[17]

Nor, as Alain-Fournier realised in 1905, were Kipling's tales just for children or soldiers. '"Wireless"', 'Mrs Bathurst' and '"They"', all collected the previous year in *Traffics and Discoveries*, were as good as anything he had ever written. Each, in its different way, turned on Kipling's fascination with new technology and the supernatural. In '"Wireless"', while the lovesick young chemist Shaynor involuntarily scribbled botched lines from 'The Eve of St Agnes' and 'Ode to a Nightingale', two men-of-war out at sea were trying to 'talk to each other' in Morse code, using early Marconi transmitters.[18] By the end, the reader was left to contemplate the transmission of radio waves as an analogy for the creative process; and although the bulk of the tale concentrated on the literary side of the analogy (Shaynor's inability to reproduce 'authentic' Keats), the romance inherent in Marconi's recent experiments, and their naval potential, were also powerfully intimated. Again, the governing notion was of inspiration coming from outside.

The new item of technology in 'Mrs Bathurst' was the cinematograph – the device through which Vickery saw his lover on screen and was convinced that he was being haunted. It was a wonderfully elliptical tale, but Kipling had already so moved to the periphery of literary fashion that none of the leading critics of the day troubled to give it serious attention. Someone who was decidedly not a literary critic, P G Wodehouse, would recall to a friend in 1928 his first encounter with the story:

Listen Bill, something really must be done about Kip's 'Mrs Bathurst'. I read it years ago and didn't understand a word of it. I thought to myself: 'Ah, youthful ignorance!' A week ago I re-read it. Result, precisely the same. What did the villain [Vickery] do to Mrs Bathurst? What did he tell the Captain in his cabin that made the Captain look very grave and send him up country where he was struck by lightning? Why was the other chap who was struck by lightning, too, introduced? And, above all, how was Kip allowed to get away with six solid pages of padding at the start of the story?[19]

Even if Kipling *had* retained his literary readership, 'Mrs Bathurst' would still have baffled the critics, for it was, in effect, the first modernist text in English. Deliberate obliqueness, formal fragmentation, absence of a privileged authorial point of view, intense literary self-consciousness, lack of closure – all the defining qualities of modernism were present and correct. But 1904 was also the year of 'Bloomsday', from which literary modernism was about to take off on a different flight-path.

In '"They"', the third of this trio of remarkable stories, it was the motor car that represented new technology. The narrator driving around the Sussex countryside in the spring got lost and found himself at a country house belonging to a blind woman who looked after several elusive children. Returning twice more, in summer and autumn, he eventually realised that the house and surrounding woods were a meeting-place for grieving parents to make contact with the ghosts of their dead children. The real situation was only revealed at the end when the narrator, who had thought the children merely shy, was permitted a brief reunion with his own dead child. Still unsuspecting, and imagining that the children were playing a game of hide-and-seek with him, he positioned his chair in the firelit hall with its back to a shadowy screen behind which he knew the children were concealed:

> The little brushing kiss fell in the centre of my palm – as a gift on which the fingers were, once, expected to close: as the all-faithful half-reproachful signal of a waiting child not used to neglect even when grown-ups were busiest – a fragment of the mute code devised very long ago.
>
> Then I knew. And it was as though I had known from the first day when I looked across the lawn at the high window.[20]

Beerbohm, as one might expect, refused to be enchanted. 'I was told it was a good ghost story,' he observed. 'But it is metallic. The house and garden and children all seem made of zinc.'[21] Looked at more sympathetically, the story was written by Kipling in order to move on from his grief at Josephine's death five years earlier. With the Mowgli stories he had allowed himself an improved version of the past; with "They", he allowed himself an improved version of the present so that he could leave the past behind. But it was not quite as simple as that. In a final exchange the narrator told the blind woman that he knew he could never come to the house again. Within the dynamics of the story, this indicated the narrator's understanding that the love between his dead child and himself had transcended the normal boundary between life and death – and also his acceptance that, once he left the house, the usual taboos would come back into force. For Kipling himself, it was an implicit recognition of the dangers of fictional consolation that he had been permitting himself, and acceptance of the fact that he must never do it again.

One of the incidental pleasures of ' "They" ' was Kipling's celebration of the richly storied English landscape, which the narrator drove through on his successive trips to the house. A few weeks after finishing the story, Kipling expanded 'on the practical, moral and sentimental side of motoring' in a playful letter to the journalist Filson Young for inclusion in his book *The Complete Motorist*:

> To me it is a land full of stupefying marvels and mysteries; and a day in the car in an English country is a day in some fairy museum where all the exhibits are alive and real and yet none the less delightfully mixed up with books. For instance, in six hours, I can go from the land of the *Ingoldsby Legends* by way of the Norman Conquest and the Barons' War into Richard Jefferies' country, and so through the Regency, one of Arthur Young's less known tours, and *Celia's Arbour*, into Gilbert White's territory . . . in England the dead, twelve coffin deep, clutch hold of my wheels at every turn, till I sometimes wonder that the very road does not bleed. *That* is the real joy of motoring – the exploration of this amazing England.

It was this excited discovery of layer upon layer of English history that he wanted to communicate in his two volumes of Puck stories, *Puck of Pook's Hill* (1906) and *Rewards and Fairies* (1910), and in the verses he contributed to C R L Fletcher's *A History of England* (1911). He wished, he told Edward Bok in July 1905, 'to give children *not* a notion of history but a notion of the time sense which is at the bottom of all knowledge of history and history rightly understood means love of one's fellow men and the lands one lives in'.[22] The Puck stories started from the idea that the present was the moving edge of the past, that without a perception of the slowly accumulating deposits of time the present made no sense.

Kipling in his autobiography credited his cousin Ambo Poynter with the original idea of a story about Sussex in Roman times, with 'an old Centurion of the Occupation telling his experiences to his children'.[23] Ambo even provided the centurion's name, Parnesius. That was presumably after the Kiplings' move to Rottingdean in the summer of 1897, since that December Kipling was telling Charles Norton that he and Uncle Ned were 'deep in the Roman occupation of Britain (this with an eye to stories)'.[24] The idea, however, lay dormant until the autumn of 1904. 'Rud at work on a fresh idea,' noted Carrie on 25 September, 'a set of stories, the History of England told by Puck to Children'.[25]

When his journalist friend H A Gwynne visited Bateman's a fortnight later, Kipling asked if he could bring 'from some London toyshop a donkey's head mask, either in paper or cloth sufficiently large to go over a man's head, *and* also a pair of gauze fairy wings'. He reassured his friend:

> Don't think I'm mad but the kids are next month doing a little piece of *Midsummer Night's Dream*, in the Quarry. I've got to be Bottom with the ass's head and Elsie is going to be Titania. Hence the wings. But if I don't have a proper donkey's head I'll get into trouble from Elsie. John is going to be Puck *but* I don't think he wants wings.

Granted that 'Weland's Sword', the opening story in *Puck of Pook's Hill*, begins with the two children Una (Elsie) and Dan (John) acting out scenes from *A Midsummer Night's Dream*, this sounds as though Kipling was keen to have a real-life run-through before turning the scene into fiction.

By early January 1905 he gave Bok a rough check-list of the main characters whom Puck brings from the past to tell their stories to the children: 'a Roman legionary, last of the Roman soldiers left in Britain; a young Norman baron who came over with William the Conqueror; a medieval adventurer who had an interest in a gold mine on the West African coast . . . an old Sussex iron master who cast guns for the Armada and persons of that sort'.[26] He wrote the Norman stories first, featuring the adventures of Sir Richard Dalyngridge, before going back in time to the tail-end of the Roman occupation, and introducing the centurion Parnesius. In 'A Centurion of the Thirtieth', 'On the Great Wall' and 'The Winged Hats', Parnesius told the children how he and his friend Pertinax held Hadrian's

Wall against the invading Winged Hats who came raiding across the North Sea. Kipling completed the volume with 'Hal o' the Draft' about a medieval craftsman; 'Dymchurch Flit', which described how the Pharisees (fairies) left England; and 'The Treasure and the Law', in which the children were told by a Jewish physician how he was instrumental in forcing King John to sign the Magna Carta.

The ten stories taken together, especially the Norman and Roman tales, reflected a more subtle view of the colonial experience than he had hitherto presented. Parnesius might seem to be simply an Anglo-Indian subaltern in fancy dress, but in fact he was a more problematic figure, explaining to Una that his family had lived on Vectis (the Isle of Wight) for generations. Rome to him was not really Home. He was a British Roman and therefore a colonial settler, an equivalent to a Cape Colonist. This connection was quietly reinforced when Parnesius further explained that 'the Roman-born officers and magistrates looked down on us British-born as though we were barbarians'.[27] Besides the implied parallel to British snobbishness towards colonial troops during the Boer War, Kipling was raising the wider issue of national identity, and how this derived from definitions of who was inside and who outside the tribe. The stories did not assert that Roman, Norman, Saxon or any other single strain was the real 'English' strain – it was the mixture that was important. In his 1920 speech 'England and the English', Kipling quoted with approval Defoe's witty couplets from *The True-born Englishman*:

> A true-born Englishman's a contradiction,
> In speech an irony, in fact a fiction,
> A metaphor intended to express
> A man akin to all the Universe.[28]

For the adult reader, the lines would have made a fitting epigraph to *Puck of Pook's Hill*.

The rewards for the child reader were of course of quite another order. Like the *Jungle Books* and the *Just So Stories*, though in a rather different way, the Puck stories empowered the child. This was implicit in the basic format: rather than Una and Dan travelling from the present back into the past, the past travelled forward to them in the present. Una and Dan were thus always on home ground and always in charge. They were never made to feel like strangers; the characters from the past behaved like guests and were treated as such. The children were even at times allowed to know more than the grown-up characters whose stories made up the informal history lessons. In 'A Centurion of the Thirtieth', Elsie coached Parnesius in how to use Dan's catapult and explained that what he called 'stretching leather' was really 'laccy – elastic'. The two then had an animated conversation about their respective childhoods and discovered that 'Good families are very much alike.'[29] Una and Dan were never merely passive listeners; they actively took part in the stories, asking questions and expressing opinions.

There were further developments in *Rewards and Fairies*. The children, now a year older, had acquired different interests and were not always together. In 'The Wrong Thing', Dan, working on a model boat, was told the story of how the medieval craftsman Hal was knighted by Henry VII and nearly murdered by a jealous fellow craftsman. In 'Marklake Witches', Una, who was learning milking, was told the story of a young Regency woman's 'triumph' in reducing her father and his dinner-guests to tears with her singing. The children were also more prepared to form independent judgements about the people they met. After 'the lady' had told the children in 'Gloriana' how Queen Elizabeth (that is, herself) had sent two young adventurers off to die for their country in the war against Philip of Spain, Una's view was made clear: she 'felt that she disliked the lady as much as she disliked the noise the high wind made tearing through Willow Shaw'. Dan, by contrast, said that he could not see what else the young men or the Queen could have done: all had their duty to do. 'The lady' then asked Dan whether he would have blamed the Queen 'for wasting those lads' lives' if Philip had won. 'Of course not,' replied Dan. 'She was bound to try to stop him.' At which the Queen said approvingly: 'You have the root of the matter in you.'[30]

Rewards and Fairies was different, too, in the way that from story to story it constantly shuttled backwards and forwards in time. So the 'Flint' Age of 'The Knife and the Chalk' was immediately followed by the late-eighteenth-century Philadelphia of 'Brother Square-Toes' and 'A Priest in Spite of Himself', followed in turn by the Anglo-Saxon times of 'The Conversion of St Wilfrid' and the English Civil War period of 'A Doctor of Medicine'. While these lively time-shifts offered contrast, repeated motifs also suggested continuity. So the children's 'particular friend', old Hobden the hedger, the archetypal countryman, often appeared at the end to mark the children's transition from past to present.[31] Equally, at some point in their tale each of the characters from the past asked a variant on the question 'What else could I have done?' Or two stories would be linked in an unexpected way, as were the Elizabethan 'Simple Simon' and the Regency 'Marklake Witches' by the discovery of an invention before its time: iron ships in 'Simple Simon', the stethoscope in 'Marklake Witches'.

Like *Puck of Pook's Hill*, the volume contained several excellent poems. In 'The Looking Glass' the rhythm suggestively complemented Queen Elizabeth's reluctance to confront the mirror:

> Backwards and forwards and sideways did she pass,
> Making up her mind to face the cruel looking-glass.

'The Way Through the Woods' (which prefaced 'Marklake Witches') hauntingly evoked the sense that much more than an old road had been lost:

> You will hear the beat of a horse's feet
>   And the swish of a skirt in the dew,
>   Steadily cantering through
> The misty solitudes,
>   As though they perfectly knew
> The old lost road through the wood . . .
> But there is no road through the woods!

There was also 'If–', probably still the most famous poem in English. The poem's enormous popularity has done it a disservice, yet it still has an impact, not least in the final stanza:

> If you can talk with crowds and keep your virtue,
>   Or walk with Kings – nor lose the common touch,
> If neither foes nor loving friends can hurt you,
>   If all men count with you, but none too much;
> If you can fill the unforgiving minute

With sixty seconds' worth of distance run,
    Yours is the Earth and everything that's in it,
    And – which is more — you'll be a Man, my son!'[32]

In his autobiography Kipling was typically unstuffy about both the poem and its success. He felt that the lines had been 'anthologised to weariness' and claimed they had done him no good with 'the Young', who were always complaining to him that they had to write them out 'as an impot'. As for the content of the poem, he said that it 'contained counsels of perfection most easy to give'.[33] And that was the point: the long list of conditions that made up the single thirty-two-line sentence of the poem was, of course, impossible to fulfil. No one got to be 'a Man' if these were the requirements. Though admirable in themselves, and worth aiming at, the standard was unattainable; this was the test that everyone fails. A prime model was Donne's 'The Undertaking', which Kipling had used as an epigraph for the first part of 'William the Conqueror'. In Donne, it was the lover, not the child, who was faced with the tangle of impossible conditions:

If, as I have, you also do
    Virtue attir'd in woman see,
And dare love that, and say so too,
    And forget the He and She;

And if this love, though placèd so,
    From profane men you hide,
Which will no faith on this bestow,
    Or, if they do, deride:

Then you have done a braver thing
    Than all the Worthies did;
And a braver thence will spring,
    Which is, to keep that hid.[34]

Not so much a stockpile of wholesome pieties, but rather a latter-day 'metaphysical' poem, 'If–' was both playful and rueful in its depiction of the ethical assault-course confronting the child or young adolescent.

And, as so often with Kipling's work, it was far more interesting than the clichés.

The year Kipling started in earnest on the Puck stories, 1904, was also the year that he finally managed to sell off Naulakha. He had been trying to dispose of his Vermont home since 1901, dropping the asking price from $30,000 to $10,000 to a give-away $5,000. Was the sale of Naulakha the break with the past that allowed Kipling to take an imaginative plunge into his own corner of Sussex? Certainly, it was only after the sale that he really got to work on the Puck stories, his most enduring tribute to Bateman's and particularly its gardens and grounds.

It was Bateman's that usually provided the background for a Kipling who has only occasionally been given his due: the sensitive and loving father to his two surviving children, Elsie and John. This is the Kipling one constantly encounters in over 200 letters to them. These letters were initially printed so that John could read them more easily and were often illustrated with deft sketches, for instance of Kipling trying to play golf. On one occasion, in 1907, a letter turned into an impromptu *Just So* story, as Kipling described how he and Carrie journeyed across Canada by private Pullman under the expert management of their black major-domo William. The point of the letters was always to maintain the sense of family unity, the new Family Square that he enjoyed with Carrie, Elsie and John. He became typically adept at letting his children know how much he loved them, while not embarrassing them with gush: 'Mother has packed and unpacked herself into fiddlestrings but she says that so long as she hasn't you two horrid little brats to look after she can stand most things. Seriously, she lies down for an hour in the evenings before going to sleep and you don't know how large and long the days are without you two.'[35]

Elsie, educated at home, was the recipient of many fewer solo letters than her brother; but those she did receive have the charm peculiar to Kipling's fiction for children, here specifically geared to her and her interests and concerns. The letters would begin with a pet name, usually 'Bird', but sometimes 'Fipps' or 'Ploomp'. Once it was, extravagantly, 'Ducky Dicky-Bird', followed by an invitation to get her own back, to play: 'This I consider *quite* the lowest title for you that even *I* have invented. Please tell me how angry it made you.' The letter itself, apart from nicely judged family details (a joke about John, something about the garden), would often contain some snippet of a private game. For a while, there were references to the sayings of a fictitious Mr Campbell, through whom Kipling could pass on good advice without sounding preachy or could just have fun sounding sententious: 'A taste in practical botany (said Mr Campbell) is always laudable.'[36] (The naming of this Polonius figure after the master Kipling had most disliked at school suggests an even more private level to the game and another bit of retrospective revenge.)

As Elsie became older, there was the added pleasure of sharing his work with her, and even of collaboration. At first he kept this low-key and carefully pitched to her age. In 1908, while twelve-year-old Elsie was in London for four months with her governess undergoing treatment for mild curvature of the spine, he was busy with 'Marklake Witches' in which Elsie, as usual, appeared as Una. He encouraged her to make an appropriate contribution to the story. 'My only bother,' he wrote from Bateman's, 'is I can't think of a place for Una and Philadelphia Bricksteep [later Bucksteed] to sit in while Phil is telling her story. They can't sit on stools because Una has the only one – there isn't a shaw nearby and there isn't a cow-lodge. Can you offer me a suggestion? Sixpence for a good one.' In time such collaborations took more serious form, and father and daughter even wrote a one-act play together called *The Harbour Watch*, in which Pyecroft (a naval Mulvaney, who had earlier appeared in 'Mrs Bathurst' and several other stories) dealt with a case of desertion. 'The Vedrennes-Eadie Company, Royalty Theatre, is anxious to produce *our* play – the Pyecroft one,' Kipling informed his daughter in March 1913. 'At present we haven't quite decided the terms but if we agree 'twill be produced on the 22nd of next month as a curtain raiser. Shall you go? I shan't.'[37] The play was duly staged – on 23 April, appropriately St George's Day as well as Shakespeare's birthday – and according to Carrie's diary went down well.

The letters could be more serious. While Elsie was in London for those four months in the summer and autumn of 1908, Kipling missed her desperately, though he was careful in his letters not to fuel her homesickness. Writing to her just before going up for a visit, his impatience broke through the banter: 'On Thursday you'll go and wash yourself in the Paddington baths and on Thursday evening – *unberufen!* [touch wood] *unberufen – unberufen!* I see you, *all clean*, at the Leonards. This thought so paralyses my pen that I can write no more.' Kipling did everything he could to foster the trust between his children, nowhere more so than in a letter of February 1913. Kipling and Carrie were off on a short trip to Egypt, leaving Elsie, now seventeen, with a group of other English girls in Paris. In addition to encouraging Elsie to make the most of this opportunity, he rather touchingly (but also sensibly) urged her to write to her brother at public school, giving him 'a full true and particular account (much fuller than you'd write to *us*) of your feelings and experiences in your new life. *He'll* understand because, you see, he goes out into the cold hard world three times a year – and he remembers what his first day at school was like. Tell him fully and you'll find that he'll sympathise with you no end and that you'll have another bond of sympathy between you.'[38]

John himself was sent as a boarder to St Aubyn's School, Rottingdean, in September 1907. The decision to send the ten-year-old boy away to school (having previously been taught at home with Elsie) was not an easy one. 'The fact is,' Kipling would confide to his old friend Dunsterville, 'that parents are too much interested in their own progeny to give them enough of that judicious letting alone which makes and builds up a kid's character. It's a hard saying but it is true.'[39] Kipling and Carrie put off boarding school as long as possible, but they were sensible as well as besotted parents. Their imminent trip to Canada also formed a natural point of separation.

Kipling's letters to John that autumn were a careful mixture of concern and encouragement. 'I know exactly how homesick you feel at first,' he sympathised on 12 October. 'I can remember how I felt when I first went to school at Westward Ho!' But he pointed out that at least John was in familiar surroundings, 'full of all the people you have known all your life with Aunt Georgie round the corner'. Inevitably, there were also more self-conscious passages, as though suddenly remembering that he was 'Rudyard Kipling' writing to his son, rather than 'Daddo' as he usually signed himself:

> I am rather pleased with you about one thing. You know I never mind jumping on you when you have done something I don't like – the same way I generally tell you when you have behaved decently.

Well, from all I can discover, you behaved yourself like a man when you felt homesick. I understand that you did not flop about and blub and whine but carried on quietly. *Good man!* Next time it will come easier to you to keep control over yourself and the time after that easier still.[40]

This and other similarly bracing paragraphs – absent from his letters to Elsie – may have reflected contemporary assumptions about the importance of the stiff upper lip, but also revealed how Kipling agonised over his son, or 'Dear old Man', as he was soon calling him.

A letter to Edmund Gosse, after Kipling's return from Canada in November 1907, provided a rather different expression of that natural anxiety. Gosse had just published *Father and Son*, describing his Plymouth Brethren upbringing by his marine biologist father. Gosse *fils* was no favourite of Kipling, and the idea of a son writing with critical affection about his father could well have been abhorrent. In practice, the book aroused such strong memories of his own miseries in Southsea that he found himself deeply moved and impressed, and wrote at once to Gosse to say so:

It's *extraordinarily* interesting – more interesting than David Copperfield because it's true. I had a few years in my boyhood somewhat under the shadow of the same terrific Doctrine and curiously enough, the same idea of avoidance of my surroundings by 'natural magic' (in my own case by discovering a charm. I used to make 'em out of old boxes stuffed with wool and camphor-scented.) It is a strange shadow to lay on a young mind and they that do it must be more sure of themselves than most of us.

But the delicacy of the psychology, the inferential revelation of the milieu and, above all, the wonderful realisation of your father have given me very deep delight. I don't say pleasure because the thing is too near certain of my own experiences to only please.

The devil of it is that that life still persists – I could give you awful instances – and I have a notion that your book will undam some tides of revolt in some darklingly Christian homes. I only hope and pray it will be so.

As the reviews *won't* say the book 'ought to be in the hands of all parents and teachers'. Much – much good ought to be done by a cheap edition. But I bet you nine tenths of the reviews will cheerily miss the whole point of it.

Life has separated us a good deal and we have a ten year old at school (his first term!) over whom we very humanly agonise (the last thing a parent learns is when not to love over-much) but when we meet you'll find there's precious little difference except about the hair . . .[41]

'Over whom we very humanly agonise'; Kipling could only hope that the absent John was not going through torments similar to those once suffered by the absent Ruddy. His letters to his son were full of homely news and details: going to the village with Elsie to buy peppermints, spreading mushroom spawn, planting a small oak, the arrival of new pigs or the pups Betty and Jack, a description of a grown-up friend falling into the pond, and an account of the great flood of autumn 1909, which left the kitchen awash, obliterated paths and carried away garden seats and hives. The tone was often gently humorous: 'I have been digging in the garden. Mother has been weeding in the garden. Elsie played tennis in the garden to-day. (This is not a French exercise but a story of our news.)'[42] From time to time, when he wanted to impress on John the importance of a particular event, Kipling would pull out all the stops, as he did in a long letter on 20 May 1910 describing the day of Edward VII's funeral. 'The stillness all over the fields and in the air was much deeper than the ordinary stillness of a Sunday,' he told his son. '. . . It was absolute *stillness*. I listened long and often but except for the bees there was nothing. You see, all England – literally all our Empire, – was getting ready for the King's burial.' After a short account of the memorial service in the local church, he tried to catch something of the human drama and the human significance of the occasion, the last sentence even imagining John in middle age:

All the Sunday school children were there. As they settled down into their places one of the boys (happy boy!) managed to kick a tin under the benches with his feet, and instantly you saw all the boys' faces lighted with one grin of pure joy . . . But seriously it is a great day to have lived through. I expect it must have been impressive at your school service at Rottingdean but here in the quiet green country it was tremendously impressive. One saw just the ordinary every day people, who after all make up the world, just grieving for the loss of their own King and friend as they would grieve for any-one of their own blood and kin. The number of medals was astonish-ing. I won't afflict you with the moral of it old man but it's a gentle hint to us all to play the game and do our work, for the King did his and died in the doing of it just as much as if he'd been shot on active service, and he was a great King. We are too near to realise how big a man he was but when you are my age you'll see it clearly.[43]

Jerome K Jerome encountered the Kiplings *en famille* when they were all staying in the same Swiss hotel at the start of 1909. If the weather prohib-ited skiing or skating, guests entertained themselves with political debates and amateur theatricals. Most of the English visitors were die-hard Tories, leaving Jerome, a Liberal, to feel as though he was taking on single-handed the whole of the right wing of the Conservative Party. However, unlike 'the peppery old colonels and fierce old ladies of Bath', he found his fellow writer 'always courteous' and Carrie 'still a beautiful woman', though her hair had now turned white. 'Kipling's boy and girl were there. They were jolly children. Young Kipling was a suffragette and little Miss Kipling played a costermonger's Donah [sweetheart]. Kipling himself combined the parts of scene shifter and call-boy.'[44]

Jerome's account confirms one's impression that Kipling the Edwardian family man was quite different, almost another person, from the embit-tered and embattled reactionary figure of popular reputation. However, just occasionally in a family context someone would catch a glimpse of that other side. The young Bob Boothby, a contemporary of John's at St Aubyn's, wrote to his mother after tea with Kipling: 'He is a very strange little man – I think there is a savage dog in him trying to get out.'[45] Did John ever see that savage dog in his father? Certainly there is no hint of a growl in the letters. The prep-school John was a typically sporty boy, but the author of *Stalky & Co.* and 'the flannelled fools at the wicket' did not complain. 'Of course, being *my* son, he is crazy on cricket,' Kipling told Dunsterville in 1908, 'and discourses to me about overhand bowling and when he comes home makes me *bowl* to him at the nets.'[46] It is hard to picture Kipling bowling – probably he was happy enough to purvey a slow military medium while John whacked him around.

John left St Aubyn's in 1911 at the end of the summer term. He and his father had accepted that his poor eyesight would debar him from the Navy, but with the Army still a possibility John was sent to Wellington College in Berkshire, a feeder for Sandhurst. Kipling and Carrie had done a recce of the school the previous autumn. 'It's a simply glorious building,' he wrote to John encouragingly, 'with huge iron gates and quadrangles and inner courtyards standing in the middle of the most splendid grounds that ever you saw.' The grounds, he added temptingly, had playing fields that were 'a dream of delight'. He was also careful to emphasise that Pearson's House (where John was to go) seemed '*very* delightful' and that each of the thirty boys had his own 'cubicle to work and sleep in – with a big couch, desk, chair and any amount of knickknacks on the walls which are wood'. In sum, he concluded his report, you have 'a sort of big world of your own among trees and gardens and shrubberies and huge playing fields – more than a hundred acres'.[47]

John duly started at Wellington in the Michaelmas term of 1911 and stayed until the end of the Lent term in 1914. The fact that he went at the relatively advanced age of fourteen suggests that he was struggling somewhat academically, and his school career bears this out.[48] He started in the next-to-bottom form and moved up the school always in the slow lane. By the end of his second year, the summer term of 1913, things were looking awkward: if he failed to reach a particular form in two terms' time, he would be in danger of having to leave. As his father gently, but rightly, pointed out, it would be a major news story if John were asked to go: 'in your case, remember, everyone would know that *you* had been superannuated'.[49] In the event, John did not reach the requisite level, but left voluntarily at Easter 1914; and, still hoping to get a berth at Sandhurst, went to a crammer in Bournemouth.

Throughout his son's unspectacular school career Kipling remained involved and supportive, never saddling him with unrealistic expectations. Indeed, his pleasure at John's small successes, usually at sport, are rather touching. 'I read out the P.S. announcing that you had got the Young Cup,' he wrote after the news of John's triumph in winning the House running cup. '. . . . I do *not* say that Fipps [Elsie] squealed like a stuck pig or even like a locomotive, but she let the house know the fact in one long clear high yell. She tore upstairs howling: – "Mother! Mother!

He's got it!", as if it was small-pox.' Another time, when John got beaten for 'larking on a Sunday', his father sensibly played the situation down, agreeing that it was stupid the boys were not allowed to play tennis to let off steam. And on the subject of homosexuality, Kipling was at least direct, warning his son to avoid 'any chap who is even suspected of beast-liness' and adding that 'whatever their merits may be in the athletic line they are at heart only sweeps and scum and *all* friendship or acquaintance with them ends in sorrow and disgrace'. For all the homophobia, the fact that Kipling was able to raise and discuss such a difficult topic – not usually brought up by Edwardian fathers – suggests an unusual bond of trust and understanding. This bond was equally apparent in a letter later in 1912, after John had evidently been having a go at Carrie. Kipling was sympathetic but firm:

> Another time you want anything, *don't* take it out of Mother. She was quite upset after your performances last Sat. I told her it was only your cheerful way of expressing yourself. I don't know whether you saw how near I came to laughing when you protested that it 'was no pleasure to *me*, Sir, to have to say these things'. Of course it was a great pleasure and you thoroughly enjoyed it – same as I used to do when I was a youngster and my people allowed me to jaw and ass about over *my* grievances. But, as I have said, next time you want to blow off steam – try it on *me* not Mother. I may not be so sympa-thetic but I shall be amused.[50]

A further test of the father–son bond came when, to John's potential embarrassment, Kipling was asked to deliver a paper to the College Literary Society. Its title, 'The Possible Advantages of Reading', suggests how carefully Kipling approached his assignment and tried to gear it to his audience. Presented on 25 May 1912, the paper – and Kipling's deliv-ery – struck just the right note. 'The resources of our national literature and the benefits to be derived from a study of the classics,' said the report in the *Wellingtonian*, 'were presented to us intermingled with stories amus-ing and thrilling, witty and serious.' It concluded in stumbling admira-tion: 'The Society was deeply impressed . . . and carried away from that meeting feelings of delight, of fascination, which it is impossible to describe.' The Kipling charm clearly carried the day.

If Kipling as paterfamilias was a largely sympathetic figure, so too was Kipling the dutiful nephew and son of a dying older generation. The first to go was Aunt Aggie Poynter in June 1906, 'the dearest and sweetest of my mother's sisters', as he called her in a letter to Mrs Hill.[51] She died of cancer, fuelling Kipling's fear that this was the family complaint. She was followed two years later by Uncle Alfred, Aunt Louie's husband. Kipling promptly had his aunt to stay at Bateman's and did his best to offer comfort and support. One of the means he adopted was to resume his old role of literary mentor, going to endless trouble with the poems she was later to publish in *Afterglow*. The next death was that of Uncle Crom, his old headmaster, in May 1910, and a few months later, most heart-rending of all, his parents too were dead.

Alice died first, on 23 November of heart failure. Though she had been in declining health for some time, Kipling took comfort in the fact that her final illness only lasted four days. He and Trix were there at the end, and Lockwood told Edith Plowden they were 'all the world to me'. Of Alice, Lockwood would only say to Edith: 'You have lost a friend who loved you, while I – but it cannot be written of.' Trix promptly broke down again, so that by Christmas Day Lockwood was almost at the end of his tether, as he tried to find an experienced nurse. He laid much of the blame for Trix's state at her husband's door, tartly remarking to Edith that he was a man 'who would give a brass monkey depression'.[52] But Lockwood's difficulties did not last long. Having made provision for Trix, he went to stay nearby with his friends the Wyndhams, and there on 26 January 1911 he died of a heart attack. Kipling took the double blow very hard. Dear as his mother had been, his father had been even dearer. 'Now that I have no one to talk to or write to I find myself desolate,' he confessed to Mrs Hill a fortnight later.[53] To Edith Plowden, at Lockwood's funeral on 30 January, he had put it even more bleakly: 'I feel the loneliest creature on God's earth today.'[54]

All the time, Kipling remained deeply committed to the development of his other family, the Empire. If, in hymns like 'Recessional' and in his almost mystical veneration of Rhodes, his imperialism suggested a displaced religious fervour, it also reflected his overriding need for family. For him 'Mother England' was no empty phrase. He desperately wanted England to act as a caring and protective parent to her imperial children;

and he became increasingly frustrated when, under a succession of Conservative and Liberal governments, the mother of Empire refused to take on that demanding role.

For some years his favourite imperial child was South Africa, which he and his family continued to visit annually until 1908. The first winter after the Boer War saw him there in the unaccustomed role of pacifier, publishing in *The Times* 'The Settler' as a coda to Joseph Chamberlain's recent placatory tour to the Cape. To Milner he offered a wry account of his intentions: 'Personally – and I mean poetically – I am bound to his [Chamberlain's] chariot wheels, because he is all that we have and we owe him gratitude for the past. So I have made – God forgive me – a peaceful and reconciliatory poem of the situation as it ought to be.'[55] At least one reader, Edward VII's friend Reginald Viscount Esher, found the results 'rather rough'.[56] The final stanza suggests why:

> Here, in the waves and the troughs of the plains,
>   Where the healing stillness lies,
> And the vast, benignant sky restrains
>   And the long days make wise –
> Bless to our use the rain and the sun
>   And the blind seed in its bed,
> That we may repair the wrong that was done
>   To the living and the dead![57]

The poem may also support the idea that Kipling briefly considered becoming a 'settler' himself. In a letter to H A Gwynne a few weeks later he mentioned the possibility of buying land and building a house in the Colesberg-Norvalspont region of the Cape Colony. Though nothing came of that plan, his commitment to imperial South Africa showed in the increasingly active part he played in local politics, to the extent of even making electioneering speeches in 1904 on behalf of the Progressive Party, of which Jameson, now Prime Minister of Cape Colony, was leader. 'I've been addressing the 'orny-'anded – mechanics, loco-drivers, fitters and boiler men – at Salt River,' Kipling told a journalist friend, 'on roaring hot nights in the open by the light of flare lamps. Rather like a coaster selling winkles but it was great fun.'[58]

Not that his summers and autumns were exactly apolitical; rather that in England he operated more indirectly, trying to pull strings rather than standing on the hustings. Apart from a period when he fell out with *The Times* over the introduction of their Book Club (a threat as he saw it to authors' rights and sales), he always had an open billet there for poems. But useful as he found it, *The Times* was too venerable, too mainstream, too Establishment; what he wanted was a younger, feistier paper openly committed to imperial issues and with an editor he could lobby at will. He found the perfect vehicle in the *Standard* when, on Chamberlain's recommendation, Gwynne became editor in late 1904. 'You have an unrivalled chance of preaching your Imperial Labour party views; Army and Navy, reform; protection and all the rest that is vital,' Kipling wrote congratulating Gwynne, who must soon have realised that 'your' really meant 'my'. Over the next few years Kipling pleaded, pushed and cajoled Gwynne on a range of Empire-related topics. Compulsory national service was a favourite; so was the future of South Africa, especially after the Liberals came to power in 1905 and proposed, in effect, to hand control of the Transvaal and the Orange River Colony back to the Boers. 'I wish you could arrange for a regular correspondence in the Standard,' he urged Gwynne in February 1906, 'pointing out how the Boers will win and what use they will make of the victory if the Franchise is gerrymandered to their liking. It will be absolutely, as Milner says in his magnificent speech – sheer Krugerism backed by British bayonets.'[59]

By that stage Kipling's South African hopes had all but collapsed. Milner, their chief architect, had resigned as High Commissioner the previous year – a resignation that prompted 'The Pro-Consuls' (the opening and closing lines of which Kipling would later use to give Aunt Louie a workshop on the sonnet). When the verses originally appeared in *The Times* in July 1905, he was more preoccupied with the basic message – that the imperial task mattered more than those who performed it – and with the Horatian overtones of the title, encouraging the reader to look for parallels between the Roman and British Empires. Such analogies cropped up regularly in his work and letters during these years. They lay in the background of the Parnesius stories in *Puck of Pook's Hill*, with the two young centurions on Hadrian's Wall doubling as two subalterns on the North-West Frontier. Gloomily contemplating the impact on South Africa of the Liberal Government, Kipling naturally reached for a Roman equivalent. 'As you know the whole English ministry went to smash at the elections,' he lamented to Mrs Hill in early 1906, 'and we sat like so many Mariuses in the ruins of Carthage while the Dutchman and the rebel *and* the native crowed over us.' Setting off almost two years later for what he knew would be his last winter at the Cape, he had obsequies, if not specifically Roman ones, in mind. 'We're off,' he told Uncle Alfred on Boxing Day 1907, '. . . to see the corpse of South Africa decently buried at the next elections there.'[60] His auguries proved accurate. Within a few months Jameson had lost the Cape Colony elections and been succeeded as Prime Minister by J X Merriman of the South African Party.

Although Kipling was always to remain bitter about the débâcle in South Africa, his disappointment had already been somewhat cushioned by his visit to Canada the previous autumn. It was on this trip that his double-sense of family came out most strongly. Writing home to the children as he and Carrie traversed the country, his letters began 'Dear Family' or 'Very dear Family'; while after his return, writing up his travels for his Empire readership in the *Morning Post*, he called the series 'Letters to the Family'. The conceit was nothing new – he had been using it in poems for years, sometimes to unfortunate effect. In 'The Young Queen', the 1900 poem that Meredith so disliked, Mother England saluted Australia as 'Daughter no more but Sister, and doubly Daughter so –', raising incestuous possibilities that Kipling could not have intended.[61] By his Canadian trip, however, the idea of the imperial family had become more than a literary metaphor; it was a bond he passionately believed in and was taking every opportunity to promote. In his *Morning Post* Letters, he cast himself as a kind of older brother figure, filling in the rest of the family on a visit to 'our Eldest Sister' (Canada). He reported (with a few minor reservations) how well she was progressing, reflected on matters of mutual family interest and took every chance to bolster proper family feeling. The sense of kinship was constantly asserted by the use of an imperial 'we' and by occasional interjections like 'Truly we are an odd Family!'[62]

The trip itself was a personal triumph. Kipling and Carrie toured the country in the comfort of their railway car ('the private Cathedral') and were royally treated wherever they went. Buoyed up by an adulation and attention he was no longer receiving in England, Kipling blossomed as a public speaker and delivered a number of well-received speeches. 'I have preached on the National Spirit like a blessed book,' he told a friend after his 2 October speech in Winnipeg on 'Growth and Responsibility'.[63] Four days later, he was discoursing 'fluently about Oriental labour at Vancouver and Victoria', while at McGill University in Montreal, on the 23rd, talking about 'Values in Life', he teasingly reassured his predominantly student audience that 'the only penalty youth must pay for its enviable privilege is that of listening to people known, alas, to be older and alleged to be wiser'. More seriously, he urged the students not to be materialistic, not to be 'smart' – and, striking a deliberately personal note, not to succumb to 'a certain darkness into which the soul of the young man sometimes descends'.[64] It was, however, a public warning that permeated his 'Letters to the Family' series. The 'loss' of South Africa, the 'canker and blight that has settled on England for the last couple of years', the pressing need for the imperial family to club together: each was announced early and each recurred throughout the Letters as sub-themes. The chief threat to the 'family', as Kipling insisted in his final flourish, was 'that very Democracy which depends on the Empire for its proper comforts, and in whose behalf these things are urged'.[65]

Several of the stories collected in 1909 in *Actions and Reactions*, Kipling's next volume of adult fiction, complemented the imperial concerns of 'Letters to the Family'. Of these, the allegorical 'The Mother Hive' was the most original, the most apocalyptic and, as its title suggests, the most familial. England was portrayed as the 'Old Hive', so overcrowded and overstretched in its resources that it was overrun by touchy-feely, sharing-caring Wax-moths (the Liberals). The traditional codes, discipline, hard work and sense of hierarchy that had maintained the hival community broke down, and the hive itself became a freak show of 'Oddities – albinos, mixed-leggers, single-eyed composites, faceless drones, half-queens and laying sisters'. These Oddities (Utopians, arty types, free-loaders) were fed, nursed and protected by a small, diminishing band of healthy bees who stuck to the accustomed ways. This band secretly raised a new Queen and awaited the nemesis that the old Queen had foretold. Eventually the judgement fell, and the 'Veiled Figures' of the Bee-master and his son (Jehovah and Jesus?) came to cleanse and fumigate the infected hive. Only the plucky cluster of loyalists under the young Queen survived, swarming on the bough of a nearby oak and 'waiting patiently within sight of the old Hive – a handful, but prepared to go on'.[66] Kipling was working on 'The Mother Hive' during the summer of

1907, shortly before he and Carrie set off for Canada. The story was another of his *nuzzur-wattus*, averters of the Evil Eye, though he was also tormenting himself here with a vision of the worst that could happen.

The fear that, for all his and others' efforts, the imperial family might simply fall apart continued to haunt Kipling over the next few years, though it ceased to feature as a significant concern in his fiction. After *Actions and Reactions* the closest he came to finding imaginative expression for this fear was in a different medium. Haggard, following a visit to Bateman's in the autumn of 1911, noted that Kipling read him two plays he had written and that 'we discussed others, especially one that would deal with the fall of the British Empire'.[67] There is no evidence, however, that this Gibbonian drama ever found its way on to paper.

Kipling's dislike of the Liberals was always acute; during their years of dominance, acute dislike turned to obsessive hatred and a desire to attack with every verbal means at his disposal. When the Conservatives were annihilated in the January 1906 election, he was as usual wintering in South Africa and effectively *hors de combat*, though his letters told how bitterly he took the Liberal victory. The moment he returned in May he went straight into action.

Docking in Southampton on the morning of 5 May, he delivered a speech that evening at the Royal Academy to an audience that included his current *bête noire*, the Liberal Prime Minister Sir Henry Campbell-Bannerman. His theme was that 'the man with the Words shall wait upon the man of achievement, and step by step with him try to tell the story to the Tribe'. He wound up with a parable about the recent election and the danger to national prosperity. In 'a land where the magic of words is peculiarly potent and far-reaching', a tribe wanted rain. When the rain-doctors' magic produced only 'patchy, local, circumscribed, and uncertain' results, the tribe complained. The rain-doctors retorted by asking the tribe what it had been doing recently:

And the Tribe said, 'Oh, our head-men have been running about hunting jackals, and our little people have been running about chasing grasshoppers! What has that to do with your rain-making?' 'It has everything to do with it,' said the rain-doctors. 'Just as long as your head-men run about hunting jackals, and just as long as your

15. Naulakha: 'a house designed for work and play'.

16. Josephine Kipling at Naulakha, the 'Best Beloved' of the *Just So Stories*.

17. The author of
the *Jungle Books* in
his lair at Naulakha.

18. Kipling's brother-in-law, Beatty Balestier, who was to drive him
away from his lair.

19. Phil Burne-Jones's portrait of Kipling, 1899.

20. Phil Burne-Jones's companion portrait of Carrie, 1899.

21. The Woolsack, the house lent to the Kiplings by Cecil Rhodes
for their winters at the Cape.

22. Bateman's, Sussex: 'The Very-Own House'.

23. From Max Beerbohm's *Lives of the Poets*: Kipling composing
'The Absent-Minded Beggar'.

24. From Max Beerbohm's series 'The Old Self and the Young Self':
Young Self: 'I *say*! Have you heard the latest about Mrs Hauksbee?'

25. Kipling's surviving daughter, Elsie, in 1901.

26. Kipling's son, John, in 1901.

27. Carrie, John, Rud and Elsie Kipling, in Muizenberg, 1908.

28. (*Inset*) Second-Lieutenant John Kipling of the 2nd Battalion Irish Guards: 'My Boy Jack'

29: Kipling delivering a recruiting speech at Southport, June 1915.

30. Max Beerbohm's 1921 cartoon 'On the Shelf', reflecting Kipling's post-war neglect.

31. The new Rector of St Andrew's University, October 1923.

little people run about chasing grasshoppers, just so long will the rain fall in this manner.'[68]

It was a beginning, but, as he admitted to Gwynne, 'too dam [sic] allusive – not to say elusive'.[69] There was a continuation of this allusive/elusive approach in 'The Mother Hive' and in a poem like ' "The City of Brass" ', where a light Arabian Nights gloss was given to Liberal England:

They chose themselves prophets and priests of minute understanding,
Men swift to see done, and outrun, their extremest commanding –
Of the tribe which describe with a jibe the perversions of Justice –
Panders avowed to the crowd whatsoever its lust is.[70]

While the literary Kipling relished the obliqueness of parable and the ingenuity it required, his anxiety about what the Liberals were doing to the Empire soon demanded a more direct outlet. 'Letters to the Family' provided this, especially its stark opening sentence: 'It must be hard for those who do not live there to realise the cross between canker and blight that has settled on England for the last couple of years.'[71] From then on, in his frequent attacks on the Liberals, the oblique and the direct tended to go hand in hand.

Many were prompted by particular occasions. ' "The City of Brass" ', written in late May 1909, was obviously triggered by Lloyd George's 'People's Budget', presented the previous month. (Carrie's diary for April showed the couple in a complete panic about how the Budget's proposed tax changes would affect their savings.) When Edward VII died in May 1910, Kipling pushed his friend R D Blumenfeld, editor of the *Daily Express*, to do a piece blaming the Liberals for the King's death:

Symposium by present Cabinet '*How it feels to kill a King*'? The point is that those vanity-drugged little beasts killed him just as surely as though they had hoisted [?] him with a Portuguese bomb and I do hope that when they open their mouths you will jump down it. Could you call 'em The Regicides?[72]

Blumenfeld wisely declined this extraordinary suggestion, and Kipling's own fulsome tribute – 'The Dead King', published on 18 May in *The*

Times and the *Morning Post* – barely hinted at his more hysterical feelings:

> When he was bowed by his burden his rest was refused him.
> We troubled his age with our weakness – the blacker our shame to
>   us![73]

Against the Suffragettes (whom he saw as Liberal-inspired), he came up in 1911 with 'The Female of the Species', complete with infamous refrain: 'The female of the species is more deadly than the male.' The following April, to coincide with Asquith's introduction of the Home Rule Bill for Ireland, Kipling produced 'Ulster', the last stanza of which was virtually a pledge to go down fighting:

> Believe, we dare not boast,
> Believe, we do not fear –
> We stand to pay the cost
> In all that men hold dear.
> What answer from the North?
> One Law, one Land, one Throne.
> If England drive us forth
> We shall not fall alone![74]

Perhaps most extreme of all was his reaction in the summer of 1913, when it was (correctly) rumoured that the Attorney-General Sir Rufus Isaacs was about to become Lord Chief Justice. Isaacs had been implicated the previous year in the Marconi Scandal – involving insider dealing on the Stock Exchange and much unpleasant anti-Semitic rhetoric – and Kipling, always quick to spot a possible Biblical parallel, saw a resemblance to the story of Elisha's servant Gehazi taking money from Naaman under false pretences. His poem, 'Gehazi', though not published for another couple of years, was soon being passed around privately in Tory circles. The final stanza imagined Isaacs as a leper:

> Thou mirror of uprightness,
>   What ails thee at thy vows?
> What means the risen whiteness

Of the skin between thy brows?
The boils that shine and burrow,
  The sores that slough and bleed –
The leprosy of Naaman
  On thee and all thy seed?
Stand up, stand up, Gehazi,
  Draw close thy robe and go,
Gehazi, Judge in Israel,
  A leper white as snow![75]

As nasty as the nastiest of Pope, this vision of Gehazi's punishment could only have been written by a deeply troubled man.

For all his current fixation with politics, Kipling had no desire to be a parliamentarian. He was, however, increasingly prepared to make speeches and attend political meetings, prophesying the twin dangers of civil war and German invasion. 'Make no mistake about it, old man,' he told Gwynne in March 1914, *'an Ulster or an Ireland handed over to the Celt means an appeal for outside intervention* as in 1688. That is what I fear horribly.'[76] Naturally National Service remained a top priority. When the National Service League Caravan held a meeting in Burwash in September 1913 as part of its East Sussex tour, Kipling's participation turned the event into news:

> Standing unceremoniously on the edge of the caravan, cigarette in hand, and speaking simply and unconventionally, Mr Rudyard Kipling, in terse sentences, uttered the gravest warning. The meeting was spellbound as the distinguished speaker brought home to them a comparison of what had happened in the Balkans and the terrible plight that England would be in under similar circumstances.[77]

A few months later, when the pro-Ulster British Covenant was established, Kipling was a much-publicised signatory.

This most exposed, somewhat hysterical phase of Kipling's life culminated in his famous Tunbridge Wells speech of 16 May 1914. To a highly vocal and partisan crowd of some 10,000, he launched an all-out attack on the Liberal Government and its Home Rule policy. From the start it was obvious he was going to take no prisoners.

He began by branding the Liberals a gang of crooks who, having voted themselves parliamentary salaries, were prepared to go to any lengths to hang on to money and power. They were, he jeered, like 'a firm of fraudulent solicitors (laughter and a VOICE: 'Rub it in') who had got an unlimited power of attorney from a client by false pretences, and could dispose of the client's estate as they pleased (laughter)'. The Marconi Scandal was a weapon ready to hand, and he used it twice. First, to smear the Cabinet: 'We know that two at least of them found it necessary to supplement their official incomes of £7,000 and £5,000 by taking part in a Stock Exchange flotation which was floated (about the time the Titanic sank) in a way that was too much even for the Stock Exchange (hear, hear).' And again later, to support the claim that the Ulster crisis was only the thin end of the wedge:

Ireland is sold to-day. To-morrow it may be the turn of the Southern counties to be weighed off as the make-weight in some secret bargain (laughter). You laugh. Why not? Three years ago you would have said the Marconi Scandals were impossible, and the appointment of the present Lord Chief Justice was impossible (hear, hear). Six months ago you would have said that the plot against Ulster was impossible (hear, hear). Nothing is impossible in a land without a constitution (hear, hear), nothing except peace.

The Home Rule Bill itself, which Kipling believed to be a direct threat to the British Empire, came in for some of his most slashing invective. It 'broke the faith of generations'; it 'officially recognised sedition, privy conspiracy and rebellion'; 'it subsidised the secret forces of boycott, outrage, intimidation, and murder'; and, most damningly of all, it provided 'an independent stronghold in which all those forces could work together, as they have openly boasted that they would work together for the destruction of Great Britain'. What, he asked, were the politics of the Irish Nationalists whose support the Liberal Government had bought with the Home Rule Bill? The result, according to Kipling, was a 'despotism of secret societies, a government of denunciation by day and terrorism by night', whose methods were those of 'oppression and hate and fear'. There followed an impassioned defence of those involved in the Curragh Mutiny – by soldiers not prepared to enforce Home Rule in

Ulster – before he spelt out his main message in the closing peroration. The Home Rule Bill was tyranny. Civil war was imminent unless the Government went to the polls to 'refer these grave matters to the judgement of a free people'. Finally, he warned, 'if they do not, all the history of our land shows there is but one end for us – destruction from within, or destruction from without'.[78]

This powerful speech duly made its splash, and Press reaction lined up in predictable columns. The *World* was ecstatic: 'Never since the days of the poet shepherd-king has a slinger hurled smooth stones with deadlier aim against a swaggering braggart than did this poet-journalist.' The *Daily News* was derisory: 'We shall not insult our readers by replying to this farrago of futile venom.' And the *Globe* tried to sound measured: 'If the Government wants to know how their record impresses the typical English mind, they could not do better than read Mr Rudyard Kipling's speech at Tunbridge Wells – a speech which puts what other people are thinking into serious and unflinching English.'[79]

If Kipling felt gratified by all the attention, he did not show it. Barely two months later one of his predictions cancelled out another, as civil war in Ulster was averted by the declaration of war against Germany. 'My cold possesses me,' Carrie noted in her diary on 4 August. To which Kipling added laconically: 'Incidentally Armageddon begins.'[80]

18

My Boy Jack

Kipling had been prophesying war for years, but it is an assumption too far that he positively wanted such a war, even encouraged it. He knew just how unprepared England was and recent trips to the Continent had shown him that France was in little better state. Besides, war meant a direct threat to his two families – John and the Empire.

His son was at the War Office as early as 10 August, applying for a commission in Kitchener's New Army. Although no doubt suitably proud of his son's eagerness to join up, there is nothing to suggest that Kipling put any pressure on the already military-minded John. A week later, on his seventeenth birthday, John heard that he had been turned down because of his eyesight. Once he had calmed down and stopped talking of enlisting in the ranks, he realised that he would need the help of his uniquely well-placed father in order to get in as an officer. 'Bobs', Kipling's old friend Lord Roberts, was now Colonel of the Regiment of the Irish Guards; and on 10 September Kipling went to London to see Roberts and ask him to nominate John for a commission. Two days later, John's commission in the Irish Guards duly arrived (backdated to 16 August), and on the 14th he was reporting for duty at Warley Barracks in Essex.

'I'm thankful to see Kipling hasn't written a poem yet,' the young poet Charles Sorley remarked perkily a few days after the outbreak of war.[1] He

spoke too soon. On 1 September 'For All We Have and Are', Kipling's
call to arms, was in all the papers:

> For all we have and are,
> For all our children's fate,
> Stand up and take the war.
> The Hun is at the gate! . . .
> No easy hope or lies
> Shall bring us to our goal,
> But iron sacrifice
> Of body, will, and soul.
> There is but one task for all –
> One life for each to give.
> What stands if Freedom fall?
> Who dies if England live?[2]

Duty, service, sacrifice: these were also the keynotes of his recruiting
speech in Brighton on 7 September. By then the Germans had been
briefly halted at Mons and, even while he was speaking, they were being
pushed back from the gates of Paris in the Battle of the Marne. The
original venue for the meeting was the Dome, but the crowd proved so
large that a second, overflow meeting had to be arranged in the Corn
Exchange. Kipling spoke to both audiences and was warmly received. 'All
the interests of our life of six weeks ago are dead,' he told his listeners.
'We have but one interest now, and that touches the naked heart of every
man in this island and the Empire (applause). Each long day, each rush of
men to our self-conscripted armies, and every new burden laid upon the
country, binds us yet closer in a brotherhood of service and sacrifice.' He
concluded simply, but resonantly: 'If we do our duty, we shall not fail.'[3]

His duty, as he saw it, was to raise confidence at home. So, in addition
to patriotic poems and speeches, he wrote a morale-boosting series of articles called 'The New Army in Training' for the *Daily Telegraph* in
December. 'Kipling's little 6d book on the New Armies is very good,' the
poet Ivor Gurney observed when the series came out as a booklet the following February.[4] On the other hand, yet another young poet, Edmund
Blunden, later said that it was this pamphlet that permanently turned
him off Kipling: 'It was so hideous a dismissal of such creatures [as me]

into the bottomless pit of war that I never could forgive. To him they were the merest cannon-fodder.'[5]

Moreover, eager to believe the worst of the Germans, Kipling was all too ready to accept and disseminate rumours of their 'atrocities' in Belgium. One much-publicised rumour was that the Germans cut off the right hands of Belgian boys to stop them later joining the armed forces. He worked this detail elliptically into his first story of the war, ' "Swept and Garnished" ', written in white heat in three days in late October and published in English and American magazines in January 1915. A crude revenge story – a brutalised version of ' "They" ' – it related how Frau Ebermann, a stereotypical German *Hausfrau* in bed with a fever, was visited in her immaculate Berlin flat by the ghosts of five Belgian children, killed in the German invasion of their country. The children told the disbelieving Frau Ebermann that there were thousands in their situation and that they had come to Berlin to wait for their parents to collect them. Her apparently safe and tidy flat had, along with the Kaiser's palace, become a rendezvous for dead children, awaiting their parents – presumably after Germany had been defeated by the Allies, and Berlin occupied. Before the children left the distraught Frau Ebermann, the elder girl pulled at the sleeve of one of the boys, who cried out. At which point, 'Frau Ebermann looked and saw.'[6] Most English readers would have known exactly what she saw and, Kipling must have hoped, would have had their anti-German animus reaffirmed.

The story's simultaneous appearance in the States was important. America had declared itself neutral, and Kipling was busy trying to mobilise old friends in support of the Allies. The month he was writing ' "Swept and Garnished" ', he plied the former President, Theodore Roosevelt, with the same tales of German atrocities. Roosevelt, sensibly cautious, advocated the need for 'authoritative statements, backed by official authority'.[7] Edward Bok, still editor of the *Ladies' Home Journal*, was another to be bombarded. Kipling told him of a young Belgian refugee (met on his Red Cross rounds) whose father, mother and sister had been killed in front of him and who was in a state of deep shock. There was now, he went on, a hospital in London that dealt specifically with Belgian women and small girls who had been raped. He urged Bok to send someone over to check the reports and make them known. As for Bok's suggestion that he might write a poem on how America would be next to suffer,

Kipling proudly declined, saying that it might be mistaken as a plea for help. Besides, his duty was to the Empire and to the Allies: 'I have given my only son to the Army: I am giving my time and substance to the work that lies before us.'[8]

He had indeed given his son to the Army and was already suffering for it. On 21 September, a week after John left for Warley, Carrie noted that her husband was prostrated with pains in his face. This led to four days in bed tossing and turning with a high temperature. He only began to pick up when John was allowed out on leave the following weekend. From then on, he was in a state of almost constant anxiety about John, which naturally mounted as news of the deaths of sons of friends began to come in. His letters to John betrayed deliberately little of his feelings, sticking to safe topics like what to call the small Singer car he had bought him: 'Why not call her Car-uso (he's a great singer). So was David. So was Melba. You might christen her "Depèche Melba" which is a foul pun.'[9]

November brought news of the death in France of Roberts. He had, as Kipling put it in his quickly penned elegy, 'passed in the very battle-smoke/Of the war that he had descried'.[10] There were visits to Indian troops in the New Forest and to the newly arrived force of 30,000 Canadians camped on Salisbury Plain: both breezily written up in 'The New Army in Training'. Christmas, with John present, was spent at Cherkley Court with the Canadian financier Max Aitken, one of whose other guests was another mutual friend, the Tory leader, Andrew Bonar Law. Among other things, they discussed the newly established post of 'Canadian Eye Witness' at the Front, with a brief to send war news back to Canada. Aitken was desperate to secure the post, and Kipling and Bonar Law in their different ways were both in a position to help. By late January 1915 the entrepreneurial Aitken had got himself appointed and, with Kipling's assistance, was soon making a reputation for himself as a war correspondent. Kipling was in touch with older friends too, telling Dunsterville in February that John had just finished a signalling course in London and was expecting to be sent to the Front. Kipling's pride in his son was clear; so too was his wistful self-identification with John. 'He's rather like what I was, to look at, at his age. . . .'[11]

Soon afterwards, on 23 March, Rider Haggard recorded in his diary that the casualty figures for officers in the recent inconclusive 'victory' at Neuve Chapelle had risen to 724; and that Kipling, whom he had seen the previous day, had remarked: 'Heaven save us from more such "victories"!' Kipling seemed greyer and smaller, his friend also noted, and neither he nor Carrie looked well. Haggard knew what to attribute this to: 'Their boy John, who is not yet 18, is an officer in the Irish Guards and one can see that they are terrified lest he should be sent to the Front and killed, as has happened to nearly all the young men they knew.' The only point during their visit when Kipling perked up was when Haggard observed that at least it had been a Liberal Government that had declared war, rather than a Conservative one, which would have been savaged by the Radicals. To which Kipling, 'with his usual wit', replied that:

this fact was the one thing that made him believe that we should win in the end. In it he saw the hand of the Almighty himself who had created the Radical Party and borne with it during its eight long years of rule, merely that it might be in power when the great crisis of our fate arrived and thus constrain its louder-voiced and more unpatriotic elements to silence.

When Haggard asked him what he had been occupying his mind with, Kipling answered that he had been writing stories and added: 'I don't know what they are worth, I only know they ain't literature.'[12]

Yet, at the time of this remark, he had started, and may well even have finished, one of his greatest stories, 'Mary Postgate'. Its central figure was the middle-aged, unimaginative and deeply repressed companion of a Miss Fowler. When the latter's orphaned young nephew, Wynn, entered the household, Mary became his surrogate mother and 'always his butt and his slave'. Wynn joined the Flying Corps on the outbreak of war and was soon killed on a trial flight, without having been in action. The two women decided that Mary should burn all his more personal effects in 'the destructor', the garden-incinerator.[13] Going to the village for paraffin, Mary witnessed the death of the publican's small daughter, killed by a bomb dropped by a German plane. Later, while burning Wynn's possessions, she discovered the German airman, who – after dropping the bomb – had fallen from his plane and was now dying. Mary, tending the bonfire, watched with mounting pleasure as the German slowly died.

Kipling began the story in early March. German planes had only started bombing raids on England two months earlier, so his use of detail was right up to date. More significantly, John had told his parents that he was about to be sent to the Front. At the time of writing, Kipling, only too well aware of the life-expectancy of officers, was terrified that his son would soon be killed. 'Mary Postgate' thus, almost certainly, began as another of his superstitious attempts to avert the evil eye: if he wrote a story in which he imagined his deepest fear, the gods might spare John.

This is not to ignore the story's more obviously shocking aspects: that Kipling was also gratifying his non-combatant fantasies of killing a German and that this imaginative gratification had its sexual counter-point within the story. Specifically, in a succession of sentences inter-spersed throughout the final scene (as Mary attended to the burning of Wynn's possessions and watched the German pilot die), Kipling made it quite clear that she had an orgasm. 'She wielded the poker with lunges that jarred the grating at the bottom [of the 'destructor'], and careful scrapes round the brickwork above'; 'the exercise of stoking had given her a glow which seemed to reach to the marrow of her bones'; 'she thumped like a pavior through the settling ashes at the secret thrill of it'; 'an increasing rapture laid hold on her. She ceased to think. She gave herself up to feel'; 'the end [the German's death, but also her orgasm] came very distinctly in a lull between two rain-gusts. Mary Postgate drew her breath short between her teeth and shivered from head to foot'; 'she scandalised the whole routine [of the household] by taking a luxurious hot bath before tea, and came down looking, as Miss Fowler said when she saw her lying all relaxed on the other sofa, "quite handsome!"'[14]

It was presumably this final scene that would lead Stanley Baldwin's son Oliver to describe 'Mary Postgate' as 'the wickedest story ever writ-ten'.[15] It was shocking, and was meant to be. But it also had the inevitability, the sense of waste, of tragedy. The story might have had its origins in Kipling's own terror, superstition and wish fulfilment, but Mary was imaginatively transformed into something far more than a conduit for his tortured feelings. Her repressed life, thwarted love and grotesque con-summation, evoked with an absolute conviction of detail and nuance, compelled an appalled compassion. It was arguably the finest short story inspired by the Great War.

In the event John did not go to the Front as soon as expected; so perhaps Kipling felt that writing 'Mary Postgate' had worked as a *nuzzur-wattu*, at least in the short term. Instead, John was sent off to Dublin. 'Dear F,' he wrote his father from Brown's Hotel (off Piccadilly) on the evening of 16 March:

Just a line to say I am off to Dublin to night to bring back a party of 34 recruits to Caterham.

You can faintly imagine what Dublin will be on St Patrick's day & the state of the recruits 'falling in'.

I have to march 'em right through the town.

So I will have my hands full till Thursday evening.

Well good bye old things, wish me luck.

Can the 'front' present a worse prospect than this little 'Dublin Stunt'?

'*Je pense que non*'.

Love to Jerry [the secretary at Bateman's].

Yours ever,

John [16]

John's other letters at this time struck a similarly cheerful, nonchalant note – chatting about his car or route marches, or a night on the 'Razlle-Dazlle' at various music halls and nightclubs. Meanwhile Kipling, having refused to write the history of the first Battle of Ypres, helped Aitken with his account of the month-long second Battle of Ypres. This was the battle at which poison gas was first used by the Germans, and Aitken's vivid description of how a small Canadian force bravely held out against overwhelming German numbers made his reputation as a war correspondent. At the end of May, John wrote to say that he was again on stand-by for France; again it came to nothing. In early June the Kiplings offered Bateman's to the War Office for use as a hospital, but their offer was declined. Later that month, Kipling gave a recruiting speech at the Southport Municipal Gardens. The photograph in the local paper accompanying the report of his speech showed him in suit, wing-collar and soft hat, flanked by Army and Navy officers, local town councillors and the clergy. In an inset snapshot, he was leaning forward, in full flow, bare-headed. Though his left hand was holding notes, he probably did not refer to them; he always, according to Haggard, learnt his speeches by heart.

He began in typically arch fashion: 'Ladies and gentlemen, I am here to speak on behalf of a system in which I do not believe, and in which, I daresay, a good many of you do not believe either – the system of voluntary service.' After a brief reminder that for years he and others had been advocating National Service, he launched into the Germans: 'There is no crime, no cruelty, no abomination that the mind of man can conceive which the German has not perpetrated, is not perpetrating, and will not perpetrate if he is allowed to go on.' In a world now divided up into 'human beings and Germans', he told his laughing and applauding audience, 'our strength and will alone can save us'. Stressing 'the horror' of Belgium's fate, he insisted that should Germany triumph, far worse awaited England. And, if England and the Allies fell, no one in the world would be safe – which in turn meant that no retreat, no terms, were possible. Roughly one-tenth of the British male population had already joined up. Now was the time for the rest of the fit and eligible to do so. He finished his peroration with a well-worn crowd-pleaser:

> In the old days – days that seem now so small and so far off – the days when we dealt in words, there used to be a saying which ran: 'What Lancashire thinks to-day, England will think to-morrow.' (Applause.) Let us change that saying for three years, or for the duration of the war, to 'What Lancashire does to-day, England will do to-morrow.' (Loud applause.)[17]

'Kipling has been making a good speech,' the uncritical Rider Haggard noted. 'It says exactly what we all think, neither more nor less, pointing out the terrible things that defeat would mean to this nation.'[18]

John was told in early July that he would definitely be the first ensign sent to France after 17 August (his eighteenth birthday); but even then, he would have been considered too young, had he not already done a year's service. 'So going in early was a damned good move after all,' he wrote jubilantly to his father on 5 July. Kipling's reply by return was the epitome of paternal anxiety thinly overlaid by pride. There followed for John visits to music halls and tea at Bateman's with a brother-officer, Rupert Grayson. On 18 July a 2nd Battalion of the Irish Guards was officially formed. 'That's us,' John wrote excitedly, '– a regular battalion – what ho!!'[19] Kipling, making his own will, at the same time gave his formal consent for John (still not yet quite eighteen) to be sent on active service.[20]

In fact, Kipling reached France before his son, leaving on 12 August for a fortnight at the Front as a war correspondent. He was shocked and moved by the devastation he saw and the desolation of the shell-smashed towns: 'The stillness was as terrible as the spread of the quick busy weeds between the paving-stones; the air smelt of pounded mortar and crushed stone; the sound of a footfall echoed like the drop of a pebble in a well.' He marvelled at the courage and endurance of the ordinary French people: women sorting hops in a flattened village; 'a girl at work with horses in a ploughed field that is dotted with graves'. Naturally the French forces came in for their fair share of praise, particularly the artillery; and to underline British and French solidarity, he described in some detail a distant glimpse of Lord Kitchener and General Joffre reviewing a French Army Corps. He took care, too, to ram home his line on German inhumanity. 'Remember *we* knew the Boche in '70 when *you* did not. We know what he has done in the last year. This is not war. It is against wild beasts that we fight. There is no arrangement possible with wild beasts.' Perhaps, as he claimed, he really was reporting a French woman verbatim; though it sounds more like a Franglais version of parts of his Southport speech, or of his own meditation shortly afterwards on a group of German prisoners whom he dismissed as hypnotised Yahoos:

> They were the breed which, at the word of command, had stolen out to drown women and children; had raped women in the streets at the word of command; and, always at the word of command, had sprayed petrol, or squirted flame; or voided their excrements on the property and persons of their captives. They stood there outside all humanity. Yet they were made in the likeness of humanity. One realised it with a shock when the bandaged creature began to shiver, and they shuffled off in response to the orders of civilised men.[21]

As before, he wrote up his experiences in a series of articles for the *Telegraph*, subsequently published as a sixpenny booklet, *France at War*.

John, by an odd coincidence, had also recently seen Kitchener though at rather closer quarters. Kitchener, having succeeded Roberts as Colonel of the Irish Guards, had come down to Warley on 13 August to inspect the new battalion. John's friend, Rupert Grayson, would recall how, after introductions and port in the Mess, the officers were grouped with their new Colonel for the usual photograph:

> As one of the junior ensigns, I was standing next to John Kipling, the son of Rudyard Kipling, on a form in the back row. As usual, John was superbly smart, for he was meticulous about his appearance. Kitchener was seated between Lord Kerry and our commanding officer, the Hon. L.J.P. Butler. Unfortunately John, from his superior height, had noticed a grease-spot on the Field-Marshal's cap, which he immediately pointed to; and in the intense hush which precedes the taking of a photograph, his resonant voice broke the silence: 'I told you, Rupert, that Kitchener would never make a guardsman.'[22]

It was a story that Kipling, who thought Kitchener 'a fatted Pharo in spurs', would have enjoyed.[23] After the photograph, John and his friend beat a hasty retreat before any questions could be asked, John going to Bateman's to stay briefly with his mother. John, Carrie noted in her diary on the 15th, 'looks very straight and smart and young, as he turns at the top of the stairs to say: "Send my love to Daddo."'[24] Just after midnight on the morning of his eighteenth birthday, after spending the crossing from Southampton on picket duty, he was docking in Le Havre. '*This is the life,*' he wrote home on landing.[25]

Though father and son were now briefly both in France, they did not meet. Kipling was first in Verdun, later Paris. After entraining north to Lumbres, John was billeted in 'a splendid little village . . . about 20 miles from the firing line', which was where he stayed for most of September while his father was with the Dover Patrol and the Harwich Flotilla. The two, however, corresponded regularly. John's letters home mixed safe snippets of news with requests (and thanks) for a vast array of items. These included civilian and khaki socks, braces, slippers, towels, a service lamp, pyjamas, 'that *stiff* hair brush of Dad's', stocking puttees, writing paper and envelopes, 'some literature: Nashs (Sept.), Royal, Strand, Pearsons etc.', tooth and shaving powder, clean shirts, chocolate, chocolate biscuits, a naval oilskin, collar studs, front and back, a good strong toothbrush and a replacement aluminium Identification Disc. From his quarters, there were also stories of Grayson misbehaving with a local girl and of his own penchant for the Mayor's pretty daughter, Marcelle. In one letter, to his parents' delight, he described the antics of a huge ravenous sow, which made off with one of his men's emergency ration bag and was chased round the farmyard by the entire billet armed with rifles and sticks. In another, more grimly, he described a court martial at which, as he put it, 'one man came very near the extreme penalty & I didn't like it at all'.[26]

Kipling responded with anecdotes of his French tour; how a soldier at Troyes had known all his works; a 'fruity' account (John's appreciative word) of attending a show at the Palais Royal Music Hall; and advice, repeated in no fewer than three letters, about using overhead rabbit-wire in the trenches to ward off bombs. To this well-intentioned guidance, John replied with the kindly impatience of the professional to the amateur: 'Surely you know it is a standing order never to have any thing over the top of a trench, even rabbit wires. If the Bosch comes, he has you like rabbits underneath it.' On 10 September he thanked his father for sending 'the mags'. If these included the September issue of *Nash's Magazine* (as seems likely, since he specifically asked for that issue), he would have come across 'Mary Postgate'; one wonders what he made of it. By then, though he could not directly say so, John knew that 'the greatest battle in the history of the world' (as General Haking had put it in a recent briefing) was about to take place nearby – and that he was going to be in it. On 23 September he sent a quick message to say they were on the move; and two days later at 5.30 pm:

Dear F –

Just a hurried note as we start off tonight. The front line trenches are nine miles off from here so it won't be a very long march.

This is THE great effort to break through & end the war.

The guns have been going deafeningly all day, without a single stop. We have to push through at all costs so we won't have much time in the trenches, which is great luck.

Funny to think one will be in the thick of it tomorrow.

One's first experience of shell fire not in the trenches but in the open.

This is one of the advantages of a Flying Division; you have to keep moving.

We marched 18 miles last night in the pouring wet.

It came down in sheets steadily.

They are staking a tremendous lot on this great advancing movement as if it succeeds the war won't go on for long.

You have no idea what tremendous issues depend on the next few
days.

This will be my last letter most likely for some time as we won't
get any time for writing this next week, but I will try & send Field
post cards.

Well so long old dears.

Dear love

John

Love to Jerry

JK [27]

After some initial gains in the Battle of Loos, the British advance again
came to a grinding halt. On the afternoon of the 27th, near Chalk Pit
Wood, John was wounded and reported missing.

'Mary Postgate' had contrasted two reactions to Wynn's loss. When Miss
Fowler asked Mary whether she had cried yet, Mary said she could not: 'It
only makes me angry with the Germans.' To which her employer replied:
'That's sheer waste of vitality . . . We must live till the war's finished.'[28] In
Mary's displaced rage and Miss Fowler's tough stoicism, Kipling accu-
rately anticipated his own reactions to John's loss.

The tough stoicism was at once apparent. The day the telegram from
the War Office arrived at Bateman's, Bonar Law's daughter, Isabel, was
visiting Elsie. The Kiplings waited until Isabel had gone before breaking
the ominous news to their daughter. The displaced rage came later.
Haggard noted shortly before Christmas that he had seen Kipling in
town: 'R.K. expressed his opinion of the Government and individual
members thereof in language too strong to write down even in a private
diary.'[29]

At first, ill with gastritis and worry, Kipling concentrated on trying to
find out what had actually happened to John. 'Wounded and missing' did
not necessarily mean 'dead', as he and Carrie were no doubt told *ad infini-
tum*. Friends rallied round. Aitken came over from France with what little

he had been able to pick up. Gwynne started enquiries through Roman Catholic channels. Walter Page, the American Ambassador in London, did what he could; so too did the Prince of Wales. The Red Cross was approached; leaflets appealing for information were dropped behind German lines. Over the succeeding weeks and months, Kipling sought out anyone who might have information.

Rupert Grayson had been wounded the same day as John and brought back to England, but he could only tell the grieving father 'how we awaited the grey dawn and of the casually tense trivialities before we went into action'.[30] All John's colonel could relate was that he had been seen to fall, hit in the foot or leg, but then to get up and go into a shed that almost at once fell into German hands. 'I do hope and pray,' Lieutenant-Colonel Butler wrote, 'that you may hear he was carried off by the Germans and looked after by them.'[31] Though intended to be consoling, this last hope may have terrified Carrie as much as the awful uncertainty. Dorothy Ponton, a governess and secretary at Bateman's, remembered Carrie's dread that John 'had been taken prisoner by the Germans who might take vengeance on him for being the son of Rudyard Kipling'.[32] By early November, Kipling himself seemed to have accepted the fact that John was dead. He forced himself to spell it out in a letter to Dunsterville on the 12th:

Our boy was reported 'wounded & missing' since Sep. 27 – the battle of Loos and we've heard nothing official since that date. But all we can pick up from the men points to the fact that he is dead and probably wiped out by shell fire.

However, he had his heart's desire and he didn't have a long time in trenches. The Guards advanced on a front of two platoons to each battalion. He led the right platoon over a mile of open ground in face of shell and machine gun fire and was dropped at the further limit of the advance after having emptied his pistol into a house full of German m.g.'s. His C.O. and his Company Commander told me how he led 'em: and the wounded have confirmed it. He was senior ensign tho' only 18 yrs & 6 weeks, had worked like the devil for a year at Warley and knew his Irish to the ground. He was reported on as one of the best of the subalterns and was gym instructor and sig-naller. It was a short life. I'm sorry that all the years work ended in that one afternoon but – lots of people are in our position and it's something to have bred a man. The wife is standing it wonderfully tho' she of course clings to the bare hope of his being a prisoner. I've seen what shells can do and I don't.[33]

In fact, whatever he might tell Dunsterville and indeed himself, like Carrie he desperately went on hoping. Even a year later, he was still pleading with the War Office to keep his son's name on the missing list.

In the meantime, Haggard too was busy interviewing the wounded. On 27 December 1915 he talked to a young Guardsman called Bowe, brought over to his house by a 'very well educated' soldier called Frankland. Bowe had been about forty yards away from John when he entered Chalk Pit Wood and disappeared. He told Haggard that Lieutenant Kipling must have been blown to pieces, or buried, by a shell – or captured and murdered by the Germans. Since nothing was yet certain, Haggard kept these grim conjectures to himself. The following day he heard more in a letter from Frankland:

Bowe now says that as they left this wood he saw an officer, who *he could swear* was Mr Kipling, leaving the wood on his way to the rear and trying to fasten a field dressing round his mouth which was badly shattered by a piece of shell. Bowe would have helped him but for the fact that the officer was crying with the pain of the wound and he did not want to humiliate him by offering assistance.[34]

Again, Haggard decided not to pass this on, though personally convinced of its truth. Various other eye-witness accounts also exist, including that of Sergeant Kinnelly:

Mr Kipling was about 50 yards in front of his platoon and was shouting 'Come on boys!' He was the bravest officer I ever saw. A couple of shrapnel burst right over his head and I saw him fall. On the way back someone said, 'Poor Mr Kipling is dead'. Then I came on Mr Kipling myself and I am sure he was dead. The ground where he lay was heavily shelled.[35]

The report which finally persuaded Kipling that his son was dead was the one given him in person by Sergeant Farrell in December 1917. According to Farrell, he had seen John shot in the head and in the late afternoon had himself put John in a shell-hole on the left side of Chalk Pit Wood.

For many years, Kipling and Carrie tried without success to locate John's grave. Their efforts were defeated by their son's lack of an identification disc and a clerical error. John's unidentified body lay in No Man's Land from 1915 to 1917, when it was dug up and reburied with the headstone 'AN UNKNOWN LIEUTENANT OF THE IRISH GUARDS' in Plot 7, Row D, Grave 2 of St Mary's Advanced Dressing Station Cemetery. Three-quarters of a century later, in 1992, an officer of the Commonwealth War Graves' Commission spotted that the body of the 'unknown lieutenant' had been recovered from Block G25 C68, a sector unoccupied at the time by the Irish Guards. Block H25 C68, however, was precisely the area where John had last been seen. Since he was the only Irish Guards lieutenant still unaccounted for, the grave and remains were clearly his. The headstone now reads: LIEUTENANT JOHN KIPLING, IRISH GUARDS, 27TH SEPTEMBER 1915, AGE 18'.[36]

'For pain of the soul there is, outside God's Grace, but one drug,' the Abbot would observe to the grieving artist John of Burgos in 'The Eye of Allah' written in 1924; 'and that is a man's craft, learning, or other helpful motion of his own mind.'[37] Kipling's first application of this principle in the weeks following Loos was to write up his recent naval experiences in a series of lively sketches and poems called *The Fringes of the Fleet*. The *Daily Telegraph* again ran the series before they appeared in booklet form in December 1915. The following September, Ivor Gurney told Marion Scott how he had read most of the booklet 'in a shell hole, during one of the most annoying times we have had. It was during heavy fatigue, and the Bosches spotted us and let fly with heavy shrapnel and 5.9s'.[38] Kipling would have been pleased to learn that what had proved a vital displacement activity for himself had also helped a private soldier get through part of the Battle of the Somme.

The intense personal feelings associated with the writing of *The Fringes of the Fleet* were reflected in Kipling's subsequent dealings with Edward Elgar. In January 1916 Lord Charles Beresford, former Admiral of the Channel Fleet, asked Elgar to set the poems in the booklet. Elgar made a start, but Kipling was at first unwilling to give permission. When he relented, Elgar selected four of the six poems – 'The Lowestoft Boat', 'Fate's Discourtesy', 'Submarines' and 'Sweepers' – and set them for four baritones and orchestra in what he called 'a broad saltwater style'. On 17 June 1917, with Elgar conducting, *The Fringes of the Fleet* began a two-week run at the Coliseum as part of a wartime variety programme. So popular did the item prove that the run was extended, two performances a day, till the end of July, and *Fringes* was then sent to Manchester, Leicester, Chiswick and Chatham, for a week each, before returning to the Coliseum in early October. It was towards the end of the provincial leg that Kipling tried to call a halt to further performances. 'I fear the songs are doomed by R.K. he is perfectly stupid in his attitude,' an exhausted Elgar grumbled to a friend in September.[39] In fact, he was to complete the second, and a third, stint at the Coliseum before Kipling finally withdrew his consent in December. The story is usually told by Elgarians to Kipling's discredit; yet despite the songs' painful associations, he *did* give his permission, and there were regular performances over a period of six months.

Back in early 1916 the Kiplings went again to Bath. Carrie took the cure; he visited soldiers in the local hospital. It was around this time that, following a suggestion of Elsie's, Kipling developed his idea of scrapbooks for sick and wounded troops, which he passed on to May Gaskell, the instigator of the Red Cross Library. The scrapbooks were a great success. 'The typhoid and dysentery cases were too weak to hold books at all, and needed pictures,' Mrs Gaskell remembered:

> Mr Rudyard Kipling had realised this need, and asked us to make brown-paper scrapbooks of a few pages, not too crowded with pictures, the recipe being as follows: 'Size about 14 × 11 inches, four sheets, i.e. eight leaves. *Outside* a nice coloured picture. Fill both sides of the paper – contents – attractive pictures, plain and coloured, *very* short stories, little jokes and anecdotes, short poems. Anything amusing or pretty. Remember the books are for grown men.'[40]

Late February brought news of the death of their old friend Henry James and of a huge German onslaught on the great French fortress system at Verdun. Pondering on the terrible losses that the war had already inflicted, Kipling began a new story in April, eventually called 'On the Gate'.

The basic proposition was simple, but arresting: Heaven, imagined as a direct reflection of Earth, was swamped by the administrative and salvational complications caused by the vast numbers of war dead. The resultant story was ingeniously worked out and, because of (rather than in spite of) its elaborately arch manner, curiously moving. St Peter was the central figure, tackling the heavenly emergency with compassionate good humour and a little help from some of Kipling's favourite writers and divines. The passage in which St Peter, chatting with Death, despatched a bureaucratic Seraph to supervise admissions on the Gate gives the flavour:

> 'I'm just off on an inter-departmental inspection which will take me some time,' said St Peter. 'You *must* learn to act on your own initiative. So I shall leave you to yourself for the next hour or two, merely suggesting (I don't wish in any way to sway your judgement) that you invite St Paul, St Ignatius (Loyola, I mean) and – er – St Christopher to assist as Supervising Assessors on the Board of Admission. Ignatius is one of the subtlest intellects we have, and an officer and a gentleman to boot. I assure you' – the Saint turned towards Death – 'he revels in dialectics. If he's allowed to prove his case, he's quite capable of letting off the offender. St Christopher, of course, will pass anything that looks wet and muddy.'[41]

Haggard's wry private comment two years later, when Kipling read him the story, was that if Kipling had published it at the time, 'it would have been caviare to the General . . . because the keynote of it is infinite mercy, extended even to the case of Judas'.[42] Carrie's veto, Kipling told Haggard, was the reason it had so far remained unpublished – the only known instance of her interfering with his production line. While the act of writing such a story at such a time would have had some therapeutic value for him, it could have none for her.

In this celebration of the saint's patience and sympathy, one can see the fifty-year-old Kipling reaching out for these qualities himself. It was, however, entirely in keeping that in 'The Neutral' (later retitled 'The Question'), also written in 1916, he used Peter's denial of Jesus as a means of expressing his deep rage, on this occasion directed against America's continuing neutrality:

> Brethren, how must it fare with me,
>   Or how am I justified,
> If it be proven that I am he
>   For whom mankind has died –
> If it be proven that I am he
>   Who, being questioned, denied?[43]

More savagely still, Kipling was to base his anti-Papal poem of 1918, 'A Song at Cock-Crow', on Peter's triple denial; yet a later story, 'The Church that was at Antioch', depicted Peter once more as a warmly human and admirable figure. Good Peter for prose, bad Peter for verse. More generally, the First World War signalled a profound change in Kipling's use of the Bible. Previously his work had been strongly marked by allusions and attitudes drawn from the Old Testament. After John's death, perhaps surprisingly, the New Testament predominated.

This shift from Old to New was not simply from the retributive to the redemptive, for the New Testament also offered the most powerful instances of sacrifice and betrayal. From the very start of the war, Kipling had been claiming that the Allies, and England in particular, were offering themselves as a sacrifice for the whole of mankind. After John's death, the idea became an obsession. In June 1916, he wrote a long letter to his French friend André Chevrillon in which, after repeating his usual sacrificial line, he went even further, managing to turn England into Jesus. He had, he told Chevrillon, been roughing out an interview between Judas and one of the Sanhedrins shortly before the payment of the thirty pieces of silver. Both Judas and the priest agreed on the virtues of Jesus (unnamed). He might, they asserted, be a bit strict, a bit selfish, but in himself Jesus was a reasonable citizen. What made him dangerous were his principles, which were deeply conservative and – for the sake of peace in the region – must be stopped from spreading. In this little allegory, which Kipling never intended for publication, Jesus was clearly England, Judas America (and perhaps also the Liberals), and the Sanhedrins the Germans. In 'On the Gate', Judas had been cast as one of the redeemed; now, only a couple of months later, he was the great betrayer. Kipling's letter to Chevrillon continued on a more personal note, the bereaved parent watching key dates on the calender come round again. And from bereaved parent it was only a short step to German-hating Englishman: 'Never believe again, that the English do not know how to hate: It was a long lesson and we were slow learners but we have our teaching by heart at last.'[44]

Yet while Kipling's own feelings were yo-yoing so violently during the Somme summer and autumn of 1916, a poem of his, written during the Boer War, was one of the things sustaining an overworked young VAD nurse in London. 'When the groans of anaesthetised men made the ward a Bedlam,' Vera Brittain would write in *Testament of Youth*, 'and the piteous impatience of boys in anguish demanded attention just when the rush of work was worst and the heat least endurable, I kept myself going, with the characteristic idealism of those youthful years, by murmuring under my breath two verses from Kipling's "Dirge of Dead Sisters":

(When the days were torment and the nights were clouded terror,
    When the Powers of Darkness had dominion on our soul –
When we fled consuming through the Seven Hells of fever,
    These put out their hands to us and healed and made us whole.)

(Till the pain was merciful and stunned us into silence –
    When each nerve cried out on God that made the misused clay;
When the Body triumphed and the last poor shame departed –
    These abode our agonies and wiped the sweat away.)'[45]

For Kipling himself, the countdown to the first anniversary of John's disappearance brought on a recurrence of the physical pain he had felt in 1915. Accompanying this was a kind of paranoia, reflected in his obsessive splicing together of his hatred of the Germans with his hatred of the Socialists. The visible expression of this paranoia was his coining of the neologism 'Boschialist' ('the Socialist with Hun leanings', as he glossed it), which he offered to Blumenfeld at the *Daily Express*: 'The lower grade of Boschialist is the Hunnomite which is a beautiful word because it verges on the obscene. Here is the example: – Ramsay MacDonald might at present (till we know more about him) be described as a Boschialist. Whereas Haldane is indubitably a Hunnomite.' Five days later, on 11

September, he was gloating to Dunsterville about improvements on the Western Front: 'It's a scientific-cum-sporting proposition with enough guns at last to account for the birds and the Hun is having a very sickly time of it . . . They tell me the whole earth gets up bodily like a pancake. If we can give the Hun one more winter underground he will be quite malleable by the spring.'[46]

The letters to Blumenfeld and Dunsterville are repellent, even slightly mad. Against them one might put 'My Boy Jack', a bleakly poignant elegy for John, in which one can either imagine two speakers or a single character's speech and thoughts. Kipling included the poem in another collection of war articles, *Sea Warfare* (where 'The Neutral' also appeared), published in December 1916:

> 'Have you news of my boy Jack?'
> *Not this tide.*
> 'When d'you think that he'll come back?'
> *Not with this wind blowing, and this tide.*
>
> 'Has any one else had word of him?'
> *Not this tide.*
> *For what is sunk will hardly swim,*
> *Not with this wind blowing, and this tide.*
>
> 'Oh, dear, what comfort can I find?'
> *None this time,*
> *Nor any tide,*
> *Except he did not shame his kind –*
> *Not even with that wind blowing, and that tide.*
>
> *Then hold your head up all the more,*
> *This tide,*
> *And every tide;*
> *Because he was the son you bore,*
> *And gave to that wind blowing and that tide!*[47]

There was rather less of the angry, bitter Kipling in 1917. One reason was that though his *bête noire* Lloyd George had become Prime Minister with the resignation of Asquith, Lloyd George's reformed Coalition Government now had several of his closest friends (including Milner, Bonar Law and Stanley Baldwin) in positions of power. Another reason was the approach in January by the Irish Guards to write their history during the war. Colonel Proby's tactful letter proposed this 'not as a business matter, but as a memento of your son's service in the Regiment'.[48] Kipling accepted at once and was soon hard at work amassing factual and anecdotal material for this labour of love. Also tempering the bitterness was the United States's entry into the war in April; and Kipling was soon eagerly responding with 'The Choice', in which the spirit of America made lots of Kiplingesque protestations about being able 'to live with ourselves again' and choosing 'that the Flesh should die/And not the living Soul!'[49]

April brought too the publication of A Diversity of Creatures, his first collection of adult stories since Actions and Reactions in 1909. Unusually, Kipling dated each of the fourteen stories, to make it clear that all but the final two, ' "Swept and Garnished" ' and 'Mary Postgate', had been written (and in most cases published) pre-war. The volume lived up to its title with a wide cast of characters: two drug addicts suffering from pre-natal trauma; a flamboyant music-hall impresario; Stalky, young and middle-aged; laconic Sussex farm labourers; visiting colonial dignitaries; an international group of twenty-first-century administrators; a bewitched, squinting terrier; and an aesthete-turned-foxhunting-man. The collection opened with a Wellsian futuristic fantasy, 'As Easy as A.B.C.', and closed with the threatened village life of 'Mary Postgate'. There was comedy and tragedy; fantasy and farce; something for the highbrow, something for the lowbrow. The supernatural country-house canine love story 'The Dog Hervey' turned on a misunderstood quotation from Doctor Johnson. An officious and stuck-up JP was publicly ridiculed by a music-hall song in 'The Village that Voted the Earth was Flat'. Horace was a major presence in 'Regulus', Surtees in ' "My Son's Wife" ', Jane Austen in 'Mary Postgate'.

The anonymous reviewer in the Athenaeum, while enthusiastically praising the volume, pointed out that 'various as the contents are, we are well acquainted with their different kinds'.[50] It was another reminder that, by this time, English readers were largely reading the Kipling they expected to read. (Significantly, the Athenaeum review nowhere referred to 'Mary Postgate'.) This was as true of those hostile to Kipling as of those who enjoyed him. The Orientalist Ronald Storrs read the book in the summer of 1917 and noted his responses in his diary:

> Read Kipling's Diversities . . . All his youth R.K. gaped upon high officials from an Indian Grub Street, and now, admitted to share the breezy shop of Colonial Ministers, he records with smug pride their uninteresting indecorums. Yet with a gift of writing, for immediate effect, almost beyond belief. But for stimulus and constructive criticism and suggestion, young Britain should be fed on Wells.[51]

Storrs's comments cast little light on the stories (only 'The Vortex' included a Colonial Minister), but provided a perfect example of an antipathetic reader finding exactly the Kipling he expected to find: a talented literary bounder, showing off that he had 'made it'.

Kipling spent part of May visiting the Italian Front. As on his trip to France in 1915, he was accompanied by his Boer War friend Perceval Landon, a Bateman's regular in the Edwardian years and from 1912 a frequent user of Keylands, a cottage on the estate. The trip produced more articles for the *Daily Telegraph* under the title 'The War in the Mountains'. Shortly after his return Kipling learnt from Bonar Law, via his cousin Stan, that Lloyd George was eager to award him any honour he was prepared to accept. He refused crossly, and a mixture of indignation at Lloyd George's approach, ever-present thoughts of John and contempt for the mishandling of the war in the Middle East fuelled the angry 'Mesopotamia':

> Our dead shall not return to us while Day and Night divide –
>   Never while the bars of sunset hold.
> But the idle-minded overlings who quibbled while they died,
>   Shall they thrust for high employments as of old?[52]

In September, two years after John's death, Kipling became a member of the War Graves Commission, another public act of private memorial to his son. By the end of that month he was working on a new story. 'In the Interests of the Brethren' centred on an unofficial Masonic Lodge ('Faith and Works 5837') set up by Lewis Burges, a middle-aged London tobacconist, and his friends. As the war slowly ground on, the Lodge had evolved into a rendezvous and place of worship for soldier-masons on leave from the Front. For Burges, whose son was killed in Egypt, it became both a personal lifeline and a means of contributing to the war effort. 'All Ritual is fortifying' and 'We must all do what we can', Burges repeatedly observed to the narrator – advice that we can see Kipling patiently giving himself in writing the story. As with 'On the Gate', the keynote here was sympathy: for the bereaved and for the troops, both finding temporary comfort at the Lodge. September 1917 was the month that, at Craiglockhart War Hospital, Wilfred Owen was showing Siegfried Sassoon drafts of his sonnet 'Anthem for Dead Youth', and Sassoon suggested changing 'Dead' to 'Doomed'.

Kipling's older friends continued to thin out. Jameson died in November after earlier asking Kipling to become a Rhodes Trustee, a position he happily accepted. Work progressed on his regimental history. He saw a good deal of Trix, who had come to live nearby, and also of Aitken, now Lord Beaverbrook and soon to become Minister of Information. Kipling had also – building on an imitation Horace ode – started up a game with friends like George Saintsbury and C R L Fletcher about an imaginary fifth book of Horace's odes. He claimed that he had come across a copy in the Vatican Library, that another existed at Uppsala and a third was supposedly held in the Bodleian. Other Latinist friends and acquaintances including Charles Graves (uncle of Robert) and Ronald Knox took up the game. They translated the imitation ode into Latin and also Kipling's earlier, Horatian piece, 'The Pro-Consuls'; and with some assistance and much interest from Kipling, they went on to produce *Q. Horati Flacci Carminum Liber Quintus a Rudyardo Kipling et Carolo Graves Anglice Redditus* . . . in 1920. Horace and Jane Austen (whom Kipling read aloud to Carrie and Elsie) were his great literary stand-bys during the war. A later letter to Herbert Baker, in which he approvingly called Horace 'the soundest Platitudinarian that ever was', spelt out nakedly why reading him was such a welcome activity: 'Having but a few shreds of Latin I have to worry about his *nuances* which diverts one from thinking.'[53]

Kipling seems to have needed as much diversion as he could find during 1918. Advising Beaverbrook on propaganda, delivering a rousing speech at Folkestone (17 February), and performing his other official tasks

provided some constructive relief. So in a different way did 'En-dor', written in March, a rejection of spiritualist offers (probably by Trix and
others) to get in touch with John. Here, in a rare return to the Old
Testament, Kipling took as his starting-point the episode where the witch
at En-dor raised the spirit of Samuel for Saul. While fully acknowledging
the aching temptation of such a course, Kipling's poem sanely concluded:

> *Oh, the road to En-dor is the oldest road*
> *And the craziest road of all!*
> *Straight it runs to the Witch's abode,*
> *As it did in the days of Saul,*
> *And nothing has changed of the sorrow in store*
> *For such as go down on the road to En-dor!*

Early in April he was engaged on 'Epitaphs of the War', a series of
aphoristic poems, which represented a kind of poetical counterpoint to
the work he was doing on the War Graves Commission and with his
regimental history. These often brilliant pieces had, in their mixture of
the mandarin and the demotic, much in common with the Imagist
experiments that Ezra Pound and his group had been attempting in the
years just prior to the war – to the point where one wonders whether
Kipling might have come across a copy of Pound's Imagist anthology *Des
Imagistes* (1914), or his volume *Lustra* (1916), and have been partly imitating them:

A DRIFTER OFF TARENTUM

He from the wind-bitten North with ship and companions
    descended,
    Searching for eggs of death spawned by invisible hulls.
Many he found and drew forth. Of a sudden the fishery ended
    In flame and a clamorous breath known to the eye-pecking gulls.

THE BEGINNER

On the first hour of my first day
    In the front trench I fell.
(Children in boxes at a play
    Stand up to watch it well.)[54]

337

The kind of thoughts Kipling was trying to divert himself from can be guessed from a long diary entry by Haggard on 22 May, after he had spent most of the day at Bateman's. His host was still suffering from bouts of the internal pain that had begun in September 1914, though a recent X-ray had cleared him of cancer or a tumour. The two friends had talked of 'the soul and the fate of man':

> Rudyard, apparently, cannot make up his mind about these things. On one point, however, he is perfectly clear. I happened to remark that I thought that this world was one of the hells. He replied that he did not *think*, he was *certain* of it. He went on to show that it had every attribute of a hell, doubt, fear, pain, struggle, bereavement, almost irresistible temptations springing from the nature with which we are clothed, physical and mental suffering, etc., etc., ending in the worst fate that man can devise for man, Execution!

At some point in the conversation Kipling asked how much older Haggard was, and on being told ten years older, grimly remarked: 'Then you have the less time left in which to suffer.' This was also the occasion on which Kipling read Haggard 'On the Gate' and made his remark on literary inspiration: 'We are only telephone wires.'[55]

Ironically, given the Horace hoax that he and his friends were busy cooking up, Kipling that summer was himself the victim of a hoax. On 27 May *The Times* published a new Kipling poem called 'The Old Volunteer' – except that it was not his, despite a passable forgery of his signature. The verses, he crossly pointed out, were pretty feeble, and *The Times* should have known better than to print them on spec. Things, as Kipling later chose to remember them, rapidly turned farcical when the paper sent Mr H Smale, an ex-Detective Inspector from Scotland Yard, down to Bateman's to investigate:

> It was a Detective out of a book, down to the creak of Its boots. (On the human side at lunch It knew a lot about second-hand furniture.) Officially, It behaved like all the detectives in the literature of that period. Finally, It settled Its self, back to the light, facing me at my work-table, and told me a long yarn about a man who worried the Police with complaints of anonymous letters addressed to him from

unknown sources, all of which, through the perspicacity of the Police, turned out to have been written by himself to himself for the purpose of attracting notoriety.[56]

At the time, however, Kipling was deeply upset by the affair and grateful for the support of his nephew Oliver Baldwin, who was staying in the house.

Already at a low ebb, the effect of the hoax and Mr Smale's insinuations was to induce just the sort of persecution complex Mr Smale imputed. In July Kipling told his friend Ian Colvin (Scotland Yard's candidate for the hoax): 'My theory from the first was and is that the "old Volunteer" was a Hun trick meant to discredit and annoy.'[57] In August he was offering another of his paranoid neologisms, 'Bolshewhiggery', to Blumenfeld at the *Express*, as well as encouraging him not to capitalise the word 'Hun' any more and always to use 'it' and 'which' when referring to Germans.[58] With September, as the third anniversary of John's death approached, Kipling's German-hate level went up another notch. Writing to Stanley Baldwin from Newquay on the 21st, he described gleefully how a mob of locals had tried to lynch four Germans, a man and three women, who had been living in the town for well over a year; and he was careful to explain that local feeling only boiled over when, as a result of recent German torpedoing, the corpses of local fishermen began to be washed up in the harbour. His evident relish in the whole business – and obvious disappointment that a town councillor rescued the Germans from the mob – was repellent. As in 1896 and 1899, and on and off during the war, the combination of extreme private anguish and national threat had tipped him over some edge of hysteria.

As the war itself at last moved towards an end, Kipling became tormented with the idea that Germany was not going to be made to pay in full, and for ever, for being 'Evil Incarnate'. The phrase was from his October poem 'Justice', which might more accurately be called 'Retribution'. Rage and anger spluttered through the lines as he shouted that Germany must be punished so that:

> our dead shall sleep
> In honour, unbetrayed,

> And we in faith and honour keep
> That peace for which they paid.[59]

What he meant, beneath the patriotic bluster, was so that *he* did not want to feel that John had died in vain.

A number of his 'epitaphs of war' were plainly inspired by John's death. They need to be read alongside the outbursts of hate and cries for vengeance. One, simply entitled 'A Son', achieved some stoical balance:

> My son was killed while laughing at some jest. I would I knew
> What it was, and it might serve me in a time when jests are few.

Another epitaph, 'Common Form', was more multi-faceted. At one level, it again attacked the Conservative and Liberal Old Guard whose lies had betrayed the younger generation; at another level, it glanced wryly at disillusioned poems like Sassoon's 'Base Details'. But the couplet also asked to be read more literally, and Kipling bitterly included himself as one of the lying fathers:

> If any question why we died,
> Tell them, because our fathers lied.[60]

The news did not reach Bateman's until 12 November that the Armistice had been signed. 'A world to be remade without a son' was all that Carrie could bring herself to record in her diary.[61]

19

Debits and Credits

'I'm as busy as the Devil in a gale of wind at all sorts of jobs that don't seem to matter much,' Kipling told Dunsterville in July 1919. 'Nothing matters much really when one has lost one's only son. It wipes the meaning out of things.'[1] One of the jobs he was busy at was his two-volume history of the Irish Guards, and for all his despair this did mean something. He continued interviewing survivors, reading diaries and letters, compiling material, writing it up. For the next three years the history formed the centre of his working life. 'It is being done with agony and bloody sweat,' he remarked once to his secretary Dorothy Ponton, though she recorded that he also declared: 'This will be my great work.'[2]

Miss Ponton left a lively first-hand account of the volumes as they progressed. After boning up on the details of a particular engagement or episode, Kipling did a first draft in his microscopic handwriting, which she typed up. He would then redraft, and she would retype, and so on until he was satisfied; and the copy would be put aside to wait the final revision. When she admitted to making 'pot-shots' at illegible phrases, he reassured her: 'Continue the pot-shots. They sometimes give me an idea; anyway I like 'em better than blanks.' When he began typing his drafts, the initial results were even harder to read. 'The beastly thing simply *won't* spell,' he would complain.[3]

Not surprisingly, so personal a project created an atmosphere of pervasive anxiety. Miss Ponton recalled the consternation when the fourth revision of a particular chapter disappeared, and the relief when the missing draft eventually turned up in a book in Kipling's study. Carrie added to the general anxiety by the obsessive control she exercised over all of Kipling's manuscript material. Apart from private letters, reputedly not a scrap of paper with his handwriting or signature on left the house without her permission. So when at the same time as the missing chapter, another single page of manuscript that Kipling thought he had passed on to his secretary went astray, Carrie's suspicions were instantly aroused. Fortunately Kipling soon located the page and came to apologise to Miss Ponton. "'Here it is. I'd only forgotten to tear it off my block. Sorry!" he said. "Thank you. I'm glad it has been found," replied I politely. "And I'm glad I didn't say 'Quite certain it was given out,'" added he.'[4] It was a glimpse of one aspect of the Kiplings' marriage after thirty years: Carrie the tough, wary administrator who kept everything running, her husband the smoother of ruffled edges.

By the end of July 1922 Kipling had finished the manuscript and sent it off. The effort had left him 'yellow and shrunken', Carrie observed, and, in fact, by now in his mid-fifties, he was soon to undergo further X-rays, followed in the autumn by an operation, which for a month or two left him weak and exhausted.[5] In January 1923 he worked on the proofs, and on 16 April *The Irish Guards in the Great War* (Edited and Compiled from their Diaries and Papers by Rudyard Kipling) was in the shops. The volumes sold for a pound apiece, and Kipling's royalties went to a fund for the widows of those who had served in the regiment.

John Buchan, who had already published a *History of the South African Forces in France* and a *History of the Great War*, greeted the books enthusiastically in *The Times*. Saluting Kipling as 'the greatest living master of narrative', Buchan praised the 'clearness and speed' with which particular engagements were evoked, the handling of 'vivid concrete detail' and the sheer quality of the descriptive writing. He picked out the way in which 'an under-current of interpretation' ran through the volumes, 'a kind of Greek chorus which subtly presents the mind of the soldier' through the use of 'frequent passages in brackets quoting the actual words of men and officers'. Kipling, he claimed, 'has earned the gratitude of his country by capturing, before the memory of it dies, the very soul and spirit of her battle purpose, and he has presented a great regiment with an incomparable record of its deeds'. Buchan concluded with a tactful glance towards

John Kipling: 'The young Second Lieutenant who fell at Loos shares in a noble monument.'[6]

'The generation that I tried to write for conked out between '14 and '18,' Kipling had told Dunsterville sadly that March.[7] If Edmund Blunden was typical, the more literary survivors of that generation did not share Buchan's enthusiasm. In a review in the *Nation and Athenaeum*, Blunden declared that although Kipling had 'chronicled' the Irish Guards 'with decision and skill', he had failed to capture 'the multitudinous enigma of war atmosphere'. 'The fact is,' Blunden insisted, 'that Mr Kipling appears not perfectly to understand the pandemonium and nerve-strain of war.' To demonstrate his point, he gave some instances where what he called the 'mere languidness' or exaggeration of Kipling's language conflicted with the survivor's 'memory'. For example: 'While they watched drowsily the descent and thickening of a fresh German shell-storm, preluding fresh infantry attacks'; or 'What had been a Brigade ceased to exist – had soaked horribly into the ground.'[8] Impatient with yet another non-combatant's account – perhaps especially from someone famous for his soldier writing – Blunden was determined to put the combatant point of view. Only those who had been there in the trenches would ever know, or could hope to express, what it had really been like.

In the history itself, '1915 Loos and the First Autumn', the opening chapter of the volume about the 2nd Battalion, began by covering the events leading up to John's death. John himself was only mentioned by name in the main text on three occasions, once moving forward in an attack with the 1st Scots Guards, once as wounded and missing, and finally as simply missing. Given that John disappeared on the first afternoon the battalion went into action, there was no way that he could feature more prominently without Kipling drawing disproportionate attention to the loss of his eighteen-year-old son, and that would have been quite inconceivable. However, one can sense something of John's aching absence in small, eloquently reticent details in those few pages before Loos. He was there in the round-up of Special Reserve Officers in the 2nd Battalion who, Kipling told the reader, 'hailed from every quarter of the Empire, and represented almost every profession and state of life in it, from the schoolboy of eighteen to the lawyer of forty'. He was there as one of those (all unnamed) who on 6 August took part in the Battalion's 'first route-march, of sixteen miles, in the flat country, filled with training troops, that lies round Warley'. He was there (very much there, by Rupert Grayson's account) a week later when Kitchener 'was photographed with a group of all the Officers of the 2nd Battalion and Reserve Battalions, and expressed his belief that they would be a credit to the Guards Division then, as we know, being formed in France'. And so on throughout the build-up to 27 September 1915 and the three occasions when his father could fleetingly, legitimately, name him. It is telling that one of the few passages where Kipling openly criticised the early military conduct of the war immediately followed the last reference to his son. The way he summed up the Battalion's first day in action had a dreadful ironic flatness:

Of their officers, 2nd Lieutenant Pakenham-Law had died of wounds; 2nd Lieutenants Clifford and Kipling were missing, Captain and Adjutant the Hon T. E. Vesey, Captain Wynter, Lieutenant Stevens, and 2nd Lieutenants Sassoon [R.E., not Siegfried] and Grayson were wounded, the last being blown up by a shell. It was a fair average for the day of a debut, and taught them somewhat for their future guidance. Their Commanding Officer told them so at Adjutant's Parade, after they had been rested and cleaned on the 2nd October at Verquigneul; but it does not seem to have occurred to any one to suggest that direct Infantry attacks, after ninety-minute bombardments, on works begotten out of a generation of thought and prevision, scientifically built up by immense labour and applied science, and developed against all contingencies through nine months, are not likely to find a fortunate issue. So, while the Press was explaining to a puzzled public what a far-reaching success had been achieved, the 'greatest battle in the history of the world' simmered down to picking up the pieces on both sides of the line, and a return to autumnal trench-work, until more and heavier guns could be designed and manufactured in England. Meantime, men died.[9]

There were also other, newer deaths to be mourned in these post-war years. Theodore Roosevelt died in January 1919, Madam Balestier in March, Uncle Edward Poynter in July. Kipling was a pall-bearer at his uncle's funeral and marked Roosevelt's passing with the poem 'Great-

Heart'. Carrie wrote of her mother's death: 'We have kept very close together all these years, writing twice each week, and her death tears up all the roots I have left of my child home and life.' Carrie spoke for them both when she recorded of Georgie Burne-Jones's death early the following year: 'A great loss to us. Aunt Georgie was of our dearest – always deeply loving.'[10] When Kipling was later asked to do a memoir of the Beloved Aunt, he gave a pungent refusal. 'This here biography and "reminiscence" business that is going on nowadays is a bit too near the "Higher Cannibalism" to please me,' he told Sydney Cockerell. 'Ancestor-worship is all right but serving them up filletted or spiced, "high" (which last is very popular) has put me off.'[11] The melancholy procession continued with the passing of Colonel Feilden and his wife, their closest Burwash friends, in the next couple of years. Milner, Haggard and Aunt Louie Baldwin all died in May 1925, and cousin Phil Burne-Jones in June 1926.

Kipling's own health during this period was poor, and Carrie's diary frequently referred to him in pain or as having had a bad night. They relied most on the judgement of their friend, the surgeon Sir John Bland-Sutton, but a bevy of other doctors was also consulted. All sorts of diets and remedies were tried, but none brought any lasting relief. Kipling's condition made him quick to sympathise with others suffering from similar symptoms. When Dorothy Ponton had a gastric attack, Kipling produced a box of Jenner's absorbent lozenges. '"Try them!" he recommended. "I take them myself when my inside cupboards are disarranged."'[12] In February 1921, on Bland-Sutton's advice, he had all his teeth removed and went through further discomfort while getting used to his false set. In August 1922, after the completion of the Irish Guards history, he was in a particularly bad way and was again X-rayed. What he dreaded was the discovery of cancer – of which Aunt Aggie and Aunt Georgie had died – but the tests showed no sign of it. Ulceration of the colon was now put forward as the explanation, and he was put on another new regime: a milk diet, enemas, Epsom salts. For a time this seemed to help, but by November the pain had returned even more insistently, and Bland-Sutton decided to operate. The operation left the patient 'looking drawn and considerably aged', Haggard thought after spending a day at Bateman's the following March.[13] From then on the 'inside cupboards' continued to give trouble, particularly after eating. There were other alarms too. Kipling went down with pneumonia in the autumn of 1925 and only recovered after months of rest and nursing.

As in the past, travel or at least a change of scenery was one answer, and in the post-war years the Kiplings' life once more took on a loose yearly frame. Bateman's was always their home-base, but January or February would often be spent in Bath, enabling Carrie to take the cure. During the summer there would usually be a motor tour of northern France to visit the war cemeteries, and in the autumn another motor tour of Scotland or the West Country. In February 1920, after Aunt Georgie's funeral, the Kiplings revisited the Isle of Wight, where they had spent the summer of 1891 with Wolcott, Madam Balestier and Carrie's sister Josephine. In a darker trip down memory lane, they came back via Southsea. 'Rud takes me to see Lorne Lodge near St Bartholomew's Church and near Outram Rd', read Carrie's diary entry for 25 February, 'where he was so misused and forlorn and desperately unhappy as a child – and talks of it all with horror.'[14]

In northern France that summer they identified Chalk Pit Wood and, had they only known it, went very close to John's unmarked grave. These battlefield tours became a feature of their post-war life, partly in remembrance of John and partly in Kipling's capacity as a member of the War Graves Commission. In May 1922 when George V made a State visit to the Belgian war cemeteries, Kipling wrote a poem in anticipation of the event, 'The King's Pilgrimage'. For the ceremony itself, he acted as the King's speech-writer, a role he was to play on subsequent occasions. Sometimes on their travels the Kiplings went a little further afield. In spring 1921 they got as far as Algiers; in spring 1926 they took a villa near Monte Carlo. After Elsie's marriage in 1924, the longer trips were intermingled with shorter ones to visit her in Brussels or Madrid or Paris. Besides offering opportunities for recreation and mourning, these motor tours and pilgrimages provided Kipling with background detail for the stories he began to write once he had finished his Irish Guards history.

Elsie's marriage to Captain George Bambridge took place on 22 October 1924. Wounded several times during the war and awarded the MC, George had been one of the young officers to come to Bateman's with material for the regimental history, and had become a family friend. After leaving the Army, he joined the Diplomatic Service and was appointed Honorary Attaché at the British Embassy in Madrid. Elsie broke the news of her engagement to her parents on 23 May 1924. George 'is a nice man we have all greatly liked,' Carrie commented in her diary, 'but we don't like losing her – and I am appalled at the change it will make.' In his understated way Kipling expressed much the same consternation in a July letter to George Saintsbury: 'We've known him for five years and he is – so far as potential sons-in-law can be – very good and sound. But he is taking away Elsie. Therefore I'm not *too* happy.' Something that may have helped to reconcile the superstitious Kipling was that George's birthday fell on 27 September, the day of John's death. The London wedding, after plenty of preliminary bustle with the dress, invitations and financial settlements, went off well. Carrie noted that there were more than 1,000 at the church service at St Margaret's, Westminster, over 500 at the reception and 400 presents. Elsie, she said, looked 'quite charming in her pretty coat and hat', before adding: 'We sadly return to face an empty side to our life and for the present are too weary to meet it.' The happy couple left a few days afterwards for Brussels, where George had recently taken up a new posting. On 3 November, only ten days later, Kipling was writing wistfully to Saintsbury: 'Since the Child married, the house has become resonant and silent and enormously empty.'[15]

Both the Kiplings took Elsie's departure hard. Carrie's diary showed how much she missed her daughter's company and support in keeping up her husband's health and spirits. Some entries also hinted at earlier strains between herself and Elsie, and even a certain jealousy of the bond between father and daughter. In February 1925, after a visit to the Bambridges in Brussels, Carrie observed: 'Happy in my thoughts of a re-found Elsie who has seemed to me sometimes to be dead.' In August 1926 she tartly recorded that Kipling had sent Elsie £1,600 'which we can ill spare'.[16] Even before the marriage, Carrie, not always well herself, had been finding her role as major-domo and wife-manager of the genius an increasing struggle. Her husband's health was now a regular cause for concern, and, leaving all arrangements to her, he tended to be unaware of how much had to be done. Reliable servants were hard to find and harder to keep. There were frequently friends to be entertained – on average about 150 visitors a year. The unwelcome and the uninvited, still a significant problem, had to be fended off. And always there was what Stanley Baldwin used to call 'the business end of the Kipling fiction foundry' to be seen to.[17] Even if some of her burdens were self-imposed, Carrie had much to cope with, and it is not surprising to find her describing herself in September 1926 as having 'a tired heart'.[18] She was also capable of great kindness and thoughtfulness. Realising the pressure that Bonar Law's daughter, Isabel, was under prior to her marriage in 1920, Carrie had her down to Bateman's for a few days to relax and recuperate. Years later in Palestine, the Kiplings made a point of visiting Isabel's brother's grave in the cemetery at Gaza, Carrie sending Isabel photographs of the cemetery and Charlie's grave, and a warmly affectionate letter describing it all.

Kipling's way of filling the gap was to write to Elsie, sometimes as often as twice a week. As with his pre-war letters to his children, he did everything possible to hold her attention. He packed in descriptions of visits and visitors, village talk, gossip about friends and relations, teases at her expense, comments on the news, politics, plays, the Duchess (their Rolls-Royce), the dogs – anything, in fact, that he thought might interest her. There were requests for her to supply in return the minutiae of her new life. 'Please send us,' he begged a few months after the marriage, '– you *can never send* too much – every detail of your little entertainments – food, service and decor, and how the guests behaved.' When she did so, he was touchingly grateful: 'Your way of describing and observing things is delicious, and fills us with joy.'[19]

At times he even seemed to notice someone or something expressly in order to tell Elsie about it. A visit to the Poet Laureate, Robert Bridges, in August 1925 elicited a careful, wry pen-portrait: 'The manner of the man was, though dignified enough, quite as self-conscious as is good for anyone. The diction – low, even and smooth and, as one might put it, aggressively "Oxford".' The West Country motor tour the same autumn produced a couple of long descriptive letters, designed to make Elsie feel as though she was there too, speeding 'along utterly empty roads, in hot thick sunshine, and the Duchess shoving the miles behind her like a dream'. At Tollund on the edge of Exmoor, he told her, they went to look at an old farmhouse which had apparently once belonged to Carrie's family:

We found it, utterly lost and secluded, and in a huge hall, were welcomed by a huge, grey-bearded, heavily-paunched, asthmatic old farmer, who identified me at sight. The ceiling above us was grimy black and polished brown by the wood-smoke of ages: but it was an amazing mixture of allegorical conceits, angels (Gabriel blowing a real *trombone*, my dear, to entice an offensively dead man to rise), Latin inscriptions, and a huge pendentive in the centre. All of which he explained. There was a lovely linenfold oak screen in filthy condition, a refectory table, a young nephew (or son) with an immensely over-dressed young wife and a boy of 2½: old apple-trees, a pond, silence, green stillness and decaying stone farm buildings. They were very polite.

The following day he and Carrie reached Westward Ho! 'with my heart in my mouth over old days'. In 'blinding sun and a soft bland air', they walked on the links, basked on Pebble Ridge, and went to Clovelly ('jam *and* Devonshire cream at the bottom of the vertical street'). There followed a slow walk back up to the car. 'Strong exercise: but the sight of *hedges* of fuchsia in the combe and in front of the whitewashed houses, was alone worth the price.'[20] His love for Elsie and pride in her were everywhere apparent in the zest of these letters, in the keenness of his interest in all her doings. It came out too in letters to friends and relations, the writing immediately lifting off at the mention of her name. The beginning of his description to Haggard in February 1925 of visiting Elsie in her new home in Brussels was typical: 'The young couple were giving a fancy Ball (1850 epoch) and, at the same time, were on the edge of 'flu. The ball was a great success; particularly as they introduced the esurient Belgae to sausage and mash *and* beer at 3-a.m.! Then they devoted 'emselves to their colds—.'[21]

Elsie was not the only 'child' to move on around this time. In the immediate post-war years the Kiplings had come to think of various young relations and friends as surrogate children. 'We all love to have him and deplore his leaving,' Carrie observed after a short stay by Ollie Baldwin in November 1919. 'A hint of a son about the house always crosses with his visits.'[22] They were equally devoted to his sister Lorna, with whom they travelled round northern France in 1921 and whom Kipling described to Haggard as 'practically, my child . . . since her baby-dom'.[23] To a lesser extent the same was true of Crom Price's children, Teddy and Dorothy, whom Kipling had helped to support and always took a quasi-parental interest in. Naturally these ties loosened in time as Teddy went to India and Lorna Baldwin married. Only in one case was there a permanent rift – with Ollie, on political grounds, when he became a Labour MP in 1929.

Kipling's post-war friends tended to be the tried and true-blue like Dunsterville, Gwynne and Haggard. However, he did establish some newer friendships. Like many others, he had thrilled to stories of T E Lawrence's heroic exploits in the desert and made a point of meeting him. On 2 November 1918, just after a first encounter, he was telling Dunsterville all about it: 'The Arabian Nights are tame and unconvincing beside his adventures: and having made his Kings he is now going back to teach history at Magdalen College, Oxford!'[24] He was soon in correspondence with Lawrence himself, trying unsuccessfully to invite him to Bateman's, commiserating with him over disappointed plans ('we are all sitting in the middle of wrecked hope and broken dreams'), and encouraging him to keep going: 'You will not go out of the game – except for the necessary minute to step aside and vomit. You are young, and the bulk of the men now in charge are "old, cold and of intolerable entrails" and a lot of 'em will be dropping out soon.'[25] When, a few years later, Lawrence was circulating the manuscript of The Seven Pillars of Wisdom among friends, Kipling was an early reader – though according to Sassoon, who had it from E M Forster, he 'disapproved strongly'.[26]

In the same letter to Dunsterville in which he enthused about meeting Lawrence, Kipling observed: 'We in England at present are sitting stupefied like children at a cinema, among the wrecks of Empires.'[27] The film he found himself, or told himself, he was watching over the next few years was less an epic than a low-grade political thriller, as Britain and Europe continued to suffer from serious unrest. Kipling instinctively still blamed the Germans abroad and Labour and the Liberals at home, to which roll of honour he now added the Bolsheviks and the Jews. Sometimes he was able to squeeze some of these elements together to produce a composite enemy wax-doll, as in a letter in November 1919 about the Germans to his French friend André Chevrillon:

Do you notice how their insane psychology attempts to infect the Universe? There is one Einstein, nominally a Swiss, certainly a

Hebrew, who (the thing is so inevitable that it makes one laugh) comes forward, scientifically to show that, under certain conditions Space itself is warped and the instruments that measure it are warped also . . . the phrase that sticks in my mind is that 'Space is warped'. When you come to reflect on a race that made the world Hell, you see how just and right it is they should decide that space *is* warped, and should make their own souls the measure of all Infinity . . . Einstein's pronouncement is only another little contribution to assisting the world towards flux and disintegration.[28]

It was at this juncture that Gwynne, still editor of the *Morning Post*, was sent a typescript of the infamous *Protocols of the Elders of Zion*, a document purporting to contain Jewish plans to destabilise Christian civilisation through control of the financial markets, as a step towards world domination. Gwynne excitedly sent copies to various right-wing friends, including Kipling, and to the *Post*'s proprietor Lady Bathurst. Gwynne himself was willing, indeed eager, to accept the authenticity of the *Protocols*, and over the next few months he and some like-minded hacks knocked out a series of articles heavily influenced by them. Run in the *Post* in July 1920, they were collected the following August in *The Cause of World Unrest*. The *Protocols* too were published for the first time that year in England, under the restrained title *The Jewish Peril*.

A year later the real source of the *Protocols* was exposed by Philip Graves in *The Times*. Unpicking a trail as intricate as any spy story, he showed conclusively that they had been largely plagiarised from *Dialogues aux Enfers entre Machiavel et Montesquieu, ou la Politique de Machiavel au XIX. Siècle. Par un Contemporain* – an anti-Napoleon III tract written by a Paris lawyer called Maurice Joly and published anonymously in Geneva in 1865. Around 1901, these 'Geneva Dialogues' had been loosely paraphrased into Russian and adapted, probably at the instigation of the Okhrana organisation (State police) for the purposes of anti-Jewish and anti-Liberal propaganda. The *Protocols of the Elders of Zion*, as this paraphrased version was known, were published in 1905 by Professor Sergei Nilus, who naïvely believed them to be genuine. Right-wing organisations like the Okhrana then seem to have used Nilus's book during the Russian Revolution of 1905 to blame social ills and unrest on a worldwide Jewish conspiracy. The *Protocols* resurfaced again in the wake of the

Russian Revolution of 1917 and in a climate of enormous European upheaval and disintegration were widely debated and translated, before Gwynne and others took them up in England.

In fact, and perhaps somewhat surprisingly, Kipling was not one of these. His view, he told Gwynne, was that the *Protocols* were 'some sort of fake . . . *not* in any way a serious programme prepared before the campaign'.[29] However, as his reaction to the 'Old Volunteer' hoax had underlined, he too was extremely susceptible to conspiracy theories, so that – despite seeing through the *Protocols* – he still desperately wanted to believe that some sort of Jewish world plot ('the campaign') did exist. This paranoid delusion came across unequivocally in Haggard's diary entry in December 1919: 'Kipling . . . is of opinion that we owe all our Russian troubles, and many others, to the machinations of the Jews.'[30] Before the war, Kipling had not on the whole (despite 'Gehazi') been anti-Semitic.[31] But by summer 1923 he was encouraging Haggard to write a trilogy about the Wandering Jew, who would turn out to have been responsible for most of Europe's troubles over the past 2,000 years; and one can increasingly see anti-Semitic elements beginning to enter into his own work.

If Kipling wanted to blame things on the Jews (and the Germans and what was left of the Liberals), Haggard preferred the trade unions and the Bolsheviks, and he was soon urging Kipling to help him form an anti-Bolshevik society. In January 1920, the editor of *The Times*, Wickham Steed, asked Haggard to be President of a council dedicated to fighting Bolshevism in England – an organisation that could count on support from the various Churches and even on unofficial Government backing. The upshot was a letter in *The Times* on 3 March, above Haggard's, Kipling's and other signatures, proclaiming the formation of the Liberty League in order to 'combat the advance of Bolshevism in the United Kingdom and throughout the Empire'. *The Times* gave the League its unqualified endorsement, and next day it ran a substantial news story, 'The Bolshevist Peril'.

The Liberty League never really got off the ground. The day after its formal launch in *The Times*, the new 'League among Leagues' was thoroughly sent up by G G in the *Daily Herald*'s 'Way of the World' column. After drawing attention to some of the absurdities of the letter, G G did for the drum-beating duo in some excellent light verse:

Two Hearts that Beat as One . . .

'Every Bolsh is a blackguard,'
Said Kipling to Haggard.
   – 'And given to tippling,'
Said Haggard to Kipling.

'And a blooming outsider,'
Said Rudyard to Rider.
   – 'Their domain is blood-yard,'
Said Rider to Rudyard.

'That's just what I say,'
Said the author of 'They'.
   – 'I agree; I agree,'
Said the author of 'She'.[32]

From there on, it was fiasco all the way. Haggard did become President, but within a few weeks one of the other founders, Lieutenant-Colonel Maitland Edwards, ran off with the subs, and the League was wound up not long afterwards.

Early that summer, while he was still embroiled with the Liberty League, Kipling had a visit from Clare Sheridan, the daughter of an old English friend, the financial adventurer Moreton Frewen.[33] She had a roving commission from the New York *World* to write up post-war Europe in a series of articles, and she made use of family contacts to gain access to notables like Kipling and Winston Churchill. The visit to Bateman's went well. Kipling sailed a model ship on the pond with her son, Dick, and sat on the lawn chatting to her daughter Margaret. Sheridan, joining in, steered the conversation towards the war, and Kipling launched into a predictable tirade – 'that the war had not been fought to a finish, that justice had not been done, that Germany had not been made to pay, and the possibility of future war had not been eradicated'. America, he insisted, had made the Allies agree to peace too early and had pulled out on Armistice Day without properly finishing the job. As he spoke, Sheridan would record in due course, he 'let loose the whole force of his relentless, imperialistic, pro-French bitterness, a bitterness engendered perhaps in no small measure by the loss of a beloved and only son'. America, he remarked, had entered the war 'two years, seven months and four days too late' and had grown rich through huge war loans made to England and the Allies. But, he claimed defiantly: 'They have got the gold of the world, but we have saved our souls!'[34]

Sheridan was struck by his combination of sadness and anger, as 'eyes of sorrow looked out ever so proudly from beneath the fiercest tangle of bushy eyebrows'. He strongly advised her to go to France, where she would 'see the great open wound' and the people 'living anywhere, everywhere, in holes in the ground, but living – working'. Bolshevism, he told her, making another of his composite enemy wax-dolls, 'was the result of German propaganda. Ireland was the work of German propaganda. The anti-French sentiment here and in the United States was the result of German propaganda.' Eventually, inevitably, Kipling brought the conversation back to 'the all-absorbing American topic' and repeated another of his pet theories that 'America – the real America – died in 1860', in other words with the Civil War. On Europe his parting shot was: 'Go and see it all for yourself . . . But – begin with France.'[35]

When the New York World published all this and more two years later in September 1922, it made international news. Kipling had impeached the United States's war record. He had impugned its national identity. He had damaged relations between Britain and America. The accusations flew, and the headline writers had a field-day. Kipling himself was shocked. A two-year-old conversation – which he had thought, naïvely but genuinely, was a private chat with an old family friend – had reappeared as a formal newspaper interview. However, there was little he could do except issue a blanket denial in The Times: 'I did not give Mrs Clare Sheridan an interview, and did not say the things I have seen ascribed to me.'[36] The Daily Chronicle summed up the débâcle cruelly but appositely: 'As a man of letters Mr Rudyard Kipling is one of our national glories. As a politician he simply does not count.[37]

The new generation of writers did not even think him a national glory. Rather, according to T S Eliot in the Athenaeum in May 1919, Kipling was 'a laureate without laurels', 'one of the Minor Prophets' and 'very nearly a great writer'. In fact, Eliot's review of The Years Between was an unusually perceptive attempt to read Kipling – his main argument being that Kipling was the heir of Swinburne, both poets producing what he called a 'poetry of oratory' and persuading 'not by reason, but by emphatic sound'. However, as Eliot acknowledged, that was not how Kipling was normally treated in serious literary circles. There, he was not even 'anathema'; he was 'merely not discussed'.[38]

Virginia Woolf, reviewing Kipling's next publication (*Letters of Travel 1892–1913*) in July 1920, found an ingenious way of simultaneously praising and dismissing him. She characterised his writing as like the 'notes' of a brilliant adolescent, where 'every word . . . has been matched with the object with such amazing skill' that, when they were all 'stitched' together in a book, they became 'literally, unreadable'. Warming to her subject, she then wrote off Kipling's 'passion' for the Empire as the preoccupation of a noisy toddler and finished by doubting whether his stilted Empire types, or indeed the Empire itself, actually existed outside his work: 'Whether grown-up people really play this game, or whether, as we suspect, Mr Kipling makes up the whole British Empire to amuse the solitude of his nursery, the result is curiously sterile and depressing.'[39]

The following year, Beerbohm dismissed him more wittily and more brutally in a cartoon called 'On the Shelf' in which a large fat John Bullish man gazed up at the small, solitary Buddha-like figure of Kipling, squatting on a high shelf like an ornament. And towards the end of the decade, in a piece included in *Scrutinies* (a collection of essays dedicated to 'killing off' the generation of Bennett, Shaw and Wells), Robert Graves stung with a breezy waspishness:

Kipling is a great man in the most traditional sense, the Lloyd-George-Northcliffe sense; he is usual, traditional, the subject for mass-admiration, and no more to be argued away than the design on a postage stamp. The previous superior critics found that out long ago. There is no point in parodying him; you can't outdo him. There is no point in suggesting that he is no real poet; that has been a popular commonplace since 1886. There is no point in suggesting that he cannot write prose: he can, like any Frenchman. It is definitely untrue to say that he is unreadable; a set of Kipling has a certain sinister fascination for the reader, particularly the reader recovering from influenza. Like bound volumes of *Punch*; you go over them again and again. And finally, he is the literary aspect of the British Empire, the only possible literary aspect of a complex organisation to which even the superior critics and the most superior critics unaccountably and inevitably belong.[40]

Tellingly, *Scrutinies* contained no similar despatch of Hardy. He was pre-eminently the older literary figure whom the post-war generation sought out and paid homage to; Woolf, Graves, Sassoon and others left memorable accounts of their visits to the 'famous Dorchester magician' at Max Gate.[41] Apart from being politically more congenial than Kipling, Hardy (born in 1840) was a survivor from a much earlier period. He was, in effect, a literary grandfather, a much less threatening relationship for younger writers, particularly those, like Woolf and Sassoon, who had started to make their reputations during the war.

Kipling's contact with this new literary generation was fairly minimal, certainly with the Bloomsbury-Garsington set. When he and Carrie met Lytton Strachey in June 1923, she commented laconically in her diary that he was 'a new person to us'. In fact, Strachey would not have been new to Kipling as a writer. He had read *Eminent Victorians* when it came out in 1918 and predictably disapproved. ('It seems to me downright wicked in its heart,' he told C R L Fletcher.) But he was sufficiently interested or curious to read *Queen Victoria* and in his own way showed a keen appreciation of Strachey's special qualities as a biographer. 'Yes – isn't Strachey's Victoria felinely malignant,' he observed to Elsie in April 1925, 'but his life of Edward VII as P. of W. gives one a real insight into the terrific domination of that resolute little piece of half German goods. Why Edward stayed on the rails, even occasionally, wholly beats me.'[42]

The odd literary accolade that did come Kipling's way tended to be from other 'non-serious' writers like A A Milne. On the publication of *When We Were Very Young* in 1924, Kipling wrote Milne a highly appreciative letter; to which Milne replied: 'If you can remember what you once said to Tennyson you will know what your letter makes me want to say to you. I am proud that you like the verses.' When Tennyson had praised 'The English Flag', Kipling had written back: 'When a private is praised by his General he does not presume to thank him, but fights all the better afterwards.'[43]

Indeed, in so far as Kipling was sought out by the younger literary generation at all, it was by teenage hopefuls like Maurice Cranston (a future professor of political thought) and Rupert Croft-Cooke (a voluminous autobiographer). Cranston, as a precocious fourteen-year-old, got himself an invitation to Bateman's with a female relation. He would recall an outdoor Kipling and an indoor Kipling. Walking with his young visitor in the garden, Kipling was easy and expansive. Learning that Cranston wanted to be an author, he reminisced freely about his own early work and fame, though there was a kind of posthumous undertow to the reminiscences, 'rather as an unsuccessful and unhappy man might relate the biography of a successful and happy brother lately dead'. Back inside the house, in the drawing-room with the ladies, Kipling at once withdrew into a 'silent simulation of nonentity'.[44]

The adolescent Croft-Cooke secured his invitation on the strength of some Sussex poems he had sent Kipling. On the fateful day, 10 October 1922, he turned up rather nervous on his 'stuttering motor-cycle'. Kipling, with 'his vast bushy eyebrows greying, his thick glasses and his bald pate' and 'his little legs in plus-fours', seemed a combination of father-figure and imp, and instantly charmed away his young visitor's diffidence. At first there was chat about cars, then tea with Carrie, 'a gentle motherly person, with dignity but without condescension', and Elsie, 'cheerful, hungry and in tweeds'. After tea ('home-made blackberry jam' and 'piles of home-made cakes'), Croft-Cooke was taken up to the study. Kipling, 'all energy and smiles', talked to him about past writers like 'a fellow adolescent', 'as though after a study tea at school we were smoking illicit cigarettes over a discussion of "favourite authors".' Of Wilde, Kipling remarked: 'No, I've never cared for his work. Too scented.' Of Bunyan: 'Go home and read him. Read the *Pilgrim's Progress* half a dozen times before you try to write prose.' Kipling also gave the would-be writer a couple of invaluable tips:

'Never look over your shoulder at the other man. Paddle your own canoe and don't worry about anyone passing you. Keep going in your own time. If you're going to do anything you'll do it; if not, watching others succeed only embitters failure. And failure in writing shouldn't be bitter.

'You'll get a lot of criticism written and spoken, some of it honest, some not, some careful, a good deal thoughtless. But remember this. You and only you who are being criticised will know what is valuable, what is helpful, whether it is praise or blame. Every now and then someone will say a thing which stops you in your tracks. "He's right", you'll say, and be the better for it.'[45]

This is the Kipling – enthusiastic, sympathetic, fun – whom one encounters in the reminiscences of other young friends of the time. Stanley Baldwin's younger son, Arthur, recalled how during Christmas 1921 at the Baldwin home, Astley Hall, they played 'games like "Slosh" and "Pots and Cannons", exchanging the while quips in an affectedly laborious dog-French, at which Kipling was, of course, particularly ingenious'. The adults also participated in a form of 'Consequences': 'You have to write a passage, fold the paper over leaving one or two words visible, then pass it on to your neighbour to continue. Kipling's opening lines in one of these rounds were masterly. After fifty years I can still quote them: "It's a perfect Hell of a night", pouted the Duchess, unfastening her gaiters.' Arthur's literary bonus, while still a boy at Eton, was to receive a crash-course in the English classics. This comprised a dozen of Kipling's favourites, with a snappy letter of personal recommendation:

> *Hazlitt* isn't as out of date as he looks. He makes one take notice. *Crashaw* is for words and emotions. *Swift* is purely for style. *Coleridge* is an out-of-the-way bird with a habit of approaching the ordinary at extraordinary angles. M. *Aurelius* is the heavy lead and awful stodge in most places but about $\frac{1}{10}$ percent of him goes. *Donne* may or may not catch hold of you. Anyhow, keep him for a bit and see if he doesn't affect you later. Anyway, he will teach you words and tropes and such things . . .[46]

Another of Kipling's surrogate sons, Rupert Grayson, who visited Bateman's often, would offer a vividly affectionate snapshot:

> R.K. was one of the kindest men I have ever known, and quite the most natural. He always addressed his personal friends as: 'Old Man,' and when he shook hands he offered his hand with the palm upwards – parallel to the sky. Invariably he smoked cherry-wood pipes, burning out four or five a month. He liked odd walking-sticks, and kept a strange assortment by the window-door of the lounge leading to the ornamental lake.[47]

Grayson also painted an appreciative portrait of the Kiplings together – how close they were, Carrie's 'most infectious laugh', and how 'at table they passed the conversation from one to the other like a ball in a juggler's act'. Kipling's voice, he added, 'was always soft, but when he wished to impress you it would drop to a stage-whisper'; while his talk was 'a spicy mixture of biblical invocation and barrack-room slang'. Grayson particularly remembered his quick-wittedness on the occasion of an 'American woman complimenting him on his wide vocabulary. "Mr Kipling," she said, "has it ever occurred to you that the only word in the English language where s-u is pronounced as s-h-u is the word sugar?" "Sure," he said, smiling.'[48]

Or take Thelma Cazalet, whose parents lived not far away, and who became something of a substitute daughter after Elsie's departure. She too recalled how charmingly disconcerting Kipling could be. After meeting the noted mimic and impersonator Ruth Draper, Kipling asked Thelma whom she would like to 'personate'. When she asked him to go first, he replied that he would like to be Buddha, 'because he has attained what he called supreme and absolute enlightenment on all the realities of life'. On Thelma asking for 'a more possible attainment', he 'grinned, after the model of Beetle in *Stalky & Co.*, and said, "Well, what about a better Rudyard Kipling?!!"' He also showed her a more emotional side than he was usually prepared to reveal to male friends. One day, leaving Bateman's, she happened to exclaim: 'How you must love your lovely home!' To which Kipling replied with tears in his eyes: 'I used to think I could not live anywhere else. But now there are no more laughing voices and running footsteps, so I don't care where I live; nothing really matters now.' With Thelma gripping his hand in sympathy, he added 'with something like a twinkle, "If I do retire some day to a boarding-house, you promise to come and see me, won't you?"'[49]

With other chance-met acquaintances, the results were hit and miss. Lady Gregory, lunching with him in the summer of 1920, found Kipling 'friendly and unaffected'.[50] The future King Faisal of Iraq, encountering him not long afterwards, was less impressed. After being questioned for ten minutes about the size, number, origin and significance of camel brands in the Hejaz, he looked over Kipling's shoulder and asked a friend in Arabic: 'Does this man take me for a camel dealer?'[51] When a couple of years later Beverley Nichols realised that he was going to be at lunch with

Kipling, he was somewhat apprehensive. At Oxford in 1920 he had, as an *enfant terrible* of English letters, claimed in the *Morning Post* that it was the 'white-hot bitterness' of Sassoon's poems – and not 'the flamboyant insolence of Rudyard Kipling' or the sonnets of Rupert Brooke – that expressed what the young thought of the war. At the lunch Kipling introduced himself straight away with the words: 'You're the young man who was so rude to me in the *Morning Post*, aren't you?' Nichols admitted that he was and started to apologise. ' "Sorry? What for?" said Kipling. "I used to be much ruder to people when I was your age . . . Besides," said Kipling, "that was a jolly good phrase – flamboyant insolence – I liked it." '[52]

One thinks of Kipling as always hitting it off with children, but this was not always the case. Enid Bagnold, author of *National Velvet* and wife of Sir Roderick Jones of Reuters, saw a good deal of the Kiplings in the post-war years. She recalled various visits with her children to Bateman's, where Kipling kept up 'a charade at all times' and had 'a special one for boys'. Over one lunch he tried out his routine on eight-year-old Timothy, who had recently gone to prep school at Summerfields. 'Do they give you extra chu?' Kipling quizzed him:

> Timothy went scarlet. He had no idea what was asked. We were so few at such a large table that I couldn't whisper, 'prep'. Kipling said it again with the same result and the subject dropped. After lunch he made Timothy fire a revolver and the thing kicked.

Bagnold's view, not unlike that of Cranston, was that he used his 'Kipling-talk' as a defence mechanism and that there was an almost complete split between his 'marvellous gift' and his blimpish public self. She recalled a luncheon party at Lady Colefax's, during which Kipling had begun to tell her a story ('Once there was a man who had a baby'), when they were interrupted by their hostess, and the 'marvellous gift' was instantly switched off. Bagnold thought him 'heroic and stoic' – indeed, wondered whether he was 'a quite unconscious homosexual'. Either way, he was condemned to 'plough through a dull second part of his life to its end with the ghost of that enormous cake of success he had eaten too young'.[53]

It was after another luncheon at Lady Colefax's in January 1930 that Harold Nicolson would offer the definitive description of the eyebrows.

'Rudyard Kipling's eyebrows are really very odd indeed!' he commented. 'They curl up black and furious like the moustache of a Neapolitan tenor.'[54] The eyebrows were especially prominent in a photograph of Kipling taken after his installation as Rector of St Andrew's University in 1923. He stood bare-headed and smiling, right hand raised in salutation. The appointment was one traditionally made by the students themselves and suggests that, outside literary circles, Kipling still retained a certain ground-swell of popularity. He and Carrie received a rapturous welcome from the students on their arrival on 9 October, and two days later after opening the Students' Union she mentioned 800 handshakes. In between, on the 10th, he gave his Rectorial address on 'Independence', a nicely judged blend of the entertaining and the pragmatic. Pushing a favourite theme, he urged on his young audience the absolute importance of owning yourself, since 'yourself is the only person you can by no possibility get away from in this life, and, it may be, in another'.[55]

As before the war, the academic honours piled up in inverse proportion to his literary standing in England: honorary degrees from the Sorbonne and the Universities of Edinburgh and Strasbourg in the early 1920s, and an honorary fellowship from Magdalene College, Cambridge, in 1932. One honour that he was not at all keen on was the imminent prospect of a Kipling Society. This was something, he told Dunsterville in December 1922, he could not actually prevent, but he did not want. When the society was eventually established in 1927, he burst out to the first President, Dunsterville himself:

> As to your dam [sic] Society – how would *you* like to be turned into an anatomical specimen, before you were dead, and shown upon a table once a quarter? It makes me feel naked as well as ridiculous . . . The whole thing is unutterably repugnant . . .[56]

In his other official capacities, as a member of the War Graves Commission or a trustee of the Rhodes estate, as Vice-President of the London Library or Vice-President of the Society for the Prevention of Venereal Disease, one imagines him polite and conscientious, but very much 'on duty'. Away from Bateman's or the company of close friends, where he was likeliest to be found in relaxed mood was at one of his several clubs. His favourite was the Beefsteak. The company was varied, the talk uninhibited, and there was always a chance of being plunged by 'some one or something' into 'what you might call a general "rag," each man's tongue guarding his own head'.[57] In such surroundings, Kipling would unwind and be the most engaging of company.

After a lunch at the very end of the war, David Lindsay, twenty-seventh Earl of Crawford and tenth Earl of Balcarres, made a long note of Kipling's conversation. He had apparently been 'ruminating over two great subjects: one the American débâcle, the other Col. Lawrence who has fought over Allenby's flank from Aden to Aleppo', and was wondering how best to write them up: as fact or fiction. Kipling also related how he would 'sit quietly in No.2 Buffet, Charing Cross Station, and listen to the soldiers talking – quick oblique elliptical references to the war, to its facts and fictions, its tragedies and comedies – to all the amazing facts of prowess artlessly told by the actors'.[58] Years later, Hugh Walpole recorded spending 'a wonderful morning with old Kipling in the Athenaeum'. *Debits and Credits* had recently appeared, and Kipling 'was sitting surrounded by reviews of his new book, beaming like a baby'.[59]

Debits and Credits, published on 15 September 1926, was Kipling's first adult volume of stories for nine years, although in between he had published *Land and Sea Tales for Scouts and Guides* in 1923, a rag-bag of previously uncollected items. The new book's backbone was eleven major stories written over the previous three years – a considerable feat, given his state of mind and health. However, although the author might have been 'beaming', the English reviews were mainly anodyne: the piece in the *Nation* ('Chiefly Debits') was unusual in its outright hostility. For more alert – and appreciative – reviews he had to look to the States. In the *Saturday Review of Literature*, Christopher Morley made much of the poems interleaved between the stories, especially four new additions to the imaginary Fifth Book of Horace's Odes, and called attention to Kipling's literariness, dubbing him 'the subtlest of highbrows'.[60] A notably perceptive review was by the young Edmund Wilson, associate editor of *New Republic*. Although complaining of the continuing simplicity and banality of Kipling's ideas, Wilson argued that it was Kipling who had invented 'the whole genre of vernacular stories . . . in which we are made to see some comedy or tragedy through the half-obscuring veil of the special slang and technical vocabulary of the person who is telling it'. He also praised Kipling's ventriloquism, what Wilson called his 'unrivalled collection of . . . marvellous language exhibits: the kitchen chatter of a Sussex cook, the eloquence of a Middle Western realtor and several varieties of war slang'. 'I cannot believe,' he daringly concluded, 'that James Joyce . . . would ever have written the Cyclops chapter of *Ulysses*, if he had never read Kipling'.[61]

Wilson, the first to spot Kipling's modernist affiliations and influence, might also have made a connection between *Debits and Credits* and Eliot's *The Waste Land*, that other archetypal modernist text, published the same year as *Ulysses*. Among other quintessentially modernist features, he could have pointed to the intense literary self-consciousness of Kipling's collection, as reflected in the constant allusions to earlier writers, but also in the subversive games that were played. Official literature (Jane Austen, Swinburne, Shakespeare) was regularly placed in conventionally unliterary contexts (the officers' mess, the Navy, the trenches, school) and mixed up with unofficial literature (*Uncle Remus*, limericks, hymns), so that there were no firm boundaries between high culture and low culture, no fixed categories. There was an equally self-conscious employment of links and cross-references between different parts of the work. As with *The Waste Land*, these connections could be subtly unobtrusive, a matter of a repeated detail or phrase (the English as the lost tribes of Israel in 'Sea Constables', picked up in 'The Propagation of Knowledge'). They could, more portentously, involve mythic patterning: the collection opened with 'The Enemies to Each Other', a version of Genesis and the Fall, and ended with 'The Gardener', whose final phrase, 'supposing him to be the gardener', evoked the possibility of redemption and the Resurrection.

Again, as with Eliot's poem, there was continual parody and pastiche of past writers. Enjoyable as a virtuoso performance in itself, this also served a double function – of giving the illusion of collapsing the distance between present and past, so that the two appeared contemporaneous, while at the same time reinforcing the sense that everything was running down and fragmenting – that after the war all a writer could do was recycle the past. Moreover, again thoroughly modernist, textual self-reference occurred in some form or other in most of the stories. 'Somehow I had tuned myself to listen-in to tales of other things,' reflected the narrator in 'The Prophet and the Country'. Or, as Anthony remarked to the shell-shocked Humberstall in 'The Janeites': 'An' did you find out what *Tilniz* meant? I'm always huntin' after the meanin' of things meself.'[62] The sustained self-referentiality was intensified by the extent to which, quite apart from including two new Stalky stories, Kipling deliberately alluded to his own previous work. 'A Madonna of the Trenches' contained an infinitely richer reworking of the same revenant motif he had employed nearly forty years before in 'By Word of Mouth'. More obliquely, the phrase 'thrown away' at the beginning of 'The Gardener' glanced back at 'Thrown Away', another early Indian story. (In 'The Gardener', the phrase was used apparently casually of Helen's dead brother George, a former Inspector of Indian Police.) The connection was, in fact, anything but arbitrary, since both stories dealt with the covering up of socially unacceptable facts (suicide and illegitimacy).

The argument for a modernist reading of *Debits and Credits* (or more widely of Kipling) would not of course be based on the modernists' influence on him, but on his influence on them. Kipling would then be cast as the literary father who could not or must not be acknowledged, much as Wordsworth in the 'Preface' to the *Lyrical Ballads* went out of his way to deny Gray as a poetic parent. The closest that one can demonstrate Kipling engaging with the modernists in the 1920s was his reading of Strachey – though in 1935 he did question an American visitor, Arthur Gordon, 'almost sharply' about T S Eliot, Gertrude Stein and E E Cummings. On Gordon saying that they were good, Kipling asked him to recite some of their lines. When he was unable to, Kipling laughed and said: 'You see, that's the trouble with verse that doesn't rhyme. But let's not be too harsh where poets are concerned. They have to live in no-man's-land, halfway between dreams and reality.'[63] The obvious point of the anecdote was Kipling's good-humoured assertion of his old-fashionedness; although if he *had* read some Eliot, it is not inconceivable that his last sentence was a half-memory of 'The Hollow Men'.

There is nothing inherently odd about offering a modernist reading of Kipling. Addressing the Royal Society of Literature on 7 July 1926, shortly before the publication of *Debits and Credits*, he made at least one statement that was to become a modernist truism: 'The true nature and intention . . . of a writer's work does not lie within his own knowledge.'[64] This anticipated by some years Eliot's famous pronouncement that 'what a poem means is as much what it means to others as what it means to the author'.[65] Kipling's 1926 speech also gave the sixty-year-old writer the opportunity to reassess the debits and credits of his own literary career. 'In every age some men gain temporary favour because they happen to have met a temporary need of their age,' he wryly observed.[66] This was exactly the point that Eliot would be making five years later about himself: 'When I wrote a poem called *The Waste Land* some of the more approving critics said that I had expressed the "disillusionment of a generation", which is nonsense. I may have expressed for them their illusion of being disillusioned, but that did not form part of my intention.'[67]

There was also an important personal element running through *Debits and Credits*. The volume started with a covert allusion to Elsie and her marriage, while John's death was obliquely alluded to in no fewer than five stories. These included 'The Eye of Allah', the story of the destruction by the Church of a primitive microscope, in which the central character was an illuminator of manuscripts, John of Burgos. John, who brought the microscope back to England from Spain, revolutionised his work through the magnified shapes that the instrument revealed to him. As an artistic pioneer, he was Kipling's surrogate in the story. His mistress having died in childbirth, John was shown transmuting his desolation into the figure of the Magdalene for his 'Great Luke'. The need for the artist to transform personal suffering into art, and the partial remedy that this afforded, were two of the many strands underlying this highly complex story. In a tight-lipped exchange, John confided his loss to Lady Anne, the Abbot's ailing mistress:

'I left all in the hands of God.'
  'Ah me! How long since?'
  'Four months less eleven days.'
  'Were you – with her?'
  'In my arms. Childbed.'
  'And?'
  'The boy too. There is nothing now.'
Anne of Norton caught her breath.
  'I think you'll be glad of that,' she said after a while.
  'Give me time, and maybe I'll compass it. But not now.'
  'You have your handiwork and your art, and – John – remember there's no jealousy in the grave.'

'Ye-es! I have my Art, and Heaven knows I'm jealous of none.'

The parallel with Kipling's own situation is obvious enough. Not quite so transparent, but equally loaded with association, was the moment a little later when John gave Brother Martin some copying to do and told him to take his time. 'My Magdalene has to come off my heart first,' the artist explained, referring both to his dead mistress as his personal Magdalene and to the Magdalene she would become in his art.[68] The comment also anticipated the depiction of Helen Turrell as a modern Magdalene in the volume's next and concluding story, 'The Gardener'; she too, like John of Burgos and Kipling, had a son who would not 'come off' her heart.

Kipling had never been able to grieve openly for the loss of his son and had felt obliged in public to maintain a properly stoical front. Now, to write a story about a woman who was also unable to grieve openly and had to keep up appearances was the nearest he could come (in the controlling metaphor of 'The Burden', the accompanying poem) to 'rolling away the stone' and assuaging his innermost feelings. In the French cemetery, surrounded by the sea of black crosses, looking hopelessly for her 'nephew' Michael's grave, the gardener's words 'I will show you where your son lies' brought Helen a moment of release from her years of silent pretence.[69] This pretence was a necessary lie, which society and her own sense of propriety had required her to live out, though the reader was clearly expected to sympathise with the emotional cost and suffering involved. Helen was rewarded for her stoicism by having the word she could not say spoken for her and by being permitted to find the grave, a consolation denied to Kipling himself. For him, the act of creating in Helen's situation an 'objective correlative' for his own stoically endured suffering, and the final admission of the crucial word 'son', had to be vicarious compensation enough.

Debits and Credits began with Elsie and the 'debit and credit' of her marriage; it closed with John and the 'debit and credit' of his death. Kipling's decision to end the volume with 'The Gardener', his ultimate war story, turned the collection into his private memorial to John, the fictional counterpart of *The Irish Guards in the Great War*.

20

Pallbearers

'A train has to stop at some station or other,' Kipling remarked to a friend a few weeks before his death. 'I only wish,' he added sadly, 'it wasn't such an ugly and lonesome place, don't you?'[1] But before reaching that last desolate stretch of the track there had been bright patches, bursts of creativity, even a few final triumphs.

The Kiplings' yearly pattern of travelling continued: a spell in Bath perhaps; always a winter–spring trip to somewhere warm, usually driving back through France; an autumn motor tour to Scotland or the Midlands; and in between short jaunts to Paris. In 1927 they went to Brazil, a glimpse of a new world, which Kipling wrote up enthusiastically for the *Morning Post*. In 1929 and 1931 it was Egypt and Palestine, visiting war cemeteries; 1930 the West Indies; 1932 and for the next three years the south of France, Monte Carlo and Cannes. While novelty sometimes prompted the location, health was always the main issue. And not simply Kipling's, for Carrie too was increasingly unwell, diagnosed as diabetic in 1928 and having to be hospitalised for a time in Bermuda in 1930.

For Kipling the acute internal pain, the specialists, the diets, the fear of cancer persisted. One of the less obvious benefits of the Brazilian trip, he told Stanley Baldwin, 'was a steady, unremitting sweat for five weeks in a tropical climate where there is neither fever nor sunstroke! Practically Bath treatment while you sat still with a few clothes on.'[2] In 1928 he was

367

told (not for the first time) to stop smoking, but having been a heavy user of pipes, cigars and cigarettes all his life, he could not give up. The dull diets he did stick to, compensating by feeding his characters well, while he made do with boiled and mashed chicken and fish. When at last, in May 1933, two Paris doctors correctly diagnosed his problem as a duodenal ulcer, it was considered too risky to put him through the required operation.

Not surprisingly, he struck many – including his publisher Harold Macmillan – as 'a somewhat sad figure' who had 'retired from the world'.[3] On occasions he could be morose. Dean Inge, sitting next to him at the Lord Mayor's Banquet in 1929, a few months after Labour had won the election, found Kipling 'quite the most pessimistic Tory I have ever met. He is convinced that the middle-class will be skinned alive by the Socialists, and that the Government has made irreparable mistakes in India, Egypt and elsewhere.'[4] If Inge, known as 'the gloomy dean', could find Kipling pessimistic, there must have been times when he was very depressing indeed. Predictably, like many English Tories in these years, he developed an enthusiasm for Mussolini, telling Gwynne in April 1926 that 'Mussolini rides the [Bolshevik] storm quite serenely' and Elsie, a couple of years later, that 'M. has taught his people quiet, cleanliness *and* punctuality.'[5]

Yet he could still be an engaging companion as Harold Nicolson discovered, lunching with him only weeks after the doom-mongering at the Lord Mayor's Banquet. Kipling entertained the table with the story of how he had once been on a yacht with Theodore Roosevelt, Henry Cabot Lodge and others, and they had been making fun of people who carried mascots, 'until someone suggested that they should all empty their pockets on the table. It was found that all of them possessed some object, a bit of stick, a knife, or something, which they would hate to lose and always carried with them.'[6] With children, and particularly the children or grandchildren of old friends, Kipling was usually at his most natural. His godson Bonar Sykes, grandson of Bonar Law, enjoyed happy visits to Bateman's as a prep-school boy: 'The Kiplings could not have been more welcoming. The paddle-boat, dogs and happy atmosphere have remained a warm memory. Kipling himself showed me many of his treasures in the house and garden . . .'[7]

Many reminiscences about the late Kipling mention his dogs, and after

Elsie married and left home a succession of Aberdeen terriers played a key role in his life at Bateman's. Inevitably, their names had some personal and literary significance. Wop, acquired in 1926, was called after the character in William Black's novel *A Daughter of Heth* who had provided the nicknames 'Wop of Asia' and 'Wop of Europe', which Kipling had used of himself and his cousin Margaret in early Indian letters. There was also James, presumably named in memory of Henry James, and Malachi, taken from Thomas Moore's line 'When Malachi wore the collar of gold' and from Kipling's own story, 'The Dog Hervey', in which Malachi was the name of the narrator's pet terrier. James, Thelma Cazalet recorded, 'was a special favourite. This dog always lay under the table with his head on his master's feet; and when he died Kipling was really heart-broken.'[8] James's resentment in 1932 at the introduction of the six-month-old Malachi (or Mike) prompted an affectionate description from Kipling to his sister: 'I take the poor old chap for walks with Mike in the morn. It's rather like trying to co-ordinate a bath-chair and a baby-Austin, and one has to cover every yard of the road thrice – once to get back Mike: once to speed up James and once to get over the ground.' Malachi quickly won over Kipling, if not James, with his shrewdness and sense of humour, as Trix was soon being told:

> He has taken now to climbing up in a window-seat, carefully nosing his ball through the window and then coming to me with a long tale that he has lost it, so that I may go out into the garden, find it, and throw it for him. The only time he drops his toy is when he sees me with my fishing-rod, which he knows means business, and sits beside me on the bank with a corrugated brow watching the water. So far, he hasn't seen me catch anything but he knows quite well what I'm after.[9]

But for all their playfulness and intelligence, it was the unconditional affection that dogs give to their owners that most appealed to Kipling; and it was this quality that he celebrated in a late flurry of charming dog stories, three of which (narrated by Boots, an Aberdeen terrier, modelled on James) were collected in 1930 in *Thy Servant A Dog*. The last of them, 'Toby Dog', which ended with Boots's bewildered distress at the death of his friend the foxhound achieved considerable poignancy. Not long before his own death, Kipling also wrote '"Teem": a Treasure-Hunter' about a truffle-hunting dog. In the story, 'Teem' – clearly a surrogate for Kipling himself – began his career abroad before being transported to his adopted country England, where his art was misunderstood. One passage was particularly suggestive about Kipling's attitude to the nature and value of his gift. A frustrated 'Teem' tried to explain to his friend, the English sheepdog, about his truffle-hunting ability:

> 'But, ma Tante,' I cried, 'I have the secret of an Art beyond all others.'
>
> 'That is not understood in these parts,' she replied. 'You have told me of it many times, but I do not believe. What a pity it is not rabbits! You are small enough to creep down their burrows. But these precious things of yours under the ground which no one but you can find – it is absurd.'
>
> 'It is an absurdity, then, which fills Persons' chimney-places with Pieces and Thin Papers. Listen, ma Tante!' I all but howled. 'The world I came from was stuffed with things underground which all Persons desired. This world here is also rich in them, but I – I alone – can bring them to light!'[10]

The allusion was not only to stories that lay everywhere waiting to be unearthed; it also, more specifically, referred to the kind of 'layering' effect that Kipling aimed for in his later work, where each story (like this one) was intended to operate on a variety of different levels. Or, as he had observed insouciantly a few years earlier to the shipowner, Sir Percy Bates: 'Yes, the Eye of Allah *was* an allegory. Several of my tales are.'[11]

Bates was one of the new close friends Kipling made towards the end of his life. There were others, Lord Dunsany for instance, but on the whole it was to relations and established friends that he turned. Elsie and George, Trix (now more or less recovered), Cousin Stan (Prime Minister for much of the period) and Aunt Edie, the last of the Macdonald sisters, who had determinedly taken to her bed but remained an active correspondent and family archivist: these always had first call on his love and interest. He kept, however, in regular touch with a wide circle of English, French, Anglo-Indian, American and South African friends – friends who by now included the Royal Family, since the Kiplings, besides being regular attenders at the annual Buckingham House garden parties, were also invited to less official gatherings at the Palace. Kipling, furthermore, wrote several Christmas broadcasts for George V in the early 1930s, and these involved some pleasant but probably taxing sessions with that famously inarticulate monarch.

Bates came nearest to filling the gap left by Haggard, though there was never the same degree of intimacy. When Bates's son ran away from boarding school, Kipling was full of helpful advice and support. The two went to Naval Reviews and exchanged anti-socialist gibes. Occasionally Bates would be given a glimpse of his new friend's more vulnerable, sensitive side. 'I have made it a rule, ever since I was a youngster,' Kipling told him, 'not to keep letters. They are as bad as old photographs for harrowing up the mind.'[12] As a mark of particular trust and affection, Bates was invited to participate in the writing of 'The Manner of Men', a story about St Paul's shipwrecked voyage to Rome. Kipling deluged Bates with detailed questions about Mediterranean traders, their tonnage and dunnage, cargoes and embargoes, galleries and undergirting, and was suitably grateful for his help and suggestions.

It was to Bates in June 1930 that Kipling remarked: 'It don't pay to build dams with the Beaver. But I knew *that* ages ago.'[13] He had by then been long estranged from Beaverbrook – they fell out over the Treaty of Ireland not long after the war – though Carrie and Gladys Beaverbrook had remained friends until the latter's death in 1927. Earlier in 1930 itself, with Beaverbrook and the other major press baron, Lord Rothermere, trying to oust Baldwin from the leadership of the Conservative Party, Kipling had lent his cousin a crucial hand. The campaign to topple Baldwin hinged on a by-election in St George's Westminster on 20 March, with the Beaverbrook-Rothermere candidate, Sir Ernest Petter, tipped to defeat Baldwin's man, Duff Cooper. Three days before polling day, Baldwin delivered a notable speech on the issue of Press dictatorship and his own hounding by Beaverbrook and Rothermere. The final withering denunciation had Kipling's distinctive stamp, and is usually accepted as his. 'The newspapers attacking me,' Baldwin claimed:

... are not newspapers in the ordinary acceptance of the term. They are engines of propaganda for the constantly changing policies, desires, personal wishes, personal likes and dislikes of two men

[Beaverbrook and Rothermere]. What are their methods? Their methods are direct falsehood, misrepresentation, half-truths, the alteration of the speaker's meaning by putting sentences apart from the context, suppression, and editorial criticism of speeches which are not reported in the paper . . . What the proprietorship of these papers is aiming at is power, but power without responsibility – the prerogative of the harlot throughout the ages.[14]

Beaverbrook and Rothermere had overreached themselves. By setting up an *ad hominem* campaign against a politician known for his honesty, they had succeeded only in making Baldwin's position once again rock-solid. With a little help from Kipling, Baldwin gave them the lie, and that week Duff Cooper romped home with a majority of nearly 6,000.

Kipling was not always such a warm supporter of his cousin. After the election of a National Government in 1931 under Ramsay MacDonald (but with the Conservatives under Baldwin as the dominant force), he liked to complain to his more right-wing cronies that Stan had always been a secret socialist and needed watching.

Yet it was not the 'Beaver', or even his cousin's political trajectory, that preoccupied Kipling during these final years. Besides his by now ingrained anxiety about England and the Empire, he had never stopped worrying about Germany, and the rise of Hitler and National Socialism confirmed his worst fears. One response was to remove the sign of the swastika from his books; unlike the Nazis, he had adopted it as a traditional Eastern symbol of prosperity and creativity, not as a supposed emblem of Aryan purity. (Kipling, incidentally, pronounced the word to rhyme with 'car's ticker'.) Another response, showing some prescience, was to lobby influential friends (including Baldwin) on the need for rearmament, air-raid shelters and other defensive measures. 'Get someone to work out the amount of cellar-room and the rest of it,' he exhorted Gwynne in March 1934; 'and *keep pegging away with figures*. Absurd? Yes. But the only way of putting the wind up the people is by going on just those lines.'[15] However, he reserved his major warning for the speech – broadcast by the BBC – that he delivered to the Society of St George on 6 May 1935, the day of George V's Silver Jubilee.

With a quiet intensity that he maintained throughout, he began by giving his account of what had happened to England over the last two decades. There were those, he declared, 'who, for various motives, dissociated themselves from the War at the outset', and survived it. They had helped to put about a theory that the war 'had been due to a sort of cosmic hallucination which had infected the nations concerned with a sort of cosmic hysteria. This theory absolved those who had not interested themselves in the War, and by implication condemned those who had, thus supplying comfort and moral support where needed. Naturally the notion bore fruit.' He put forward his version of the tale that the English had been telling themselves:

> All pain, whether it comes from hitting one's head against a table or from improvising a four years' war at four days' notice, is evil. All evil is wicked, and since of all evils war gives the most pain to the most people, the wickedest of all things is war. Wherefore unless people wish to be thought wicked they must so order their national life that never again shall war in any form be possible.

His deeply patriotic audience, appreciating the ironic edge to the last sentence, applauded loudly. In the push to realise the 'national ideal of an ever-rising standard of living', he went on, 'we chose' – dramatic pause – 'we *chose* – not to provide that reasonable margin of external safety without which even the lowest standard of life cannot be maintained in this dangerously congested island'.[16]

With that phrase 'reasonable margin of external safety' he introduced one of the main thrusts of his speech: defence. The threat from 'our opponent' followed immediately afterwards. Kipling pointedly contrasted Germany's 'national life and ideals . . . based on a cult, a religion as it now appears, of war' – he gave the word 'cult' a Germanic intonation – with England's preoccupation with material improvement. For the last decade, he insisted, Germany had been building up for yet another war, its fifth in recent history; and England had made this all the easier, not only by drastic cuts to its armed forces but also, he implied, through a commitment to the League of Nations. And all, he said, in order 'to set the world a good example'. While England was following this righteous path, the world beyond its shores (a clear tilt at the Soviet Union) had become characterised by 'state-controlled murder and torture, open and secret', by 'state-engineered famine, starvation and slavery', and by 'state-imposed godlessness, or state-prescribed paganism'.[17]

Having painted this gloomy picture of a vulnerable, wrong-headed England, faced by an implacable enemy in a hostile world, Kipling went on to offer what hope and consolation he could:

> Nevertheless, the past year or two has given birth to the idea that our example of state-defended defencelessness has not borne much fruit, and that we have walked far enough along the road which is paved with good intentions. It is now arranged that in due time we will take steps to remedy our more obvious deficiencies. So far, good. But if that time be *not* given to us – if the attack of the future is to be on the same swift, all-in lines as our opponents' domestic adminis-trations, it is possible that before we are aware – before we are aware – our country may have joined those submerged races of history who passed their children through fire to Moloch in order to win credit with their Gods. And yet – and yet – the genius of our race fights for us in the teeth of doctrine. The abiding springs of English life are not of yesterday or of the day before. They draw from the immemor-ial continuity of the nation's life under its own sovereigns. They are fed by a human relationship more intimate and more far-reaching than any that the world has ever known. They make part of a mystery as incommunicable as it is unpurchaseable.

After a few more compliments to the monarchy, he invited the society to drink to 'England and the English'. The toast – 'England, this precious stone set in a silver sea' – was proposed and drunk, and Kipling retired to sustained applause.[18]

For many of his audience – at the dinner, listening at home on the wireless, or reading the papers – he had again spoken their thoughts, and the letters of thanks and congratulation soon poured in. 'Someone had to say it,' Kipling commented to Bates a couple of days later, 'and I'd nothing to lose or gain. So I did.' However, he added, not everyone had been so enthusiastic: 'The Church has already been at me seriously. I'll agree with 'em just as soon as they leave their Offertory-boxes unlocked and the communion plate in the aisle between services.'[19] More impor-tantly, in his sharp division between those who had been involved in the war and those who had dissociated themselves from it, Kipling had entirely ignored all those combatants who, as a direct result of their war experience, had become pacifists, pinning their hopes on the League of Nations. Sassoon, a strong supporter of the League, was simultaneously fascinated and horrified:

Hester and I [he wrote to Max Beerbohm on 17 May] 'listened in' to Kipling's speech, which was most extraordinary. He spoke with fanaticism in his voice, like a suave precise professor of military law, also like a prophet who has been disregarded for a decade and a half and was taking his chance to get his own back. Hester and I sat there feeling almost frightened by his intensity, but we decided afterwards that modern European nations aren't Old Testament tribes, and that Kipling was exaggerating a bit.

With his letter, Sassoon enclosed a poem, 'Silver Jubilee Celebration', which in his best hard-hitting vein conveyed more fully his reaction – and that of many of his generation – to Kipling's 'planned post-mortem on the post-war years':

Suavely severe – not one bleak syllable blurred –
In dulcet-bitter and prophetic tones
(Each word full charged with dynamite deferred)
He disinterred a battlefield of bones . . .
And then reminded us that our attempt
To put all war behind us with the last one
Had been a dream administrators dreamt;
In fact a virtuous fallacy – and a vast one.

Meanwhile his audience, mystified at first,
Sat spellbound while he preached with barbed conviction,
Who, through implied anathemas, re-cursed
Our old opponents in that four-years friction.
And if indeed it was the astringent truth
He told with such incomparable concision –
That we must now re-educate our youth
With 'Arm or Perish' as their ultimate vision –

Let us at least be candid with the world
And stitch across each Union Jack unfurled
'No bargain struck with Potsdam is put over
Unless well backed by bombers – and Jehovah!'[20]

Sassoon had been present at Hardy's funeral in Westminster Abbey in January 1928. The pallbearers were Stanley Baldwin, Ramsay MacDonald, E M Walker (pro-Provost of Queen's College, Oxford), A B Ramsay (Master of Magdalene College, Cambridge), Shaw, Galsworthy, Kipling, Barrie, Gosse and Housman: a highly distinguished cross-section of the great, the literary and the learned. Years later, Sassoon would describe his most treasured moment:

> what he found unforgettable was a meeting between Kipling and Bernard Shaw, who hated each other. Due to an uncertainty in the seating arrangements, they found themselves facing each other. The person in charge ventured an introduction. Kipling's face was purple. He looked at Shaw with aversion. Still he was being introduced. 'How do you do, sir?' he managed to sputter out as if he were greeting Lucifer.
> 'How do you do, sir?' Shaw replied urbanely.[21]

It was a good, well-polished story, and clearly some such 'convergence of the twain' did take place. According to Shaw's secretary, Blanche Patch, it was Gosse who effected the introduction, and the uncertainty was not about seating arrangements but about who should pair as pallbearers, and the tall Shaw and small Kipling had plainly been mismatched. In her version, Kipling 'shook hands hurriedly and at once turned away as if from the Evil One'.[22]

Hardy, with his relish for the incongruous, would have enjoyed the story. Only a couple of months before his death, he had observed tartly that Kipling 'had given to party what was meant for mankind'.[23] The remark, an allusion to Goldsmith's lines on Edmund Burke, placed Hardy among those who felt Kipling had misapplied his great ability. For Sassoon, on the other hand, Kipling was the butt, the blimpish reactionary nonchalantly bested by the suave Fabian. Even writers who deeply admired Kipling's work felt the need to put him down. Take

Somerset Maugham, who met Kipling several times between the wars, later edited a selection of his prose, and would describe him as the only English short-story writer to rival the great Europeans. Yet he too, like Sassoon on Hardy's funeral, had a party piece featuring Kipling at his most bufferish and Anglo-Indian. 'To the end,' Somerset Maugham would say, Kipling 'had the mind of a 5th-form boy at a second-rate school. He dined with me on the day after Gene Tunney beat Jack Dempsey. "Gene is a white man," he said. I made a bet with myself that his next two words would be "pukka sahib". They were.'[24]

Kipling as professional writer could also be inadvertently amusing. Vera Brittain recalled how, writing *Testament of Youth*, she wanted to quote the eight lines from Kipling's 'Dirge of Dead Sisters', which had helped to sustain her as a VAD nurse in the First World War. To secure permission to use the lines without charge was a complicated process. She listed the required stipulations:

(1) Make due acknowledgement in a form dictated by himself.
(2) Reproduce the lines exactly as they appeared in *The Five Nations* without omitting any part of either verse.
(3) Write additional letters to his publishers in Britain, the United States, and Canada.
(4) Send him copies of both my English and American editions when the book appeared.

One short quotation thus involved five letters and two presentation copies. I felt thankful that everyone wasn't Kipling; he must, I thought, have collected a good free library over the years.[25]

Presumably she was unaware of the copyright hassles that had plagued Kipling in earlier days; all the same, her story graphically and comically conveyed the Fort Knox barriers that he and Carrie had built around the use of his name and his work.

Brittain had another, intriguing connection with Kipling. In *Radclyffe Hall: A Case of Obscenity?*, her documentary account of the 1928 court case about the lesbian novel *The Well of Loneliness*, she mentioned that Kipling, together with Marie Stopes and others, sat behind counsel at the Appeal proceedings on 14 December. He does not seem to have attended the original trial on 9 November at Bow Street Magistrates' Court, when permission was refused for a bevy of distinguished witnesses (including E M Forster, Leonard and Virginia Woolf, Vita Sackville-West, Hugh Walpole and Julian Huxley) to speak on behalf of the book's literary merits. Why Kipling was at the Appeal is unclear. Presumably he was not there on behalf of the defence, to judge by an exchange in October between himself and Walpole. The latter, who considered the novel 'tiresome' and 'stupid' but was against censorship, asked Kipling what he thought of it and noted his reply: 'No, he doesn't approve of the book. Too much of the abnormal in all of us to play about with it.'[26] It is just conceivable, as a previous biographer of Kipling has suggested, that the homosexual Walpole was using the latest literary hot topic in order to sound out someone he suspected of also being homosexual.[27] However, in context, the far likelier explanation is that Walpole was putting out a feeler to Kipling to see if he would be prepared to defend the book at the magistrates' hearing, should literary witnesses be permitted. In fact, it is not even clear whether Kipling ever read *The Well of Loneliness*. He need not have done; James Douglas had recently 'exposed' it in the *Sunday Express*.

On 16 November the chief magistrate delivered his judgement that, in Vera Brittain's words, 'the book was an obscene libel, and that it would tend to corrupt those into whose hands it might fall'.[28] Carrie noted on 13 December, the day before the Appeal, that the Director of Public Prosecutions called to discuss the novel with her husband. Next day Kipling was in court to hear the Appeal dismissed with costs. It is a reasonable surmise that Kipling contributed one, if not both, of the literary references to lesbianism mentioned by the Attorney-General as he opened the case for the Crown: Paul's Epistle to the Romans I, 24–8 and Juvenal's *Satires* VI, 327–9. St Paul had become a particular hero of Kipling's, and in 1928 he had written one story, 'The Church that was at Antioch', with the saint as a central character and had started another, 'The Manner of Men'. Moreover, although Kipling in his time had dealt fairly explicitly with some contentious subjects (syphilis, for instance, in 'Love-o'-Women'), he did not approve of the literary treatment of homosexuality. So, what more natural than to offer the Crown chapter and verse, and then turn up the next day to see how things went? When, a couple of months later, a similar case was brought against the novel in the States, and the opposite verdict was returned, Kipling probably took it as yet one more sign of American 'lawlessness'.

This involvement in *The Well of Loneliness* case was, however, unusual. His literary encounters were now of a more accidental or socially unavoidable nature. Carrie's diary mentioned a boring lunch with Baroness Orczy, the creator of *The Scarlet Pimpernel*, and there were letters politely turning down invitations from Elizabeth Russell (Elizabeth von Arnim). In the right circumstances, however, Kipling could still be a fascinator. Buchan never forgot his 'devouring interest in every detail of the human comedy, the way in which in conversation he used to raven the heart out of a subject', while Walpole recalled a conversation between Kipling and P G Wodehouse at the Cazalets' showing that Kipling, a genuine fan of the younger writer, had lost none of his old complimentary touch. ' "But tell me, Wodehouse," asked Kipling, "how do you finish your stories? I can never think how to end mine." '[29]

There was a particularly tantalising encounter with R C Sheriff in January 1930.[30] Sheriff's play, *Journey's End*, set in the trenches during the war, was in certain respects distinctly Kiplingesque. He had virtually 'invented' the Army speech that Sheriff employed for the dialogue, while the doomed subaltern, Raleigh, and the conscientious middle-aged officer, Osborne, were both familiar Kipling types. With a young Olivier as the disillusioned Stanhope, *Journey's End* had made a major impression on first being staged in 1928, appearing the same year as Edmund Blunden's *Undertones of War* and Sassoon's *Memoirs of a Fox-Hunting Man*, the first of the great prose reminiscences of the war. Had Kipling seen the play? If so, what had he thought of it? Did he and Sheriff hit it off? Or was the meeting what Wodehouse would have called a 'frost'?

When *Limits and Renewals*, Kipling's last collection of adult stories, came out in April 1932, it caused little stir. The best *The Times* could say was that 'his capacity for combining the superficially incongruous in theme, diction, setting, and moral inference is technically the most interesting thing in the book'.[31] Most of the fourteen stories had been written in a two-year flurry after the publication of *Debits and Credits*; eleven had appeared in English and American magazines, while three were previously unpublished. The volume was framed by 'Dayspring Mishandled', a story of aborted revenge, and 'Uncovenanted Mercies', a vision of Hell. Within that frame there were medical stories, stories about St Paul, a First

World War story, an Indian story, a naval story, a dog story and a couple of excellent farces; cracking up (from war experience or personal suffering) and healing (through medical means, laughter or some kind of divine mercy) were the volume's main preoccupations.

The highlight was 'Dayspring Mishandled'. Like Hardy's late poems, it had the power of a highly condensed novel. The story covered over thirty years, from the early 1890s to the mid-1920s, and described the enmeshed lives of James Manallace, 'a darkish, slow northerner of the type that does not ignite, but must be detonated', and Alured Castorley, 'a mannered, bellied person . . . who talked and wrote about "Bohemia", but was always afraid of being "compromised"'. As young men, they both fell (unrequitedly) in love with the same woman and worked for the Fictional Supply Syndicate, turning out romantic pot-boilers. On one occasion, the love-sick Manallace found himself producing a fragment of pseudo-Chaucerian poetry, as unusable as it was involuntary. Later, he became a popular historical novelist, while Castorley turned into the leading Chaucerian expert of the day. During the war the two men were thrown together, and Castorley said something unmentionable and unpardonable about the woman they had both loved, and whom Manallace had devotedly nursed through the last stages of paralysis. From that point Manallace pursued his revenge, creating a fake Chaucerian manuscript out of the fragment of verse he had written years before; authenticating the manuscript as genuine made Castorley's scholarly reputation and gained him a knighthood. Manallace, on the point of exposing the hoax and bringing down Castorley (now a sick man), stayed his hand when he discovered that Castorley's wife had rumbled him – and was keenly urging him on because she wanted to marry Gleeag, the family doctor. The story ended at Castorley's funeral: with Manallace taking out his black gloves, the coffin crawling sideways 'through the noiselessly-closing door-flaps' and Lady Castorley's eyes turning towards Gleeag.[32]

Kipling wrote the story in a fortnight in late 1926. 'It is not at all a nice tale,' he told Elsie, 'but it came by itself, and it called itself "Dayspring Mishandled", which, at least, is a pretty title.'[33] Though he did not say so, he almost certainly borrowed the forgery idea from his friend, Ian Colvin, who had once nearly pulled off a similar hoax on The Times with some 'early' Keats sonnets. However, the story's narrative obliquity and its moral and other dilemmas owed a different debt, which was to Henry

James's treatment of literary themes. A pseudo-Jamesian story about a pseudo-Chaucerian fragment: what could be more apt for a tale about forgery and pastiche? 'Dayspring Mishandled' offers, once again, an example of readers tending to read the Kipling they expected to read. If his work were regularly given the kind of close attention, and literary trust, accorded to the acknowledged modernist giants, it would be taken for granted that Manallace's Christian name 'James' was a knowing nod, a gesture of homage, to the author of 'The Aspern Papers'. Indeed, there was something eminently Jamesian about Kipling's reluctance to let the reader know what dreadful thing Castorley said to Manallace. In his last great story, he had fully imbibed the lesson of the master: 'So long as the events are veiled the imagination will run riot and depict all sorts of horrors, but as soon as the veil is lifted, all mystery disappears and with it the sense of terror.'[34]

The two stories about St Paul – decidedly *not* a figure of interest to James – were 'The Church that was at Antioch' and 'The Manner of Men'. This renewal of Kipling's interest in writing about the Roman world was spurred by seeing the 1926 silent film, *Ben-Hur*. He saw it twice, in June 1927 and January 1928, and according to Carrie was much struck. There was also an increasingly strong personal identification with Paul – so much so that he described the apostle as 'a small hard man with eyebrows' who had 'the woman's trick of taking the tone and colour of whoever he talked to', a chameleon attribute often remarked of Kipling himself and one of which he was well aware. 'At His Execution', the poem following 'The Manner of Men', underscored the connection. Here Paul/Kipling was 'made all things to all men': he was a consummate ventriloquist ('In each one's tongue I speak'), a travelling communicator between peoples ('In City or Wilderness/Praising the crafts they profess'), and one who had given away self in the cause, and now asked for its return: 'Restore me my self again!'[35]

St Paul, the closest thing to a presiding figure in *Limits and Renewals*, was imaginatively quarantined off from his Jewishness in the two stories. Indeed, 'The Church that was at Antioch' was at heart deeply anti-Semitic. '*Never* decide upon the evidence, when you're dealing with Hebrews!' declared the city's Roman Chief of Police, whose nephew Valens was eventually murdered by a vengeful Jew whom, with Roman fair-mindedness, he had previously allowed to go free.[36] Valens's dying words explicitly echoed Christ's on the cross, turning him into a sacrificial victim of the Jewish mob. The underlying theme of the story, as Kipling more bluntly put it in another context, was that 'Israel is a race to leave alone. It abets disorder.'[37]

Some of Kipling's late verse was equally anti-Semitic. 'The Waster', for instance, a 1930 poem, nonchalantly flaunted its prejudice in its refrain, replacing the rhymes 'the Jew', 'the Hun', 'the Jew' at the end of successive stanzas with 'etc.'. The opening stanza read:

> From the date that the doors of his prep-school close
> > On the lonely little son
> He is taught by precept, insult, and blows
> > The Things that Are Never Done.
> Year after year, without favour or fear,
> > From seven to twenty-two,
> His keepers insist he shall learn the list
> > Of the things no fellow can do.
> (They are not so strict with the average Pict
> > And it isn't set to, etc.)[38]

The adroit satire on the English public-school code did not make the verses any the less racist.[39] Another late poem, untitled and never intended for publication, purported to trace the history of the Jewish race, and its feud with the Arabs, from Old Testament times to the present day. Again the considerable metrical and other ingenuity in no way dispelled the verses' inherent unpleasantness. The following two quatrains were characteristic:

> We do not know what God attends
> The Unloved Race in every place
> Where they amass their dividends
> From Riga to Jerusalem.

> But all the course of Time makes clear
> To everyone (except the Hun)
> It does not pay to interfere
> With Cohen from Jerusalem.[40]

Less vitriolically, two other strands recurred through the later verse: warnings of future threat and meditations on pain. The most striking poem of warning was 'The Storm Cone' of 1932, deriving much of its power from the menace of the undefined. In Kipling's own mind the ship in danger probably represented England threatened by the seas of German military aggression; but if so, the lines transcended their occasion, suggesting by the tragic intensity of the voice a threat of more existential proportions:

> This is the midnight – let no star
> Delude us – dawn is very far.
> This is the tempest long foretold –
> Slow to make head but sure to hold . . .
>
> It is decreed that we abide
> The weight of gale against the tide
> And those huge waves the outer main
> Sends in to set us back again.
>
> They fall and whelm. We strain to hear
> The pulses of her labouring gear,
> Till the deep throb beneath us proves,
> After each shudder and check, she moves!
>
> She moves, with all save purpose lost,
> To make her offing from the coast;
> But, till she fetches open sea,
> Let no man deem that he is free![41]

One of the most memorable poems in *Limits and Renewals*, 'Hymn to Physical Pain', preceded a medical story, 'The Tender Achilles'. This poem, interpreted confessionally, offered an appalling glimpse of the darker side of Kipling's last years, celebrating the capacity of physical pain temporarily to blot out mental and spiritual anguish:

> Dread Mother of Forgetfulness
> Who, when Thy reign begins,

Wipes away the Soul's distress,
    And memory of her sins.

The trusty Worm that dieth not –
    The steadfast Fire also,
By Thy contrivance are forgot
    In a completer woe . . .

And when Thy tender mercies cease
    And life unvexed is due,
Instant upon the false release
    The Worm and Fire renew.

Wherefore we praise Thee in the deep,
    And on our beds we pray
For Thy return that Thou may'st keep
    The Pains of Hell at bay![42]

There was also 'Hymn of Breaking Strain', finished in late 1933 and originally written as part of a masonic-style ceremony for graduating Canadian engineers, which had been inaugurated with Kipling's assistance after the war. The poem presented his final word on his deep conviction that life constantly tested one beyond one's limits and that it was only through stoically accepting this condition that one could renew oneself:

Oh, veiled and secret Power
    Whose paths we seek in vain,
Be with us in our hour
    Of overthrow and pain;
That we – by which sure token
    We know Thy ways are true –
In spite of being broken,
    Because of being broken.
      May rise and build anew.
      Stand up and build anew![43]

Or, as he more prosaically explained this last verse to one of the ceremony's founders, 'not only in spite of being broken, but through the mere fact of being broken (and also taught humility etc.) a man may start again on his job . . .'[44]

In January 1934 Kipling urged his friend, the architect Sir Herbert Baker, to take a break from work and write his autobiography while he still could:

> Lucky is he who sees the distant signal against him in time – as the late years have taught me . . . It can't hurt one to break away after the initial wrench, and it may do heaps of good. Also, as one picks up the other side of life, one can set in order, and in some fashion, digest and regurgitate (one of the foulest words in the English Language!) the history of one's own days.[45]

Baker preferred to wait, while he completed the rebuilding of the Bank of England, but a year and a half later Kipling was following his own advice.

He started his autobiography on 1 August 1935, telling Carrie that he was going to 'deal with his life from the point of view of his work'.[46] By Boxing Day he had completed the eight-chapter manuscript (published posthumously in 1937 as *Something of Myself*, an apt title but probably not his). The first seven chapters covered his life chronologically up to the receipt of the Nobel Prize in 1907, with frequent glances forward to later events; the eighth, 'Working-Tools', discussed his literary daemon, told a few anecdotes about his work and offered some tips to the literary beginner. He revised the manuscript as he went along and would presumably have done more: there were numerous careless factual mistakes, which a little research would have corrected. There is no reason to think, however, that he ever intended to carry the main body of the story beyond 1907. Like many of his stories, *Something of Myself* is probably best described as a 'completed fragment'.[47]

Kipling had a strong feeling that the book would be his swansong. In October he had turned down an offer to do the life of Lord Byng because, Carrie noted, 'he must put his affairs in order'. In December he changed solicitor and in the New Year made and signed a new will. On 2 January 1936, a few days after his seventieth birthday, he wrote Aunt Edie a letter full of a sense of ending:

Bless you for your note which has just come in. He who put us into this life does not abandon His work for *any* reason or default at the end of it. That is all I have come to learn out of my life. So there is *no* fear!

I was hoping for your letter, my dear; and it makes me feel better to have got it.

Ever your loving

RUDDY

P.S. Just now, in our valley where it has been raining for about three weeks, I feel like the enclosed gentleman.[48]

In effect his last word, the autobiography was a thoroughly characteristic performance: immediate and reticent, insouciant and oblique. It was a final display of the 'layered' manner he had been perfecting for more than thirty years, and of which he now gave a short summary during a discussion of *Rewards and Fairies*. 'I worked the material in three or four overlaid tints and textures,' he explained, 'which might or might not reveal themselves according to the shifting light of sex, youth, and experience.'[49]

He seems to have had a number of objects in mind. He wanted to give a brief account of his life, emphasising particularly his good luck on the writing side. This note was struck in the opening sentences: 'Looking back from this my seventieth year, it seems to me that every card in my working life has been dealt me in such a manner that I had but to play it as it came. Therefore, ascribing all good fortune to Allah the Dispenser of Events, I begin: —.' He wanted to present a childhood that was half Bombay idyll, half Southsea hell, suggesting how both experiences had benefited him as a writer. He wanted to depict his years at USC, and later as a reporter in India, as providing a hard but necessary training-ground. He wanted to convey his sense that his early fame (the 'notoriety', as he archly called it) had been 'a sort of waking dream' outside his control.[50] After a sketchier though still vivid treatment of the Vermont period, South Africa and the Boer War, he wanted to leave himself settled at Bateman's and awarded the Nobel Prize. The final chapter was a form of postscript, a quick skim over aspects of his work and the literary life as he had experienced it. Woven more obliquely, but quite deliberately, into this narrative were strands reflecting his political anxieties, his hatred of radicals and Liberals, and cryptic warnings against disarmament, Ireland, the Germans, the Jews. Kipling wanted to 'regurgitate' the history of his own days on a national as well as a personal level.

What he did *not* want to bring up were the most painful and personally important episodes of his adolescent and adult life. There was no mention of his infatuation with Flo, his relationship with Mrs Hill, his engagement to Caroline, his friendship with Wolcott, his court case with Beatty, or the deaths of Josephine and John. Carrie ('the wife') made occasional brief appearances, as did his sister, Trix. Friends like 'Stalky', Haggard, Norton, Doubleday, Rhodes, Jameson, Gwynne and Colonel Feilden fared somewhat better, while there were more frequent loving glimpses of Lockwood and Alice, Uncle Ned and Aunt Georgie. Read in an age that equates confession with honesty, the omissions are striking. But a half-Victorian like Kipling was never going to write a frank autobiography; the 'Higher Striptease', as he might have dubbed it, was a kind of writing he would have considered tasteless, tactless and self-indulgent.

Of course, any autobiography – evasive or otherwise – leaves the author exposed to psychological scrutiny. E M Forster, reviewing the book in March 1937, found support for a pet theory: 'There are at least two Kiplings. One of them is Kim, the Little Friend of all the World, the other is also a boy, but sneering and cocky.' Forster also read *Something of Myself* as proof that 'an immature person' could be 'a great writer'. When Kipling 'turns from his "job" to his "Daemon",' Forster insisted, '. . . he enters another world at once, the world of inspiration, and he moves with authority there'.[51] Similarly, it could be argued, the autobiography provided a classic example of someone trying with difficulty to preserve conflicting elements of his personal myth. It was integral to Kipling's myth, as presented in his autobiography, that he was the son of parents so perfect that they could only be designated the 'Father' and the 'Mother'. *Equally* integral to his myth was that, by being left with the Holloways in Southsea, he had in effect been orphaned. He emphasised this image of himself as abandoned child by repeated self-identification with Robert Browning's Fra Lippo Lippi, the quintessential orphan-artist. Yet Kipling appeared oblivious that this orphan myth clashed with his other myth of Lockwood and Alice as ideal parents.

That said, *Something of Myself* showed that Kipling had lost none of his sheer button-holing power or his daring. He might have claimed to envy Wodehouse's ability to finish stories, but he knew exactly how his autobiography should finish. In the last couple of pages, with the phrase 'Nor did I live to see', he suddenly shifted the narrative into a posthumous tense, as though writing from the grave. And he ended with the two words with which logically all autobiographies should end: 'Left and right of [my] table were two big globes, on one of which a great airman had once outlined in white paint those air-routes to the East and Australia which were well in use before my death.'[52]

His actual death came quickly. En route to the south of France for their usual winter break, the Kiplings put up at Brown's Hotel in London. On 12 January 1936 they visited Elsie and George in Hampstead. That night Kipling had a massive haemorrhage and was taken to the Middlesex Hospital, suffering from a perforated duodenum. When the surgeon, his friend Sir Alfred Webb-Johnson, came to see him prior to the operation and asked him, 'What's the matter, Rud?', Kipling answered, 'Something has come adrift inside.' Which Webb-Johnson felt 'brilliantly summarised the matter'.[53] Over the next few days he improved, weakened, rallied, relapsed. In the early hours of Friday the 17th, Carrie and Elsie were summoned from Brown's for a last vigil. They stayed in the hospital all that day while Kipling lingered on; and they were there when he died a few minutes after midnight on 18 January, his forty-fourth wedding anniversary.

Though inevitably overshadowed by George V's passing a couple of days later, Kipling's death sent almost as many shockwaves round the world as his near-fatal illness had done in 1899. It symbolised an end. For some, like General Sir Ian Hamilton, it marked the close of an era of European history: 'His death seems to me to place a full stop to the period when war was a romance and the expansion of the Empire a duty.'[54] For others, like P G Wodehouse, it meant the end of a literary era and of a portion of his own life: 'Doesn't Kipling's death give you a sort of stunned feeling? He seems to leave such a gap. I didn't feel the same about Doyle or Bennett or Galsworthy. I suppose it is because he is so associated with one's boyhood. It has made me feel older all of a sudden.'[55]

For T H White, the experience would assume an almost existential quality:

I stood outside the hospital in London, where Kipling was dying, on the night he died. I just stood there for a bit. I don't know why, and can't say that I felt anything in particular: or at least it was not a feeling with any known label. It was one of these modern feelings. 'Am I being dramatic? What is death anyway? There isn't any God. Why stand here? etc. etc. etc.' I must have looked at the great barrack of a wall half resentfully, also blankly, confusedly, self-consciously: I was thinking of myself more than of the little beetle-browed dusky man snuffing it somewhere inside. But the fact remains that I stood. There were no other people in the side street and I had not gone there on purpose.[56]

Even someone as antipathetic as Virginia Woolf felt compelled to acknowledge the event in her diary, though with a self-conscious unwillingness: 'I open this, forced by a sense of what is expected by the public, to remark that Kipling died yesterday; & that the King (George 5th) is probably dying today. The death of Kipling has set all the old war horses of the press padding round their stalls.'[57]

Alongside the predictable tributes, Rebecca West – in the course of a long, shrewdly tough appreciation in the *New Statesman* – took Kipling to task for 'the black exasperation in which [he] thought and wrote during his later years':

He had before him a people who had passed the test he had named in his youth – the test of war; and they had passed it with a courage that transcended anything he can have expected as far as war transcended in awfulness anything he can have expected. Yet they had only to stretch out a hand towards bread or peace or power or any of the goods that none could grudge them in this hour when all their governors' plans had broken down, for Kipling to break out in ravings against the greed and impudence of the age.[58]

Edwin Muir observed more sympathetically in the *Listener* that while Kipling 'was inclined to look upon society in general as a larger edition of the Army, and so reformers always had to him a suggestion of insubordination', there remained in his stories 'a warm human sympathy which nothing could suppress'.[59]

Kipling was cremated privately at Golder's Green on 22 January. His

immediate predecessor at the crematorium had been Saklatvala, the celebrated Indian communist, and Kipling's Union Jack-draped coffin arrived
to the strains of Saklatvala's supporters singing the Red Flag. The funeral
in Westminster Abbey was held the following day, when Kipling's pallbearers included Stanley Baldwin (still Prime Minister), Sir Roger Keyes
(Admiral of the Fleet), Sir A Montgomery-Massingberd (Field Marshal),
Sir Fabian Ware (editor and instigator of the Imperial War Graves
Commission), and H A Gwynne (editor of the *Morning Post*). Six of the
most celebrated writers of the day had helped to carry Hardy's coffin in
1928; not a single writer did so for Kipling. Nor were there many writers
among the distinguished congregation of politicians, newspapermen, cler-
gymen, ambassadors and other dignitaries that packed the Abbey for the
service. Kipling was, as his obituarist observed in the *Times Literary
Supplement*, 'a national institution', but by his death no longer a literary
one.[60]

One writer who did attend the funeral was Vera Brittain. In its imme-
diacy, its economy, its assured handling of phrasing and detail, her
account of the service showed that some of the most valuable portions of
Kipling's legacy had been passed on long before his death:

> I sat in the North Transept, watched the clergy and choir move with
> uplifted crosses to the Poets' Corner before the marble urn contain-
> ing Kipling's ashes, and heard the Dean utter the Committal Prayer
> standing beneath the outstretched hand of Addison's statue.
>
> After the quiet singing of the 'Recessional' I moved with the con-
> gregation to the South Transept, and saw the purple-covered tomb,
> surrounded by wreaths of spring flowers, situated in odd companion-
> ship between the graves of Charles Dickens and Thomas Hardy.[61]

Notes

ABBREVIATIONS

Birkenhead   Lord Birkenhead, *Rudyard Kipling* (1978).
Carrington   Charles Carrington, *Rudyard Kipling: His Life and Work*, 3rd edn
                     1978.
CK's diary   Charles Carrington's notes from Carrie Kipling's diary, kept from
                     1892–1937 and held at Sussex University.
Critical Heritage Roger Lancelyn Green (ed.), *Kipling: The Critical Heritage* (New
                     York, 1971).
Definitive Verse   *The Definitive Edition of Rudyard Kipling's Verse* (London, 1989).
Early Verse   Andrew Rutherford (ed.), *Early Verse by Rudyard Kipling
                     1879–1889* (Oxford, 1986).
KJ   Kipling Journal.
KP   Kipling Papers held at Sussex University
Letters   Thomas Pinney (ed.), *The Letters of Rudyard Kipling*, Vols 1–3,
                     1872–1910 (1990, 1996).
'O Beloved Kids'   Elliot L Gilbert (ed.), *'O Beloved Kids': Rudyard Kipling's Letters to
                     his Children* (1983).
Orel   Harold Orel (ed.), *Kipling: Interviews and Recollections*, Vols 1 and
                     2, (Totowa, New Jersey 1983).
Record of a Friendship Morton Cohen (ed.), *Rudyard Kipling to Rider Haggard: The Record
                     of a Friendship* (1965).
Seymour-Smith   Martin Seymour-Smith, *Rudyard Kipling* (1989).
SOM   Thomas Pinney (ed.), *Rudyard Kipling: Something of Myself And
                     Other Autobiographical Writings* (1990).
Wilson   Angus Wilson, *The Strange Ride of Rudyard Kipling* (1977).

Kipling's novels, travel writing and collections of stories are indicated simply by title and
year of publication; the page reference unless otherwise stated is to the standard

Macmillan edition. The place of publication for all other works is London unless otherwise stated. I am grateful to A.P. Watt & Co, London, and the National Trust for permission to quote published and unpublished material, and to other copyright holders, listed in the Acknowledgments.

1: RUDDY IS COMING

1   Frederic W Macdonald, *As a Tale that is Told* (1919), 115.
2   A W Baldwin, *The Macdonald Sisters* (1960), 32.
3   *The Macdonald Sisters*, 44.
4   Edith Plowden, *Fond Memories*, KP 28/18.
5   *As A Tale that is Told*, 334.
6   *The Macdonald Sisters*, 107.
7   This *In Confession* book, which probably belonged to Alice's sister Louisa, is now in the Worcester Records Office.
8   *The Macdonald Sisters*, 86, 85.
9   *The Macdonald Sisters*, 98.
10 *As A Tale that is Told*, 58.
11 *The Macdonald Sisters*, 19.
12 Hannah Macdonald's diary, 6 August 1874, Worcester Records Office.
13 Arthur R. Ankers, *The Pater* (Otford, 1988), 7.
14 Mrs A M Fleming to Stanley Baldwin, 27 March 1945, KP 1/20; and Lockwood Kipling to Edith Plowden, 17 July 1908, KP 1/10.
15 *The Pater*, 60.
16 James Craig, 'John Lockwood Kipling: The Formative Years', *KJ* December 1974, 5.
17 Birkenhead, 8.
18 *Fond Memories*, KP 28/18.
19 *The Macdonald Sisters*, 113, 112, 113.
20 *The Macdonald Sisters*, 114.
21 *Fond Memories*, KP 28/18.
22 *Fond Memories*, KP 28/18.
23 Louisa Baldwin to Agatha Poynter, 18 June 1868, Worcester Records Office.
24 *The Macdonald Sisters*, 114.
25 Louisa Baldwin to Agatha Poynter, 23 June 1868, Worcester Records Office.
26 Hannah Macdonald's diary, 2 November 1868, Worcester Records Office.
27 Louisa Baldwin to Agatha Poynter, 9 November 1868, Worcester Records Office.
28 Hannah Macdonald's diary, 9 October 1868, Worcester Records Office.
29 RK to his godson, Bonar Sykes [c.1930], *KJ*, March 1996, 42.
30 RK to André Chevrillon, 22 October 1919, KP, 14/37.
31 RK to André Chevrillon, 22 October 1919, KP, 14/37.
32 SOM, 4.
33 SOM, 4–5.
34 W E Gladstone Solomon, 'Lockwood Kipling and the Bombay School of Art', *KJ*, March 1938, 24.
35 Alice Kipling to Mrs Rivett-Carnac, 28 August 1870, KP 1/13.
36 Charles Allen (ed.), *Kipling's Kingdom* (1987), 40.
37 Orel 1, 10.
38 RK to André Chevrillon, 22 October 1919, KP 14/37.

39   *The Macdonald Sisters*, 115
40   *Fond Memories*, KP 28/18.

2: THE HOUSE OF DESOLATION

1   Louisa Baldwin's diary, 27 May 1871, Worcester Records Office.
2   Royal Navy Records, Kew.
3   SOM, 5.
4   Oxford Records Office.
5   General Register Office.
6   Oxford Baptismal Records.
7   Birkenhead, 16.
8   Mrs A M Fleming, 'Some Childhood Memories of Rudyard Kipling', *Chambers's Journal*, March 1939, 169; and Mrs A M Fleming to Miss Oldbury, 3 March 1939 (with thanks to Barry Henderson).
9   Birkenhead, 17.
10   Hannah Macdonald's diary, 29 August 1872, Worcester Records Office.
11   Louisa Baldwin's diary, 10 September 1872, Worcester Records Office.
12   Hannah Macdonald's diary, 13 October 1872, Worcester Records Office.
13   For instance, Louie Baldwin's diary, 22 September, 13 October, 15 October 1872, Worcester Records Office.
14   SOM, 8.
15   SOM, 9.
16   Georgiana Burne-Jones, *Memorials of Edward Burne-Jones Vol. 11, 1868–1898* (1904), 45.
17   SOM, 9.
18   SOM, 10.
19   *Sydney Morning Herald*, 25 January 1936.
20   SOM, 9.
21   Mrs A M Fleming to Stanley Baldwin, 11 April 1945, KP 1/20.
22   'Some Childhood Memories of Rudyard Kipling', 168.
23   SOM, 6.
24   George Eliot, *Middlemarch* (Penguin, 1965), 191.
25   M Davies, *Unorthodox London* (1876), 374.
26   'Some Childhood Memories of Rudyard Kipling', 168.
27   SOM, 6.
28   *Wee Willie Winkie and Other Stories* (1895), 291.
29   SOM, 6, 8–9.
30   SOM, 11, 11–12.
31   Birkenhead, 26.
32   SOM, 8.
33   *Letters* 3, 278.
34   'Some Childhood Memories of Rudyard Kipling', 169.
35   Orel 1, 10.
36   Lennox Robinson (ed.), *Lady Gregory's Journals (1916–1930)* (1946), 271.
37   Roger Lancelyn Greene, *Kipling and the Children* (1965), 43.
38   *Fond Memories*, KP 28/18.
39   *Early Verse*, 477–9.

40 SOM, 12.
41 SOM, 11.
42 SOM, 12.
43 *Traffics and Discoveries* (1904), 302.
44 SOM, 11.

3: BEETLE IN LOVE

1   'Some Childhood Memories of Rudyard Kipling', 172.
2   'Some Childhood Memories of Rudyard Kipling', 172.
3   SOM, 12.
4   'Some Childhood Memories of Rudyard Kipling', 173.
5   RK to Edith Macdonald, 30 December 1930 and 7 September 1933, KP 11/10.
6   SOM, 13.
7   Mrs A M Fleming, 'More Childhood Memories of Rudyard Kipling', *Chambers's Journal*, July 1939, 510.
8   SOM, 13, 14.
9   SOM, 13.
10 SOM, 15.
11 Major-General L C Dunsterville, *Stalky's Reminiscences* (1928), 41.
12 *From Sea to Sea and Other Sketches*, 2, (1900), 48.
13 Alice Kipling to Cormell Price, 24 January 1878, Sotheby's Catalogue, *New York Times*, 2 December 1964.
14 *Stalky's Reminscences*, 31–2.
15 George Charles Beresford, *School-days with Kipling* (New York, 1936), 1.
16 *Kipling and the Children*, 45.
17 Lockwood Kipling to Cormell Price, 15 June 1878, Sotheby's Catalogue, *New York Times*, 2 December 1964.
18 *Letters* 1, 6.
19 Lorraine Price, 'Uncle Crom', *KJ* June 1994, 26.
20 *School-days with Kipling*, 196.
21 *Stalky's Reminscences*, 26.
22 British Library, Add MSS 45337.
23 Notes by Mrs Fleming on Flo Garrard, KP 32/32.
24 *Early Verse*, 55–6.
25 Lockwood Kipling to Edith Plowden, 5 October 1880, KP 1/10. The suggestion that 'The Lesson' might have been addressed to Edith is presumably a Lockwood tease.
26 Alice Kipling to Edith Plowden, 18 November 1880, KP 1/10.
27 Lockwood Kipling to Edith Plowden, 21 December 1880, KP 1/10.
28 Mrs Fleming on *Schoolboy Lyrics*, KP 32/32.
29 *Early Verse*, 60–2.
30 *Early Verse*, 94.
31 Cecil Y Lang (ed.), *The Swinburne Letters: Vol. 5, 1883–1890* (New Haven, 1962), 51.
32 *School-days with Kipling*, 237.
33 SOM, 22, 21, 22.
34 Anonymous review in *The United Services Chronicle*, No. 8, 20 March 1882; R E Harbord (ed.), *The Reader's Guide to Rudyard Kipling's Work* (Canterbury, 1963), 2,

1282.

35   *Letters* 1, 10–11.
36   *Stalky's Reminiscences*, 48.
37   RK to Major-General L C Dunsterville, 20 January 1927, KP 14/51.
38   *The United Services Chronicle*, No. 4, 30 June 1881.
39   Lockwood Kipling to Cormell Price, 2 December 1881, Sotheby's Catalogue, *New York Times*, 2 December 1964.
40   *Early Verse*, 27.
41   *Early Verse*, 160–1.
42   *Definitive Verse* 169.
43   *Stalky's Reminiscences*, 50.
44   *Letters* 1, 18.
45   *Definitive Verse*, 329.
46   *Letters* 1, 20–1.
47   *Letters* 1, 22–3.
48   Birkenhead, 53–4. Trix was presumably the source of this letter; I have been unable to trace the original.
49   KP 24/3.
50   *Letters* 1, 16.
51   Alice Kipling to Edith Plowden, 28 April 1882, KP 1/10.

4: ECHOES

1   RK to André Chevrillon, 22 October 1919, KP 14/37.
2   SOM, 25–6.
3   *Letters* 1, 24–5.
4   *Letters* 1, 28.
5   Alice Kipling to Edith Plowden, 24 February 1883, KP 1/10.
6   Lockwood Kipling to Edith Plowden, [?] 1883, KP 1/10.
7   Lockwood Kipling to Edith Plowden, [?] 1883, KP 1/10.
8   *Early Verse*, 178.
9   *Early Verse*, 184.
10   SOM, 32.
11   *Early Verse*, 184–5.
12   *Letters* 1, 34.
13   *Early Verse*, 192.
14   *Letters* 1, 39.
15   Birkenhead, 72.
16   *Letters* 1, 45.
17   Lockwood Kipling to Edith Plowden, 16 March 1885, KP 1/10.
18   *Letters* 1, 52.
19   Orel 1.
20   Orel 1.
21   *Letters* 2, 140.
22   *Letters* 1, 71.
23   Orel 1.
24   *Letters* 1, 71.
25   *Early Verse*, 226–7.

26 *Early Verse*, 225.
27 *Early Verse*, 231.
28 *Early Verse*, 223–4.
29 *Letters* 1, 76.
30 *Early Verse*, 256.
31 *Letters* 1, 57.
32 Thomas Pinney (ed.), *Kipling's India: Uncollected Sketches 1884–88* (1987), 43–4.
33 *Plain Tales from the Hills* (1890), 277–85.
34 SOM, 33.
35 *Letters* 1, 74–5, 76, 75.
36 *Letters* 1, 55.
37 *Letters* 1, 133, 69.
38 *Letters* 1, 80.
39 *Letters* 1, 84.
40 SOM, 209.
41 SOM, 209–11.
42 *Letters* 1, 90.
43 *Letters* 1, 90–1.

5: ANGLO-INDIAN ATTITUDES

1 *Letters* 1, 83, 84 (note).
2 *Letters* 1, 95, 101.
3 *Letters* 1, 103.
4 *Letters* 1, 103.
5 *Letters* 1, 104–5.
6 *Letters* 1, 106–107.
7 *Letters* 1, 80.
8 *Letters* 1, 107–9.
9 *Letters* 1, 109.
10 *Letters* 1, 110–11.
11 *Early Verse*, 109.
12 Andrew Rutherford in his annotation of 'The Second Wooing' in *Early Verse* takes 'right' to be a misprint for 'sight'. This is possible (for all Rud's efforts, *Quartette* was still riddled with typographical errors), but 'right' offers so much stronger a reading and is so characteristic of Kipling's oblique way of settling personal scores that I have taken it to be correct.
13 *Letters* 1, 133.
14 *Quartette* (Lahore: The 'Civil and Military Gazette' Press, 1885), 105, 87, 88, 89, 103.
15 *Wee Willie Winkie and Other Stories* (1895), 127.
16 SOM, 122.
17 *Quartette*, 53, 63, 58.

6: BOUNDARY-CROSSING

1 Lockwood Kipling to Margaret Burne-Jones, [10 October?] 1885–31 January 1886,

    KP, 1/1.
2   *Letters* 1, 118.
3   Seymour-Smith, 48–50.
4   *Letters* 1, 125, 127.
5   *Plain Tales from the Hills*, 154.
6   *Letters* 1, 99.
7   SOM, 176.
8   *Letters* 1, 139.
9   KP 32/24.
10 *Definitive Verse*, 23.
11 Orel 1, 74.
12 *Letters* 1, 139.
13 *Definitive Verse*, 14.
14 Lockwood Kipling to Edith Plowden, 27 July 1886, KP 1/10.
15 Carrington, 101.
16 Wilson, 109.
17 *Letters* 1, 130–2.
18 *Early Verse*, 327–8.
19 Lockwood Kipling to Edith Plowden, 6 July 1886, KP 1/10.
20 *Critical Heritage*, 34, 35.
21 Orel 1, 70–2.
22 *Letters* 1, 141.
23 *Letters* 1, 141.
24 RK to Thacker Spink & Co., 3 February 1887.
25 I am grateful to Dr Nelson Wattie for this translation.
26 *Plain Tales*, 132–3.
27 *Plain Tales*, 27, 54, 35, 42, 129.
28 *Plain Tales*, 302.
29 *Plain Tales*, 27, 28, 32, 34.
30 *Plain Tales*, 28–9.
31 *Plain Tales*, 330–1.
32 *Plain Tales*, 328, 332, 331, 332, 335–6, 336.

7: OUT OF INDIA

1   *Letters* 1, 151.
2   *From Sea to Sea* 1, 98.
3   *From Sea to Sea* 1, 98.
4   *From Sea to Sea* 1, 98, 98–9, 100–1.
5   Orel 1, 92.
6   *Letters* 1, 149.
7   Orel 1, 96.
8   *Letters* 1, 158, 190.
9   Carrington, 153.
10 *Letters* 1, 178, 172 (note).
11 Orel 1, 98.
12 *Letters* 1, 205.
13 *Letters* 1, 212, 208, 209.

14 *Letters* 1, 216.
15 *Letters* 1, 150.
16 *Letters* 1, 223.
17 Lockwood Kipling to Edith Plowden, 28 August 1888, KP 1/10.
18 SOM, 42.
19 SOM, 120.
20 *Soldiers Three and Other Stories* (1895), 75.
21 *Letters* 1, 92.
22 *Wee Willie Winkie and Other Stories*, 312.
23 Orel 1, 103.
24 *Wee Willie Winkie and Other Stories*, 273.
25 *Definitive Verse*, 69–70.
26 Carrington, 155.

8: CHARTING THE ORIENT

1 *From Sea to Sea* 1, 216.
2 *From Sea to Sea* 1, 218, 224.
3 *From Sea to Sea* 1, 232.
4 *From Sea to Sea* 1, 243, 245.
5 *From Sea to Sea* 1, 249.
6 *From Sea to Sea* 1, 250, 253.
7 *From Sea to Sea* 1, 274, 275, 277.
8 *From Sea to Sea* 1, 304, 310–11. Mrs Hill later stated that the feverish Kipling did not in fact see Canton but remained in bed on the boat and based his account on what she and her husband told him (*Letters* 3, 137 note 2).
9 *Letters* 2, 9.
10 *From Sea to Sea* 1, 279, 282, 287.
11 *From Sea to Sea* 1, 373, 349, 408.
12 *From Sea to Sea* 1, 319, 315, 349.
13 This and the previous comment about understanding Japan occur in Kipling's fourth letter from Japan to the *Pioneer* and are reprinted in Hugh Cortazzi and George Webb (eds.), *Kipling's Japan: Collected Writings* (1988), 69, 74. Kipling cut both remarks when he republished the Letter in *From Sea to Sea*.
14 *From Sea to Sea* 1, 433.
15 *From Sea to Sea* 1, 319, 322.
16 This is the version of the passage as Kipling originally wrote it and as reprinted in *Kipling's Japan*, 54–5. He subsequently shortened and slightly adapted the exchange, cutting out, for instance, the sentence beginning 'They stand high . . .' when republishing the Letter in *From Sea to Sea*.
17 *Kipling's Japan*, 92.

9: KNOCKING ABOUT THE STATES

1 *Kipling's Japan* 151, 152. Kipling omitted these passages when he republished the Letter in *From Sea to Sea*.
2 Orel 1, 105.

3   Orel 1, 105.
4   *Letters* 1, 310.
5   *From Sea to Sea* 1, 474–5, 477–9, 478.
6   *From Sea to Sea* 1, 478, 482.
7   *From Sea to Sea* 1, 475, 471–2, 494, 497.
8   *Letters* 1, 314–15.
9   *From Sea to Sea* 2, 13, 14, 15.
10 *Letters* 1, 320, 323.
11 *From Sea to Sea* 2, 43, 44, 47, 46.
12 *Letters* 1, 324.
13 *From Sea to Sea* 2, 50, 55, 56, 57.
14 *From Sea to Sea* 2, 62, 68, 81, 82, 88.
15 *From Sea to Sea* 2, 120, 128, 129.
16 *From Sea to Sea* 2, 130, 131, 137, 138, 137.
17 *From Sea to Sea* 2, 140, 135–6, 136.
18 *From Sea to Sea* 2, 138, 139.
19 *From Sea to Sea* 2, 140.
20 *From Sea to Sea* 2, 147, 149, 149–50.
21 *From Sea to Sea* 2, 163, 166–7.
22 Orel 1, 105–6.
23 *Letters* 1, 334.
24 *From Sea to Sea* 2, 171, 172, 174–5, 175–6, 176, 177, 178, 181.
25 *From Sea to Sea* 2, 188, 191, 197.
26 *From Sea to Sea* 2, 54.
27 *Letters* 1, 325.
28 *St James's Gazette*, 6 July 1889.

10: LONDON AND FAME

1   *Early Verse*, 467.
2   *Letters* 1, 349 (note).
3   KP 32/32.
4   *Letters* 1, 354.
5   *Letters* 1, 356.
6   A V Baillie, *My First Eighty Years 1864–1944* (1951), 52–3.
7   Orel 1, 119.
8   Coulson Kernahan, *'Nothing Quite Like Kipling Had Happened Before'* [no date], 13.
9   A B Paine, *Mark Twain: A Biography Vol. 11* (New York, 1912), 880.
10 Orel 1, 119.
11 *Critical Heritage*, 50, 50, 49–50, 48.
12 RK to George Saintsbury, 23 December 1923, KP 17/28.
13 Edmund Gosse, *Portraits and Sketches* (1912), 221.
14 *Letters* 1, 353.
15 *Letters* 1, 374.
16 Phyllis Grosskurth, *John Addington Symonds: A Biography* (1964), 275.
17 Herbert M Schueller and Robert L Peters (eds.), *The Letters of John Addington Symonds Volume III, 1885–1893* (Detroit, 1967–9), 381.
18 *Letters* 1, 348.

19   *The Letters of John Addington Symonds Volume II, 1885–1893*, 409, 422, 518.
20   *Letters* 1, 348.
21   *Early Verse*, 470–2.
22   *Letters* 1, 96, 97, 358.
23   *Letters* 1, 355, 372.
24   *Definitive Verse*, 234.
25   SOM, 128.
26   *Letters* 1, 357, 364–5.
27   *Letters* 1, 365, 356.
28   SOM, 48–9, 49, 48.
29   Orel 1, 116.
30   *Letters* 1, 370, 2, 43.
31   *Letters* 1, 362.
32   *Letters* 2, 7.
33   Edmonia Hill to W M C, 3 October 1930, KP 16/5.
34   *Letters* 2, 9, 8.
35   *Letters* 1, 378–9.
36   KP 32/32.
37   SOM, 52.
38   SOM, 50; and Peter Green, *Kenneth Grahame* (1959), 113–14.
39   Max Beerbohm, *The Yellow Book*, 2 July 1894, 283.
40   Charles Neider (ed.), *The Selected Letters of Mark Twain* (1982), 201.
41   Margaret Ross (ed.), *Friend of Friends* (1952), 20.
42   *Definitive Verse*, 399, 414.
43   Carrington, 198.
44   T S Eliot (ed.), *A Choice of Kipling's Verse* (1941), 11.
45   *Letters* 1, 366.
46   SOM, 48.
47   *Our Book of Memories: Letters of Justin McCarthy to Mrs Campbell Praed* (1912), 237.
48   Leonard A Björk (ed.), *The Literary Notebooks of Thomas Hardy* (1985), 14.
49   Charles Eliot Norton (ed.), *Letters of James Russell Lowell* (1894), 450.
50   *Critical Heritage*, 50, 51, 52, 53, 54.
51   Lockwood Kipling to Edith Plowden, Autumn 1890, KP 1/10.
52   SOM, 54.
53   *The Light that Failed*, 89.
54   KP 32/32.
55   Carrington, 613.
56   *The Light that Failed*, 112.
57   Reproduced with the kind permission of Josias Cunningham, owner of the inscribed copy of the novel.
58   SOM, 47.

11: AN AMERICAN WIFE

1   Preface to *The Light that Failed*.
2   *The Light that Failed*, 44, 140.
3   *The Light that Failed*, 3, 128.
4   *The Light that Failed*, 117.

5   *Record of a Friendship*, 100.
6   *Critical Heritage*, 82, 84, 86, 116.
7   Rayburn S Moore (ed.), *Selected Letters of Henry James to Edmund Gosse 1882–1915: A Literary Friendship* (1988), 80.
8   *The Light that Failed*, 32.
9   *Letters 2*, 19.
10 *Life's Handicap* (1891), 52, 55, 57, 61.
11 *Life's Handicap*, 83. Kipling's description here of Ortheris as 'the artist' subtly reinforces his self-identification with the character which is also hinted at in the half-pun in Ortheris's name ('author is').
12 *Life's Handicap*, 150.
13 *Letters 2*, 23.
14 *Athenaeum*, 4 October and 8 November 1890.
15 *Athenaeum*, 22 November and 6 December 1890.
16 RK to Edmund Gosse, 6 December 1890, KP 15/13.
17 *Athenaeum*, 6 December 1890.
18 Wilson, 277–8, 278.
19 Arthur Waugh, *One Man's Road* (1931), 171–2.
20 *One Man's Road*, 186.
21 Carrington, 224.
22 *Vermont Phoenix*, 13 November 1891.
23 Seymour-Smith, 156.
24 Quoted with permission of the Kipling Manuscript Collection, Rice Library, Marlboro College, Marlboro, Vermont.
25 *Letters 2*, 30.
26 Florence Emily Hardy, *The Early Life of Thomas Hardy 1840–1891* (1928), 295.
27 Carrington, 229.
28 *Letters 2*, 37.
29 Introduction to *Mine Own People* (New York, 1891), 23, 14–15.
30 Leon Edel (ed.), *Henry James: Letters Vol. IV, 1895–1916* (Cambridge, Mass., 1984), 70.
31 SOM, 59.
32 Christchurch *Press*, 19 October 1891.
33 Harry Ricketts (ed.), *One Lady at Wairakei* (Wellington, 1983), 51, 31. The story, never collected by Kipling, was first published on 30 January 1892 in the Saturday Supplement of the *New Zealand Herald*.
34 SOM, 61.
35 Orel 2, 273.
36 SOM, 59.
37 SOM, 61.
38 Ann Thwaite, *Edmund Gosse* (1984), 332.
39 SOM, 62.
40 *Henry James: Letters Vol. III, 1883–1895*, 364–5.
41 *Letters 2*, 44, 46, 45.
42 *Edmund Gosse*, 332.

12: AN AMERICAN HOME

1   These and other details are recorded in the diary that Carrie kept throughout the

Kiplings' married life. The diary itself does not survive (it was probably destroyed by their second daughter Elsie), but Carrington was allowed to make extensive notes and transcriptions from it while working on his official biography. These notes provide an invaluable source of information about the details of the Kiplings' daily life and particularly of when Kipling was writing what. The disappearance of the original diary is probably not a major loss, for it is unlikely to have contained anything much more informative than the short, factual details or occasional comments that Carrington was allowed to transcribe.

2   *Definitive Verse*, 84, 165.
3   Orel 1, 120–1.
4   *Letters of Travel (1892–1913)* (1920), 5.
5   *Letters of Travel*, 5, 11, 13, 12.
6   *Letters* 2, 52.
7   *Letters of Travel*, 16, 19.
8   *Definitive Verse*, 182.
9   *Letters of Travel*, 30, 31, 32.
10 CK's diary, KP 1/8.
11 *Letters* 2, 108.
12 *Letters of Travel*, 35, 34, 35.
13 *Letters of Travel*, 49.
14 Janet Adam Smith (ed.), *Henry James and Robert Louis Stevenson: A Record of Friendship and Criticism* (Westport, Connecticut, 1979), 213.
15 SOM, 65.
16 SOM, 65–6.
17 *Letters* 2, 54.
18 Charles Allen (ed.), *Kipling's Kingdom* (1987), 46.
19 *Letters* 2, 76, 81.
20 *Letters* 2, 98–9, 66 (note).
21 *Letters* 2, 86.
22 Orel 2, 253, 254.
23 *Letters* 2, 110.
24 *Letters* 2, 104.
25 *Many Inventions* (1893), 275.
26 *Letters* 2, 89–90.
27 SOM, 70.
28 *Letters* 2, 105, 106.
29 CK's diary, KP 1/8.
30 *Letters* 2, 115, 116, 117.
31 CK's diary, KP 1/8.

13: TROUBLE WITH BEATTY

1   *Definitive Verse*, 330.
2   *Letters* 2, 143.
3   *Letters* 2, 129.
4   *Letters* 2, 139.
5   *Philadelphia Ledger* reported 18 May 1894 in the *Vermont Phoenix*. From the Howard Rice Jr. Collection, Marlboro College, Marlboro, Vermont.

6   *Letters 2*, 129.
7   *Selected Letters of Henry James to Edmund Gosse*, 113.
8   *Letters 2*, 134.
9   SOM, 67–8.
10 *Record of a Friendship*, 31–2.
11 *The Jungle Book* (1894), 273–4.
12 *The Jungle Book*, 157.
13 *Letters 2*, 144.
14 Orel 2, 238.
15 *Definitive Verse*, 120, 123, 123–4, 124.
16 Orel 2, 238.
17 Carrington, 270.
18 *Letters 2*, 156.
19 *The Day's Work* (1898), 51.
20 *Letters 2*, 165.
21 *Letters 2*, 228.
22 *The Day's Work*, 319.
23 *Letters 2*, 228.
24 *Letters 2*, 173.
25 CK's diary, KP 1/8.
26 SOM, 73, 72.
27 SOM, 73.
28 *The Second Jungle Book* (1895), 114, 109.
29 *The Second Jungle Book*, 263, 294.
30 Lockwood Kipling to Carlo Placci, 28 November 1895, Manuscript Section, Biblioteca Marucelliana, Florence.
31 *The Day's Work*, 387, 365.
32 *The Day's Work*, 361.
33 *Letters 2*, 213.
34 *The Day's Work*, 187.
35 CK's diary, KP 1/8.
36 *Vermont Phoenix*, 10 August 1894.
37 *Letters 2*, 156.
38 *Letters 2*, 181, 182.
39 Mary Cabot, 'The Vermont Period: Rudyard Kipling at Naulakha', reprinted in *English Literature in Transition, 1880–1920*, 29 (2), 165, 166, 169.
40 Carrington, 592.
41 *Letters 2*, 214.
42 *Letters 2*, 215, 221, 225–6.
43 *Definitive Verse*, 325.
44 SOM, 76–7.
45 'Rudyard Kipling at Naulakha', 188.
46 CK's diary, KP 1/8.
47 *Windham County Reformer*, 15 May 1896. Quotations from this paper and the *Vermont Phoenix* are from the Howard Rice Jr. Collection, Marlboro College, Marlboro, Vermont.
48 *Vermont Phoenix*, 15 May 1896.
49 *Windham County Reformer*, 15 May 1896.
50 *Vermont Phoenix*, 15 May 1896.
51 'Rudyard Kipling at Naulakha', 190.

52 'Rudyard Kipling at Naulakha', 187–8.
53 *Selected Letters of Henry James to Edmund Gosse*, 140.
54 CK's diary, KP 1/8.
55 *Letters 2*, 240.
56 'Rudyard Kipling at Naulakha', 194.

14: RECESSIONAL

1 'Rudyard Kipling at Naulakha', 195.
2 *Letters 2*, 266.
3 *Letters 2*, 259, 256.
4 Hon. Evan Charteris, *The Life and Letters of Sir Edmund Gosse* (1931), 225, 237.
5 *Definitive Verse*, 172.
6 *Definitive Verse*, 121, 126, 343.
7 *Letters 2*, 282, 273.
8 *Critical Heritage*, 187, 189.
9 *Letters 2*, 279.
10 *Critical Heritage*, 192, 194, 195, 193.
11 Randolph S Churchill, *Winston S Churchill: Volume 1, Youth 1874–1900* (1966), 322.
12 *Selected Letters of Henry James to Edmund Gosse*, 152.
13 Richard M Taylor (ed.), *The Personal Notebooks of Thomas Hardy* (1978), 39.
14 *Letters 2*, 263, 297, 173. But see Kipling's 1909 comment on James: "he is head and shoulders the biggest [contemporary writer] of them all and will in the end be found to be perhaps the most enduring influence. It's very amusing to see men who, so to say, blaspheme his manner unconsciously saturated with his technical methods" (*Letters 3*, 394).
15 *Letters 2*, 266.
16 'Rudyard Kipling at Naulakha', 194.
17 *Letters 2*, 309, 346, 344.
18 *Letters 2*, 296.
19 *KJ*, June 1986, 28, 38.
20 *Definitive Verse*, 323.
21 CK's diary, KP 1/8.
22 British Library Add MSS 45100.
23 CK's diary, KP 1/8.
24 *Definitive Verse*, 328–9.
25 SOM, 86.
26 Orel 1, 131, 132.
27 This account is based on Dr H I Bell's report published in *The Times* on 20 December 1937. Bell was Keeper of the Manuscripts at the British Museum, which had recently been presented with the manuscript of 'Recessional' by Stanley Baldwin, who had been given it for that purpose by Elizabeth Norton, Sally's surviving sister. Elizabeth was presumably told this version by Sally herself, though the outline of the story had been known for years, Beerbohm referring to it in a 1913 letter to Holbrook Jackson.
28 British Library Add MSS 45100.
29 *Record of a Friendship*, 33–4.
30 Carrington, 325.

Notes

31 *Letters 2*, 306.
32 *Critical Heritage 1, 257.*
33 Letters 2, 311.
34 Carrington, 326.
35 Marguerite Steen, *William Nicholson* (1943), 68. I am grateful to my colleague Dr Robert Easting for more information than I could possibly use about this traditional shepherds' counting system.
36 *Definitive Verse*, 359.
37 *William Nicholson*, 68.
38 Angela Thirkell, *Three Houses* (1931), 83, 88, 86.
39 Sir Harry R Ricardo, *Memories and Machines* (1968), 44–5.
40 Winifred Gérin, *Anne Thackeray Ritchie: A Biography* (Oxford, 1981), 26.
41 Orel 1, 33.
42 *KJ*, June 1994, 21.
43 *Letters 2*, 359.
44 The following quotations from J E C Welldon's speech are taken from J A Mangan's incisive study of Welldon and other proselytising imperialist headmasters in *The Games Ethic and Imperialism* (1986), 35–6, 36.
45 *Stalky & Co.* (1899), 210–11.
46 *Letters 1*, 80.
47 *Letters 2*, 381.
48 Carrington, 328.
49 *Letters 2*, 328, 336, 335.
50 *Letters 2*, 336.
51 Margaret Lane, *Edgar Wallace* (1938), 98, 99, 100.
52 *Letters 2*, 341, 342.
53 *Critical Heritage*, 216.
54 *Letters 2*, 353.
55 Alice Kipling to Louisa Baldwin, 17 January 1899, *Baldwin Papers*, Worcester Records Office.
56 CK's diary, KP 1/8.
57 CK's diary, KP 1/8.
58 James Agate, 18 January 1936, *Ego 2* (1936), 319.
59 Birkenhead, 373.
60 *Winston Churchill: Volume 1, Youth 1874–1900*, 435.
61 Bernard Falk, *He Laughed in Fleet Street* (1933), 291; and Mildred Howells (ed.), *Life in Letters of William Dean Howells* Vol. 2, (New York, 1929), 101.
62 CK's diary, KP 1/8.
63 Carrington, 352.
64 Birkenhead, 198.
65 KP 32/34.

15: REPUTATIONS

1 *Critical Heritage*, 221.
2 *Henry James: Letters Vol. IV, 1895–1916*, 70.
3 James Hepburn (ed.), *The Letters of Arnold Bennett Vol. II, 1889–1915* (1968), 78.
4 *KJ*, March 1993, 35.

5   Newman Flower (ed.), *The Journals of Arnold Bennett 1896–1901* (1932), 81.
6   Paul F Mattheisen, Arthur C Young, Pierre Coustillas (eds), *The Collected Letters of George Gissing Vol. VI, 1895–1897* (Ohio, 1995), 194.
7   George Gissing, *The Whirlpool* (1897), 449–50.
8   *The Collected Letters of George Gissing*, Vol. VII, 412.
9   *The Letters of Arnold Bennett*, Vol. II, 78.

16: A SADDER AND A HARDER MAN

1   *Letters* 2, 369.
2   Edward Bok, *An Autobiography* (1921), 254–5.
3   Lockwood Kipling to Sally Norton, 4 July 1899, KP 1/9.
4   Lockwood Kipling to Sally Norton, 22 July 1899, KP 1/9.
5   *Letters* 2, 376.
6   *Three Houses*, 86.
7   *Henry James: Letters Vol. IV, 1895–1916*, 124; and *Critical Heritage*, 21.
8   *Critical Heritage*, 245–6, 244.
9   *Letters* 3, 8.
10 Duff Hart-Davis (ed.), *End of an Era: Letters and Journals of Sir Alan Lascelles 1887–1920* (1986), 6.
11 *Definitive Verse*, 459.
12 Lockwood Kipling to Sally Norton, 21 November 1899, KP 1/9.
13 SOM, 88.
14 *The Reader's Guide to Rudyard Kipling's Work* Vol. 3, 1530.
15 *Letters* 3, 10–11.
16 *Letters* 3, 10.
17 Lockwood Kipling to Sally Norton, 5 February 1900 and 21 November 1899, KP 1/9.
18 *Definitive Verse*, 297.
19 Frederick R Karl and Laurence Davies (eds.), *The Collected Letters of Joseph Conrad* Vol. II (Cambridge, 1986), 207.
20 CK's diary, KP 1/8.
21 Leo Amery, *Days of Fresh Air* (1939), 150.
22 Nourah Waterhouse, *Private and Official* (1942), 76.
23 SOM, 91.
24 Mark Twain, *Following the Equator: A Journey Around the World* (New York, 1989), 708.
25 RK to Sir Herbert Baker, 22 February 1934, KP 14/7.
26 *Letters of Travel*, 88.
27 Apollon Davidson, *Cecil Rhodes and His Time*, translated from the Russian by Christopher French (Moscow, 1988), 327–8.
28 SOM, 101.
29 *Letters* 3, 14.
30 *Letters* 3, 26.
31 SOM, 93, 94.
32 *Letters* 3, 26.
33 CK's diary, KP 1/8.
34 *Letters* 3, 15–16, 22, 31.
35 *Letters* 3, 23.
36 *Letters* 3, 53.

37   *Definitive Verse*, 187.
38   C L Cline (ed.), *The Letters of George Meredith* Vol. III (1970), 1370.
39   Kingsley Amis, *Rudyard Kipling* (1975), 112.
40   *KJ*, July 1942, 16.
41   *Critical Heritage*, 21.
42   *Letters 3*, 181.
43   *Letters 3*, 41.
44   SOM, 101, 99, 100.
45   *Definitive Verse*, 300.
46   *Letters 3*, 41. 42.
47   *Letters 3*, 53.
48   *Definitive Verse*, 319.
49   *Letters 3*, 72 (note).
50   *Kim* (1901), 81, 90–1.
51   *Letters 3*, 11.
52   *Kim*, 111.
53   H A Vachell, *Now Came Still Evening On* (1946), 125.
54   *Critical Heritage*, 22, 271.
55   David Garnett (ed.), *The White/Garnett Letters* (1968), 85.
56   *Henry James: Letters Vol. IV, 1895–1916*, 210–11.
57   *Letters 3*, 73.
58   *Letters 3*, 64 (note).
59   Charles Neider (ed.), *The Autobiography of Mark Twain* (New York, 1959), 287.
60   *Letters 3*, 81.
61   *Definitive Verse*, 301, 304, 302.
62   Michael Davie and Simon Davie (eds.), *The Faber Book of Cricket* (1987), 312.
63   *Definitive Verse*, 304.
64   SOM, 129.
65   *Letters 3*, 85.
66   *Letters 3*, 87.
67   *Definitive Verse*, 209, 210.
68   *Letters 3*, 87.
69   *Three Houses*, 79–80.
70   CK's diary, KP 1/8.
71   SOM, 103.
72   *Letters 3*, 113–14, 113.

17: FAMILY AND FOES

1   Ford Madox Ford, *Return to Yesterday* (1931), 4, 6–7.
2   *Letters 3*, 115.
3   W Sorley Brown, *The Life and Genius of T W H Crosland* (1928), 131.
4   R J Minney, *Viscount Southwood* (1954), 823.
5   L Thompson (ed.), *Selected Letters of Robert Frost* (1965), 72.
6   Denys Sutton (ed.), *Letters of Roger Fry* (1972), 355.
7   William Rothenstein, *Men and Memories Vol. 2, 1900–1922* (1932), 25.
8   *Letters 3*, 192–3, 159.
9   W J Strachan (ed. and trans.), *Towards the Lost Domain: Letters from London, 1905*

(Manchester, 1986), 102.

10 *Letters* 3, 249, 243.
11 J G Riewald, *Sir Max Beerbohm, Man and Writer* (The Hague, 1953), 29.
12 S N Behrmann, *Conversation with Max* (1960), 57.
13 A G Gardiner, *Prophets, Priests, and Kings* (1908), 293.
14 Michael Millgate, *Thomas Hardy: A Biography* (Oxford, 1982), 452.
15 *Letters* 3, 283, 285, 286, 291.
16 *Just So Stories* (1902), 65.
17 *Three Houses*, 88.
18 *Traffics and Discoveries* (1904), 238.
19 P G Wodehouse, *Performing Flea: A Self-Portrait in Letters* (1953), 41.
20 *Traffics and Discoveries*, 332.
21 David Cecil, *Max: A Biography* (1964), 251.
22 *Letters* 3, 152, 150–1, 189.
23 SOM, 108.
24 *Letters* 2, 324.
25 CK's diary, KP 1/8.
26 *Letters* 3, 162, 173.
27 *Puck of Pook's Hill* (1906), 152.
28 *A Book of Words* (1928), 178.
29 *Puck of Pook's Hill*, 144, 148.
30 *Rewards and Fairies* (1910), 50.
31 *Rewards and Fairies*, 34.
32 *Rewards and Fairies* 51, 87, 176.
33 SOM, 111.
34 Theodore Redpath (ed.), *The Songs and Sonnets of John Donne* (2nd ed. 1983), 289–90.
35 *Letters* 3, 269.
36 'O Beloved Kids', 67, 63.
37 'O Beloved Kids', 69, 162.
38 'O Beloved Kids', 64, 147–8.
39 *Letters* 3, 326.
40 'O Beloved Kids', 46.
41 *Letters* 3, 278.
42 'O Beloved Kids', 90.
43 *Letters* 3, 431, 432.
44 Joseph Connolly, *Jerome K Jerome* (1982), 155.
45 Robert Rhodes James, *Bob Boothby: A Portrait* (1991), 26.
46 *Letters* 3, 325–6.
47 'O Beloved Kids', 113, 114.
48 Mark Baker's 'John Kipling at Wellington', *KJ*, June 1982, sets out what is known or can be reliably deduced about John's time at Wellington College.
49 'O Beloved Kids', 165.
50 'O Beloved Kids', 144, 133, 127, 140.
51 *Letters* 3, 215.
52 Lockwood Kipling to Edith Plowden, 23 November and 25 December 1910, KP 1/10.
53 RK to Edmonia Hill, 10 February 1911, KP 16/5.
54 *The Macdonald Sisters*, 134.
55 *Letters* 3, 127.
56 Maurice V Brett (ed.), *Journals and Letters of Reginald Viscount Esher Vol. 1* (1934), 382.

57 *Definitive Verse*, 213–14
58 *Letters* 3, 147.
59 *Letters* 3, 166, 203.
60 *Letters* 3, 215, 293.
61 *Definitive Verse*, 188.
62 *Letters of Travel*, 121, 122.
63 *Letters* 3, 275.
64 *A Book of Words*, 17, 21, 20.
65 *Letters of Travel*, 119, 205.
66 *Actions and Reactions* (1909), 95, 106.
67 *Record of a Friendship*, 69.
68 *A Book of Words*, 6, 7, 8.
69 *Letters* 3, 212.
70 *Definitive Verse*, 315.
71 *Letters of Travel*, 119.
72 RK to R D Blumenfeld, 8 May 1910, KP 14/19.
73 *Definitive Verse*, 226.
74 *Definitive Verse*, 233.
75 *Definitive Verse*, 243.
76 RK to H A Gwynne, 10 March 1914, KP 15/15.
77 *Kent and Sussex Courier*, 3 October 1913.
78 *Kent and Sussex Courier*, 22 May 1914.
79 *Kent and Sussex Courier*, 22 May 1914.
80 CK's diary, KP 1/8.

18: MY BOY JACK

1   Jean Moorcroft Wilson (ed.), *The Collected Letters of Charles Hamilton Sorley* (1990), 185.
2   *Definitive Verse*, 329–30.
3   *Brighton Observer*, 11 September 1914.
4   R K K Thornton (ed.), *Ivor Gurney: Collected Letters* (Manchester, 1991), 13.
5   Barry Webb, *Edmund Blunden* (1990), 43.
6   *A Diversity of Creatures* (1917), 418.
7   Elting E Morison (ed.), *The Letters of Theodore Roosevelt: The Days of Armageddon 1914–1919* (Cambridge, Mass., 1954), 530.
8   RK to Edward Bok, 28 October 1914 (Syracuse University).
9   *'O Beloved Kids'*, 172.
10 *Definitive Verse*, 204.
11 RK to Lionel Dunsterville, 24 February 1915, KP 14/51.
12 *Record of a Friendship*, 81, 82, 84.
13 *A Diversity of Creatures*, 421.
14 *A Diversity of Creatures*, 439–41.
15 Norman Page (ed.), *A Kipling Companion* (1984), 106.
16 *'O Beloved Kids'*, 178–9.
17 *The Southport Guardian*, 23 June 1915.
18 *Record of a Friendship*, 84.
19 *'O Beloved Kids'*, 188, 190.
20 Carrington, 503.

21   *France at War* (1915), 16, 43, 28, 51.
22   Rupert Grayson, *Voyage Not Completed* (1969), 70.
23   CK's diary, KP 1/8.
24   'O Beloved Kids', 18.
25   'O Beloved Kids', 195.
26   'O Beloved Kids', 198, 199, 214, 215.
27   'O Beloved Kids', 213, 219, 222.
28   *A Diversity of Creatures*, 428.
29   *Record of a Friendship*, 85.
30   *Voyage Not Completed*, 84.
31   *The Times*, 3 February 1998.
32   Dorothy Ponton, *Rudyard Kipling at Home and at Work* (Poole, 1953), 20.
33   RK to Lionel Dunsterville, 12 November 1915, KP 14/51.
34   *Record of Friendship*, 87.
35   *The Times*, 3 February 1998.
36   Foreword to Rudyard Kipling, *The Irish Guards in the Great War: The Second Battalion* (Staplehurst, 1997), 8. This version has been questioned by Tonie and Valmai Holt in their recent biography of John Kipling, *'My Boy Jack': The search for Kipling's only son* (Barnsley, September 1998).
37   *Debits and Credits* (1926), 372.
38   *Ivor Gurney: Collected Letters*, 146.
39   Jerrold Northrop Moore, *Edward Elgar: A Creative Life* (Oxford, 1984), 706.
40   Lady Maud Warrender, *My First Sixty Years* (1933), 292.
41   *Debits and Credits*, 334.
42   *Record of a Friendship*, 101.
43   *Definitive Verse*, 328.
44   RK to André Chevrillon, 22 June 1916, KP 14/37.
45   Vera Brittain, *Testament of Youth* (Virago, 1978), 280–1.
46   RK to R D Blumfeld, 6 September 1916, KP 14/19; and to Lionel Dunsterville, 11 September 1916, KP 14/51.
47   *Definitive Verse*, 216–7.
48   Colonel Douglas Proby to RK, 8 January 1917, KP 23/3.
49   *Definitive Verse*, 186.
50   *Critical Heritage*, 320.
51   Ronald Storrs, *Orientations* (1937), 297.
52   *Definitive Verse*, 301.
53   RK to Sir Herbert Baker, 22 February 1934, KP 14/7.
54   *Definitive Verse*, 367, 391, 389.
55   *Record of a Friendship*, 99, 100, 101.
56   SOM, 131–2.
57   SOM, 264.
58   RK to R D Blumenfeld, 22 August 1918, KP 14/19.
59   *Definitive Verse*, 394.
60   *Definitive Verse*, 387, 390.
61   CK's diary, KP 1/8.

19: DEBITS AND CREDITS

Notes

1   RK to Lionel Dunsterville, 9 July 1919, KP 14/31.
2   *Rudyard Kipling at Home and at Work*, 34.
3   *Rudyard Kipling at Home and at Work*, 34.
4   *Rudyard Kipling at Home and at Work*, 35.
5   CK's diary, KP 1/8.
6   *The Times*, 17 April 1923.
7   RK to Lionel Dunsterville, 28 March 1923, KP 14/31.
8   *Critical Heritage*, 332.
9   *The Irish Guards in the Great War: The Second Battalion*, 15–18, 18, 28.
10 CK's diary, KP 1/8.
11 Quoted SOM, 251.
12 *Rudyard Kipling at Home and at Work*, 31.
13 *Record of a Friendship*, 122.
14 CK's diary, KP 1/8.
15 CK's diary, KP 1/8; and RK to George Saintsbury, 4 July and 3 November 1924, KP 17/28.
16 CK's diary, KP 1/8.
17 Thomas Jones, *A Diary with Letters 1931–1950* (1954), 447.
18 CK's diary, KP 1/8.
19 RK to Elsie Bambridge, 17 December 1924 and 21 January 1925, KP 12/13.
20 RK to Elsie Bambridge, 30 August, 5 October and 6 October 1925, KP 12/13, 12/14.
21 *Record of a Friendship*, 130.
22 CK's diary, KP 1/8.
23 *Record of a Friendship*, 139.
24 RK to Lionel Dunsterville, 2 November 1919, KP 14/31.
25 Malcolm Brown and Julia Cave, *A Touch of Genius: The Life of T E Lawrence* (1988), 156.
26 Rupert Hart-Davis (ed.), *Siegfried Sassoon Diaries 1923–1925* (1985), 68.
27 RK to Lionel Dunsterville, 2 November 1919, KP 14/31.
28 RK to André Chevrillon, 10 November 1919, KP 14/37.
29 Keith M Wilson, *A Study in the History and Politics of the* Morning Post *1905–1926* (Lampeter, 1990), 182.
30 *Record of a Friendship*, 110.
31 Angus Wilson, for instance, strongly argues for 'the special civilising contribution of the Jews to society in "The Treasure and the Law"', the final story in *Puck of Pook's Hill*, and one could also point to the sympathetic portrayal of M'Leod, the Jewish paterfamilias in 'The House Surgeon' (1909), among other examples.
32 *Record of a Friendship*, 112–13.
33 CK's diary mentions a visit by Clare Sheridan and her daughters on 1 May 1920, and I am assuming that this was the visit Sheridan later wrote up for the New York *World*. It is possible, however, that the so-called interview took place on another later visit or that Sheridan conflated comments that Kipling made on different occasions.
34 *World*, 10 September 1922.
35 *World*, 10 September 1922.
36 *The Times*, 13 September 1922.
37 *Daily Chronicle*, 12 September 1922.
38 *Critical Heritage*, 322, 325, 326, 323, 322.
39 Mary Lyon (ed.), *Virginia Woolf: Books and Portraits* (1979), 81, 82, 83.
40 Edgell Rickword (ed.), *Scrutinies By Various Writers* (1928), 75–6.
41 *Siegfried Sassoon Diaries 1923–1925*, 182.
42 CK's diary, KP 1/8; RK to C R L Fletcher, 12 July 1918, KP 15/5; RK to Elsie

Bambridge, 5 April 1925, KP 12/13.

43　Ann Thwaite, *A A Milne: His Life* (1990), 276–7.

44　Maurice Cranston, BBC Home Service, 14 April 1954.

45　Orel 2, 362, 263, 364, 365.

46　Orel 2, 356.

47　*Sunday Dispatch*, 19 January 1936.

48　*Voyage Not Completed*, 87, 92, 83.

49　Thelma Cazalet-Keir, *From the Wings* (1967), 35, 36.

50　*Lady Gregory's Journals (1916–1930)*, 271.

51　*Orientations*, 506.

52　Orel 2, 380, 381.

53　*Enid Bagnold's Autobiography* (1969), 194, 195.

54　Stanley Olson (ed.), *Harold Nicolson: Diaries and Letters 1930–1964* (1980), 14.

55　*A Book of Words*, 245.

56　RK to Lionel Dunsterville, 20 November 1927, KP 14/51.

57　SOM, 85.

58　John Vincent (ed.), *The Crawford Papers: The Journals of David Lindsay, twenty-seventh Earl of Crawford and tenth Earl of Balcarres* (Manchester, 1984), 396.

59　Rupert Hart-Davis, *Hugh Walpole* (1952), 274.

60　*Critical Heritage*, 334.

61　Edmund Wilson, 'Kipling's Debits and Credits', *New Republic*, 6 October 1926.

62　*Debits and Credits*, 185, 159.

63　Orel 2, 385.

64　*A Book of Words*, 284.

65　T S Eliot, *The Uses of Poetry and the Uses of Criticism* (1967), 130.

66　*A Book of Words*, 285.

67　T S Eliot, *Selected Prose* (1963), 368.

68　*Debits and Credits*, 371, 373.

69　*Debits and Credits*, 414.

20: PALLBEARERS

1　Carrington, 580.

2　RK to Stanley Baldwin, 17 April 1927, KP 11/3.

3　Harold Macmillan, *Winds of Change 1914–1939* (1966), 185–6.

4　W R Inge, *Diary of a Dean* (1949), 142.

5　RK to H A Gwynne, 10 April 1926, KP 15/15; and to Elsie Bambridge, 18 February 1928, KP 12/17.

6　*Harold Nicolson: Diaries and Letters 1930–1964*, 14.

7　*KJ*, March 1996, 43.

8　*From the Wings*, 35.

9　RK to Mrs A M Fleming, [1932] and 12 June 1932, KP 11/9.

10　*'Thy Servant a Dog' and Other Dog Stories* (1938), 179–80.

11　RK to Sir Percy Bates, 8 September 1931, KP 14/13.

12　RK to Sir Percy Bates, 14 November 1933, KP 14/13.

13　RK to Sir Percy Bates, 18 June 1930, KP 14/13.

14　Anne Chisholm and Michael Davie, *Beaverbrook: A Life* (1992), 305.

15　Birkenhead, 346.

16   BBC radio broadcast transcript, 6 May 1935.

17   BBC radio broadcast transcript, 6 May 1935.

18   BBC radio broadcast transcript, 6 May 1935.

19   RK to Sir Percy Bates, May 1935, KP 14/13.

20   Rupert Hart-Davis (ed.), *Siegfried Sassoon: Letters to Max Beerbohm with a few answers* (1986), 24, 25.

21   S N Behrmann, *Tribulations & Laughter* (1972), 108–9.

22   Orel 2, 326.

23   *The Personal Notebooks of Thomas Hardy*, 285.

24   Ted Morgan, *Maugham*, (New York, 1980), 505.

25   Vera Brittain, *Testament of Experience* (1979), 88.

26   *Hugh Walpole*, 296.

27   Seymour-Smith, 120–1.

28   Vera Brittain, *Radclyffe Hall: A Case of Obscenity?* (1968), 101.

29   John Buchan, *Memory Hold-the-Door* (1940), 150–1; and *Hugh Walpole*, 366.

30   CK's diary, KP 1/8.

31   *The Times*, 7 April 1932.

32   *Limits and Renewals* (1932), 4, 32.

33   RK to Elsie Bambridge, 29 December 1926, KP 12/15.

34   Leon Edel, *Henry James: A Life* (New York, 1977), 467.

35   *Limits and Renewals*, 93, 323, 251.

36   *Limits and Renewals*, 92.

37   SOM, 130.

38   *Definitive Verse*, 525.

39   Christopher Ricks has an interesting discussion of the poem's racism in *T S Eliot and Prejudice* (1988), 25–7.

40   Birkenhead, 355.

41   *Definitive Verse*, 824.

42   *Limits and Renewals*, 245–6.

43   *Definitive Verse*, 384.

44   RK to H E T Haultain, 9 January 1934, KP 15/23.

45   RK to Sir Herbert Baker, 22 January 1934, KP 14/7.

46   SOM, xviii.

47   'Completed fragment' is Professor Pinney's phrase in his introduction to SOM.

48   CK's diary, KP 1/8; and RK to Edith Macdonald, 2 January 1936, KP 11.10.

49   SOM, 111.

50   SOM, 3, 45, 47.

51   *Listener*, 10 March 1937.

52   SOM, 134.

53   Birkenhead, 357.

54   Martin Green, *Dreams of Adventure, Deeds of Empire* (New York, 1978), 283.

55   *Performing Flea: A Self-Portrait in Letters*, 85.

56   *The White/Garnett Letters*, 85.

57   Anne Olivier Bell (ed.), *The Diary of Virginia Woolf Vol. V, 1936–1941* (1984), 8.

58   *New Statesman and Nation*, 25 January 1936.

59   *Listener*, 5 February 1936.

60   *Critical Heritage*, 384.

61   *Testament and Experience*, 140.

Acknowledgments

For permission to reproduce material, published and unpublished, I should gratefully like to acknowledge the following: The National Trust and A.P. Watt & Co. Ltd, for Kipling's work and letters and that of his family; the Rice Library and Howard C. Rice Jr Collection, Marlboro College, for Wolcott Balestier's letter and various newspaper items; *English Literature in Transition* for Mary Cabot's memoir; Mrs Valerie Eliot and Faber & Faber Ltd for quotations from T S Eliot; Earl Baldwin for extracts from Hannah MacDonald's diaries, and the letters of Louisa Baldwin and Alice Kipling; Bodley Head for permission to quote from Thelma Cazalet-Keir's autobiography *From the Wings*; David Higham Associates for permission to quote from *The White/Garnett Letters* (Jonathan Cape, 1968) and Barbara Levy, literary agent of the Siegfried Sassoon estate. Every effort has been made to track down the holders of copyright, and I apologise for any unforeseen omissions, which I would be glad to rectify in later editions.

For permission to reproduce illustrations, as listed at the beginning of the book, I should like to thank Haileybury College Governing Body; the Houghton Library, Harvard University; The Howard C. Rice Jr Collection, Marlboro College, Vermont; the Library of Congress, Washington, D.C.; Julia MacSwiney; the National Portrait Gallery, London; The National Trust; the Library of the Groot Schuur Estate, Cape Town.

Like anyone now working on Kipling, I owe a great debt to Professor Thomas Pinney for his magnificent edition of Kipling's letters and to the late Professor Andrew Rutherford for his edition of Kipling's early verse.

For travel grants to help with my research, I should like to thank: the British Academy and Victoria University of Wellington.

For help with my research, and general encouragement, I should like to thank the following, with apologies if I have inadvertently left anyone out: Professor John Bayley, Molly Brennan (Marlboro College Library), the late Gavin Ewart, Andy Gibson, Diane Hadley (Victoria University of Wellington Library), Lois Hey, Bette Inglis (University of Sussex Library), Andy Klisuric, Professor Robert Langenfeld, Lisa Lewis, Lt-Col D J Patrickson, Professor Thomas Pinney, Margaret Short, Jane Stafford, Margaret Sutton, David Tansey, and various staff members at the Berg Library, Berkeley University Library, Library of Congress, Cornell University Library, Houghton Library at Harvard University, London Library, Rochester University Library, Syracuse University Library, and Worcester Records Office.

More particularly I should like to thank: Douglas Matthews for his exemplary index; my literary agent Deborah Rogers for her generous enthusiasm and practical help and her assistant Stephen Edwards; my editor Jenny Uglow for her great patience, faith and incisive reading, her assistant Jonathan Butler and their colleagues at Chatto & Windus who dealt so sympathetically and efficiently with the difficulties of having an author on the other side of the world; my friends Hugh Roberts and David Kynaston, Hugh for his many invaluable suggestions and contributions to the first half of the biography and David for his selfless and expert support from start to finish; and my wife Belinda for her unfailing good humour and support.

414

Index

NOTE: Works by Kipling appear directly under title; works by others appear under authors' names